FLOWERS OF THE FIELD

FLOWERS OF THE FIELD

A Secret History of
Meadow, Moor and Wood

STEVE NICHOLLS

Head of ZEUS

An Apollo Book

III

OPEN GROUND

Foreword

I've always had a deep fascination with nature, in particular with bugs and birds, as far back as I can remember. But until I went to university, plants were simply the things that some animals ate. Of course, in pursuing the caterpillars of different butterflies or moths, I had to learn something of the habits of specific plants. And while in pursuit of birds, I always took time to enjoy the great spectacles of bluebells, wild daffodils or ramsons (wild garlic) in the woods along the River Tees and in the valleys of the North Yorkshire Moors, close to my childhood home in Middlesbrough. But in the early 1970s I travelled to the other corner of the country, to go to the University of Bristol, a decision partly driven by its proximity to Slimbridge, home of what was then the Wildfowl Trust (now the Wildfowl and Wetlands Trust). This was set up by my childhood hero, Peter Scott, after he found a rare lesser white-fronted goose amongst larger flocks of greater white-fronts that traditionally winter on this stretch of the Severn Estuary. This area also draws wintering Bewick's swans from Siberia and a host of waders and other birds, so I spent many happy days there when I probably should have been ploughing through scientific texts and journals.

My decision to study at the University of Bristol turned out to be a good one in a number of other ways too. When I arrived in Bristol I was interested in birds, reptiles and insects, but on my first day there, feeling lost at having moved so far from home, I bumped into David Parker, a fellow zoology student who was to become my closest friend and fellow adventurer into the world of natural history throughout our undergraduate years. And he knew about plants. Gradually, by osmosis, I began to pick up some botany until I reached a threshold of knowledge that finally ignited my own interest. My passion for birds and insects remained (my PhD, also at the University of Bristol, was on dragonflies), but I began to spend more time searching out wildflowers, both rare and common, and delving into their natural history and biology. That lifelong curiosity about the biology of Britain's wildflowers is one strand of this book.

I spent many happy years at Bristol University, moving on to postdoctoral research after receiving my PhD, and I assumed I would pursue my interest in the natural world from within academia. But the BBC's Natural History Unit is just a few hundred metres from the university's biology department, and I was frequently invited to appear on Radio 4 nature programmes as a bug expert. Later I began to act as a natural history consultant for TV programmes, including *Living Planet*, the David Attenborough series that followed his ground-breaking *Life on Earth*. During this time, I began to realize that I was far more of a generalist than a specialist. Since procuring grants for academic research meant becoming ever more specialized, I jumped at the chance to join the BBC Natural History Unit when a job came up.

Making natural history programmes is a very satisfying experience. Apart from travelling to all kinds of places that I would be unlikely to visit otherwise, I discovered that film-making is a heady mix of art and science. I've had the chance to work with top scientists in many fields, to showcase their work and to document the very latest discoveries. At

Welsh poppy, in the wild a native of damp rocky woods but now so widely grown in gardens that it has become naturalized right across the British Isles.

the same time, the final programme also needs to be a work of art, to be illustrated by stunning images backed by evocative music and the whole woven into a compelling story.

I had begun to photograph wildflowers during my undergraduate days, mostly as a scientific record of what I had found, but after joining the Natural History Unit, I was lucky enough to work with some of the finest wildlife cameramen on the planet and that helped me to develop a much better eye for images. Not long after I joined the BBC I met my wife, Vicky, who, although a mathematician and engineer by training, is also a fine artist. We would eventually end up running our own natural history production company together, but working with her has also opened my eyes to even more possibilities for wildflower photography. It's far more of a challenge to try to capture the essence of each wildflower in an artistic way than simply to record where it is living. In this way, I discovered that wildflowers could provide deep satisfaction for both halves of my brain – the logical, scientific side and the aesthetic and artistic side – in equal measure. For me, wildflowers can only be truly appreciated by combining both science and art. And that's what I've tried to do in this book.

Without knowing it at the time, I think the seeds for this book were sown back in 1989 when I came across a book called *The Flowering of Britain*, by writer Richard Mabey and photographer Tony Evans. The book also inspired a documentary that aired as part of the BBC's *World About Us* series. In both book and TV programme, the idea was to capture the beauty and natural history of Britain's wildflowers in both words and pictures. Tony Evans admitted that trying to make every image in the book a work of art was something of a challenge, though he succeeded admirably. And when I embarked on the photographic side of this project, my admiration for Evans' work and his dogged determination only grew.

Another inspiration – and indeed my title – comes from a much older book. In 1851 the Reverend Charles Alexander Johns published *Flowers of the Field*, a book that became known as the amateur botanist's bible. His detailed text was illustrated by around 200 engravings based on beautiful watercolours, some by his sisters, others by Emily Stackhouse, a botanical artist who, like Johns, lived in Cornwall. He had already published many other books on British natural history, but *Flowers of the Field* was by far the most popular. It ran to fifty editions and was in print for over a century. Johns described a wide range of plants along with their uses but was inspired by the beauty of wild flowers as much as by their scientific interest. Many of his early books exhorted his readers to reach God through an appreciation of His works in nature. *Flowers of the Field* lacked these biblical overtones, so it was ironic that it was so often referred to as the botanist's bible. In this book, I've mixed art and science in a similar way, although using modern technology that Johns could never have dreamed of, and I'll be more than happy with a fraction of the success of the Reverend Johns' book.

I spent seven years travelling around Britain to gather the photographs, continually challenging myself to see these wildflowers through different eyes, trying to capture the beauty of individual plants – or parts of plants – as well as their harmony with the landscapes in which they were growing. After more than thirty years of making wildlife films, it should have come as no surprise to me that things are never as easy as you imagine at the start. It's rare to find the perfect plants growing in the perfect spot and even rarer to encounter this happy scenario when the light also just happens to be perfect! But the task of trying to take better and better photographs over those seven years gave me the perfect excuse to spend long days in the field and to travel to all manner of beautiful locations, from the machair grasslands of the Outer Hebrides to the chalk cliffs of Kent.

Sea rocket forms large clumps at the top of white shell-sand beaches along the Atlantic shores of South Uist, Outer Hebrides.

There are about 3,500 species in the British flora, which conventionally includes ferns, horsetails and conifers as well as flowering plants. This is far too great a number to cover in depth with either photographs or text, so my first decision had to be which species or families of plants to include. I've unashamedly focused mainly on our more spectacular wildflowers. In part this gave me more scope for the photographic part of the project, but these are also the most well-loved and popular of our plants. I've devoted individual chapters to our most familiar wildflowers such as bluebells, wild daffodils, fritillaries and ramsons, all of which grow in spectacular and photogenic displays. But the final choice of which wildflowers to include was driven by the scientific aspects of the book too – those plants that have the most interesting natural history stories to tell. Other chapters therefore cover groups of plants (for example, orchids, alliums and primulas) in which the plants, although individually beautiful, are also windows on to some of the most fundamental concepts in biology.

Then came the question of how to arrange these chapters in a way that placed the detailed stories in a broader context, and that also

highlighted the diversity and history of the broad range of habitats in which these plants grow. And for that, I turned for inspiration to the National Vegetation Classification, known fondly to botanists and ecologists across the country as the NVC.

I'll deal with more detailed aspects of the NVC in later chapters but, in short, it's an attempt to create at least some kind of scientific order from the bewildering variety of habitats across the British Isles. The NVC recognizes nearly 600 different categories of habitat, so you might legitimately wonder whether it has created less or more bewilderment. However, it does break down these habitats into a few broad categories, published in five definitive volumes. Broadly, terrestrial habitats fall across three of these volumes and, with a little further simplification on my part, these form the three main sections of *Flowers of the Field*. Two sections cover the distinctly different habitats of 'Woodland' and 'Grassland'. The third covers the NVC volume that describes shingle, sand, saltmarsh and cliffs. I've called this section 'Open Ground', since most of these habitats remain open naturally. Most grassland, on the other hand, would revert to woodland if left to its own devices.

I've written an introduction to each of these sections, describing the history and variety of woodlands, grasslands and open habitats as well as the unique challenges faced by plants living in each of these places. These introductory chapters also briefly cover the natural history of some of the more conspicuous and characteristic plants of these places that don't have their own dedicated chapter. The principal players, with their own chapters, are then grouped together in the appropriate section. However, plants are extremely adaptable, and those chapters that tell the stories of larger families inevitably touch on species characteristic of other sections. The orchid family, for example, is at home in grassland, woodland and open habitats but since a small majority (including some of the most spectacular) live in grassland, I've included the orchid chapter in this section.

On those cold, rainy days when I couldn't be in the field with my camera, I began to read through all the scientific papers I could find on my chosen plants, both in the UK and elsewhere in their range. Although the flowers that form the principal subjects of the following chapters are either British natives or widely naturalized here, I've also included the stories of these plants beyond the British Isles. This provides a broader framework in which to understand their behaviour in the British context, and therefore deepens our understanding of them. The behaviour of a plant growing in the UK may sometimes be very different from that of the same plant growing in another part of Europe or elsewhere. They may be on the edge of their range here, or vanishingly rare, whilst growing like weeds in other places. And the details of their biology may differ. For example, if a plant is pollinated by different insects in mainland Europe, its reproductive strategies there may be very different.

I make no apology for diving deep into the biology of these plants. Indeed, this was one of the main reasons I set out to write this book. I want to take the reader on a journey through both nature and science, to use popular and familiar wildflowers to explore cutting-edge research and show, for example, that molecular biology and folklore are just two sides of the same coin. Though I've tried to tread the narrow line between over-simplification and biological accuracy, general readers may occasionally find that the complexities of such processes as polyploidy or heterostyly make their head spin. But they should console themselves with the fact that such topics often trigger the same reaction in many practising botanists! And these intimate details are part of the joy of our wildflowers.

I love the fact that I can wander through a cowslip meadow or bluebell wood and let the sights and smells still my soul or, in a different mood, let these same plants bring to mind some intriguing and deep biological questions. Primulas inspired Charles Darwin and a long line of botanists since to ponder the reasons for heterostyly (the presence of different kinds of flowers in the same species) whilst orchids are the perfect plants through which to appreciate the intricacies of polyploidy (multiples of the basic number of chromosomes). Without knowing it, many people already appreciate the effects of polyploidy when they revel in the sheer variety of our wildflowers. How much more satisfying are our days in the field when we appreciate just how that diversity came to be.

After thirty-five years of making science and wildlife documentaries, I don't believe any story is too difficult to tell – so long as it is told well. And, as an avid collector of natural history books, I am sure that some of the stories in the following pages have never been told for a general readership. I hope that more than three decades of making popular wildlife and science TV documentaries has equipped me to do these stories justice and to inspire an even deeper appreciation of British wildflowers.

part

I

WOODLANDS

Introduction

AFTER THE ICE

We are currently in the middle of an ice age – the Quaternary Ice Age – which began about two and a half million years ago. In its four and a half billion-year history our planet has been through several such extended ice ages, some in the ancient past so severe that the whole Earth, from poles to tropics, was completely buried under ice. During these periods of 'snowball Earth' it's a wonder that life (mostly microscopic at the time) survived at all, to evolve into the rich diversity we see around us today and into a species capable of contemplating that diversity. Luckily for us, more recent ice ages, including the one we are now living in, are less severe and consist of alternating advances and retreats of the ice sheets and glaciers. Longer cold glacial periods give way to shorter inter-glacials, during which the climate warms and drives back the ice to the highest latitudes and the tops of mountains. This distinctive pattern is driven by a variety of factors, all interacting in complex ways. These include the position of the continents on the face of the Earth and the consequent pattern of ocean currents, responsible in part for triggering an ice age in the first place. Added to that, the whole planet wobbles in several different ways as it orbits the sun, like a spinning top as it slows down. This has the effect of periodically warming then cooling the higher latitudes, so driving the cycle of glacials and inter-glacials.

The current inter-glacial began around 12,000 to 10,000 years ago, and encompasses the whole of human civilization, from the birth of agriculture to walking on the moon. In the natural course of events, we may only be about halfway through this rather eventful warm period and can look forward to another 12,000 years or more before the ice returns.[1] In fact, our current inter-glacial might last even longer. Calculating how the wobbles affect the cycles of glacials and inter-glacials, some scientists think that our current warm period might last another 50,000 years.[2] Yet others believe that the human impact on the Earth's climate might be enough to disrupt these natural cycles entirely and we may never now return to a colder glacial period, at least during the current ice age.[3] Human-induced climate change could mark a sudden end of the Quaternary Ice Age.

But whatever the future holds, the past has certainly seen equally dramatic changes in climate and consequently in Britain's flora and

Left: Ancient gnarled pines in the Black Wood of Ranoch, Perth and Kinross, one of the finest remaining examples of Caledonian pine forest.

Above: Lesser twayblade, an inconspicuous orchid, grows on mossy pillows below the towering pines.

Overleaf: Lower Woods in South Gloucestershire is an example of ancient mixed deciduous woodland.

fauna. At the end of the last glacial period ice sheets extended right down to southern Britain and those places beyond the ice were bleak tundra. So much water was locked up in these massive volumes of ice that global sea levels were much lower than today and Britain was joined to continental Europe across parts of the North Sea and the Channel. Today, it's still possible to catch a glimpse of Britain at the end of the last glacial period by climbing our highest mountains. The vast plateau of the Cairngorms, towering over Speyside, is so cold and exposed that it's covered in tundra, home to plants and animals more at home in the Arctic. Like little snowballs, snow buntings bounce from rock to rock. Dotterels, with bellies that look like they've been stained with iodine, are so tame you can walk to within a few feet of them. If the howling wind calms for a moment, the creaking calls of ptarmigan, unseen in lichen-toned feathers, drift across the boulder-strewn plateau.

These areas are too bleak for trees to grow and so remain naturally open. The plants of such habitats are dealt with in the section on 'Open Ground' (see pages 349–456), yet as I explore this bit of the Arctic in Scotland, I realize that I'm also striding over the first forests to colonize Britain after the ice began its retreat. Dwarf willows hug the ground with their gnarled stems, creeping between boulders and raising tough leathery leaves just a few centimetres above the ground. In wetter, peaty patches dwarf birch grows in a similar form, natural bonsai specimens shaped by the short growing season and constant exposure to cutting winds.

When the ice began its northwards retreat around 10,000 years ago, it exposed virgin land, scoured and scraped by the slow grind of a mile or more thickness of ice over many millennia. The warming climate allowed less hardy plants to colonize this new land, a blank canvas on which today's diverse flora would slowly be painted. Meanwhile, tundra species tracked the ice sheets northwards, eventually becoming isolated on the high tops like the Cairngorm plateau. In the wake of the ice, trees began to arrive in Britain from refuges further south. The pioneering forests were made up of species like those I'd seen on the Cairngorms – dwarf birches and willows, along with juniper. At first these were just shrubs, but soon taller birches and willows arrived, together with aspen. Then Scots pine and hazel gained a roothold, followed, as the climate continued to warm, by species now familiar across the country – oak, ash, alder, elm, lime, field maple. The last trees to arrive before rising sea levels severed our land bridge to Europe were beech and hornbeam.[4]

WOODLANDS ACROSS BRITAIN

These broadly different types of forests – Arctic shrubs, birch, willow and aspen forests, pine forests and broadleaf forests – all moved north as the climate continued to improve – waves of vegetation following their favoured climactic conditions. Today, dwarf forests of birch and willow are found high in the mountains. Scots pine grows in a broad swathe across Scotland on poorer soils (though this tree has been widely planted elsewhere) where it forms the great Caledonian pine forest. In the past, the Caledonian pine forest was more widespread and may have had different origins in different areas. Some of the earliest fossil evidence for Scots pine after the Ice Age comes from Loch Maree in western Scotland. This may be where the Caledonian pine forest first grew, some 9,600 years ago, and today pine trees in this area are genetically distinct from the trees elsewhere in their natural range. It seems that, in the wake of the retreating ice, pine trees arrived in Scotland from two distinct refuges. The western trees, which colonised the area around Loch Maree, probably survived the Ice Age in Ireland, although the origin of the other trees is still unknown.[5] By 1600 these natural pine forests had been reduced to scattered fragments, to much the same extent as we see today.

The Caledonian pine forest couldn't be more different from plantations of Scots pine. In natural forests, ancient twisted pines grow from carpets of heather or bilberry and domes of colourful mosses, and they are full of special plants and animals. Red squirrels and crossbills prise open cones to feast on seeds, crested tits churr from the branches and below, orchids like creeping lady's tresses or lesser twayblade nestle in mossy pillows.

Further south in Britain, broadleaf forests predominate. Within this broad pattern there are many different types of forest, depending not only on climate but on local geology and topography. Every woodland is unique, but scientists trying to understand basic ecological principles and make comparisons and contrasts need to impose some order on this natural diversity. In the 1980s ecologists developed a comprehensive classification scheme for all of Britain's habitats. Called the National Vegetation Classification (or NVC for short), it was the first systematic survey of British vegetation and is built on a numerical analysis of the

Red squirrels are still common in Scottish pine forests and across Ireland but confined to a few scattered places in England and Wales.

Right: Hazel catkins brighten up the days of early February.

species present in any particular habitat. This has resulted in more rigorous definitions of communities and sub-communities of plants. There are twenty-five woodland communities: W1 to W25 (though only eighteen are true woodland, the others being scrub communities). Appended to this rather prosaic description are the Latin names of some of the characteristic plant species. So, the remaining fragments of Caledonian pine forest are known as W18 – *Pinus sylvatica – Hylocomium splendens* woodland. Not perhaps as evocative as 'The Great Wood of Caledon' but more scientifically useful as W18 can be divided into a number of sub-communities allowing ecologists to see, among other things, which kinds of pine forest are most threatened. But the NVC is not the end of the story.

The NVC recognizes eighteen main types of woodland. George Peterken, a woodland ecologist, has classified woodlands in a slightly different way, into twelve distinct 'stand types',[6,7] yet none of these classifications fully capture the variety of woodland in Britain. In the

mild and wet conditions along the very westernmost fringes of Scotland and Ireland, Atlantic hazel wood forms part of the Celtic rainforest. Here, hazel grows into multi-stemmed trees without any interference from humans; elsewhere, as we'll see shortly, multi-stemmed hazels are usually the result of the traditional practice of coppicing. In Atlantic hazel woods, hazel grows densely enough to shade out most other plants, but in the clean, damp air blowing in from the ocean, these woods abound in rare lichens and mosses. Such forests seem to be unique to Britain, yet they don't feature in any of the main forest classification systems.[8] Elsewhere, these western temperate rainforests consist of oakwoods, yet these also miss out in formal classifications of our woodlands.[9]

For small islands, the British Isles has (or had) an astounding variety of woodland types. At one end of the spectrum, Wistman's Wood on Dartmoor is an elfin forest of gnarled and twisted pendunculate oaks growing amongst huge moss-covered boulders. It's one of only three high-altitude oak woods on Dartmoor and looks like it should be

Wistman's Wood, on Dartmoor, Devon, one of the highest oak woods in Britain, is an elfin forest of gnarled English (pedunculate) oaks.

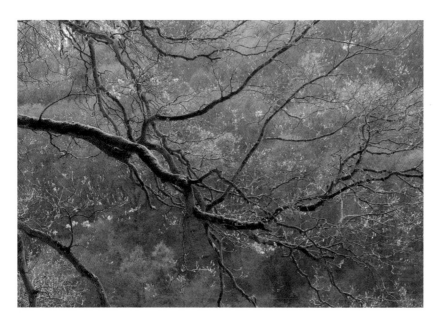

Left: Bud burst in the forests of the lower Wye Valley, along the border between Gloucestershire and Gwent.

Right: Autumn in a Cotswold beech wood.

home to moorland sprites or fairies. In complete contrast, entering one of the great beech hangars on the chalk hills of Hampshire is like walking into a cathedral. Smooth trunks rise like pillars to an arching green canopy, dense enough to shade out all but the most specialized plants. The forest floor is covered with a carpet of golden beech leaves, with few shrubs or other plants in the way to obstruct the long view of a beechwood's spectacular architecture. Although herbaceous plants may be scarce, these beech forests are famous for their fungi. Large fairy rings are common and there's always something magical about finding an earthstar, *Geastrum* spp., peeled back to reveal what looks like an egg sitting in a nest, the structure which contains the fungus's spores.

WILDWOOD

Before human activity altered natural dynamics it used to be assumed that most of Britain was forested, though as we'll see shortly that may be too simplistic a view. Today, forests across Britain are made up of different trees in different areas, reflecting local geography and geology as well as a long history of human management. But how much of this variety can be traced back to variations in the wildwood? Was there ever a period of stability during our current inter-glacial when the northward march of

trees slowed and a settled pattern of different types of natural woodland established itself? Can we look back to a period when we can discern such truly wild woods? If we can it would probably be over the few millennia of the Atlantic period – a time of optimum climate in our part of the world which began around 8,000 years ago. But during this time, humans became part of the equation. So, was the wildwood truly wild?

Humans lived across northern Europe even during the height of the last glaciation, using their intelligence to survive by hunting and gathering on land free of ice. With the retreat of the ice, these small bands of people could move north and adapt to a less harsh life as Britain's forests took root. At first these Mesolithic cultures would have had little effect on the nature of the wildwood. Doubtless, they dug waterholes or cleared off brush to allow grass to grow, to draw in game for hunting, much as North America's Indians were doing when Columbus arrived in the New World in the fifteenth century. In fact, American Indians probably had much bigger effects than Britain's Mesolithic hunters since British trees are much harder to kill. Indians killed trees by ring-barking and the dead timber and stumps then burned readily. Using such techniques, they converted large areas of forest to lightly wooded grassland, which drew large herds of deer. When the first Europeans landed on the east coast of America, they found great tracts of forest that looked more like parkland, with trees spaced widely enough that, as Giovanni da Verrazzano declared in the early years of the sixteenth century, he could have driven a carriage through it for hundreds of miles with great ease. Britain's forests don't burn (except pine forests), which limits the impact of Britain's Mesolithic cultures on the wildwood. All this would change when farming arrived on our shores around 7,000 years ago, but before then, with perhaps just a light impact from small numbers of hunter-gatherers, it's a natural question to ask what the wildwood looked like. What would it have been like to explore a more or less natural forest?

That turns out to be a surprisingly hard question to answer. If any fragment of wildwood has survived intact, it will be on tiny uninhabited islands in large lakes or other remote locations – hardly typical and even this is doubtful. Perhaps the Atlantic

Wild boar were once key creatures in the wildwood, rotavating the forest floor and helping to create the ever-changing mosaic of grasslands, scrub and woodland that characterised truly natural forests.

hazel woods are remnants of the wildwood, but if so, they are so specialized that they certainly aren't representative of the rest of Britain. Yet the quest for the wildwood resonates strongly with many people beyond the world of professional ecologists. Thanks to ancient folk tales that have found their way into Europe's great fairytales, the wildwood, with its wild beasts and wicked witches, has terrified generations of children. Yet this is a wildwood of the imagination, not the real thing. By the time such tales were being told, Europe's remaining forests had been completely altered from any natural state by generations of management for their valuable resources of timber and wood.

Today there are two competing visions of the wildwood among ecologists. One, the Tansley model, named after the influential British botanist and ecologist Arthur Tansley (1871–1955), sees the wildwood as 'trees forever' – a continuous canopy of trees with perhaps small glades created when trees die and come crashing down. The other, the Vera model, was developed more recently by the Dutch ecologist Frans Vera for northern Europe.[10] This model sees the wildwood as a mosaic of woodland, scrub and open grassland, created and maintained by big grazers and browsers, like aurochs, horses and bison, present in Europe at the time. Vera developed this idea to explain the curious abundance of pollen from grassland species in ancient lake deposits when conventional wisdom suggested that the land should have been almost entirely covered in trees.

To get a clearer idea of what this new vision of the wildwood might look like, Dutch ecologists are trying to recreate it at Oostvaardersplassen, an area along the coast east of Amsterdam. Unfortunately, several of the key big grazers – aurochs and wild horses or tarpan – are now extinct, so have been replaced by konik ponies and Heck cattle as 'ecological analogues' of those wildwood grazers. Heck cattle originated in Germany in the 1920s and 1930s when the Heck brothers attempted to back-breed the extinct aurochs. Their methodology, however, is generally seen as flawed and the end result, though an impressive beast, is no more an aurochs than the Spanish fighting bulls which formed a large part of their breeding stock. At Oostvaardersplassen Heck cattle and konik ponies are joined by red deer in an area known now as the Dutch Serengeti. The animals are left to their own devices and nature is allowed to take its course in a new style of management called rewilding. Most forms of conservation management are targeted to achieve certain aims – either to create and maintain particular habitats, like flower-rich meadows, or to benefit particular species. All of these conserve habitats and species

deemed important by humans. In rewilding, nature takes the driving seat and is allowed to develop as it will, even if it doesn't necessarily produce conventional results. As ambitious as the Oostvaardersplassen project is, it might not satisfactorily answer the question of what the wildwood looked like as there are no big predators here and studies elsewhere have shown that the presence of predators drastically alters the behaviour of their prey and therefore patterns of grazing.

Some scientists are so convinced by this new way of managing environments that they are no longer content with using ecological analogues as grazers. They are trying once again to bring back the aurochs to help rewild new areas. And they are having more success than the Heck brothers, thanks to modern scientific techniques. Some years ago I met with biologists at Wageningen University who showed me how they had sequenced the genetic code of the aurochs using sub-fossil remains from various parts of Europe. Not far away, on an area of polders, cattle breeders have assembled a herd of primitive breeds from different parts of the world. Each of these old breeds preserves some part of the aurochs' genome and the aim of the breeders was to selectively mate these cattle to reassemble as much of the original aurochs' genome as possible, using the template created at Wageningen University as a guide. To distinguish these modern animals from the historic aurochs, the scientists and breeders call them tauros and the venture itself is known as the Tauros Programme. It's an extraordinary endeavour, not quite Jurassic Park perhaps, but I still found the concept amazing as I drove around the

The woodlands of the Wye Valley have a rich diversity of tree species, including both small-leaved and large-leaved lime, the latter now a scarce tree in the wild in Britain.

polders with one of the breeders, looking for the offspring of those first experimental crosses. We eventually discovered one, a tauros standing proudly on a small rise surveying his domain, and it looked uncannily like an aurochs, even just one generation down the line – enough to send a small shiver down my spine.

Unfortunately, the Oostvaardersplassen experiment, which continued to rely on Heck cattle and konik ponies, has suffered a recent setback, at least in terms of public opinion. Several mild winters allowed the grazing herds to increase in size but in the hot, dry summer of 2018 they began to starve and many animals had to be culled to avoid further suffering. This caused a public outcry and drew a critical official report. Yet this, of course, was what the experiment was all about. Nature often goes through boom and bust cycles which might even have been important factors in structuring the wildwood. Perhaps we're not quite ready yet, in our minds and attitudes, to hand back control to nature, even though it had been doing a pretty good job for three and a half billion years before we came along. And we still don't know whether big numbers of grazers could or did create the mosaic of grassland and woodland that Frans Vera suggested.

Some lines of evidence suggest that grazers and browsers may not have had such big effects on the wildwood. Ireland was cut off by rising sea levels even before the rest of Britain, so many plants and animals moving north from Europe never made it as far as Ireland. That included many of the big grazers that roamed Europe's forests. So, using the Vera model, it might be expected that Ireland's forests would contain less grassland, which should show up as less pollen from grassland species in ancient peat and soil samples collected from there. In fact there is little difference in Irish samples and samples from further south in Europe.[11] There's still the puzzle that grassland species are present in all areas in remarkable abundance, but the effect doesn't seem to be due to large grazers. Instead, the scientists that carried out this survey suggest that we humans had already begun to open up the forest during this period and provide habitats for grassland species, as we've continued to do ever since.[12]

FOREST CLEARANCE

In the story of Britain's – indeed Europe's – woodlands, the true wildwood has long since vanished. If our Mesolithic forebears had only small impacts on the endless forest, all that changed when farming arrived in a Neolithic revolution. Agriculture arose independently in several different parts of the world – the Far East, New Guinea, South America – but our farming heritage began in Mesopotamia, between the Tigris and

Euphrates rivers in the Middle East, an area fittingly called the Fertile Crescent. This revolution began just as the glacial period was coming to an end, a time when global climate and weather patterns changed dramatically. It was once thought that these new farmers migrated across Europe and into Britain, replacing hunter-gatherer cultures, though it's more likely that it was the idea and techniques of agriculture that spread, to be adopted with enthusiasm by local cultures. In any case, agriculture needed open fields and the clearance of the wildwood accelerated.

No single person has done more to tell the complex story of Britain's woodlands across the millennia than Oliver Rackham (1939–2015). As an historical ecologist working at the University of Cambridge he de-bunked many myths about woodland history and developed the concept of 'ancient woodland', the richest and most diverse types of woodland. Despite the serious inroads into woodland made by those early farmers, Rackham always professed to have a great admiration for the rapidity with which they carved out extensive fields. Clearing trees in Britain is not easy. In many places, for example the eastern forests of North America, the forests burn readily, making the job of creating fields much easier. In the New World, cultures that were essentially Stone Age had

The Scots pines growing around Loch Maree in the Northwest Highlands of Scotland are genetically distinct from those growing elsewhere and were probably the first to recolonise Scotland after the end of the last glaciation.

widespread impacts on the great eastern forests. Most British forests are very hard to burn, so trees had to be cleared by laboriously felling them, at first with primitive stone tools.

With the advent of metal tools in the Bronze Age, the wildwood disappeared even more quickly, and by the Iron Age, it's estimated that only 50 per cent was left. These clearances took place during an extended colder and wetter period in the climate which allowed vast bogs to form in upland and western areas when trees were cleared (see Introduction to Part III, Open Ground, pages 360–361). And during this time, the composition of the remaining wildwood changed. An event called the elm decline, recorded by a drastic fall in elm pollen around 5,000 years ago, may have been due to diseases carried by bark beetles. We have seen a similar event in more recent times when Dutch elm disease ravaged our countryside. In reality, this may be a more frequent occurrence than we think. Recent research has found evidence for a drop in elm pollen as long ago as 7,300 years and the same scientists found the remains of two kinds of bark beetle (*Scolytus striatus* and *S. multistriatus*) in these early samples. These beetles are known vectors of Dutch elm disease today, suggesting that a similar epidemic was responsible for the widespread loss of elms 5,000 years ago. But there's also evidence in the samples of increasing human activity, so it's likely that the elm decline had multiple causes.[13] Lime also declined in the wildwood, probably owing in part to continued changes in the climate, but here too humans doubtless played a role. Lime leaves make excellent fodder for livestock.[14]

Forest clearances continued under the Roman occupation of Britain and although there is evidence of forest recolonising deserted farms after the Romans abandoned their northern outposts in some places, the general trend was only one way. During the Norman period only 15 per cent of our land was forested and by the fourteenth century the figure had dropped to 10 per cent. From this point, the overall percentage of forest cover seems to have remained stable since the remaining woodlands had become tightly integrated into both local and national economies.

FOREST MANAGEMENT

As soon as people began to try to clear the wildwood they would have noticed that simply chopping down a tree won't kill it. Many British trees regrow quite happily from the stumps, often sprouting a dense

The River Wye marks the border between England and Wales for much of its length. Along its lower reaches, it has carved a narrow limestone gorge whose steep slopes are clothed in rich deciduous forest.

crop of thin poles. And if these are chopped off, they will soon grow back yet again like a hydra's head. Those same people would also have realized that this regrowth was very useful – for building or for making charcoal, their main fuel before coal. Big trees also provide big timber, useful for building the great cathedrals and then later for ships as Britain built her navy.

Chopping off trees at ground level became an established technique for managing woodland. This practice is called coppicing, and the frequency with which the regrowth can be cut depends on the species being coppiced and what the regrowth will be used for. Birch is a fast-growing colonizer of open ground (as it was after the ice retreated) and can be cut every three or four years for faggots (bundles of sticks used for fuel). Oak coppice needs around fifty years or so to produce oak poles suitable for building. But the most frequently coppiced species is hazel, which can be cut every twenty or thirty years, sometimes sooner, and the poles used in many ways, from fencing and building to making charcoal. This form of woodland management has been practised for thousands of years, certainly since the Neolithic, and in a few places it's still possible to see the evidence.

The Avalon Marshes lie just an hour's drive from my home in Bristol and are rapidly becoming one of Britain's premier sites for natural history. Large reserves managed by English Nature, the RSPB, the Hawk and Owl Trust and the Somerset Wildlife Trust now protect vast areas of marshland, home to bitterns and egrets, marsh harriers and bearded tits, otters and water voles, hordes of dragonflies and even a growing population of common cranes. In winter, the marshes fill with wildfowl and provide a roost site for millions of starlings. In the ancient past this whole area, known as the Somerset Levels, was flooded as melting ice raised the sea level at the end of the last glaciation, creating a maze of waterways, dark swampy forests of alder (alder carr) and vast impenetrable reed beds from which a few islands rose. And across these marshes a thick layer of fen peat began to build up, created by dead sedges rather than the dead sphagnum moss that creates bogland peat. To supplement their winter diet, Neolithic farmers hunted the vast flocks of wildfowl that came here, but the farming revolution they began would eventually all but destroy the Avalon Marshes.

Beginning in the Middle Ages, embankments were built along the main rivers draining the levels to prevent flooding and to carry water

more efficiently to the sea. By the eighteenth century Dutch engineers had perfected the art of draining low-lying land (creating the polders on which I'd seen the reincarnated aurochs) and they were invited to turn their attention to Britain's swampy lowlands, in particular the area around the Wash in eastern England and the Somerset Levels in the south-west. Drainage ditches (locally called rhynes) were cut through the peaty base of the marshes to carry water to the rivers and the sea, and the marshes quickly dried out, to be turned into valuable farmland. But the peat that lay under these fields also proved valuable.

Peat has been dug from the levels since Roman times, but by the Victorian age and into the first half of the twentieth century, it became a major local industry. As time passed, extensive peat diggings became large lakes as the excavations flooded and when the peat extraction finished, nature recolonized the industrial landscape and the Avalon Marshes were reborn, at least in part. Today the marshes are once again truly magical places, where Glastonbury Tor rises above early morning mist as it would have done when the first farmers hunted these marshes. Avalon, after which the marshes are named, was in Arthurian legend just such an island, perhaps even the Tor itself, but hidden behind a veil of mist, accessible only to those who knew the spells, and a place where the ancient mysteries of Britain were preserved. But I've taken this detour across the marshes because something else is preserved here – something less mystical but no less ancient.

A green carpet of bilberry contrasts with the grey trunks of Scots pine in Abernethy Forest on Speyside, Scotland.

Running for more than a mile across part of this marsh is a wooden track that was constructed around 6,000 years ago, to connect two islands. It's called the Sweet Track after its discoverer, Ray Sweet, though it was built over an older track called the Post Track, named for its construction as a wooden walkway of narrow planks held in place by posts sunk into the marsh. And it's the posts that intrigue me. They are clearly cut from coppiced trees, visible evidence that Neolithic farmers were managing the woodlands around their fields in ways that would be familiar to generations of woodsmen right up to the twenty-first century.

Woodland management evolved over this time into elaborate systems that transformed the look and ecology of British forests. One of the commonest forms of management is called coppice with standards, in which some trees, often hazel, were coppiced whilst others, such as oaks, were left to grow as tall trees – the standards. The tall trees provided shelter for the coppice growth and could also be harvested when large timbers were needed. Woodlands were also divided up into sections, called coups, each cut in rotation, so there was always wood available. New coppice growth is relished by deer and livestock alike, so each coup was surrounded by a ditch and tall bank topped with an impenetrable hedge, to keep these browsers out. Though often eroded, these earthworks are still clearly visible criss-crossing many ancient woods today. Likewise, it's not hard to find the remains of charcoal hearths or evidence of iron smelting, fuelled by all that readily available charcoal. Wandering through the dappled shade of an ancient woodland today, soaking up the tranquil atmosphere, it's worth reminding yourself that such places were often hives of industry in the past.

That industrial past has created a rich and diverse ecosystem. Many of the plants we'll meet in the following chapters thrive in coppiced woodlands, flowering in abundance a year or two after cutting, when light floods the forest floor. These plants then slowly decline as the coppice grows up, only to be given a new lease of life as the next coppice cycle begins. And since most woods were made up of many coups, all in different stages, there was always prime habitat somewhere in each woodland. Insects like Duke of Burgundy fritillaries, along with pearl-bordered and small pearl-bordered fritillaries, which depended on these plants, also flourished in coppiced woodland. The fact that coppiced woodlands are full of colour and hum with life suggests to me that we humans have inadvertently taken the place of the wildwood grazers, creating a similar mosaic of scrub, forest and open ground that likely characterized the original wildwood and in which these plants and animals evolved. But this happy state of affairs wasn't to last.

In 1825, the first steam locomotive trundled along the Stockton and Darlington railway, carrying coal from the Durham coalfields first to Stockton on the River Tees, then to an even bigger port, newly built at Middlesbrough. From here it could be transported around Britain. As the railways spread and transport improved, coal became more and more important and eclipsed charcoal as a fuel. Without the need for local coppiced woodlands, woodlands began to shrink again. By the start of the twentieth century they had reached an all-time low of around 5 per cent of our land area. The First World War saw a big demand for home-grown timber, so woodland cover increased, but these were mostly conifer plantations, more often than not of non-native species, planted in dark, serried ranks. The area of woodland is greater today, at around 12 per cent, but at least half of this is still conifer plantation.

Beech forests are famous for their spectacular autumn displays of fungi. Here an earthstar grows just outside a huge fairy ring.

Only around 1 per cent of our landscape is covered in ancient woodland.

Worse still for woodland plants and animals, during the last century coppicing all but ceased in these remaining woodlands and they began to grow into high forest. Just after the Second World War, 21 per cent of woodland was still actively coppiced and around 50 per cent was high forest, the rest being classed as scrub. By the start of the twenty-first century, 97 per cent was high forest.[15] Driven by these changes, populations of woodland insects and birds have plummeted, along with the plants on which they ultimately depend. And the remaining woodlands have also become more homogenous.

In the past, as we've seen, there was a great diversity of woodland types across the country, both in the wildwood and after human management began. But during a study in Dorset scientists noticed that there was a tendency over the last seventy years for different woodlands to become

Hoddesdon Park Woods in Hertfordshire is carpeted in wood anemones in the early spring.

more similar to each other, at least in terms of the plant species growing there, in a process they called taxonomic homogenization.[16] They suggest that a similar process is likely to be happening more widely across Britain. So when assessing the value of our woodlands for biodiversity, it's not just the presence or absence of trees that defines 'good' woodland, it's the history and continuity of management and, just as importantly, how long a patch of woodland has been covered in trees.

WOODLAND CONSERVATION

Left untouched by humans, it doesn't take long for a patch of open ground to become covered in trees but such secondary woodland doesn't shelter anything like the rich diversity of plants and animals of our best

woodlands. Oliver Rackham described it as 'grassland with trees'. That's because it takes a long time for many specialized woodland plants to colonize new woodland. So it's vital to protect our remaining ancient woodland – but what exactly do we mean by 'ancient woodland'?

Ancient woodland, as conceived by Oliver Rackham, is not the same as the wildwood which, as we've seen, hasn't been wild for a very long time. To be classed as ancient woodland it must have been continuously tree-covered since 1600 (or 1750 in Scotland). Of course, a few sites might well have been tree-covered for much longer than this but virtually all will have been managed to some degree over this period. This might appear a somewhat arbitrary definition, but it reflects the very long time it takes for woodland plants and their associated animals to become established on former open sites.

One woodland, planted in 1797 as a covert for fox hunting, was surveyed 150 years later, at which time only a few typical woodland plants had established themselves. There were some bluebells, *Hyacinthoides scripta*, and primroses, *Primula vulgaris*, but just one wood anemone,

Plants of the woodland floor. *Below left:* Sanicle. *Below right:* Sweet woodruff. *Opposite:* Wood anemone

Anemone nemorosa, though it had spread into a little patch. A similar natural experiment happened when a field adjacent to Hayley Wood in Cambridgeshire was abandoned and left to become first scrub and then tree-covered. Hayley Wood itself is ancient woodland, famous for its displays of oxlips, *P. elatior*, in the spring and has been well studied by woodland ecologists including Oliver Rackham.[17] The area now known as The Triangle was abandoned in 1920 and gave Rackham and his colleagues a chance to measure the rate at which woodland plants migrated from the ancient woodland into the new woodland. Rackham found that oxlips and dog's mercury, *Mercurialis perennis*, advanced at about a metre (3 ft) a year. Sanicle, *Sanicula europaea*, and wood anemones were much slower,[18] as might be expected from the single anemone present in the fox covert described above after 150 years. Different species are limited in their speed of colonization by different factors; some have limited dispersal abilities (for example, wood anemone and the elegant woodland grass, *Deschampsia cespitosa*), some have problems in recruitment (for example, herb paris, *Paris quadrifolia*, and common Solomon's seal, *Polygonatum multiflorum*, both plants we'll meet in more detail in the next chapter), and some have both dispersal and recruitment

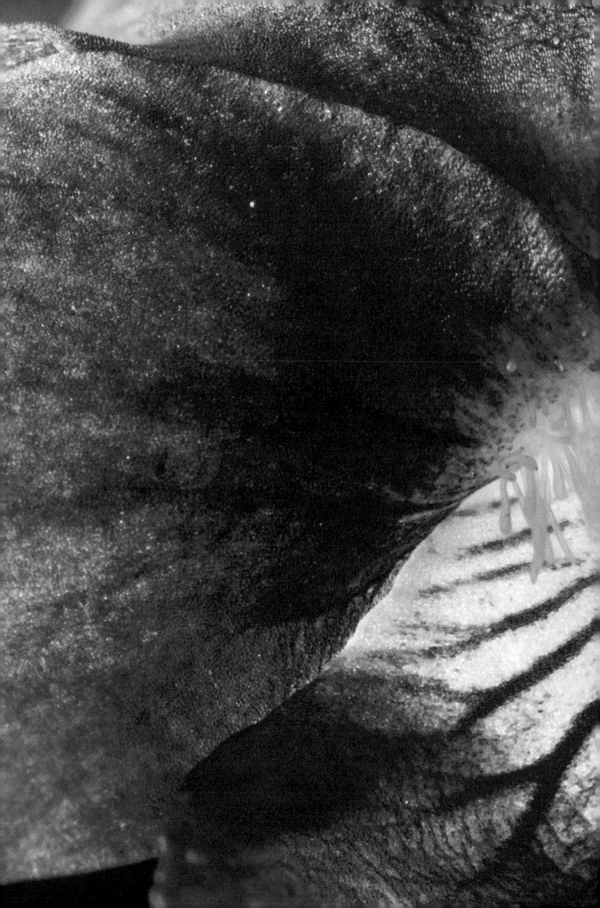

problems (including oxlip, cuckoo pint, *Arum maculatum*, and yellow archangel, *Lamium galeobdolon*).[19]

In the case of wood anemone and common Solomon's seal, along with lily of the valley, *Convallaria majalis*, their slow colonization is mainly due to the poor dispersal of their seeds.[20] And we'll see in Chapter 2 (see pages 84–86) that ramsons, *Allium ursinum*, has seeds with no means of dispersal other than gravity and yet it depends almost entirely on seed for reproduction. To aid seed dispersal some plants have evolved seeds that look like ant cocoons, hoping to fool ants into carrying their seeds back to the fertile soil of the ant nest. Others have developed structures called elaiosomes which are filled with fatty oils, a tempting treat for hungry ants. It seems like a clever trick, though it might not really be that effective. Primrose seeds have elaiosomes but those of the closely related oxlip don't. It took ants an average of just twenty minutes to find and pick up primrose seeds but it didn't take them much longer to find

Previous page: Common dog violet.

Above: Stinking iris, also more kindly known from its smell as 'roast beef plant', is one of only two species of iris native to Britain.

and pick up oxlip seeds – around thirty minutes. And both species move at about a metre (3 ft) a year. Oliver Rackham considers that oxlips could only move at that rate with the assistance of ants, despite not offering an oily feast.[21]

Because some plants take so long to colonize new woodlands, their presence at a site can be used to help identify our remaining ancient woodlands. Ecologists call such plants ancient woodland indicator species, but it's not quite as simple as it sounds. Some plants used as indicators are not strictly woodland plants. One such is the oxlip, which needs a long continuity of stable habitat to survive, but is (or was) just as happy in ancient grassland as in ancient woodland (see Chapter 9; pages 253–57). Others, such as bluebells, need the humid atmosphere of woodlands in the drier eastern counties of Britain, but in the milder, wetter west it grows in hedgerows and coastal grasslands. So bluebells are good indicators of ancient woodland in the east, but less so in the west. In the much drier climate of continental Europe they are much more strictly plants of ancient woodland.

Many of the plants in the following chapters are used as indicators of ancient woodland, and finding them means exploring some of our best woodland sites up and down the country. Of all our diverse habitats, woodlands are my favourite places to spend time. From early spring, when a strengthening sun bathes the whole forest floor in light and illuminates the whites, yellows and blues of spring flowers, to the height of summer, when only the tiniest patches of sunlight penetrate the layers of leaves, dazzlingly bright on eyes adapted to the purple-green dimness of dense shade. Then comes autumn in a blaze of new colour, in the canopy rather than on the gaudy forest floor of spring. Finally, winter reveals a skeletal framework of boughs and branches, a time when the architectural elegance of woodlands is at its most apparent. And from late winter all the way into late autumn, different plants, each with their own intriguing natural and cultural histories pop up their heads – some in spectacular displays, others more subtle in their beauty. In the following chapters I am going to explore some of the best-loved and most familiar of our rich heritage of woodland plants. I have picked species and groups that, for me, represent the essence of our woodlands and which always give me a special thrill when I find them.

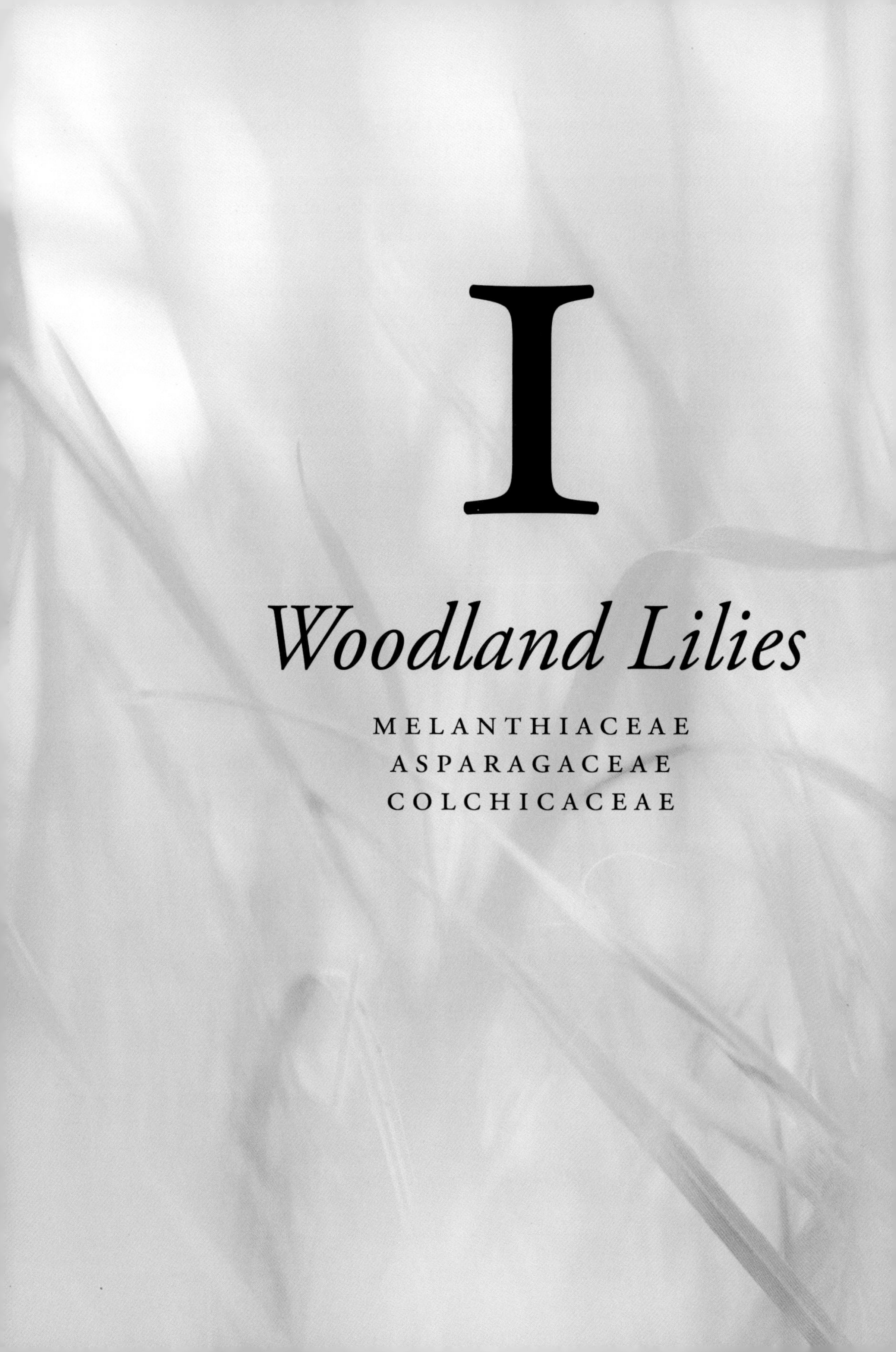

I

Woodland Lilies

MELANTHIACEAE
ASPARAGACEAE
COLCHICACEAE

Look in older field guides and you'd find all the plants in this chapter nestled cosily in the lily family, the Liliaceae. But, to borrow from human society, it was a family that had become somewhat dysfunctional. At one time it was one of the largest of all plant families, unwieldy and unhelpful as botanists began to realize that many of its members weren't related – some not even remotely so. But the story of the rise and fall of the lily dynasty is more than just a quirk of taxonomy, of interest only to hardcore botanists – it leads us on an exploration of some of the most basic concepts in natural science.

The family is named after the genus *Lilium*, the archetypal lilies, exemplified by species such as *Lilium martagon*, the martagon lily, which can be found naturalized in a few places in Britain. And how naturalized in our minds is this way of referring to a species – *Lilium martagon*. We now take it for granted that every species we come across will have such a formal two-part Latin name, genus and species – simple and effective. But it wasn't always so easy. This genus, and indeed the whole idea of giving each plant (and each animal for that matter) a unique Latin binomial, came from the work of Swedish botanist Carl Linnaeus (1707–78).

Autumn crocus (or meadow saffron) is not a true crocus. It frequents woodlands as well as meadows.

LINNAEUS: ORDER OUT OF CHAOS

Before Linnaeus, plants were described by long and cumbersome Latin phrases. Imagine botanizing with a friend and pointing out a *Plantago foliis ovato-lanceolatis pubescentibus, spica cylindrica, scapo tereti* (meaning 'plantain with pubescent ovate-lanceolate leaves, a cylindrical spike and a terete scape'). The plant would likely have withered away before you finished describing it. Today, thanks to Linnaeus, the same plant is known simply as *Plantago media* – the hoary plantain.[1] Linnaeus initially began using these brief binomial descriptions as a form of shorthand when he was studying plants eaten by cattle in Sweden. Then, with the publication of *Species Plantarum* ('The Species of Plants') in 1753, he developed this into a formal system of classification. He would later extend this to the animal kingdom as well, creating the binomial system we still use today.

In Linnaeus's system, similar species were given the same generic name, but a different species name – for example *Lilium martagon* (Martagon lily) is distinct from *Lilium pyrenaicum* (Pyrenean lily, another

lily naturalized in parts of Britain). Originally, in his shorthand, he'd intended to give each species only a number, so we might have had *Lilium 1*, *Lilium 2* and so on – a system that would have been fiendishly difficult to remember. Happily, he went on to add specific names as well – much the same as our binomials, which also evolved from longer descriptive names, though, in the Western world at least, in reverse. In Linnaeus's system I'd be Nicholls Steve. But in adopting this system, Linnaeus was, unknowingly, doing far more than just imposing some much-needed order on our understanding of the natural world.

It would be another century before Charles Darwin published *On the Origin of Species*, outlining a mechanism whereby species could split and evolve into new species, creating a pattern that Darwin visualized as a tree of life. Yet Linnaeus's system, at least at the level of species, fitted this new view of life perfectly. Linnaeus regarded species that more closely resemble each other as more closely related and therefore placed them in the same genus. But for him, the relationships between different species were simply a reflection of the mind of God, the plan behind His creation. After Darwin, botanists understood what this really meant – that more closely related species had more recently evolved from a common ancestor. Higher levels of classification, families and orders, for example, contain more distant relatives – species that still share a common ancestor, but further back in time.

Darwin's analogy of a tree, famously sketched in one of his notebooks and underscored with the words 'I think', is illuminating. The trunk gives rise to numerous large boughs, each of which in turn gives rise to branches, which then divide again into clusters of twigs. What this means for a meaningful classification of the natural world is that at each level of classification – genus, family, order, class (twigs, branches, boughs) etc. – all its members should descend from a single common ancestor, increasingly further back in time as the level of classification becomes broader. In this ideal situation, each level of classification is described as monophyletic – meaning simply that its members are all descended from a single ancestor. But the world is rarely ideal.

The problem is that we don't have a clear picture of any plant species' entire journey through time. The only direct way of observing the past is by finding fossils, but the fossil record is far from complete, even more so for plants as soft material is less likely to be fossilized. This unfortunate fact was lamented over by Darwin himself on numerous occasions. Instead, botanists had to rely on indirect methods to infer the patterns of branching on the tree of life. Linnaeus used the structure and number of the sexual organs of plants to deduce their relationships. In fact, he seemed a bit obsessed with sex. He scandalized both the church and fellow scientists by suggesting plants had sex. Many of the Latin names he gave to both animals and plants had explicit sexual connotations and his description of reproduction in flowering plants reads like an overheated romantic novel.

> *Love comes even to the plants... The flowers' leaves serve as a bridal bed, which the creator has so gloriously arranged, adorned with such noble bed curtains and perfumed with so many soft scents that the bridegroom with his bride might there celebrate their nuptials with so much the greater solemnity. When the bed has thus been made ready, then is the time for the bridegroom to embrace his beloved bride and surrender himself to her.*[2]

It's not the sort of thing you'll find in most botanical texts, but nevertheless Linnaeus's detailed – perhaps too detailed – study of the sexual organs of plants enabled him to begin to bring some order to the chaos. And as well as giving each species a binomial name, he also used

Herb paris. The most conspicuous part of its flower is its large, dark purple ovary.

the structure of flowers to place his species into higher categories. But since he had no concept of the tree-like branching pattern of evolution and since he used relatively few characters, his higher classification system was somewhat artificial – not so much a reflection of the mind of God as the mind of Linnaeus. But even before the origins of species were understood, other botanists sought a more natural classification of the vegetable kingdom.

One such person was the French botanist Michel Adanson, who created the lily family in 1763 to include genera he saw as natural kin to *Lilium*. The Liliaceae was formally named in 1789 by another French botanist, Antoine Laurent de Jussieu, who set the bar for admittance to this family by describing the key features that any plant must possess to be considered a lily, including a calyx of six equal coloured parts, six

Herb paris. Male anthers, surrounding the female parts of the flower, are held aloft, exposed to the breeze which carries the pollen of this largely wind-pollinated plant.

stamens, a single style and a three-chambered capsule. Unfortunately, he'd set the bar rather low. A great many plants possessed these features and the family grew rapidly. In the end the Liliaceae became a dumping ground for any species that didn't quite fit anywhere else.

Even as early as the middle of the nineteenth century, the English botanist and gardener John Lindley saw the Liliaceae as a problem family. Lindley was one of the first English naturalists to concern himself with uncovering the patterns of relationships in the natural world. He followed the system established by Jussieu,[3] who had abandoned Linnaeus's higher classification (though keeping the handy binomial system) in favour of one he felt more natural.[4] But Lindley recognized that Jussieu's Lily family was far from a natural grouping. When Linnaeus created the genus *Lilium* in 1753, he described only seven species, but eventually the lily family grew to 4,500 species in 300 genera.

It is only in the last few decades, with the advent of techniques that can probe the genetics of plants at the molecular level, that some semblance of natural order has been imposed on the lily family. Being able to read key sections of a plant's genetic code and compare it with others should, in theory, give a definitive answer on family relationships.

In the 1990s an international group of botanists came together to form the Angiosperm Phylogeny Group, whose mission was to use these new techniques to overhaul the whole classification system of flowering plants (Angiosperms). The work is ongoing, but new classification systems have been released from time to time, beginning with APG I in 1998. At the time of writing, the latest refinement is APG IV (2016). Of course, the system isn't perfect. It's complicated and not everyone agrees with the assumptions and interpretations that must be made, but it's better than previous systems. And it has carved a broad swathe through the lily family.

All the plants in this chapter, Solomon's seals, herb paris, May lily, lily of the valley and autumn crocus, have, despite several of their common names, been exiled from the lily family. These ex-lilies are further united by their liking for woodlands, though a few, like autumn crocus, *Colchicum autumnale*, grow happily in both woodlands and meadows and in some places lily of the valley grows on open limestone pavement.

Among the most dramatic of these woodland 'lilies' are the Solomon's seals, *Polygonatum* spp (species). They get their name from the scars (the 'seals') along the underground rhizome that mark the position of old stems. The biblical Solomon is said to have used the supposed magical properties of this rhizome to turn boulders into building material for his temple and this association with that famously wise king is widespread across Europe. In many languages, their name translates to 'Solomon's seal' (including *sceau de Salomon* in French; *Salomonssiegel* in German). The equally enigmatic name 'herb paris', on the other hand, has nothing to do with the capital of France. It comes from the Latin 'pars', meaning equal, and refers to the beautifully symmetrical four leaves held like a parasol on top of a tall stem – though sometimes that symmetry is broken by a plant with five leaves and there are a couple of forests in Yorkshire where plants with seven leaves occur.

HERB PARIS

Herb paris, *Paris quadrifolia*, pushes its leaves above ground when the soil temperature reaches 7°C. But soil temperature can vary a lot across even a small patch of woodland, so often some plants are in full leaf whilst others, perhaps only a few metres away, are just emerging. And it's hard to predict exactly when the best displays will be on show. Soil temperature in spring varies so much from year to year that there can easily be a month's difference in the timing of this plant's appearance.[5] Herb paris is fairly widespread across Britain, though nowhere is it common, and I always feel that coming across its elegant whorls of leaves catching the shifting sunspots that pattern the forest floor in early spring marks that woodland as special. It's such an elegant plant that a few nurseries have now begun to cultivate it and it makes a spectacular plant

Woodland lilies. *Left to Right:* common Solomon's seal, lily of the valley, herb paris flower, and the architectural elegance of the whole herb paris plant.

for a woodland garden, one which should really be more widely known amongst gardeners.

All of the plants in this chapter produce flowers and seeds though they can also spread vegetatively. Plants can reproduce in two ways. Sexual reproduction depends on flowers and involves pollination, followed by fertilization and the eventual production of seeds. Asexual reproduction is accomplished by vegetative growth, for example by the spreading of rhizomes or by the splitting of bulbs to form two or more daughter bulbs. Sexual reproduction often involves pollination by unrelated individuals, so seeds are genetically different from their parents and from each other. Vegetative reproduction on the other hand can only produce a genetic clone of the parent plant. The flowers of herb paris are peculiar wiry green structures that reflect the plant's fourfold symmetry – twelve stamens and four stigmas, sitting on top of a dark purple ovary, the most conspicuous part of the flower. Some of their close relatives produce much more showy flowers. Many species of *Trilliums* grow across North America and Asia and, in leaf, look very much like herb paris, but with three leaves instead of four. However, several kinds create spectacular floral displays. In the Appalachian Mountains in North Carolina and Virginia, I've wandered through woodlands carpeted with large-flowered trillium, *T. grandiflorum*, each plant bearing at its centre a single large white flower, its threefold symmetry perfectly reflecting that of the leaves. Other species produce yellow or red flowers, though *T. apetalum* is more like herb paris in having very inconspicuous flowers.

The unobtrusive offerings of herb paris, with neither scent nor nectar, but with exposed anthers, bear all the hallmarks of wind-pollinated flowers, though the dark purple ovary does seem to attract small flies, which may carry pollen from plant to plant. In the absence of either wind or bugs, herb paris also has a back-up plan – self-pollination. After the flowers have been open for a while, the anthers bend upwards to touch the stigmas and release their pollen. In addition, tiny pollen-robbing mites may also inadvertently transfer pollen to the stigmas of the same flower.[6]

But how successful the resulting seedlings are depends on the kind of woodland in which the plants are growing. In moist woods, seedlings do quite well. This results in patches of herb paris that, being the result of sexual reproduction, are all genetically different. In dry woods, few seedlings seem to reach adulthood and the plants must rely on vegetative growth. Here, herb paris produces much denser stands, all clones of a single founding individual.[7] Herb paris is very slow growing. It can take several decades to reach maturity, but the plants are extremely long-lived. Some estimates suggest that herb paris may live for more than 500 years.[8] But, as impressive as this sounds, many plants that reproduce by cloning themselves are extremely long-lived. Aspen is a tree with similar habits. There are beautiful groves of white-stemmed quaking aspens in North America that look like conventional woodland, but in reality each grove is just one single tree with many stems. And these stands are truly ancient. The oldest 'tree', called Pando – an aspen grove in Utah – is reckoned to be 80,000 years old (or at least its roots are). Even so, 500 years for an herbaceous plant, or clones of it, is still good going.

SOLOMON'S SEALS

Garden Solomon's seal, a hybrid between common and angular Solomon's seals.

The flowers of our three Solomon's seals are only a little more conspicuous than those of herb paris. But, though not large, they hang elegantly from the leaf axils in an attractive display. The most widespread species, the

Whorled Solomon's seal, a very rare plant of a few Scottish woodlands.

Overleaf: May lily, a scarce plant of acid woodlands in a few eastern counties of England.

common Solomon's seal, *P. multiflorum*, has little bunches of around two to six white flowers, each bunch emerging from the base of the pairs of wing-like leaves that are arranged along the stem. The angular Solomon's seal, *P. odoratum*, more a plant of limestone woods and crags of the north and west of Britain, has either one or two flowers in each bunch. It's sometimes hard to tell the difference between these two species, though common Solomon's seal is usually a bigger plant, with more flowers in each bunch. But a common Solomon's seal growing in less than perfect conditions and with fewer flowers can take on the stature of an angular Solomon's seal. However, each flower of the common Solomon's seal has a narrow waist around the centre, lacking in angular Solomon's seal.

Their long, elegantly arched stems mean that Solomon's seals have become popular as garden plants, but the commonest kind found in cultivation is a hybrid between common and angular Solomon's seal. This hybrid, *P. x hybridum*, has occasionally become naturalized, when it's often confused with common Solomon's seal. However, its flowers are larger and its stem has a distinct ridge running along it. True common Solomon's seal has smooth stems, and the stems of angular Solomon's seal, as its name implies, have sharp angles.

Whorled Solomon's seal, *P. verticillatum,* is a very rare plant, growing in just a few patches of woodland in Scotland. It looks very different from the other two species, both of which grow into gracefully arching stems, along which pairs of leaves arise like green wings. The whorled Solomon's seal grows vertically, with rings of leaves stacked up the stem. It's widespread in woodlands across Europe, though commonest in Scandinavia, where it is particularly abundant in birch woodlands.[9] It can survive in the dense shade of coniferous forests but rarely flowers here, instead putting up sterile shoots which, though lacking flowers, are still attractive plants with their architectural whorls of leaves. In more open sites a circle of white flowers rings the stem at the base of each leaf whorl. These flowers are pollinated by bees, but some studies have found no seedlings at all amongst stands of the parent plants, so vegetative spread is probably more important in maintaining their populations.[10]

The flowers along the lower part of the stems of common and angular Solomon's seal are all hermaphrodite (capable of producing both pollen and seeds), while those higher up are often only male, producing just pollen. Growing male flowers is less of a drain on the plant's resources and in this case, it may be a cheap way of increasing the overall floral display, a longer dangling line of bunched delicate white flowers, which makes the plant more attractive to insect pollinators.[11] And sexual reproduction does seem more important in these plants. Unlike whorled Solomon's seal, seedlings are often found amongst even dense stands of their parents, at least in the case of angular Solomon's seal.[12]

MAY LILIES

In some places, May lilies, *Maianthemum bifolium,* can cover large areas of woodland. I've seen patches covering many tens of square metres in Polish forests and on sandy soils in the Netherlands some patches reach 100 square metres (120 square yards).[13] In the forests near the source of the Mississippi in Minnesota and the higher-altitude forests of the Appalachians in North Carolina, I've seen extensive patches of a closely related plant, *M. canadense,* raising its pretty heart-shaped leaves through deep moss flowing over ancient gnarled roots, reminding me of some carefully tended Japanese planting scheme. All the plants in these patches are genetically identical since they've originated as clones of a single individual by growth of underground rhizomes. But the

plants in such clonal patches are often well spaced since the rhizomes are long. They average about a metre or so in length in most types of forest, but in fir forest in Europe, individual rhizomes reach 3.5 metres (11.5 ft) in length.[14] In this way, the May lily doesn't always form dense exclusive stands, shading out competitors. Instead it uses guerrilla tactics, infiltrating stands of other plants with its long rhizomes.

The genetic similarity of all May lilies in each patch shows that seedlings, bringing with them genetic diversity, can't easily establish themselves in existing patches. May lilies, though, do produce flowers, a pretty spike of foamy white held above their elegant leaves. Plants growing vegetatively only produce one heart-shaped leaf, but those that flower produce two leaves (the *bifolium* of their name). However, fruit formation is largely dependent on out-crossing – in other words, on the flower receiving pollen from an unrelated individual. No matter how many plants flower in a single patch, they don't count; they're all identical, so exchanging pollen between these flowers is the equivalent of self-pollination. Fruiting success depends on how close another patch is. But most clones are long-lived, which increases the chances of some cross-pollination happening, at some point in time. In fact the genetic diversity of May lilies across a local population is relatively high, so these occasional cross-pollinations seem to be enough to maintain a healthy amount of gene flow between clonal patches.[15]

The most important pollinators of May lilies appear to be hoverflies, but a study in the Netherlands showed that only one in twenty-five flowers went on to set fruit.[16] And in this population only 15 per cent of the plants actually flowered in the first place so overall very few seeds were produced despite the large size of patches of these plants. But this example isn't typical of May lilies growing elsewhere. In Poland some populations of May lilies never flower at all, others flower freely, but no seedlings are ever found and in yet others, seedlings seem abundant.[17] In other words, the strategy used by May lilies for reproduction seems to vary from place to place. Experiments have shown that seeds sown in ground from which the leaf litter has been removed produce lots of seedlings, so some form of disturbance, for example by foraging wild boar, improves the chances of seedlings establishing themselves.[18] In southern Finland seedlings also germinate and grow well after a fire, and the size of any given clonal patch in these forests correlated well with the length of time since that particular patch of forest burned. So, in this area at least, fire is the most important factor in the successful establishment of seedlings which can then grow to found new clonal patches.[19]

Although common in many areas of Europe, May lily in Britain is a rare plant of ancient woodland on acid soils. As a native plant, it's found in only four areas: in Durham, North Yorkshire, Lincolnshire and Norfolk. It's sometimes found in other parts of Britain but only with human assistance, and these naturalized or introduced populations are usually short-lived. In fact, some think that only the North Yorkshire plants are truly native. Since that was the opinion of a botanist born in Guisborough in North Yorkshire,[20] that might seem to be just another bit of typical Yorkshire jingoism (though as a fellow Yorkshireman, born only a few miles from Baker, I can attest to the fact that it really is God's own county). But the botanist in question, John Gilbert Baker, worked at Kew Gardens between 1866 and 1899, and was keeper of the herbarium there from 1890 to 1899. In that time, he wrote a monograph of the Liliaceae which, back then, was where May lilies resided, so his opinion ought to be respected.

The Yorkshire population of May lilies, in a woodland at Scarborough on the North Yorkshire coast, has had a chequered history. May lilies were discovered here in 1857 and almost immediately plants were dug up and transported south to grace London gardens. A local farmer, born in 1915, remembered as a boy that, despite decades of these depredations, the May lilies still covered about a quarter of an acre of the woodland. But since the population continued to decline, the farmer transplanted some of the May lilies on to his farm. The plants finally disappeared from their original home and so the story ended – until recently, when conservationists from the Cornfield Flowers Project took an interest. This project was set up to re-establish once abundant cornfield weeds in and around the North York Moors National Park and, although not exactly a cornfield weed, May lilies attracted the attention of the people working on this project. They began to cultivate May lilies from the transplanted population, and then, beginning in 2013, these plants were reintroduced to their original woodland home, in the hope that they would once again form a self-sustaining population.

LILY OF THE VALLEY

A more familiar woodland plant, though one with a similar biology, is the lily of the valley, *Convallaria majalis*. It is native in two distinct areas in Britain, in woodlands on sandy acid soils in the south and east and in limestone woodlands in the west and north, from the Cotswolds to the Yorkshire Dales. In the latter area, it also grows on lightly wooded limestone pavement and one unusual population in Cumbria grows in a fen. The 'lily beds' of St Leonard's Forest in Sussex are so famous that they are even marked on Ordnance Survey maps of the region. According to legend, St Leonard is credited with slaying the very last dragon in Britain, which lived in the Weald of Sussex. And where the dying beast's blood was spilled, lilies of the valley grew up.

Lily of the valley is a popular garden plant and has become naturalized widely across Britain, which has confused the overall picture of its wild distribution. There's a similar problem in Poland, where lily of the valley grows as a wild plant in many woodlands. Local gardeners have collected lily of the valley from these woods for many centuries but often these garden plants have escaped back into the wild where they form naturalized stands in places where wild plants didn't previously grow.[21]

Because these new naturalized populations originated from local wild plants it's impossible to distinguish native from naturalized plants by their genetics. This makes understanding the detailed ecology of wild lily of the valley here very difficult, but at least there was no danger of local plants being contaminated by pollen from escaped foreign plants with a very different genetic make-up, an all too common situation for many of our wildflowers. But that is now no longer the case. Wild lily of the valley was recently given legal protection in Poland, so conscientious gardeners now get their plants from cultivated stocks grown in the Netherlands. No doubt these too will eventually form naturalized colonies and cross with native plants, further complicating the picture.

Lily of the valley wasn't able to colonize Ireland under its own steam before the island was cut off by rising sea levels at the end of the last Ice Age. But it's naturalized there, and possibly has been for a considerable time. On the walls of the Cistercian Abbey at Corcomroe in County Clare, sometime between 1205 and 1210, five species of plants were carved in exquisite detail. One of these is easily recognisable as lily of the valley, perhaps carved from living specimens growing in the abbey gardens or naturalized on the nearby Burren limestone.[22]

Lily of the valley, a well-known garden plant, although much less familiar in the wild, in woodlands scattered across England and Wales.

In Britain lily of the valley is a plant of summer woodlands, often at its best in mid to late May or June. But in France and Germany it flowers a month earlier and in these countries it's a symbol of May Day at the beginning of the month. In France it's called *muguet de Mai* whilst in Germany it is *Maiblume*. Even here in Britain, one of its older names is May's lily – not to be confused with May lily. This name probably comes from its link to Whitsuntide, which sometimes falls in the second half of May. The flower is also associated with the Virgin Mary and, with its loose cascade of drop-shaped white flowers, was sometimes called Our Lady's Tears. Perhaps that is the reason why the stonemasons of Corcomroe carved its likeness so lovingly.

Like the May lily, lily of the valley forms large patches by vegetative spread which are often very dense. Each patch is usually a single clone and often roughly circular as it has grown outwards, at between 6 and 12 centimetres (2–5 in) a year, from a single founding seedling. Each patch has its own distinctive colour and all the plants in a single patch turn yellow at the same time as the growing season comes to an end. Neighbouring patches, founded by different individuals, differ in these characteristics.[23] In a similar way, May lilies as a whole produce a great many variations of their heart-shaped leaves though within each clonal patch all the leaves are exactly the same shape.

These clonal patches of lily of the valley can grow to impressively large sizes. One formed by a related species in Japan, *C. keiskei*, reached 40 metres square (48 square yards)– all the plants genetically identical. So, as for May lilies, if cross-pollination is to happen, pollinators must carry pollen from one patch to another. For this to occur, different patches must be close enough to each other. The amount of cross-pollination and therefore fruit set declines when different patches are more than 14 metres (15 yards) apart – the longest distance that the plants' pollinators are prepared to fly on a regular basis with their loads of pollen.[24]

One way around this limitation would be for the flowers to be self-compatible, so that pollen transferred between plants in a single stand could affect pollination – as of course could pollen from the same flower. Although some have interpreted the hanging flowers of lily of the valley as an adaptation to promote just such self-pollination – allowing pollen to fall on to the stigma using gravity alone[25] – other studies suggest that the flowers are self-incompatible,[26] which prevents the successful production of fruits and seeds by self-pollination. And even for those plants that do eventually manage to produce their bright-red berries, that's not the end of the story. For successful sexual reproduction the seed in those fruits must germinate and the seedling gain a roothold. And for lily of the valley, as for several other plants in this chapter, that doesn't seem to happen very often.

All the plants in any one stand are genetically identical, meaning that the stand has arisen through vegetative means alone and that no seedlings have germinated within the stand to bring genetic diversity. In another study, carried out over five years, no seedlings were ever found around existing stands, suggesting that seedling establishment in most locations is a rare event.[27] This probably explains the patchy nature of lily of the valley, even in areas where it is native. Compared to slow expansion by vegetative growth, fruits and seeds can travel quickly over much longer distances, spreading plants throughout their habitat. I know of one Cotswold wood where lily of the valley is confined to just one large patch, even though most of the rest of the wood looks perfectly suitable and could easily have been colonized by new seedlings.

However, this vigorous patch must have originated from a seedling successfully establishing itself, so seed dispersal and germination must happen, if only very occasionally. And the chances of seedlings establishing themselves is better in some places than others. Of twenty populations studied in Belgium, most followed the usual pattern of clonal patches, showing little genetic diversity within a patch. But in one population, on thin soils with a high phosphorus content, the plants showed considerable genetic diversity. In these conditions, seedlings were obviously able to establish themselves much more successfully.[28] So, for lily of the valley, as it seems to be for May lily, the amount of sexual reproduction is largely controlled by the environment the plants find themselves growing in.

TOXIC FRUITS AND THE LIMITS OF NATURAL SELECTION

Vegetative reproduction is clearly very successful for many of these woodland 'lilies', so why go to all the extra effort of producing flowers and seeds? The answer is dispersal. Fruits and seeds can be carried by animals, stuck to fur or nestled in stomachs, to be deposited some distance away, in the latter case, along with a good dollop of fertilizer. This allows plants to colonize new areas far more effectively than they could by slow vegetative spread. The fruits of lily of the valley are a tempting bright red, making them conspicuous to would-be dispersers. But the fruits are also packed with chemicals that make them poisonous to many mammals, including humans. This seems counter-productive, to say the least, if the plant is trying to enlist animals to help with fruit dispersal. Are the toxins there to protect the seeds from nibbling, gnawing mammals? Rodents collect the berries and happily munch on the precious seeds, simply avoiding the poisonous flesh, which isn't the best outcome for a plant that struggles to produce seed in the first place. Perhaps enough seeds escape to make it worthwhile for the plant. For example, rodents often hoard fruit and seeds, so any that are forgotten about stand a good chance of germinating. But that still doesn't explain why the fruits are so toxic in the first place.

Some botanists have suggested that the poisons, rather than the bright colour, attract dispersers. Rodents, not renowned for their acute vision, can more easily locate these fruits by smell, perhaps by sniffing out the smell of the toxins.[29] But birds, with far better colour vision and the power of flight, are much more efficient seed dispersers. Birds home in on bright berries and can ignore the toxins since they seem to be immune to them. So why does the plant expend all that energy in making these complex chemicals if they serve no real purpose in the fruits?

It's possible that the poisonous berries are just incidental. The old Liliaceae contained many plants with toxic fruits, which allowed botanists to carry out a detailed survey to look for correlations. The most obvious correlation turned out to be the fact that plants with toxic fruits also had the same toxins in their stems and leaves. It seems that these plants can't exclude the poisons from their fruits; their toxicity is simply the inevitable by-product of poisons manufactured in the body of the plant to protect leaves from grazers – an example of a non-adaptive trait.[30] It's tempting to see all features of an organism as having been shaped by natural selection, adapting each to some specific purpose. But it's worth remembering that sometimes we might be seeking adaptive explanations where there are none.

In 1979 the late Stephen Jay Gould, a prolific and thought-provoking writer on all aspects of natural history, and Richard Lewontin published a paper under the obscure title of 'The Spandrels of San Marco and the Panglossian Paradigm: A Critique of the Adaptationist Program'. A fuller exploration of this gauntlet thrown down to their fellow biologists is given by John Alcock, animal behaviourist-turned-orchid hunter, in a wonderfully engaging book on his near-obsessive searches for south-west Australia's orchids.[31]

In brief, Gould and Lewontin criticized biologists for intellectually dissecting animals and plants into their component parts and then describing each part as shaped by natural selection for some specific purpose. Natural selection is a much-misunderstood concept among non-biologists (and some biologists) but in essence refers to the differential survival of some varieties of genes over others. Which genes survive depends on which ones produce bodies that are better adapted to local circumstances, thus giving them the edge in the next round of reproduction. Gould and Lewontin argued that, in taking this strict 'adaptationist' approach, biologists were sometimes making-up 'just so' stories about how individual plant or animal structures or behaviours worked. Looking for the purpose behind lily of the valley's toxic fruits could be just such a story.

Gould and Lewontin saw nature as much more messy. They happily accept that many structures and behaviours in the natural world are

Below: The swelling fruit of herb paris.

Below right: Meadow saffron growing in woodland.

adapted by natural selection for a specific purpose, but not all. And in being blind to these other examples, we miss much of real interest in the history of life on our planet. They list the various other mechanisms that might account for form or function in plants and animals, including random genetic drift, where the chance survival of genes, particularly in small populations, rather than natural selection dictates which genes survive. Other mechanisms they suggest are linked growth patterns, such that if one part of an animal or plant gets bigger over time, a genetically linked structure also grows in size. It might be perfectly possible to come up with an adaptationist explanation of why this second structure is the size it is, but such an explanation would be a fiction.

Gould and Lewontin went as far as to enlist the support of the Grand Master himself, claiming that Darwin too saw other mechanisms, as well as natural selection, as responsible for the form and function of the species he studied. Darwin did indeed describe other mechanisms, though since he lacked any knowledge of genes or the mechanisms of inheritance, his descriptions are now known to be totally wrong.

Other influential scientists, such as Richard Dawkins[32] and Daniel Dennett,[33] have weighed in on the adaptationist side and argued that in reality Darwin saw natural selection as *the* agent that has shaped the natural world. They also criticized Gould and Lewontin's reasoning and pointed out several weaknesses in their analogy. As for the spandrels – these are the left-over spaces above the tops of the arches of the impressive roof of Venice's Basilica of San Marco. The spandrels of San Marco are filled with beautiful mosaics that have been so cleverly fitted into the tapering spaces between the arches that a naive 'adaptationist' viewer might assume that the spandrels were actually designed to be that shape to accommodate the works of art rather than being an inevitable consequence of the architecture.

The toxins in the stems and leaves of lily of the valley are certainly adaptive – to discourage grazers – either leaf-nibbling insects or larger grazing mammals. However, in nature's arms race predators continually adapt to find ways around a prey's defences. Deer frequently graze lily of the valley with no apparent ill effects. Even domestic cattle don't seem to be affected. But such heavy grazing damages the plants, drastically reducing the size of the shoots in the following season.

As for the relationship of humans with the lily of the valley, the evolution of a complex suite of toxins has done nothing to protect the plant – instead it encourages its destruction. In many parts of its range, lily of the valley is collected from the wild for the medicinal properties of the toxins. These toxins belong to a class of chemicals called cardiac glycosides which act on the heart, and, carefully used, extracts of the plant can be used for the treatment of cardiac problems. Since heavy grazing or cutting has such a big effect on next season's growth, there are worries that in some places their medicinal value means that lily of the valley is being over-exploited.

THE PERILS OF MEADOW SAFFRON

Many of the plants in this chapter contain toxins, and some are deadly. Meadow saffron, *C. autumnale*, contains high concentrations of chemicals called alkaloids, the most important of which is colchicine. This chemical binds to structures inside cells called microtubules. These are responsible for the cell's architecture and they also choreograph the dance of the chromosomes during cell division. By disrupting the vital work of the microtubules, colchicine prevents cell division. Today it is used in plant-breeding laboratories to induce the formation of polyploid seeds (seeds with multiple copies of each chromosome), but colchicine is perhaps one of the oldest known drugs. There are descriptions of meadow saffron and its effects from as early as the first century AD.[34]

In low doses colchicine is very effective in the treatment of gout. In recent years it has been used to treat Familial Mediterranean fever, an inherited inflammatory disease that occurs most commonly in people of Mediterranean origin. In higher doses, however, colchicine is lethal.[35] In leaf, meadow saffron is sometimes mistaken for wild garlic and there are several documented cases of fatalities amongst would-be wild-food gourmets. A woman in Austria mistakenly collected meadow saffron leaves to flavour her omelettes and though she didn't eat them herself, the two people who did died of multiple organ failure.[36] Not all such cases of mistaken identity are fatal but they can still result in very unpleasant symptoms, including vomiting and severe abdominal pains.[37] Perhaps surprisingly, lily of the valley is also sometimes mistaken for wild garlic, though – fortunately – it is less toxic than meadow saffron. Neither plant is really *that* difficult to distinguish from wild garlic. If in doubt, just crush the leaves: true wild garlic will immediately reveal itself by smell alone. In such cases a little fieldcraft goes a long way.

Of all the plants we've looked at so far, meadow saffron is the latest to flower. Its alternative name is autumn crocus, since it pushes up its crocus-like flower in late summer, well after its leaves have died down and disappeared. Of course, it's not a real crocus (the latter being members of the Iris family), and its alternative name frequently causes confusion because there are true crocuses that also flower in the autumn, and therefore better deserve the name. One of these, *Crocus nudiflorus*, has become naturalized in parts of Britain. But even the alternative name of meadow saffron is a little confusing. True saffron comes from the anthers of another autumn-flowering true crocus, *C. sativus*. And these anthers are also the surest way to distinguish true crocuses from the crocus-like flowers of *Colchicum* species. Meadow saffron has six stamens and anthers – one of the features that led to its being dumped into the old lily family – while true crocuses have only three. Meadow saffron, along with about 160 other species of *Colchicum*, is now in a separate family, the Colchicaceae, but which is closely related to the modern lily family.

Meadow saffron is sometimes called naked ladies because its flowers appear unclothed in leaves. And, according to naturalist and poet Geoffrey Grigson,[38] this turns out to be a common allusion across Europe. In France it is known as *dames sans chemise* (ladies without a chemise), while its unpronounceable Czech name *naháček* apparently means 'the naked one'.

Finally, in this saga of name confusion, even the term 'meadow' is not entirely accurate. Meadow saffron does grow in open meadows, but it also grows in woodland. Admittedly, it is largely a grassland plant, but meadow saffron is also found in woodlands on the oolitic limestone of the Cotswolds, while in Wiltshire it is almost exclusively a woodland plant.[39] In Europe, on the other hand, meadow saffron is only very rarely found in woodland. This is more typical of most *Colchicums*, which prefer open sites. I've found several species growing in spectacular abundance on the *Puszta* – the steppe grasslands of Hungary – with not a single tree in sight.

In British woodlands I often come across meadow saffron in discrete patches, frequently very small ones, even though the areas where it is absent seem much the same as those where it thrives. In Lower Woods, near Wickwar, in Gloucestershire, one patch is only a couple of square metres in extent, although meadow saffron has reliably flowered here for each of the forty years that I've been visiting these woods. Where it does grow in woodland, it can sometimes do so in large numbers, especially where trees have recently been thinned. Like its relatives in Europe and

Asia, it prefers full sunlight but can hang on in partial shade, at least for a while.

Individual plants are quite long-lived, perhaps fifteen to twenty years, though one specimen in a German botanic garden reached the age of fifty years.[40] This means they can persist through typical coppice cycles of around this period, benefitting when the shrub layer is cut back. In shadier sites, the flowers grow tall and lanky and quickly fall over. They are far better appreciated in old meadows, such as Eades Meadow in Worcestershire,* where they put on an impressive display in the autumn sunshine. Meadow saffron is widely distributed across Europe and in some places forms really dense stands, where they make up perhaps half of the ground cover. Unfortunately, even in the best sites, they never reach such dominance in this country.[41]

In the past such displays were not welcome sights. Thanks to their toxicity, farmers saw these plants as noxious weeds infesting their meadows and often tried hard to eliminate them. Meadow saffron grows a surprisingly large bunch of leaves each summer and, packed with toxins, these can be dangerous to livestock. Later in the season, the flowers, too, are toxic. In his *Flora Britannica*, Richard Mabey quotes a twentieth-century agricultural report that suggests that children were sent out into pastures in the early morning to pick any meadow saffron flowers before the cattle were turned out on to the field. The same may have been true in the Rhineland, to judge from the work of the French poet Guillaume Apollinaire. The first lines from his poem, 'Les Colchiques' ('The Autumn Crocuses', 1913) paints an unusual picture of the autumn countryside:

> *The meadow is poisonous but pretty in autumn.*
> *The cows grazing there are slowly poisoned*

Apollinaire goes on to describe local schoolchildren arriving to pick the poisonous flowers:

> *The school children come clamoring*
> *Wearing jackets and playing the harmonica*
> *They pick the crocuses...*

---

* Eades Meadow is also worth a visit in spring when it puts on an equally fine display of green-winged orchids.

Above: Autumn crocus (or
meadow saffron) in bud.

Left: Reaching for the light.
The flowers of autumn crocus
grow taller in woodland than
in open meadows.

The toxins in meadow saffron evolved to protect the plant from grazing; they make the leaves taste bitter and, with a little experience, cattle learn to avoid them. In many cases though, meadow saffron appears not to be a problem for cattle. German Hinterwälder cattle instinctively avoid the plant, while other breeds, like Belted Galloways, now frequently used in conservation grazing, suffer no ill effects after eating meadow saffron leaves.[42]

We now have the opposite problem, in fact. Meadow saffron has proved rather too easy to eliminate. Even though cattle may avoid eating the leaves, trampling in spring quickly kills the plants. Early cutting of the meadow does the same, a trick used by farmers to eliminate the plant in the past. The cessation of coppicing in woodlands has similar effects. The plants can persist for some time in shady conditions, but after a few seasons of producing lank, sickly flowers they stop flowering altogether and resort to vegetative reproduction by producing daughter corms below the ground. And, finally, the plants die.

CONSERVING MEADOW SAFFRON

Today the populations of meadow saffron across much of northern Europe are highly fragmented. For many plant species this creates a problem as genetic diversity in each isolated patch declines, making the plants less resilient. As the population gets smaller and more isolated in each of these tiny patches, so reproductive success also declines. It's a negative feedback loop – genetic diversity declines, lowering reproductive success, which makes the population smaller and more prone to the loss of even more genetic diversity, which goes on to further lower reproductive success and shrink the population to even lower numbers – a repeating loop that hastens the eventual demise of these isolated populations. It's one reason why conservation organizations are switching their strategy from protecting such isolated patches as nature reserves to working at a landscape scale, joining up populations by encouraging sympathetic management of land between reserves. In the UK this strategy emerged from a government report, *Making Space for Nature: A Review of England's Wildlife Sites*, published in 2010 and led by the distinguished ecologist, Professor John Lawton. The review found that most wildlife sites in our crowded islands were too small and too isolated to be effective in halting the loss of biodiversity. Lawton called for nature reserves to be 'bigger, better and joined up'. And most conservation organizations have responded. For example, across the country the local Wildlife Trusts have launched a series of 'Living Landscape' projects to address the problems uncovered by Lawton. The RSPB too has launched a similar series of projects under their umbrella of 'Futurescapes'.

Such a large-scale approach is clearly better than preserving small and isolated reserves, but in our enthusiasm to embrace the new way, we shouldn't forget good old-fashioned targeted local management – and meadow saffron is a good case in point. A study in Belgium, where populations of meadow saffron are now highly fragmented, showed that, unusually, successful reproduction wasn't affected by the degree of isolation. But local population size and environmental conditions had major effects.[43] So conserving meadow saffron is all about getting the conditions right on each site to increase the local population and to encourage flowering and sexual reproduction, which will maintain healthy levels of genetic diversity. Flowering is strongly inhibited by competition and by shade. Meadow saffron flowers most freely in meadows that are mown to open up the vegetation after its leaves have died back in summer and appropriate management soon reaps its rewards in the form of spectacular displays of autumn crocuses.

It was once thought that these flowers were heterostylous – having two distinct flower types, with different length stamens. Many plants show heterostyly, probably as an adaptation to encourage cross-pollination, though botanists are still puzzling over the details. It has been most thoroughly explored, from Darwin's time onwards, in the Primulas (see Chapter 9, pages 255–64), so that's where I've delved more deeply into the mysteries of this botanical conundrum. In fact, it turns out that meadow saffron flowers aren't heterostylous after all; it's simply that the stamens continue to grow throughout the life of the flower. Meadow saffron flowers can self-pollinate and this becomes easier as the stamens grow tall enough to allow the anthers to approach the female stigma.[44] So, early in the life of each flower, the separation of anthers and stigma means cross-pollination is more likely and later, as a fallback plan if the pollinators have failed to do their duty, it can produce seed by self-pollination as the anthers reach up towards the stigma.

Autumn flowering is a risky business. An early winter or, more likely in our climate, a very wet autumn can be disastrous. But, if the going gets tough, meadow saffron postpones flowering until the following spring. The flower buds are suppressed until early February, then grow extremely fast to produce flowers in early spring. Originally, spring-flowering meadow saffrons were thought to be a different genetic variety, var. *vernum*, but closer observations showed that the following year, these spring-flowering plants revert to their normal pattern.[45] They're just adapting to the vagaries of each year.

If pollination is successful meadow saffron produces seeds that are dispersed by ants. In meadows, trampling by cattle opens up the sward and creates sites free from competition where the seeds germinate well. In woodlands, loose piles of twigs and branches create shelter for growing seedlings. So grazing meadows at the right times of year or leaving some brash wood from coppicing can help expand populations of meadow saffron.

The fruits don't form immediately. Instead they emerge in spring with the leaves and gradually produce their crop of black seeds. These seeds are miniature biochemical factories. Colchicine is transported to the seeds from the growing leaves, where it is gradually converted to another chemical, colchicoside. Exactly what purpose this serves for the plant is unclear, but modern medicine has found a good use for it. Colchicoside is a very effective muscle relaxant. The life cycle of meadow saffron is not suited to intensive cultivation, so colchicoside still derives from plants collected from the wild in Central and Eastern Europe.[46] However, experimental cultivation has shown that growing plants in optimal conditions can triple the amount of alkaloids the plant produces.[47, 48] Thus there is a financial incentive to develop commercial cultivation techniques that will take the pressure off wild populations.

All of these woodland 'lilies' are attractive plants, and several kinds are familiar in gardens, grown either for their architectural interest or for their flower displays. But none of them come close to creating the displays of another refugee from the lily family. Ramsons, or wild garlic, turn woodlands across the country white in early spring. Their flowering is as eagerly anticipated as that of bluebells, both by naturalists and wild-food gourmets alike – so it seems only fitting to give ramsons a chapter of their own.

2

Ramsons

AMARYLLIDACEAE

ALLIUM URSINUM

Smell is perhaps the most potent of the senses in stimulating deep memories. Whenever I walk through a damp forest, rank with ramsons (wild garlic) in late April or May, the smell triggers a cascade of such memories. I'm taken back to a childhood spent exploring the wooded valleys on the northern slopes of the North Yorkshire Moors and the floodplain woodlands along the Tees. Some of these woods had vast carpets of ramsons, their clusters of starry white flowers giving the forest floor the appearance of a late snowfall. I would come home reeking of garlic, which at the time I didn't find at all pleasant. My young palate found garlic, wild or otherwise, extremely distasteful – it was far too continental a flavour for a North Yorkshire family in the 1960s! My palate has now matured, as has my appreciation of a wider range of cuisine, and my fondness for garlic, both its taste and smell, knows no bounds. I love that smell! It is redolent of spring woodlands where bright sunlight turns newly opening leaves a blinding green and coaxes all manner of woodland flowers into bloom.

That same smell can mean different things to different people. In interviews with people across the country for his *Flora Britannica*, Richard Mabey found some people for whom the smell evoked motorcycle racing. The reason was simple. The TT races are held on the Isle of Man during

May, along lanes bordered by wild garlic.[1] And the Isle of Man has another connection with wild garlic – its second-largest town, Ramsey. First settled by Vikings in about AD 850, the Isle of Man became an important Viking kingdom during the eleventh and twelfth centuries[2] and the modern town derives its name from that time, from Old Norse – *hrams-á* or 'wild garlic river'. That same Norse root, of course, also gives us the most commonly used name for the plant – ramsons. The plant is also sometimes called bear's garlic, this being a direct translation of its Latin name, *Allium ursinum*.

Because wild garlic is so conspicuous – both to the eyes and to the nose – there are many other places around Britain named after this plant, from Ramsey Island off the Pembrokeshire coast to Ramshope in Northumberland. As these widespread place names suggest, ramsons grow throughout most of the British Isles. And across the country wild garlic woods have always been conspicuous features in the landscape. As far back as AD 944, a charter of land from King Edmund to Bishop Aelfric mentions a wild garlic wood as one of the markers of the land chartered.[3] Wild garlic attracts attention wherever it grows. In North America it's a different species, *A. tricoccum*, but great drifts growing along the shores of Lake Michigan inspired the local Potawatomi Indians to call this stretch of coast 'place of wild garlic' – in their language 'shikaakwa'. French explorers translated this first as Checagou and later as Chicago.

Ramsons grow across most of Europe, from the Mediterranean to Scandinavia.[4] They are absent from the evergreen areas of the Mediterranean and scarcer towards the east, where the climate is hotter and drier. But they also grow through the Caucasus Mountains and Ukraine, and in Turkey.

Some botanists describe two subspecies, *A. ursinum ursinum*, occurring over most of the plant's range, including the plant familiar in Britain and *A. u. ucrainicum*, from east and south-east Europe.[5] *A. u. ucrainicum* is said to be slightly more tolerant of drought, an adaptation to the drier climate where it grows.[6] Otherwise, the two forms differ only in whether the individual flower stalks are covered in tiny papillae or are smooth – the kind of thing that excites hardcore botanists but maybe not the rest of us. And some botanists don't think this is a big enough distinction to merit creating two subspecies, instead seeing just one form across the whole of its large range.[7]

Ramsons prefer damp woodlands, with soil that's not waterlogged yet not too dry. They also like high humidity, which is why they are

Below left: An individual ramsons flower showing six stamens and a three-chambered ovary, features that meant alliums were once classified as lilies.

Below: A ramsons flower head begins to open.

largely confined to damp woodlands. Those parts of its range where it is scarcest are those with the most continental climate – hotter and drier than this plant prefers. For example, it is quite a rare plant in Hungary and Ukraine. Elsewhere, ramsons are not only common but, where the conditions are right, carpet the ground in spectacular monocultures. It's not the only woodland plant to behave like this. Dog's mercury, *Mercurialis perennis*, for example, another early harbinger of the British spring, which grows in drier conditions than ramsons, also forms dense stands on woodland floors. Like those of ramsons, these stands shade out other species, so preventing the growth of competitors. But ramsons are unusual.

MAKING MORE RAMSONS

Most plants that form monocultures do so by rapid vegetative reproduction, by producing many daughter bulbs by division or, like dog's mercury, lily of the valley (*Convallaria majalis*) and wood anemones (*Anemone nemorosa*) to name a few, by sending rhizomes (modified stems) through the soil, from which leafy stems spring up. In these cases, large patches of the monoculture consist of clones of the original establishing plants, genetically identical and often flowering or dying back with remarkable synchrony. Wild garlic stands, on the other hand, are genetically diverse, because this plant depends largely on seed for propagation.

Above and right: Once open, each ramsons flower head consists of a tight cluster of starry white flowers.

Not only is this unusual amongst plants that form exclusive stands, but it also appears to make no evolutionary sense. Ramsons don't seem to be particularly good at producing seeds. About half of all its seeds die at the embryo stage, which means each flower produces on average as few as twenty seeds. Of those only a quarter survive dormancy over late summer and winter.[8] Then, little more than half the seeds germinate during the following spring even if given the optimum treatment[9] and in nature many remain dormant for several years.[10] But the density of plants is so high that there may be up to 9,000 seeds lying in each square metre (11 square ft) of soil in a wild garlic stand. That translates to around 250 seedlings, which seems to be enough not only to maintain the stand but to allow it to expand when conditions are right.[11] From germination, it then takes the young plant six years to reach flowering age.

A few plants, often as few as one in a hundred, produce daughter bulbs by vegetative division. And when they do they invest a lot of food reserves in their daughters, enabling the new plant to flower the next year.[12] But producing flower spikes also burns up a lot of food reserves; in fact, it takes the same resources to make one daughter bulb as it does to make just two flower spikes. Yet a daughter bulb can flower the following year, whereas plants from seed need six years to reach flowering size. Further, the effort of flowering usually means that the same plant can't produce another flower spike the following year.[13] So surely it makes more sense to adopt the same strategy as other plants that form exclusive stands – vegetative reproduction.

It is unclear what has driven ramsons to invest so much in seed production – though it clearly works, to judge by the sheets of white flowers that carpet our woodlands in spring. But to be so successful at dominating the ground flora from seed-grown plants, ramsons need to be unusual in other ways. The seedlings of most plants would have trouble finding a foothold amongst such a dense stand of their parents, but ramsons seedlings do not appear to experience such difficulties.[14]

Ramsons don't have any mechanism for dispersing their seeds, despite the fact that the seeds have elaiosomes. These structures, attached to the top of the seed, are packed with an oily food, to tempt ants into carrying the seeds back to their nest, or at least some distance from the parent plant. Yet ants seem to ignore ramson seeds, even if they trip over them. Of 1,000 wild garlic seeds diligently laid next to an ant trail by a patient botanist only two were moved at all by ants and then only about a quarter of a metre (10 in). About all a wild garlic flower can do to disperse its seeds is to fall over as the seeds reach maturity – which around three-quarters of them do. But this is hardly long-distance dispersal, meaning the seedlings are faced with the problem of establishing themselves in the green jungle of their parents.

By experimentally planting seedlings into different densities of adult plants, botanists have shown that seedlings gain the best start in moderate densities of adult plants.[15] They don't do so well when the adult plants are really densely packed, probably because the seedlings are too heavily shaded. And if the adult plants are too sparse, the seedlings often wilt, being sensitive to dry air and soil. In the right densities, the adult plants provide their offspring with a sheltered, moist environment that allows seedlings to grow to adulthood and maintain the carpet of wild garlic.

Because the seeds fall close to their parents, a monoculture of ramsons is made up of small patches of closely related, though not identical plants. To contrast this with the more usual situation in which a monoculture consists of large areas of identical clones, botanists have coined the term 'Clan of Clones' to describe the pattern in wild garlic.[16]

THE COMPLEX CHEMISTRY OF RAMSONS

In maintaining dominance over large areas of the woodland floor, wild garlic might also be helped by its complex chemistry. That chemistry is one of the most obvious things about wild garlic, giving the plant its flavour and its smell, particularly pungent as the leaves begin to die in late spring. The evocative – some might say nauseating – smell of a wild garlic wood is largely created by a chemical called diallyl disulphide, which is the breakdown product of another chemical called alliin, found throughout the plant. It is just one of a whole range of chemicals, including phenols and flavonoids, that the plant produces. Many of these compounds easily dissolve in water, so quickly wash out of the decomposing leaves and into the soil. Could these chemicals inhibit the growth of other species, helping to create wild garlic monocultures? This effect, called allelopathy, is certainly known in other species with less aromatic chemical arsenals than wild garlic.

Experiments with test seedlings of other plants showed that their root growth was strongly inhibited by the chemical cocktail from ramsons, particularly by extracts from the bulb.[17] However, the seedlings in these experiments were lettuce, wheat and tomato, plants not normally seen growing alongside wild garlic in spring woodlands. In other experiments with more likely competitors to wild garlic, for example dog's mercury

Mercurialis perennis, and ground ivy, *Glechoma hederacea*, decaying garlic leaves seemed to have no effect on seedling growth.[18] So it's still not clear whether wild garlic's pungent array of chemicals helps to prevent other species from invading its space.

The sulphurous chemicals from wild garlic can also reach remarkably high concentrations in the air. The Vienna Woods, made famous by the waltz 'Tales from the Vienna Woods' by Vienna's favourite son, Johann Strauss II, are a vast area of woodland covering low rolling hills, the first wrinkles in the Earth's crust that further south and west rise up to form the Alps. The woods fringe the city, drawing many Viennese to enjoy the fresh air or to sit in traditional Heuriger restaurants and drink alarmingly large glasses of young white wine from local vineyards. Yet, in places, the air is far from fresh. The concentration of sulphur in the atmosphere, emanating from great stands of wild garlic, reaches 7.8 parts per billion, the highest emissions reported from any plant anywhere in Europe.[19]

Those same chemicals are of great interest for their beneficial effects. Wild garlic contains a similar suite of chemicals to common garlic, *A. sativum*, which are well known to have medicinal value. In fact, in some cases the therapeutic effects of wild garlic are greater than those of common garlic.[20] Wild garlic has been used in folk medicine for many centuries and is still sold in local markets, either fresh, salted or pickled, in Ukraine, Russia and the Caucasus. Modern medicine has now highlighted the potential of wild garlic in treating high blood pressure and preventing cardiovascular disease, as an antioxidant, and as protection against colorectal cancer among others. But to fully understand the medicinal potential of this plant, we also need to understand its ecology.

Plants growing in different places across their wide range often look different in leaf length, or height and size of the flower. These are different eco-types – plants finely adapted to their local environment. And different eco-types of wild garlic often have very different chemical compositions, with different essential oils.[21] On top of that, the concentration of chemicals in the plants varies with the season, with the highest amounts in March and April, just before flowering.[22] But despite these complications, it's now clear that those vast stands of wild garlic represent a potentially valuable natural pharmacy.

Overleaf: Westridge Wood, on the scarp slope of the Cotswolds above Wotton-under-Edge in Gloucestershire, is famous for its spectacular displays of ramsons.

EATERS OF WILD GARLIC I:
HUMANS

They are also a natural larder. The leaves can be eaten fresh, especially early in the season, when they have a subtler hint of garlic. Richard Mabey reports that Oliver Rackham, Britain's foremost landscape historian and woodland ecologist, who sadly died in February 2015, used to put a few leaves of wild garlic in his peanut butter sandwiches on the many days he was working in the field.[23] The flowers are also edible and the intensity of their garlic flavour increases as the flower ages. As with common garlic, the bulbs can also be eaten – but of course digging up the bulbs destroys the whole plant and should not be encouraged.

Across the Atlantic, in North America, a similar plant may be threatened by culinary use of its bulbs. *A. tricoccum*, sometimes also called ramsons or wild garlic, but more often known as 'ramps', is a different species from our familiar plant and behaves slightly differently. European ramsons flower while the leaves are still green and growing, whereas the leaves of ramps die down before the flower stalks appear.

A. tricoccum is particularly common in the southern Appalachian Mountains. Here, there are annual ramp festivals, in which wild garlic is served up, often battered and fried (good ol' southern cookin'), in large quantities. I've spent a lot of time in the spectacular forests here, so have eaten my fair share of ramps. Whilst staying with an Indian friend on the Cherokee's Qualla Boundary Reservation in North Carolina, we cooked ramps collected from the local forests. The Cherokee have an enlightened view of plants, seeing them as a resource provided for people, but only as long as they are used with proper respect and not in excess, so I'm not too worried about ramps harvesting here. But elsewhere ramps festivals are getting more and more commercialized and some conservationists are now expressing concern about over-collection.

Where the plant is rarer, such as in Quebec Province in Canada, it is protected by law and each person limited to only fifty bulbs a year for personal consumption. But ramps poachers are collecting plants in areas where they are protected and smuggling them into provinces where they can be collected legally and where there's a ready market. Such an illegal trade in wild plants is always worrying so I'm glad there is no similar tradition of ramsons festivals in Britain.

EATERS OF WILD GARLIC II:
BEETLES AND HOVERFLIES

Of course wild garlic has evolved its flavoursome compounds for its own use. The chemicals have anti-bacterial and anti-fungal effects and probably deter many potential predators. Even so, a few species feed on wild garlic. In Europe its leaves are nibbled by a bright-red leaf beetle called *Lilioceris merdigera*. This looks very similar to the infamous lily beetle, *L. lilii*, a recently introduced but rapidly spreading pest in the UK, which has become the bane of lily growers. Lily beetles frequently devastate the various species of fritillaries growing in my garden, but I've yet to see them on wild garlic, either on plants growing in various corners of my garden or on wild plants. Lily beetles only seem able to complete their full life cycle on either *Lilium* species or fritillaries.[24] Perhaps wild garlic's chemical arsenal is just too much for them.

L. merdigera differs from the lily beetle only in having red legs (the lily beetle's legs are black) and its fondness for the flavour of garlic. It's not uncommon on wild garlic in central Europe and is sometimes found in moderate numbers on commercial plantations of common garlic[25] or on chives. Its partiality to alliums means that it is sometimes called the onion beetle. *L. merdigera* is probably a species we should be on the lookout for on our own wild garlic stands as climate change encourages European species of insects to colonize Britain. Like the all too familiar lily beetles in my garden, onion beetle larvae cover themselves in a mucilaginous mix of their own faeces, which is disgusting enough to protect them from most predators – except, in the case of lily beetles, from me!

There are also two hoverflies whose larvae specialize in wild garlic. *Portevinia maculata* is a small, dark hoverfly, the males of which can be found basking in spring sunshine on the leaves of wild garlic. The females are more elusive, flitting around the base of the plants. Their larvae feed inside the bulbs all summer long, but are most active from January to March, when, above ground, the forest floor is still bare. As the leaves begin to emerge, food resources are transferred from the bulb to the growing leaves and the bulbs begin to wither. New bulbs will be formed later as the leaves build up resources by photosynthesis. Adult *Portevinia* hoverflies don't emerge until later in the spring, so the larvae are faced with a growing food shortage as wild garlic leaves thrust up into the spring sunshine and the bulbs shrink. However, by then they are

Overleaf: Ramsons are usually appreciated for their dazzling white carpets, but each flower head is an object of singular beauty.

big enough to burrow through the soil to find other bulbs and make the best use of their dwindling food supplies.[26] In this way, each larva might destroy or damage up to ten bulbs.[27]

The second species, *Cheilosia fasciata*, doesn't occur in Britain, at least as far as we know. This genus of hoverflies is nevertheless well represented in this country, with thirty-seven confusingly similar species and one, *C. semifasciata*, so similar that it is occasionally misidentified as *C. fasciata*. However, *C. semifasciata* larvae feed on orpine, *Sedum telephium*, and navelwort, *Umbilicus rupestris*, not wild garlic. It's rather curious that only one of the wild garlic hoverflies occurs in Britain. There's no shortage of the food plant here and conditions where both occur together on the continent are not that different.

One suggestion is that it is simply down to chance. During the last Ice Age, many animals and plants had to retreat further south in Europe, to refuges such as the Iberian Peninsula and Italy. Perhaps, purely by chance, *P. maculata* ended up in a nearer refuge such as Iberia whereas *C. fasciata* ended up in, say, Italy. So *P. maculata* could have recolonized Britain at the end of the Ice Age before the English Channel flooded, but *C. fasciata* may have had too far to travel and found its way blocked by water when it reached northern France.[28] However climate change is encouraging many species of insects, from bumblebees to damselflies, to

In woodlands across the country, ramsons create the impression of a blanket of snow

expand their range into the British Isles, and none of these have found the Channel a barrier, so it might not be long before *C. fasciata* turns up here, perhaps along with onion beetles, to feast on wild garlic.

Unlike the larvae of *P. maculata*, those of *C. fasciata* feed by mining the leaves of wild garlic. Since the leaves are only available for a few months at most, this forces *C. fasciata* into a very different life cycle. It must feed and grow quickly during the spring and then, as the leaves die back, it pupates. Like all higher flies, it pupates inside the hardened skin of its last larval stage (called a puparium) which provides protection through the summer and the following winter until the adults emerge the following April, in time for the next flush of wild garlic leaves.

These two hoverflies divide up the feeding opportunities on wild garlic by adapting their life cycles to the available resources. And wild garlic provides opportunities for other creatures. As the leaves die back, they form a decomposing mat on the forest floor. This slippery carpet makes walking through late spring forests somewhat treacherous: one can end up taking an undignified slide down a slope, to emerge at the bottom reeking of wild garlic.

FOREST FERTILIZER

In wild garlic patches, the quantity of dying leaves covering the forest floor in early summer is perhaps greater than those that will fall from the trees later in the year. But, crucially, wild garlic leaves are dying and decomposing at a time when the temperatures are much higher. Decomposition is much faster and more complete, flushing huge amounts of organic matter rich in nitrogen and potassium into the soil, and the soil invertebrates respond with a surge in population. Springtail populations multiply to far above normal levels, only to fall again once the leaves have finally decomposed and disappeared.[29]

The nutrients returned to the soil are an important part of the overall food cycle of the forest. In the warm summer temperatures, bacteria act on the nitrogen-rich debris, producing large quantities of nitrates that are available to other plants growing later in the summer.

The contribution of wild garlic to the chemistry of their environment can't be overstated. In early spring wild garlic in the Vienna Woods creates a sulphurous atmosphere. Now, as the leaves die back, nitrates in water running off the forest rise above the European Union limits for safe drinking water. That can't please the Viennese, who are always proud to point out that their water supply, fed by crystal-clear springs, is the purest there is and could be bottled out of any tap as mineral water if it were legal to do so. But the content of nitrogen and potassium in a healthy, dense stand of garlic is proportionally the same as that in the annual application of artificial fertilizers to arable land.[30]

Although there is no clear evidence that chemicals from wild garlic can inhibit the growth of other plants, the physical smothering of the ground by an impenetrable slimy mat might play a role in maintaining a monoculture of wild garlic. Even so, wild garlic can only achieve dominance under certain conditions. They don't like acid soils, because in such soils aluminium is more soluble – and aluminium inhibits the growth of wild garlic, particularly the seedlings.[31] Sensitivity to dissolved aluminium limits wild garlic to less acid soils and this has raised worries over the future of wild garlic stands in places like Sweden, where acid rain is causing the acidification of the soil in many areas.

Wild garlic also prefers moist soil and often grows most vigorously along river terraces. Here the history of flooding can play a part in the density of the wild garlic stands. Many rivers are now managed to prevent flooding, which affects the soil composition. The silt deposited from flood waters enriches the soil in phosphorus, an essential nutrient for plant growth. In forests that are flooded annually, wild garlic plants are bigger and stronger, and their leaves are richer in nutrients, which are then released into the soil when they die in late spring.[32] So flood suppression in these riverine forests can dramatically alter the cycling of nutrients through the whole ecosystem, mediated by stands of wild garlic.

THE SHORT LIFE OF RAMSONS

Many aspects of the natural history of ramsons are unusual. Apart from its reliance on seeds to maintain its dense stands, each individual plant is very short-lived, averaging only around eight years or so, which is very low compared to other woodland plants, such as Solomon's seal, *Polygonatum multiflorum* (thirty-five years) or wood anemone, *A. nemorosa* (twenty-five to thirty years) and perhaps centuries for herb paris. But not all plants reach even this young age. During their life cycle there are a number of times when the chances of dying are a lot higher.

We've already seen that about half the ovules die before becoming viable embryos. More die during seed dormancy, which may last several years. Once established, growth is slow for the first two years, followed by a growth spurt in years two to five, when the bulb doubles in weight each year. But during this period the bulb relocates itself in the soil, a time when mortality increases again. Young bulbs lie quite close to the surface, a zone rich in nutrients but prone to drying out. After three years they develop contractile roots, which pull the bulb deeper into the soil, away from the danger of drying out but into a zone lower in nutrients. This period of bulb migration sees another peak in mortality, seemingly due to increased attacks by soil nematode worms.[33] Finally, after just eight years or so most of the lucky survivors die of old age.

Given the precarious nature of being a wild garlic plant it seems remarkable that they are at all common, let alone can carpet hectares of forest in pure stands. Yet within an hour's drive of my home in Bristol, I know of many spectacular wild garlic woods and I try to visit as many as I can during each flowering season. But wherever I might choose to live I could do the same. They are as evocative of spring in a British wood as bluebells, if less eulogized. But Mary MacRae, a poet who died from cancer in 2009, captured the many facets of wild garlic, from spring spectacle to medicinal herb in her poignant poem 'Wild Garlic', a fitting conclusion to the story of ramsons:

Allium ursinum, ramson, sometimes ransom,
Old English hramsa: all Northern Europe
has a name for wild garlic, that startling white,
its pungency. Pick and they quickly fade
but in the mass — and what mass! — overwhelming.
In Cornwall they form thick banks along the lanes
and fill damp woods, making me long to be
propped on beds of amaranth and moly —
and truly I find they're magic: the moly-garlic
Hermes gave Odysseus to protect him.

Now hostage to fortune, how willingly
I'd pay a king's ransom — in ramsons, of course,
whole armfuls of them, a wild cornucopia —
for the smallest chance of release, remission.

3

Bluebells

ASPARAGACEAE
HYACINTHOIDES
NON-SCRIPTA

I've been fortunate enough to have seen some of the world's greatest plant spectacles; enormous pitcher plants and giant *Rafflesia* flowers in the rainforests of Borneo, the transformation of barren deserts in Africa and the Americas into carpets of colour by ephemeral flowers, the bewildering diversity of the spring display in the forests of North America's Appalachian Mountains and the unique collection of strange plants growing atop South Africa's Table Mountain.

But to spend a glorious May day in a British bluebell wood is the equal of any of these. That wash of blue flowing through the forest, the perfect mirror of a clear spring sky, entrances the senses; sight, sound and smell – a scene captured succinctly in his journal by the poet Gerard Manley Hopkins. He sensed in the 'blue-buzzed haze and the wafts of intoxicant perfume' the very 'glory of God'.[1]

In our small and heavily populated islands we're used to thinking that we have to travel abroad to see nature at its best, but in the case of bluebell displays, put your passport away. There's nowhere better than Britain. We hold perhaps half of the world's population of this plant,[2] which in any case is restricted to the north-west corner of Europe. Outside of Britain it grows mainly in north-west Spain, Portugal, Ireland, France, Belgium and the Netherlands, though nowhere as densely as here.[3] The bluebell has also been introduced into Germany, Italy and Romania,

Classic English bluebells, with drooping stems and the deep blue flowers hanging to one side of the stem.

though in the hotter and drier climate of Italy it needs human help to survive. And it's been transported across the Atlantic and now grows in a few spots in North America.

Our bluebell belongs to a select group of plants, of the genus *Hyacinthoides*. At the latest count it's one of just eleven species in a genus centred largely on the Iberian peninsula and North Africa, though it's the only one to grow in such vast drifts.[4] The North African species are autumn- or winter-flowering bulbs; those of the Iberian Peninsula and north-west Europe are spring-flowering. Some are restricted to tiny ranges, such as two of the Spanish species, *H. reverchonii*, confined to a single mountain range, or *H. paivae*, growing only in the province of Galicia in the north-west corner of Spain. It's just our familiar bluebell, *H. non-scripta*, that extends outside this core area, though not very far. It is a plant that needs the Atlantic.

Thanks to the Gulf Stream, that vast river in the ocean bringing water warmed in the Caribbean and Gulf of Mexico to our northern shores, north-west Europe enjoys a climate far milder than our latitude should allow. And since, compared to land, the ocean takes a long time to warm up or cool down, the Atlantic provinces of Europe experience a less extreme climate than that endured by our central and southern European neighbours. Such conditions suit the bluebell perfectly. Its natural distribution is limited to an area where the average maximum summer temperature lies between 15 and 25°C and the winter average doesn't drop below 0°C.[5] And the reasons for this lie in its life cycle.

A YEAR IN THE LIFE OF A BLUEBELL

Bluebells can reproduce vegetatively, by bulb division. A small percentage of plants, usually the largest individuals, can produce two buds in each bulb that will later develop as two separate plants. And there is some evidence that individual clumps of bluebells, normally a very variable plant, share most of their characteristics, suggesting they may be clones, derived by vegetative reproduction.[6] But this form of propagation pales into insignificance compared to new plants that have grown from seed.

Although bluebells can produce seed if self-pollinated, they produce far more seed if they're cross-pollinated by insects. That lake of blue that we admire in spring is, in reality, a sea of nectar, at least as far as insects are concerned. It truly is, as Hopkins wrote, a 'blue-buzzed haze', alive with butterflies, bees and flies – the 'intoxicant perfume' advertising a nectar reward for obliging insects. Hoverflies and bumblebees seem to be the most effective pollinators, carrying the bluebell's white pollen from plant to plant, though they're far from perfect. Hand-pollinated bluebells produce far more seeds, which means that despite the buzz of insects in the sea of blue, bluebells are, in botanical jargon, pollinator-limited.[7] They're not producing as many seeds as they could because pollinators are too few or too inefficient.

Even so, a trip to a bluebell wood later in the summer will reveal countless seed heads, each a thing of singular beauty in its own right, packed with large black seeds. The seeds lack any mechanism for dispersal and simply drop around their parents. Here, they lie dormant over the summer, although events are already unfolding inside the seed, at the molecular level, invisible to us.

Gardeners are familiar with seeds that are tricky to germinate unless they are given a period of cold treatment – stratification – that mimics winter. During this time, chemicals that inhibit germination are broken down, so that when the temperature rises in the spring, the seed is primed to germinate. Bluebells are the complete opposite. They won't germinate at all if treated with cold, nor do they germinate as soon as they are shed. They need a *warm* temperature to break dormancy, at which point they will germinate when the temperature then falls to 11°C or below. In other words, they're adapted to germinate in the cool of autumn.

Laboratory experiments show that ideally they need to experience temperatures of 26°C to 31°C to maximize germination.[8] In reality, beneath a leafy canopy, the soil in a British bluebell wood rarely reaches this temperature, though it does get warm enough to ensure that a good proportion of seeds will germinate in the cooler temperatures of autumn. This is probably a neat evolutionary strategy on behalf of the bluebell, an insurance policy that makes sure not all its seeds germinate in their first autumn. Germinating in autumn is risky. A really bad winter could kill most of the tiny seedlings, but dormant seeds are much tougher and are therefore more likely to survive the winter, to germinate the following autumn when, hopefully, they'll face a less severe test.

The seedlings time their emergence to coincide with leaf fall, which provides the vulnerable young plant with a blanket for winter. Even so, prolonged harsh weather will kill the tiny seedlings – one reason for the bluebell's dependence on the ameliorating effect of the Atlantic. But there's a big advantage to autumn germination in a mild oceanic climate.

The erect flower heads, with paler blue flowers facing in all directions around the stem, suggest that this population has been infiltrated by genes from non-native Spanish bluebells.

Overleaf: A bluebell wood in May looking as if a lake has washed through the trees.

The young plant can grow during warm spells in winter, giving it a head start over spring-germinating plants when temperatures and light levels rise in the spring.

Even adult plants are susceptible to cold. Although the carpet of plants in spring appears uniform, look closely and you'll find lots of subtle variations – in plant size, height and number of flowers and timing of flowering, as well as colour. It's sometimes possible to trace a pattern of earlier-flowering plants that mirrors the heavier boughs of the trees above them. The reason for this is that in more open woods, the larger boughs provide some shelter and protection from frosts that would otherwise slow down growth.[9]

BLUEBELL WOODS

Tracing the subtle variations through a bluebell wood provides other insights into bluebell ecology. The bluebells on the southern and western boundaries of woods flower earlier, thanks to the greater light and warmth of these aspects. These differences are even more marked

where the woods are sloping. And light has other effects. The more hours of spring sunshine that a plant receives, the more seed capsules it can produce.[10] So, seasonal variations in spring weather can make a big difference to the number of seedlings produced each year. And within a single wood, well-lit bluebells produce nearly double the number of flowers on each stem than their more shaded neighbours, vital statistics for a plant so dependent on seed to maintain its population. For this reason, bluebells do particularly well in woodlands that are coppiced in the traditional way.

Yet, even in its heartland in Britain, not every wood is a bluebell wood and not every part of a bluebell wood is dominated by bluebells. Apart from the factors mentioned above, soil and water play a major role in determining whether a woodland will put on a show of bluebells in the spring. They don't like thin, dry chalk soils, so you won't find bluebell carpets on the steeper slopes of the chalk downs in southern England or in the ash–beech woods of the Chiltern escarpment, though they are common on the deeper, more acid soils on the Chiltern plateau and at the foot of downland slopes.[11] Nor do they like heavy or waterlogged soils. In general, they prefer the middle ground – sandy or loamy soils, not too dry but not too wet.[12]

And there are other, more subtle factors at work as well. Bluebells don't have woodlands to themselves. They're in competition with other spring-flowering plants, in ways so complex they're not yet fully understood. In Lower Woods in Gloucestershire, an ancient woodland I've been exploring for forty years, bluebell displays give way on some slopes to carpets of ramsons and elsewhere to carpets of anemones or patches of

wild daffodils. In some cases, the differences in exposure, soil, moisture, aspect or management history are obvious, but sometimes it's hard to see much variation at all between areas dominated by different plants. So, the factors dictating the patterns of the various plants in relation to each other must be very subtle.

An experiment carried out back in 1982, in a bluebell wood in Lancashire, showed that the tiniest of changes could tip the balance. In this forest, which had a river running through it, bluebells dominated on the deeper forest soils of the gentle slopes away from the river, but wood anemones took over on the terraces close to the river. Careful analysis of the soils showed very little difference in mineral content between the two areas, but a further experiment showed that, in fact, it only took a very little difference to influence the pattern of plants. Adding tiny amounts of nitrate and phosphate to the soil of the river terraces soon allowed bluebells to take over.

The critical factor was the size of the bluebells' leaves in April, a time when anemones are in full leaf. The extra nutrients allowed the bluebell leaves to overtop the anemone leaves, cutting down the light. Over a few seasons, this weakened the anemones enough for the bluebells to take over.[13] This example shows that it's hard enough to understand the detailed behaviour of a plant in isolation, let alone the subtleties of its relationships with other species.

To understand such fine details, it's likely we'll also need to understand the distribution of fungi in the soil, an even more mysterious subject. Like many plants, bluebells form an intimate association with certain fungi. A bluebell bulb begins to grow in August, producing short fleshy roots, which are immediately colonized by fungal threads. More and more fungi colonize the roots through the winter, reaching a peak in March, when the bluebell is in full growth and the shoot emerges above ground. These fungi help the bluebell, with its relatively short root system, to absorb phosphates.[14] Without these fungi, bluebells grow very poorly. Other plants with a more extensive root system don't need to rely on fungi in the same way. So perhaps some of the less obvious patterns of bluebell distribution in woodlands reflect the distribution of appropriate fungi, as has been demonstrated for many species of orchids (see Chapter 10, pages 321–23).

Bluebells are absent from some woodlands simply because they are too recent. With no mechanism for long-distance seed dispersal and very limited ability to expand by vegetative means, bluebells are slow to

Most people visit a bluebell wood to admire the flowers but, a month or two later, the empty seed heads have their own architectural beauty.

colonize new habitats. Various figures exist for the rate at which they can move, from 100 metres every century to a mere 6–10 metres (109 yards to 6–10 yards). One long-term experiment in Belgium aimed to measure this with more accuracy, at least for that part of Belgium.

In 1960 bluebells were transplanted to twenty-seven new areas, which were tracked down again more than four decades later – in 2005 and 2006. Only a handful of bulbs were planted in each site and just under half the new populations survived and spread, and, indeed, still seemed to be in the process of establishing themselves when rediscovered. The plants were smaller on average in the transplant areas, probably because there were still many young plants in the population, so even after forty-five years the population was still growing. Because, originally, only a few bulbs were planted in each site, the scientists could easily measure how far the population had spread in that time and from this could work out that in the next forty-five years the main population will spread by only another 14 metres (45 feet).[15]

It was also clear that the spread is accomplished first by one plant, germinating from a seed, appearing by chance some distance from the main population, followed by the slow colonization of the ground be-tween. Measurements from the transplanted colonies allowed the scientists to estimate that in forty-five years' time these lone pioneers would have reached some 40 metres (130 feet) from the main colony. These transplant experiments, where each new colony was started by half a dozen mature bulbs, gave the bluebells a head start in their new home when compared to natural dispersal by seeds. Even so, this long-term experiment shows how long it would take for a bluebell in a wood to become part of a bluebell wood.

For this reason, bluebells are often used as indicators of ancient wood-land. But bluebells are not really woodland plants, at least not in the sense of being adapted to grow in shade. They grow in the spring, before the canopy closes over their heads, when there's plenty of light available. They grow in woods partly to avoid the trampling hooves of livestock and partly because they need the more moist conditions found under a woodland canopy. But the further west you travel in Britain, the wetter the climate becomes, and the less bluebells need woodland to survive.

Off the coast of Pembrokeshire, the grassy slopes of Skomer Island are awash with bluebells in the spring, with not a tree in sight. Instead, I've witnessed the incongruous sight of puffins perched on a clifftop rock protruding like a miniature island from a sea of bluebells. So, while bluebells in East Anglia might well be indicators of ancient woodland, they clearly aren't in West Wales.

Despite this dependence on a delicate interplay of many different factors, bluebells are widely distributed across Britain. And over that range there's a subtle variation in colour with occasional white flowers along with more extreme variants, such as a rare form with flower bracts that reach 6 centimetres (2.3 in) in length. So, it's always worth taking in the details of bluebells in a bluebell wood as well as admiring the bigger picture.

But it's the big picture that draws most people to their local bluebell wood in April and May. In 2002 the charity Plantlife organized a survey in which people voted for a representative flower for each county.* So many votes were cast for the bluebell that it was disqualified from the county voting and instead officially declared Britain's favourite flower. But it's been a favourite for a long time before that. In the past, special bluebell trains were laid on so people could appreciate spring in some of our best bluebell woods. And such sights have also been celebrated through the ages by poets.

BLUEBELLS IN POETRY

One Victorian poet who captured the essence of a bluebell wood as well as any was Gerard Manley Hopkins. A Jesuit priest, at times he struggled with religious doubts and bouts of depression. But to reconcile his conflicting emotions and beliefs, at least judging by his writing, a visit to a bluebell wood always calmed his soul. In his journal entry for 9 May, 1871, he wrote:

> ...in the clough through the light they come in falls of sky-colour washing the brows and slacks of the ground with vein-blue, thickening at the double, vertical themselves and the young grass and brake-fern combed vertical, but the brake struck the upright of all this with winged transomes. It was a lovely sight.[16]

---

* Plantlife is a British conservation charity working both nationally and internationally to protect plants and fungi. Across the UK they manage twenty-three nature reserves.

And such sights featured in his poem 'The May Magnificat':

And azuring-over greybell makes
Wood banks and brakes wash wet like lakes
And magic cuckoocall
Caps, clears, and clinches all—[17]

But Hopkins wasn't the only writer to be inspired by such sights. Two of the Brontë sisters, Anne and Emily, penned lines on bluebells, reflecting what they meant to each of them. For Emily Brontë, like Hopkins, that sea of blue had the power to soothe the soul:

The Bluebell is the sweetest flower
That waves in summer air:
Its blossoms have the mightiest power
To soothe my spirit's care.

Anne Brontë probably wrote 'The Bluebell' after an excursion to Scarborough with the family for whom she was then governess. In her case, just a single bluebell brought to mind more carefree days of childhood:

There is a silent eloquence
In every wild bluebell
That fills my softened heart with bliss
That words could never tell…

…But when I looked upon the bank
My wandering glances fell
Upon a little trembling flower,
A single sweet bluebell.

Whence came that rising in my throat,
That dimness in my eye?
Why did those burning drops distil —
Those bitter feelings rise?

O, that lone flower recalled to me
My happy childhood's hours
When bluebells seemed like fairy gifts
A prize among the flowers.

Bluebells are not always blue. This is an uncommon white form of the English bluebell although white or pink forms of the Spanish bluebell are much more frequent.

The only surprise is that, for a poet whose words have immortalized wild daffodils, along with several other wildflowers, we hear little of bluebells from William Wordsworth. In the early 1900s, Canon H. D. Rawnsley wrote *Past and Present at the English Lakes*, a travelogue in which he often followed in the footsteps of Wordsworth. In a section called 'The Bluebells of the Duddon' he encounters vast drifts of bluebells and wonders why Wordsworth didn't eulogize such sights in his lonely wanderings:

Above and right: Spanish bluebells are easily distinguished from English bluebells by their upright flowerheads and more widely-open flowers growing all around the stem.

> *Through the low bushes of the hazel swamp, where a few weeks since daffodils had sheeted the ground, were now to be seen the bluebell myriads, in open patches, not with such purple lustre as I have seen in Kentish woods, but blue-grey as is the northern sky. You scarce could distinguish at a distance the pools of blue water from the pools of sky blue blossom. Fancy heard a fairy music from innumerable bells, and ever as we passed along, when the flowers were hidden from our sight by wall or shrub, their fragrance filled the air.*
>
> *We descend from our long rest in happy bluebell land, and make our way back to Duddon Bridge, wondering why it was that Wordsworth, with his love for flowers, wrote so little of the bluebell glories of the North Country. The poet of the daisy, the celandine, the little wild geranium, the daffodil, and the foxglove, he seems hardly to have noticed the hyacinth loveliness of the end of May. And yet each year the bluebells for him were resplendent in the woodland of Fiddler's Farm, between Rydal and Ambleside; every year beneath the Loughrigg Terrace one sloping meadow shone in beauty of sapphire grey; and such a lover of the Duddon as he was, and as a visitor to Broughton, he must have often gazed, as we are gazing to-day, at the ineffable beauty of the blue-bell woods and thickets by its side.*

Rawnsley was writing during the First World War (May 1916) and for him, spending time in a bluebell wood could even, if only briefly, lessen the horrors of the trenches:

> *Yet so potent is the spell of the bluebell slope on this gorgeous Maytide afternoon, that at times, though it be for a few moments, we can forget the horrors of battle, and can feel in tune with the 'cloud-born stream' with 'each tumultuous working left behind'.*

Our infatuation with this most British of spectacles continues. Many modern poets still draw inspiration from bluebells (just search the internet for bluebell poems!) and there is even a bluebell service, in Swithland Wood, part of Charnwood Forest in Leicestershire. Here, on the third or fourth Sunday of April some 200 people gather, whatever the weather, for an open-air church service that evokes a sense of the timeless nature of ancient forests – 2,000 years of history, from Druids welcoming spring in their sacred groves to the twenty-first century.

BLUEBELLS UNDER THREAT

But while we still celebrate the spring flood of bluebells, the twenty-first century brings with it potential threats to this spectacle. The most widely publicized of these threats in recent years is that of a foreign invader – the Spanish bluebell, *H. hispanica*. Spanish bluebells grow wild in the Iberian Peninsula, one of the many species there. But they were brought to British gardens as early as 1680 and there they remained for more than 200 years. They are more vigorous than native bluebells and spread more readily, which no doubt appealed to gardeners through the seventeenth, eighteenth and nineteenth centuries. But it wasn't until 1909 that they jumped the garden fence and were recorded growing in the wild for the first time. The big surprise is not that it happened, but that it took so long. In its natural haunts, the Spanish bluebell is a much more delicate-looking plant. Centuries of garden breeding seem to have created a new plant, and it may have taken time for the plant to acquire the vigour to escape and prosper in the British countryside.

Such a thing has happened before – with the familiar rabbit (also a native of Spain). When rabbits were first introduced to these islands by the Normans[18] they were delicate little things, in need of much cosseting in enclosed warrens, looked after by full-time warreners.* It took time for the animal that we know today to emerge; a species more than capable of looking after itself as part of the British landscape.

Perhaps the same happened to the Spanish bluebell, but in any case, once out of the garden it began to spread. And its vigour gave botanists

---

* There is a supposed Mesolithic record of rabbits from Berkskire, but they are otherwise absent from Britain until the Norman period, when the first warrens were recorded on the Isles of Scillly in 1176.

concerns that the Spanish bluebell might out-compete our more delicate native and gradually replace it. That was deemed a bad thing because Spanish bluebells, while taller and more robust, are a more washed-out blue and lack the evocative scent of the natives. However, the real threat is less likely to be an all-out frontal attack, but a more insidious infiltration.

The two species are closely related and can interbreed, producing hybrids with a mixture of features. The first such hybrid was recorded in 1963, more than fifty years after the first Spanish bluebell was found in the wild, but the spread of hybrids wasn't noticed until 1987. Now hybrids are found widely across the country. The more crossing there is, the more native bluebell features will be diluted. Concerned by such possibilities, a number of public surveys have been organized to chart the march of the invader and the state of the natives.

In 2003, Plantlife and the Botanical Society of Britain and Ireland (BSBI) organized the *Bluebells for Britain* survey, in which 2,000 people took part. They found that overall there was still a broad separation between the Spanish and hybrid bluebells on the one hand and natives on the other. More than two thirds of native bluebells occurred in woodlands, whereas around two thirds of the Spanish and hybrid bluebells grew in urban settings or along roads and hedgerows. Woodlands are clearly still a stronghold of native bluebells. But there was one alarming statistic; one in six bluebell woods harboured at least some hybrid bluebells as well as natives.

Most of the 4,500 records received in the *Bluebells for Britain* survey came from England. But in 2008, scientists from the Royal Botanic Garden in Edinburgh carried out a smaller-scale survey in south-central Scotland. Here 99 per cent of records were of native bluebells and 90 per cent of the natives were growing in native-only colonies in woodland. As in the earlier survey most aliens were growing in gardens. But a closer analysis revealed cause for concern here too. Over 40 per cent of the natives were growing within 1 to 2 kilometres of the aliens, well within the flight range of some pollinating bumblebees or hoverflies.[19]

So are these aliens now poised for an all-out assault on our native bluebells? At this point it's not clear. The two species meet naturally in the Iberian Peninsula, roughly along the northern border of Portugal and Spain, though as far as I know, no one has looked to see whether the two hybridize there. And it's likely in any case that the Spanish bluebell invading Britain is a more competitive plant, having been bred for many generations for showy garden displays.

But even if there is as yet no clear scientific evidence of an impending disaster, it still pays to be cautious. We should certainly refrain from planting alien bluebells, especially in the countryside, though even this simple precaution is harder than it might seem. Many bulbs in garden centres labelled as natives turn out to be hybrids. It's fairly easy to tell a full-blown Spanish bluebell from our native species, by its paler colour and by the fact that the flowers are held more erect, are more open, and grow all around the stem. Native bluebell flowers are a more intense blue, are more tubular and all hang to one side of the stalk. But identifying a hybrid can be a lot harder. And it's not helped when bulb suppliers accidentally or deliberately mislabel bulbs. I've been caught out several times, growing bulbs supplied as natives that turned out to be hybrids that I had to remove.

For me, with a dozen or so bulbs in the corner of my garden, it was only a small job, but spare a thought for the village of Cleat in Worcestershire. They planted 7,000 bulbs in a local copse – at a cost of £1,000 – only to find that they were all Spanish bluebells, despite assurances from the suppliers in Holland that they were true English bluebells. And in another recent example, bulbs from a packet that was clearly illustrated with the robust pale blue spike of a Spanish bluebell grew into perfectly good native bluebells. Confusion is rife.

But even bluebells growing well away from aliens still face threats. Climate change is already altering our natural history. New insects, from dragonflies to bumblebees, are colonizing Britain and the increase in average temperature is also affecting the timing of many natural

An unusual form of bluebell with extremely long bracts.

events. Leaves and flowers now tend to appear earlier in spring, a change that may have an impact on bluebells. The strategy of germinating in the autumn gives the bluebell a head start over spring-germinating plants, but as spring events creep ever earlier, the bluebell's advantage is lessened. It's been suggested that bluebells could start to lose out to other spring wildflowers as our climate continues to change. At the same time, warmer springs might favour

Spanish bluebells, increasing their impact on the native species. And if that's not enough, bluebells also have to cope with a plague of grazers in their woodland homes.

Many times I've lingered in forests until dusk, photographing plants spot-lit against a dark forest by the last glancing sunbeams cutting almost horizontally through the forest gloom, only to be startled by the harsh bark of a muntjac. Or picking my way by torchlight back through the night-time forest, I often startle a roe deer, which, for the smaller of our native deer, makes a passable impersonation of a small herd of bison as it crashes off through the undergrowth. It's an unfortunate fact that, in the absence of large predators, there are just too many deer in Britain. And their grazing destroys many woodland flowers. On more than one occasion, I've returned to a woodland orchid spike that I've been watching until it's in perfect bloom, to find the whole flower neatly nipped off. But the effect of deer on bluebells is potentially more long-lasting.

Monks Wood in Cambridgeshire must be one of the most studied forests in Britain. It gained its name in 1127 when it was given to the monks of Sawtry Abbey and then over 800 years later, Monks Wood Experimental Station was built nearby. Since then it has been the subject of intensive ecological experimentation. In 1978 several exclosures were erected to protect certain areas from grazing animals and to observe the effects on the flora and fauna. Two decades later the long-term effects on the bluebells could be assessed.[20]

The bluebells remained just as abundant both inside and outside the exclosures, but the plants outside the exclosure had much shorter leaves. In the New Forest, other studies suggest that grazing here also produced smaller plants.[21, 22] Bluebells must make as much food as they can in their leaves in April and early May, before the canopy closes over them and shuts out the light. Every square centimetre of leaf is critical, so reduction in leaf area by grazing animals reduces the vigour of the plants. Bluebells seem to be a favourite late winter and early spring food of muntjac and roe deer, which is odd, because bluebells are packed with chemicals designed to make them unpalatable.[23] These chemicals seem to work on those other inveterate nibblers, rabbits, which are said not to eat bluebell leaves, though they do damage bluebell bulbs as they dig and scratch at the forest floor. For this problem at least, bluebells have a solution. Like many bulbs, they produce roots early in the season that are capable of contracting. Where rabbits are busy scraping away at the woodland floor, bluebell bulbs are found much deeper in the soil

– around 6 centimetres (2 in) down rather than the more usual 2 to 3 centimetres (0.8–1.2 in), having pulled themselves safely out of the way of those digging paws.

The bluebell's defensive chemicals are attracting interest from pharmacologists. Fifteen biologically active chemicals have been isolated from bluebells and two turn out to be very similar to chemicals extracted from members of the pea family that may have effects on HIV and cancer cells. Another chemical is toxic to nematode worms, which makes it useful as a pesticide, both to the bluebells themselves and to farmers. These recent discoveries are all the more interesting since bluebells are rarely referred to in old herbals, apart from a mention in the thirteenth century as a cure for leprosy and a few folk tales that credit the juice with curing snakebite. In most cases where modern science has discovered useful chemicals in plants, those same properties have long been understood in folk medicine.

Although deer appear immune, livestock can be poisoned by the bluebell's armoury of toxins and a few cases of livestock poisoning have been blamed on these plants. On the other hand, even if they don't feed on them, livestock can also be detrimental to bluebells. Trampling by heavy hooves or human feet is just as destructive as direct grazing. Bluebell leaves are formed as tiny, easily damaged buds at the end of the previous growing season. If they are destroyed by trampling, new ones can't be made in time for the coming season. And this has an enormous impact on the vigour of the plant and its ability to produce seeds in subsequent seasons. Even two years after only moderate trampling, the plants are still unable to produce seed-bearing flower spikes.[24] The susceptibility of bluebells to trampling raises an intriguing possibility. We saw earlier that the wildwood was shaped by the trampling and browsing of large animals. This disruption created a shifting mosaic of habitats and a rich diversity of plants and animals. Could our iconic bluebell displays be an unnatural monoculture resulting from the extinction in Britain of certain large mammals? In a re-wilded future, in which we restore both grazers and predators, what would happen to our famous displays of bluebells? Wild boar, one of the shapers of both the wildwood and modern European forests, are once again spreading through parts of Britain, and could give us a glimpse of what more natural woodland ecosystems might look like. [25] It may be no coincidence that Britain has the best bluebell displays in Europe and the fewest big mammals.

East Blean Woods, a National Nature Reserve in Kent, has extensive patches of bluebells which complement the glowing green of spring beech leaves.

4

Wild Daffodils

AMARYLLIDACEAE

NARCISSUS PSEUDONARCISSUS

D affodils might not be the first wild flowers of the year to appear, but those glowing golden carpets that light up grey winter woods certainly feel like the real harbinger of spring. On a warm March day, when the air is clear, the sky deep blue and the sun bright, their yellow trumpets provide the fanfare that most clearly heralds the arrival of spring, a dazzling signal that the new wild flower season is underway. Of course, I'm not alone in basking in this golden glow. Tens of thousands travel to wild daffodil hotspots each spring to wander through yellow-spangled woods and breathe the fresh spring air. William Shakespeare captured this same feeling in lines from *The Winter's Tale*:

Daffodils that come before the swallow dares, and take
The winds of March with beauty

And in more prosaic style, in his poem 'Daffodowndilly', A. A. Milne's daffodils declare 'Winter is dead'.

Inside a daffodil's trumpet, the anthers ripen to release crumbl[masses of pollen.

She wore her yellow sun-bonnet,
She wore her greenest gown;
She turned to the south wind
And curtsied up and down.
She turned to the sunlight
And shook her yellow head,
And whispered to her neighbour:
'Winter is dead.'

You can hardly miss the daffodil's proclamation of spring; different varieties and species appear everywhere, from ancient woodlands and pastures to roadside verges and urban roundabouts. They cheer up commuters on dreary train journeys and momentarily catch the attention of motorway drivers speeding past sunshine-yellow splashes on roadside banks.

With some justification, Britain might well be considered the daffodil capital of the world. Apart from the countless hectares of daffodils that appear each spring, the plant is linked inextricably to these islands in the minds of many through the writings of Shakespeare, Wordsworth and many others. And, less poetically, Britain produces about half the world's crop of daffodil bulbs, our most important bulb crop, worth several million pounds in the export trade alone.[1]

Our infatuation with daffodils goes back some time, reflected in numerous old names for this plant. Jan Dalton, archivist at the

Daffodil Society, has so far uncovered 125 names, most of which will be unfamiliar: Yellow Lily, Lent Cocks, Giggary, Cowslip, Asphodel, Gracy Day, Haverdrils… the list goes on.[2] Many of these names are very local[3] and their derivations lost in history. It's not even certain where the name commonly used for the whole group – *Narcissus* – comes from.

WHAT'S IN A NAME?

Their name is usually attributed to a story from Classical Greek mythology, concerning a handsome youth called Narcissus. Many versions of the story exist, including one set down later by the Roman poet Ovid in his *Metamorphoses*. In this version Narcissus was the son of a beautiful wood nymph and was so beautiful himself that 'many youths, and many young girls desired him'. In particular, a nymph called Echo became infatuated, but Narcissus failed to notice her devotion, so to punish his lack of awareness, Cupid (or the goddess Nemesis in Ovid's version) cast a spell on Narcissus. He would fall in love with the first person he met. Unfortunately for Narcissus, he stopped to drink at a crystal-clear pool, so still that his face was perfectly reflected – and that was that. He fell in love with himself and sat day after day staring at his reflection, pining for a love he could never have, and slowly wasting away.

At this sad sight, the gods relented a little and turned him into a daffodil, though which particular species depends on which version of the story. Some described the flower as papery white, perhaps *N. papyraceus*,

a multi-flowered species that graces Mediterranean roadsides as early as January. Ovid describes a daffodil with a yellow trumpet surrounded by white petals – perhaps *N. poeticus*. Other stories finish with him ending up as a yellow daffodil, the trumpet being a vessel to hold the tears of the youth as he pined away for his own reflection. In 1644 the French artist Claude Lorraine visualized the denouement of this myth in his painting *Landscape with Narcissus and Echo*. Hidden away by the banks of the pool is a clump of daffodils that writer Richard Mabey considers to be *N. pseudonarcissus* – our very own wild daffodil and the main subject of this chapter.[4] But whichever species of daffodil that Narcissus became, his name lived on in the plant.

However, other classical authors suggest a more prosaic origin and attribute the name to a feature common to all daffodils. Narcissus derives from the same origin as the word 'narcotic', coming from the Classical Greek *narkao*, meaning to be numb or in a stupor. As we'll see later, daffodils contain a huge range of poisonous chemicals with just such effects and the Roman naturalist Pliny asserts firmly that the Narcissus gets its name from this property and not the 'fabulous boy'.[5]

The plant's common name – daffodil (and its older variants; daffydowndilly, affodil, affodily, daffodily) – probably derives more recently from 'asphodel', one of the old names listed by Jan Dalton, but more usually associated with an unrelated group of plants that are common on dry Mediterranean hillsides. It may, however, refer to *asphodelus* (Greek) or *asphodilus* (Latin), a flower that was said by the Ancient Greeks to grow in the meadows of the Underworld and

haw Common lies in the heart of the Gloucestershire/ Herefordshire 'golden triangle'.

one which therefore became associated with Persephone, Queen of the Underworld.

Persephone herself is as closely associated with the return of spring as the daffodil. She was abducted by Hades, Lord of the Underworld and her mother, Demeter, a goddess of crops and fertility, was so upset that she neglected the Earth and so nothing grew. Eventually, a desperate and starving populace persuaded Zeus, father of the gods, to force Hades to release Persephone. He did so, but since Persephone had eaten food in the Underworld, she couldn't live on Earth all year round. So, she emerged from Hades each spring, and, with her arrival on the surface, flowers bloomed and crops grew. Then she returned to the Underworld each winter, and so life on Earth withered and died again.

In a Roman version of the same story, the god of the Underworld used daffodils to catch the attention of Proserpina (a Latinized Persephone) and as she paused to admire them, he abducted her into his domain. Again, Proserpina was allowed to return to Earth each spring.

So it feels appropriate that daffodils now seem to appear everywhere to herald the arrival of spring. But the daffodils that colour city parks and rural roadsides alike and that are exported around the world are not wild daffodils. Most of the plants used in urban plantings are big and blousy cultivars lacking the delicate subtlety of the wild plant, with its deep-yellow trumpet and pale petals. But the situation is more complicated – and more intriguing – than that. There's more than one kind of daffodil growing wild in Britain.

NATURALIZED DAFFODILS

Daffodils belong to the Amaryllis family, the Amaryllidaceae. There are perhaps between fifty and eighty-five species, depending on which classification you chose to follow.[6,7] Although they are familiar the temperate world over, the centre of diversity for daffodils lies in the mountains of the Iberian Peninsula, with a few more adventurous species extending more widely.[8] One of those is *Narcissus pseudonarcissus*, the species we know in this country as the wild daffodil. A few other kinds are also more widespread in nature, as well as being familiar here as garden plants.

The pheasant's eye or poet's daffodil, *Narcissus poeticus*, grows as a truly wild plant from France and Spain as far east as Ukraine, where it forms spectacular drifts in the nature reserve known appropriately as the Valley of Narcissi. Here its beautiful white flowers, with red-tipped yellow trumpets, carpet 70 hectares of flower-rich meadows. There are similar extravagant displays in the Carpathian Mountains of Romania.

Such beautiful flowers have made the poet's daffodil popular as a cultivated plant since ancient times, so it has long been transported as a garden plant well beyond its native range. The poet's daffodil was probably the narcissus that was frequently referred to in classical literature and said to be the favourite flower of the Roman poet Ovid. In fact, he may well be the poet referred to in its name. The Romans carried this flower with them, to grace the gardens of their villas, as they conquered and colonized Europe.[9] And maybe that is how the poet's daffodil made it to Britain, though there is no firm evidence for this species growing in Britain that far back. But it was definitely recorded here as a garden plant as early as 1538. By 1795 it was growing in the wild.[10] So however it got here, it is a long-established naturalized plant.

Another story suggests it was brought back from the crusades by Sir Geoffrey de Fynderne. It is sometimes called the Findern flower and was certainly growing in his village of Findern in south Derbyshire in 1860 when the historian Bernard Burke visited. It still grows there today and is the emblem of a local school, though claims that it grows naturalized in Britain only around this village are clearly erroneous.[11] Recent surveys show that the poet's daffodil now grows widely across lowland Britain,

Betty Daw's Wood, a Gloucestershire Wildlife Trust reserve near Newent, is the perfect place to appreciate the warming sun of early spring.

naturalized in hedgerows and on roadsides as well as on rough or waste ground where garden waste was dumped.

The bunch-flowered daffodil, *Narcissus tazetta*, is another species widespread in the wild, from south-west Europe to south-west Asia. And it also grows naturalized in the British Isles, though nowhere near as widely as the poet's daffodil. To complicate matters further, all three of these daffodil species, *N. pseudonarcissus*, *N. poeticus* and *N. tazetta* can hybridize. They do so in the wild, and in France, for example, it is not unusual to find swathes of natural hybrids. There is a similar confusing array of hybrids growing in Britain, but here they are most probably derived from garden escapes, since such hybrids are very popular garden plants. The poet's daffodil produces a hybrid with the wild daffodil called the Nonsuch daffodil, which has long been a favourite amongst gardeners. The eighteenth-century botanist William Curtis describes the Nonsuch daffodil (and its double form, which he calls butter and eggs narcissus) as being well known to gardeners in 1795.[12] The cross between *N. tazetta* and *N. poeticus* is known as the 'primrose peerless' and occurs naturalized in old bulb fields.

There are folk tales that suggest that these plants have been accidentally or deliberately planted outside the garden for many centuries. South of

Wild daffodils along the banks of the Teign at Dunsford natur reserve in Devon.

where I live in Bristol lies the village of Churchill. Here, it is said, a crusader returned home with two bulbs of the 'primrose peerless' for his wife, who was fond of beautiful flowers. Unfortunately, on his return, he found his wife had died some four years earlier. In his grief he threw the bulbs over the wall of the churchyard where, as daffodils are prone to do, they thrived and spread.[13]

There are records of several other species growing naturalized in Britain, in short-lived colonies. These include the miniatures *N. cyclamineus* and *N. bulbocodium*, along with *N. papyraceus* and *N. minor*. To complicate matters further, other non-native subspecies of our wild daffodil are also occasionally found here. The Spanish or greater daffodil grows wild in Spain and Portugal and, though sometimes seen as a distinct species, *N. hispanicus*, it is usually regarded as a subspecies of the wild daffodil, *N. pseudonarcissus major*.

Daffodils' readiness to jump the garden wall and establish themselves in the wild is evident from many a roadside verge in spring. They have been described as the 'cats' of the plant world, barely domesticated and ready to resume life in the wild at the slightest opportunity.[14] Daffodils also hybridize very freely, which is one reason why there is such a huge number of cultivars. Some 3,000 varieties have been described, though relatively few of those are vigorous enough to be popular and therefore familiar to gardeners.[15]

Even so, such a wide choice of plants is great news for gardeners, but makes understanding the true situation of the wild daffodil in this country very difficult. The naturalized species and hybrids cross with wild daffodils and wild daffodils themselves have been widely planted across the country. All this makes any meaningful taxonomy or any attempt to plot the natural distribution of wild daffodils in Britain a difficult, if not impossible, task. It is such a confused picture that not everyone accepts that the wild daffodil is even a true native of these islands.[16]

WILD DAFFODIL HOTSPOTS

Most botanists, however, assume the wild daffodil to be native, at least in those core areas where it is extremely abundant, several of which have become famous as daffodil hotspots. Daffodils are well known along the banks of the River Dove in Farndale on the southern edge of the North

Yorkshire Moors. Each spring the tiny moorland villages along the dale welcome the droves of daffodil enthusiasts by producing industrial quantities of cream teas. The path along the Dove is frequently crowded with admirers, but wild daffodils also grow in the neighbouring valley of Rosedale, along the banks of the North Dale Beck, not far from Rosedale Abbey. Here it's still possible to wander alone through the spring display.

In the middle of April 1802, Dorothy and William Wordsworth also wandered alone through daffodils in another of their strongholds, in the Lake District. Dorothy recorded their walk in her journal.[17]

> *The wind was furious… the Lake was rough… When we were in the woods beyond Gowbarrow park we saw a few daffodils close to the water side, we fancied that the lake had floated the seeds ashore & that the little colony had so sprung up – But as we went along there were more & yet more & at last under the boughs of the trees, we saw that there was a long belt of them along the shore, about the breadth of a country turnpike road. I never saw daffodils so beautiful they grew among the mossy stones about & about them, some rested their heads upon these stones as on a pillow for weariness & the rest tossed & reeled & danced & seemed as if they verily laughed with the wind that blew upon them over the Lake, they looked so gay ever glancing ever changing. This wind blew directly over the lake to them. There was here & there a little knot & a few stragglers a few yards higher up but they were so few as not to disturb the simplicity & unity & life of that one busy highway… – Rain came on, we were wet.*

Wild daffodils still grow aroun[d] Glencoyne Bay, on Ullswater i[n] the Lake District, where Wordsworth famously describe[d] them in his poem 'I Wandered Lonely as a Cloud', also commonly known as 'Daffodils'.

It wasn't until two years later that her brother wrote his famous lines exalting this solitary encounter. Daffodils still grow in some abundance around the Lake District, including along the banks of Ullswater, around Glencoyne Bay, where William and Dorothy saw them. And even though these daffodils now border a busy road along the lake shore, it is, surprisingly, still possible to sit alone amongst this world-famous golden host.

Further south, the Gloucestershire–Herefordshire border has such an abundance of wild daffodils, it became known as the Golden Triangle, its apices in the villages of Dymock, Kempley and Oxenhall. Many woods and meadows here are carpeted with daffodils in March and April, some of the best managed by the Gloucestershire Wildlife Trust. My favourite

place to celebrate the arrival of spring is Betty Daw's Wood, which in March is often eye-achingly yellow. Nearby, Gwen and Vera's Fields are a great place to see wild daffodils growing in a meadow. Similar large drifts flow through more open woodland at Shaw Common, just down the road and the drive between all these locations is along roads lined with wild daffodils. Just as in Farndale, there is no shortage of cream teas to round off a day's daffodil appreciation.

Each village in the area has its own daffodil weekend, on three different weekends in March, when the village halls are open to supply tea and cake. Kempley even operates a 'Daff and Ride' bus service to move visitors around the village. Recently a circular walk, the 'Daffodil Way', was marked out to take in some of the best daffodil sites in the area. And the fact that the Daffodil Way runs for ten miles illustrates the extent of daffodils in this area. Luckily there are plenty of opportunities to overdose on tea and cakes to sustain the effort.

The Weald of Sussex is another daffodil hotspot, as is South Devon, at, for example, Dunsford Nature Reserve along the banks of the River Teign. They don't form such extensive carpets here, though a few clearings in the woods still have many thousands of plants. But for me the appeal of Dunsford is the clumps of daffodils overhanging a picturesque Dartmoor river – the epitome of spring in leafy Devon. They are also

St Mary's Church in Farndale, North Yorkshire, is awash with wild daffodils in spring.

abundant in parts of the Black Mountains in Wales. Wild daffodils occur beyond these hotspots of course, but in scattered, often sparse, colonies in woods and meadows. They are generally regarded as natives where they grow in semi-natural conditions in England, particularly in these hotspots, but are seen as introduced and naturalized in both Scotland and Ireland.[18] However, is the daffodil really a native plant?

One alternative suggestion is that it was brought here by travelling monks. Like the Romans, they may have admired the plant for its beauty and used it to decorate their churches in spring or, more likely, they may have grown it for its medicinal properties. Many kinds of daffodils are important medicinal plants; indeed, it is likely that many first came into cultivation not for their beauty but for their usefulness to apothecaries. *N. poeticus* is described in the Bible, where it seems to have been used to treat cancer and before that, in the fourth century BC, Hippocrates suggests that the oil of this species is effective against uterine tumours. Pliny the Elder offers both *N. poeticus* and *N. pseudonarcissus* for the same purposes. In China, *N. tazetta* was also used against tumours and still is in parts of Turkey.

The sixteenth-century herbalist John Gerard extols the virtues of daffodil roots in healing cuts and gashes, though not from personal experience. He was liberally borrowing from earlier writers, as far back as Ancient Greece. The Romans were also said to use this plant as a poultice for wounds. And this ancient wisdom is now backed by modern science. We now know that daffodils contain a range of chemicals called alkaloids, some of which are not found in any other group of plants.[19] These chemicals have a wide range of medicinal properties, including anti-viral and anti-bacterial effects as well as inhibiting some kinds of tumours. So those early descriptions of the medicinal properties of daffodils were not that wide of the mark. And it's not too surprising that learned monks would transport such a useful plant as they established new monastic settlements. Certainly, many daffodil hotspots have intriguing associations with monks and monasteries. The only large population of daffodils near London is in Abbey Wood near Bexley, named after the medieval Lesnes Abbey.

Local folklore suggests that the famous daffodils of Farndale came originally from the less well-known site at Rosedale, around the Cistercian priory that once stood there.[20] And the Rosedale daffodils themselves may also have been early imports. Monks from nearby Byland Abbey worked iron ore in Rosedale, but before they established

Byland Abbey, these monks had previously come from Furness Abbey in the Lake District. So perhaps the Farndale daffodils had their ultimate origin in the Lake District, from apothecaries' gardens at Furness Abbey.

We might have a better idea of the origins of our wild daffodil if we had a clear picture of its original distribution. But centuries of garden escapes and hybridization along with deliberate plantings have confused that picture beyond hope of detailed understanding. However, we can perhaps glimpse a broader picture. Today the daffodil's distribution, centred on a few widely scattered hotspots, seems rather strange, with no obvious reasons for its various centres of distribution. In the past, however, it seems the plant was much more widespread.

In the sixteenth century, John Gerard observed: 'The common yellow Daffodilly or Daffodowndilly is so well knowne to all, that it needeth no description.' He goes on to say that 'The yellow English Daffodill groweth almost every where through England.'[21] When Belgian botanist Charles de l'Écluse visited London in 1581 he also described daffodils as growing in profusion in the meadows around the capital.[22] According to other descriptions, daffodils remained widely distributed until the middle of the nineteenth century, after which they underwent a somewhat mysterious decline, resulting in the plant's rather odd modern distribution.

DAFFODILS: POPULATION PATTERNS

If this was the history of wild daffodils, it's not immediately obvious what caused such a dramatic decline. For a plant like the snake's head fritillary (see Chapter 7), with its dependence on traditional haymeadows, it is evident that habitat loss has severely restricted its distribution. Yet in most of its strongholds the wild daffodil seems a remarkably unfussy plant, growing in a variety of woodlands and meadows and even along verges. But its wide tolerance in these hotspots may be misleading. Detailed ecological studies and computer modelling have shown that wild daffodils are very sensitive to small changes in local conditions. And those effects are different in pastures and woodlands, making the wild daffodil's response to changing conditions very complicated. For example, a warm summer causes populations in woodlands to increase, whilst those in open pastures decrease.

This sensitivity affects both population growth and the number of flowers produced, so a detailed understanding of wild daffodil behaviour is vital if we want to continue to enjoy those early spring displays. One of the longest-term studies started in the 1980s, when J. P. Barkham and his colleagues at the University of East Anglia began a detailed ten-year study on wild daffodils in Cumbria.

The size of the population of any species depends on how successfully it reproduces. Like many plants, wild daffodils can reproduce either by producing seed or by vegetative growth (producing daughter bulblets budded off from the main bulb). Reproduction by seed has the advantage (if the plant is pollinated by a different individual) of producing genetic variation in the population. Vegetative growth can produce only a clone of the parent plant.

For the wild daffodil, vegetative growth seems more important, with seed production being of minor importance. Not all ovules in the plant's ovary get fertilized, not all seeds that are fertilized actually germinate and of those that do germinate, very few seedlings make it to adulthood. So wild daffodils are not very effective (in most conditions) at reproducing by seed.[23]

But the effectiveness of clonal reproduction differs from place to place and from year to year depending on conditions. Clonal growth varies with the density of plants. At low densities, when plenty of moisture and nutrients are available to each plant, the bulb can build up the reserves that allow it to produce daughter bulbs. At high densities, the bulbs are stressed and this again encourages clonal reproduction, producing small daughter bulbs which are more likely to be dispersed away from the stressful conditions. So clonal growth in wild daffodils is highest at both high and low densities.

The openness of the site also plays a role. Both clonal growth and seed production are more effective in more open conditions, either in open pastures or in woodlands that have recently been coppiced. Coppicing removes the dense shrub layer in a forest and before the high leaf canopy closes in late spring, this greatly increases the amount of light reaching the forest floor. Not surprisingly, daffodils do well in woodlands still managed by coppicing and in the second or third year after cutting there is a dramatic increase in the number of daffodil flowers.[24]

As the coppiced shrubs grow back and begin to shade the site again, the number of daffodil flowers falls. This is not due to plants dying, at least not in a normal coppice rotation of a couple of decades or so.

Overleaf: Wild daffodils flower long before leaves on the trees shade the forest floor.

Rather, daffodils can switch from being a mature plant, capable of producing a flower spike, back to a sub-adult or juvenile state, in which it is more concerned with growth and survival.[25] Needless to say, since seed reproduction needs the production of flowers, as a site becomes more shaded, reproduction by seed becomes very unlikely indeed.

The number of flowers also depends on the previous season's weather, but in different ways in open and shaded sites. In shaded places, flower numbers are limited by drought in the previous summer. In open sites, drought in either spring or summer limits the number of flowers. And, as I've already noted, a hot year increases daffodil numbers in shaded sites while decreasing numbers in open sites. The longevity of plants also varies between open and shaded sites. The age at which half the plants die is eighteen years in open sites, falling to twelve years in shaded sites.[26] And plants on open sites also reach maturity sooner, in six years as opposed to ten.[27]

It's abundantly clear from the Cumbrian study that wild daffodils respond to their environment in complex ways. But how does this manifest itself in increases or decreases in population, and can this throw any light on the apparent decline of daffodils during the nineteenth century? Understanding the key factors that influence daffodils in the field allowed Barkham and colleagues to produce a computer model in which they could vary any or all of these conditions at will and monitor the responses of wild daffodils over a virtual 1,000-year period.[28]

They soon noticed that the population size varied dramatically with just tiny changes in one of the environmental factors described above. So although conditions within and outside daffodil hotspots might look very similar, it may not take much of a difference to affect their numbers. Indeed, they saw fluctuations similar to those in their model in the field over as little as ten years, the length of their study period. So if the history of daffodils in England really did follow a pattern of widespread decline during the nineteenth century, reducing the national population to its current hotspots, the factors driving that decline might be very subtle indeed.

The computer model does emphasize how important traditional coppicing is in maintaining daffodils in woodland sites. The open phase increases vegetative reproduction and therefore makes the survival of individual clumps of daffodils more likely. Indeed, without coppicing, daffodils gradually disappeared from shaded woodland sites. There has been a drastic decline in woodlands managed by coppicing over the past

century, which has had a huge impact on many plants and animals.[29] Butterflies like the pearl-bordered fritillary have suffered a massive population crash as woodlands grew too dense to support the lush growth of violets needed by its caterpillars. It is now confined to a few scattered hotspots.

In more recent years, there has also been a decline in daffodil numbers across parts of Europe: their occurrence as natives is now very scattered across, for example, Germany west of the Rhine, and in the Ardennes region of Belgium and Luxembourg. The main reason here seems to be the replacement of traditionally managed coppiced oak woodlands with spruce plantations.[30]

Barkham's computer model suggested that vegetative clumps of daffodils should gradually spread over time to colonize new areas, but experience in Europe reveals that vegetative growth simply maintains existing clumps and that only seed can spread the population and reverse the decline. As we've seen, daffodils aren't great at reproducing by seed,

The valley of the River Dove in Farndale, on the southern flanks of the North York Moors, is a well-known daffodil hotspot.

but we now know how to tip the balance in their favour. Returning woodlands to coppice management and mowing meadows after leaf die-back opens up the ground and gives daffodil seedlings the best chance of establishing themselves.

The balance between seed and vegetative reproduction also seems to account for a distinct characteristic of daffodil woods. Rather than carpeting the ground in a solid mass, in the manner of bluebells or dog's mercury, wild daffodils grow in distinct clumps, with gaps in between. The clumps and gaps are probably created in the first place by disturbance, for example during the cutting phase of the coppice cycle. But why don't the gaps close over?

If mature bulbs are planted in the gaps, they grow quite happily; so there's nothing about the immediate environment that prevents the plant from surviving. But seedlings transplanted into the gaps don't survive unless they are give a nutrient boost to speed their growth.[31] Daffodil seedlings have thin, strap-like leaves for the first two years of their growth and these suffer heavy damage from slugs. They are also easily covered by leaf litter. Vegetative growth is quite slow and would take a long time to fill in the gaps. Seeds could easily colonize the gaps, but particularly as the site becomes shaded after coppicing, seedlings rarely survive, so the gaps between clumps remain.

TENBY DAFFODILS

There is one other kind of daffodil growing in Britain that I have yet to mention – the Tenby daffodil. It is sometimes elevated to a species in its own right, but more frequently regarded as a subspecies, *N. p. obvallaris*, of the more widespread wild daffodil. As its name suggests, it once grew in great abundance in the hills and valleys around Tenby in south Pembrokeshire. Unlike the more familiar wild daffodil, with its bright-yellow trumpet offset by paler yellower petals, the Tenby daffodil is a showy bright yellow all over, perfect for decorating the lapels of patriotic Welsh folk on St David's Day.

We do not know exactly when the daffodil became the national flower of Wales. Its status as such may have evolved from an earlier affinity with the leek. St David himself ordered his troops to wear leeks on their helmets in a battle against the pagan Saxons. That might seem like an odd thing to do, but unlikely plants were often used as symbols of allegiance like this. The Plantagenets wore sprigs of common broom, *Cytisus scoparius*, which in the twelfth century was called *Planta Genista*, the origin of the name of their dynasty.

In Welsh the names for leek (*cenhinen*) and daffodil (*cenhinen Bedr* – or St Peter's leek) are similar. And in some parts of Wales daffodils are also called *Cenhinen Dewi* – Dewi's (David's) leek, so perhaps this close association of the two plants is how the daffodil became a symbol of St David's Day. But however the association of leeks and daffodils arose, the wearing of daffodils in celebration of St David's Day grew more popular through the nineteenth century and was given a later boost by the fondness of David Lloyd George – Britain's sole Welsh (and Welsh-speaking) prime minister to date – for wearing this plant. As a symbol of St David's Day in March, the daffodil, our most obvious harbinger of spring, seems more than appropriate. But Dewi's leek refers to any of the daffodil varieties so frequent in spring. It wasn't until more recently that it became clear that Wales had its own unique kind of daffodil.

As with all the other species and hybrids we've seen so far, the origins of the Tenby daffodil are shrouded in mystery, which has spawned a whole series of colourful tales. One story describes a Phoenician trading vessel foundering off the coast of Pembrokeshire. The sailors were rescued and were warmed around fires of local anthracite. Realizing the value of such coal as a fuel, the traders repaired their ship and returned the next year, with a hold full of daffodil bulbs to trade for coal.

Another story claims that Flemish colonists, sent to Pembrokeshire in 1106 by Henry I, brought the plants. Several historians have argued that since these colonists would have had a tough job carving out land and a living in Pembrokeshire a supply of daffodils was unlikely to have been high on their list of priorities.[32] However, if St David sent his men into battle adorned with leeks some six centuries earlier, who knows…?

As with some of the colonies of wild daffodil elsewhere in Britain, medieval monks travelling from France or Italy have also been fingered as possible importers of the Tenby daffodil. But this particular daffodil seems not to have occurred elsewhere in Europe, so even this more plausible route to Pembrokeshire is unlikely. Since Tenby daffodils are unique, they must have originated in the area, possibly as hybrids that found the fields and pasturelands of this part of the Welsh coastline to their liking. And the historical record certainly offers descriptions of them growing in spectacular abundance, covering some fields entirely.[33]

Like the more widespread wild daffodil, Tenby daffodils experienced a catastrophic decline in the nineteenth century, though in this case, we know exactly who the culprits were – commercial collectors. By the Victorian era, plants were big business and fields full of spectacular – and unique – daffodils were too good an opportunity to miss. Seeing easy money, a few local people began digging up the bulbs and shipping them out to markets such as Covent Garden in London.

In 1893, the curator of the Tenby museum reported that '…a man named Rees, learning of the value of the flowers at Covent Garden, sold the bulbs, the entire crop on fields, for £80'. In the same year another resident of Tenby wrote that because of 'the greed of occupiers of land, who have been sending off truck loads to the dealers, [the Tenby Daffodil] is becoming scarce'.[34]

But according to a paper read before the Cardiff Naturalists' Society in 1894 by Charles Vachell, the elimination of wild populations of Tenby daffodils can be laid at the door of one man – a Mr Shaw – who set up a nursery in Tenby and then realized that the local wild daffodils seemed different from anything else he knew. Consultation with experts from Covent Garden proved his suspicions correct and there was an instant demand for this plant, so huge that Mr Shaw was able to employ a small staff of people to dig bulbs from the local fields and pastures. The farmers on whose fields these plants grew regarded them as little more than nuisance weeds, so sold them to Mr Shaw for pennies, grateful to be rid of them. Carts heaped high with daffodil bulbs trundled into Mr Shaw's nursery, each cartload worth perhaps £160 on the London market. He kept his dealings as quiet as possible to retain a monopoly on the lucrative trade and by the time others began cashing in on the Tenby daffodil, most of the big displays had vanished.

As Tenby daffodils flourished and spread around gardens across the country, only a few hung on in out-of-the-way places in their original home. For three-quarters of a century the Tenby daffodil was forgotten and few inhabitants of Tenby were even aware of the unique plant named after their town. However, since the plants were no longer being dug up by collectors, their numbers slowly recovered, so that when botanist H. W. Pugsley visited the area in 1941, he was able to find good numbers on one or two of the hilly fields where it once thrived.[35] But in a few decades the Tenby daffodil would shoot to fame again.

In the 1970s a young boy from Essex, holidaying in Tenby, asked at the local tourist office where he could buy Tenby daffodil bulbs to take home to his aunt. No one in the office knew what he was talking about, and they were on the point of putting it down to a schoolboy prank when a workman in the building showed them a copy of the *Reader's Digest Book of British Flowers*, which showed the plant in all its glory. The prestige value of having a unique plant named after their town was not lost on the tourist office. They set about obtaining supplies, and descendants of those plants ripped from the fields around Tenby began to grow everywhere, as verges, roundabouts and parks were planted up. At least this time the plant's fame fostered a growing population around its eponymous town.

THE POETS' DAFFODILS

The vibrant spring shows of daffodils, whether wild or cultivated, have long drawn admiration from more than just botanists and gardeners. As we have seen, poets through the ages, from Ovid to Shakespeare and beyond, have eulogized these plants. But it's the displays of wild plants that really seem to capture the poet's imagination.

In the centre of Gloucestershire and Herefordshire's golden triangle, a whole group of poets began to assemble in the village of Dymock. The 'Dymock Poets' included Rupert Brooke, John Drinkwater, Wilfrid Gibson, Edward Thomas and the American Robert Frost. All were entranced by rural life here, admittedly somewhat idealized through the eyes of these poets, and they all drew inspiration for their varied literary output from long early spring walks through woods and meadows golden with wild daffodils. The informal group was started by Lascelles Abercrombie, perhaps the least known of them, who moved to the village of Dymock in the years leading up to the First World War. In 1910 he wrote 'Ryton Firs', which captures spring in this remote corner of north Gloucestershire:

But in the Spring, not too softly entangling
For lively feet to dance on, when the green
Flashes with daffodils. From Marcle way,
From Dymock, Kempley, Newent, Bromesberrow,
Redmarley, all the meadowland daffodils seem
Running in golden tides to Ryton Firs,
To make the knot of steep little wooded hills
Their brightest show

Robert Frost's poem 'The Road Not Taken' has become an American icon, but the poem's conflicted speaker was based on another of the Dymock Poets, Edward Thomas, whom he had befriended on long walks through the fields and woods of the Golden Triangle, as the opening lines make clear:

Two roads diverged in a yellow wood
And sorry I could not travel both.
And be one traveler, long I stood
And looked down one as far as I could
To where it bent in the undergrowth

John Drinkwater also made frequent references to the daffodils of the Golden Triangle. In his poem 'In Lady Street', he compared the colourful charm of rural life (he didn't have to live it!) with the grey drudgery of the city. In another poem, 'Daffodils', he describes cartloads of daffodils arriving from Gloucestershire to remind a rural immigrant to the city of the vibrancy of the countryside he has left:

Again, my man of Lady Street,
Your daffodils have come, the sweet
Bell daffodils that are aglow
In Ryton woods now, where they go
Who are my friends and make good rhymes.
They come, these very daffodils,
From that same flight of Gloucester Hills,
Where Dymock dames and Dymock men
Have cider kegs and flocks in pen,
For I've been there a thousand times.
Your petals are enchanted still
And when those tongues of Orphic skill
Bestowed upon that Ryton earth

A benediction for your birth,
Sun daffodils that now I greet.
Because, brave daffodils, you bring
Colour and savour of a spring
That Ryton blood is quick to tell.
You should be borne if all were well,
In golden carts to Lady Street.

Even after the Dymock Poets drifted away from the Golden Triangle, daffodils still made their way to London and Birmingham. In the 1920s picking daffodils was a vital source of income early in the year for the rural communities based around the villages listed by Abercrombie in 'Ryton Firs'. Even up to the 1950s children would skip school in March to harvest wild daffodils.

The commercial trade in cut flowers, supplying markets like that at Covent Garden, worked because the flowers could be transported quickly by train

The pale petals and sepals contrasting with the deep yellow trumpet differentiate the wild daffodil from many cultivated hybrids and varieties.

from the heart of the Golden Triangle. A local line, opened in 1885, connected the daffodil fields and woods to the main express line to London. The same line, which soon became known as the Daffodil Line, also transported 'Daffodil Girls' as extra pickers, along with curious tourists, straight to the centre of the action. From Victorian times onwards, large numbers of people flocked here to delight in the spring spectacle and, for a small price paid to local landowners, could carry home an armful of memories. The Daffodil Line stopped carrying passengers in 1959 and closed completely in 1964.

I have deliberately avoided the most famous lines written about daffodils, from the pen of one William Wordsworth. Instead I'll focus on an interesting botanical observation to be found in the poem's less familiar second verse.

They stretched in never-ending line
Along the margin of a bay:
Ten thousand saw I at a glance,
Tossing their heads in sprightly dance.

It was Dorothy Wordsworth who first noticed this 'sprightly dance', as she noted in her journal for that day in March.

I never saw daffodils so beautiful they grew among the mossy stones about & about them, some rested their heads upon these stones as on a pillow for weariness & the rest tossed & reeled & danced & seemed as if they verily laughed with the wind that blew upon them over the Lake, they looked so gay ever glancing ever changing.

Dancing daffodils caught the eye of other poets. John Masefield, describing how the daffodils of the Golden Triangle carpet the soils of the old red sandstone rocks that underlie the area, wrote:

Red clayed and pleasant,
which the young spring fills
with the never quiet joy of
dancing daffodils.

More recently, scientists have also turned their attention to dancing daffodils. Even in a gentle breeze, the flowers of daffodils bounce around continuously, frustratingly so if you are trying to capture a sharp photograph. The flowers of daffodils are large and stick out to one side of a tall stem. Big, conspicuous flowers held high above the ground may more easily attract insect pollinators, but also carry a risk for the plant. Like a sail, they present a large surface area to the wind, and in stronger winds could easily bend or break the stem.

But the stems of daffodils have evolved a cross-sectional shape that allows the flower to twist easily – hence their propensity for dancing. This allows the flower to orientate itself downwind, offering less wind resistance and reducing drag by about a third.[36]

In the dancing daffodil, science and poetry come together. And that, for me, is the beauty of many of our more spectacular wildflowers. Even in a country as well botanized as ours, there is always more to learn about wildflowers. Yet, when the brain is jaded by facts, those same flowers can refresh the mind in profound ways, and none more so than the displays of wild daffodils that herald the start of spring.

5

Snowdrops
& Snowflakes

AMARYLLIDACEAE

With the possible exception of the summer snowflake, *Leucojum aestivum*, most of the plants I'm going to examine in this chapter are probably not British natives. However, since they enhance our countryside in so many places, creating spectacular displays, both in the wild and in gardens, I feel they have earned their place. Snowdrops, in particular, bring enormous pleasure to a great many people, so I make no apology for exploring their natural history – on both sides of the garden fence – in the following pages.

Snowdrops and snowflakes, as their names suggest, are closely related. In many field guides they are both placed in the lily family, but as we saw in Chapter 1, the lily family had become something of a catch-all for plants that didn't conveniently fit anywhere else. Recently, using molecular techniques, the family has been revised and many species, including snowdrops and snowflakes, evicted. They now reside in the same family as daffodils, the Amaryllidaceae, and like daffodils themselves, are refugees from the lily family.

THE DIVERSITY OF SNOWDROPS AND SNOWFLAKES

Globally, there are only two species of true snowflakes, the spring snowflake, *L. vernum* and the summer snowflake, *L. aestivum*, both of which grow in this country, though whether native, introduced or a bit of both is still a matter of some debate. Originally, there were eleven species included in this genus, but molecular studies have reduced this to two, with the rest being moved to a new genus, *Acis*, which includes the popular garden plant autumn snowflake, *A. autumnalis*.[1] Along with three other *Acis* species, it flowers in the autumn, though it hasn't really established itself in the wider British countryside. However, a late holiday in the Algarve, for example, will reveal this plant in all its wild glory, white bells thrusting up in the late autumn sunshine long before the leaves appear. Curiously, though, my cultivated plants keep their leaves year round.

In all there are twenty species of snowdrops, *Galanthus*, with a distribution centred on Turkey and the Caucasus region. Indeed, the ancestor of all snowdrops might well have lived in the Caucasus before diversifying and spreading across Europe and parts of Asia Minor.[2] One species, the common snowdrop, *G. nivalis*, is sometimes seen as a British native. But as with the two snowflakes, no one is exactly sure.

Top: Common snowdrop.
Above: Greater snowdrop.
Below: Summer snowflake.

Two other species of snowdrops might also be encountered on late winter rambles through the countryside – the pleated snowdrop, *G. plicatus*, and the greater or giant snowdrop, *G. elwesii*. Both of these plants hail from south-east Europe, Turkey and Georgia and any patches discovered in the wild in Britain are definitely relics of former cultivation and also likely to be of fairly recent origin. The pleated snowdrop is said to have been brought back by soldiers returning from the Crimean War in around 1856, although there are records of it growing in British gardens since 1818.[3] However, it wasn't seen growing in the wild until 1947. The greater snowdrop has been a garden plant since 1875, but was not found growing wild until 1957.[4]

Snowdrops are popular garden plants, brightening up the dull days of February, often in concert with winter aconites, *Eranthis hyemale*. Their popularity means that several other species, like *G. woronowii*, are now often seen in early spring gardens, though less frequently than the three above. And a few, such as *G. reginae-olgae* from Greece and Sicily, and *G. peshmenii*, from a small area of Antalya province in south-western Turkey, provide an autumn flower display. Like autumn snowflakes, the flowers of these species appear before the leaves.

Whilst the common snowdrop is widespread, both in Britain and across Europe, others are restricted to tiny areas. A recently discovered species, Panjutin's snowdrop, *G. panjutinii*, seems to be confined to just five sites, covering no more than 20 square kilometres (8 square miles), in the Colchis area of southern Russia and Georgia. Unfortunately, one of those sites was near Sochi, location of the 2014 Winter Olympics, and was destroyed by construction during preparations for the games.[5]

All of these snowdrops and snowflakes look very similar at first glance, with their white pendulous flowers. And their botanical names also have similar meaning. *Galanthus* means 'milk flower', whilst *Leucojum* means 'white violet'. However, the snowflakes are fairly easy to distinguish from the snowdrops, being larger, especially the summer snowflake which can reach over half a metre (2 ft) in height. And unlike snowdrops, summer snowflakes prefer very wet woodlands or meadows, including those that flood regularly. Summer snowflakes also have multiple flowers atop each stem while spring snowflakes and snowdrops have only one.

On closer inspection, the individual flowers of snowdrops and snow-flakes look very different. All the tepals (petals and sepals) of snowflake flowers are similar in size and form a hanging white bell. In the snow-drop flower, the inner three tepals are smaller and form a cup inside the larger outer three tepals, which are splayed out like a propeller. The warmer the weather, the more these outer tepals spread wide. The outer surface of the tepals is covered in microscopic papillae which give them

a slightly velvety texture, and which perhaps helps pollinating insects, sluggish with the cold, hang on to the flower as they clamber over it.[6]

The inner tepals of snowdrops are usually marked with green and variations in the size and shape of this is one of the ways of telling different snowdrop species apart. This might be convenient for botanists and gardeners, but that is not why the snowdrop has evolved these green marks. They are green because they contain chlorophyll, the complex chemical that plants use to carry out photosynthesis. And experiments have shown that these green patches on the snowdrop's inner tepals do indeed photosynthesize.[7] In other flowers, floral photosynthesis produces food that goes directly into seed development, helping to offset the costs of producing flowers and seeds. The green patches on snowdrop tepals are probably too small to help with the costs of reproduction, but it's been suggested they may at least help offset the costs of producing nectar. The snowdrop also uses these green marks as nectar guides, to point the way for early flying bumblebees seeking the honey-scented nectar in the inner cup. Inconspicuous to us, they reflect ultraviolet light brightly, making them glowing beacons for insects sensitive to this short wavelength light.

Another way to tell different snowdrops apart is by their vernation. This is the way the leaves emerge from the bulb and push up through the soil surface, so can be clearly seen early in the season, even before the plants flower. In 'applanate' species, the two leaves are pressed together, flat against each other like hands in prayer, as they emerge. In 'explicative' species, the leaves are also pressed together, but the edges of the leaves are folded back. In 'supervolute' species, one leaf is clasped around the other. These arrangements can be used to identify different species of snowdrops – or at least that is what the gardening books will tell you. But a recent molecular study of snowdrop DNA, which set out to clarify the evolution and distribution of snowdrop species, has shown that different types of vernation can occur in a single species, as defined by its genetic chemistry.[8]

Thanks to the popularity of snowdrops amongst gardeners, any unusual variations are eagerly sought out and cultivated, and there has been an astonishing explosion in the numbers of described varieties in recent years. When the book generally known as the snowdrop bible was published in 2002,[9] the authors described a mere 500 varieties. There are now around 2,000, plenty of material for the new edition of *Snowdrops, a Monograph of Cultivated Galanthus*. Most of the varieties derive from

Below left: Pleated or Crimean snowdrop. *Below:* A single flower of the pleated or Crimean snowdrop.

the three most popular species, *G. nivalis*, *G. plicatus* and *G. elwesii*. There's a rich diversity of snowdrops to be discovered in gardens around Britain. But what about snowdrops beyond the garden fence? Can we claim at least one of these species as a British native?

SNOWDROPS: NATIVE OR ALIEN?

In the past there were plenty of botanists who believed that some populations of common snowdrops were indigenous to these islands and some still think that plants growing in the south-west might be true natives. In places such as the valleys cut into the slopes of Exmoor, they certainly *look* wild, cascading in drifts over wooded slopes down to wild rivers in late winter spate. Here they look and behave very much like the indisputably wild snowdrops growing in southern and eastern Europe.

But there are no records from before the late eighteenth century describing snowdrops in the wild anywhere in Britain. As with other conspicuous plants, like snake's head fritillaries, this is curious. They were cultivated in British gardens at least as far back as the sixteenth century. Gerard illustrates an unmistakable snowdrop in his *Herball* of 1597,[10] a plant that he calls 'the timely flow'ring bulbous violet', but which he knew in Britain only from London gardens.

However, he knew it was a wild plant further south in Europe. In the *Herball* he writes, 'These plants do grow wild in Italie and places adjacent, notwithstanding our London gardens have taken possession of them all, many years past.' Incidentally, the name 'snowdrop' appears to have first been coined in 1633, when Thomas Johnson produced a revised edition of Gerard's *Herball*, and added a note reading 'some call them snowdrops'.

A few decades later John Parkinson, in 1656, describes snowdrops in his book *Paradisi in Sole, Paradisus Terrestris: or, A Choice Garden of all Sorts of Rarest Flowers*. His specimens came from Constantinople (Istanbul) in Turkey. John Evelyn mentions snowdrops as garden plants in his *Kalendar of Horticulture* in 1664 and they slowly became more familiar to gardeners through the following century. In 1732 Robert Furber described several varieties in *The Flower Garden Displayed* and eventually in 1753 it received its new binomial name, *G. nivalis*, from Linnaeus

himself, in his *Species Plantarum* – the name which it carries to this day.

Yet snowdrops weren't seen growing in the wild until the 1770s, well over a century and a half after first appearing in British gardens. In the 1778 edition of *Flora Anglica*, William Hudson describes finding 'wild' snowdrops in meadows, hedges and orchards in Westmorland, Cumberland, Lancaster and Gloucestershire.[11] Another botanist, William Withering, later found further 'wild' colonies in Gloucestershire and Worcestershire. By 1804 Sir James Edward Smith, in *Flora Britannica*, was describing colonies from County Durham, south to Bedfordshire and west to the Malverns. He had no doubt that some of these colonies, for example those along the River Tees on the borders of Yorkshire and County Durham, were wild. His entry for *Galanthus* in the *Flora* reads 'On the banks of the Tees about Blackwell and Conniscliffe, certainly wild'.[12] I've wandered amongst snowdrops in this area many times. They grow on steeply sloping banks in clumps and drifts above the dark, peat-stained water of the Tees and they look as though they belong here, as much as those in the Exmoor valleys. Yet, walking the Teesdale Way, a long-distance path that parallels the river, it soon becomes clear that the further from riverside hamlets and cottages I progress, the fewer snowdrops grace the banks.

Common snowdrops along the River Tees in County Durham

Overleaf: Dazzling carpets of snowdrops brighten up the dark days of late winter.

And it's hard to imagine, given the numerous descriptions of these conspicuous plants after the 1770s, that earlier botanists could have missed them. This was a period when some of our most obscure native plants, growing in remote corners of the British Isles, were being discovered and described. Surely drifts of white flowers carpeting the ground when little else is in flower can hardly have been missed. The conclusion of many botanists today is that the common snowdrop was introduced to this country as a garden plant sometime in the fifteenth or sixteenth century and eventually escaped to grace the wider countryside some considerable time after that.

In some ways this botanical detective work might seem overly pedantic. You might ask, does it matter whether common snowdrops are native or not? Their status certainly has no effect on the enormous pleasure that these plants bring to many people, myself included. They are an eagerly awaited sign that the year has turned and spring is just round the corner.

One of their folk names is Eve's Comforter, derived from a legend concerning Eve after she and Adam were banished from perpetual summer in the Garden of Eden. Eve was dismayed as the seasons turned and snow ushered in her first winter. Seeing her weeping as snow fell around her, an angel took pity on Eve. He caught a snowflake and breathed on it, turning it into a snowdrop. And as the angel left, more snowdrops sprang up in his footsteps – a timely reminder to Eve that, even beyond the Garden, spring will eventually return. In the nineteenth century, Edinburgh-born chemist George Wilson, in his poem 'The Origin of the Snowdrop', captured the essence of what snowdrops mean, not just to Eve, but to all of us:

> *And thus the snowdrop, like the bow*
> *That spans the cloudy sky,*
> *Becomes a symbol whence we know*
> *That brighter days are nigh.*

We can be thankful, if not to angels, then to gardeners over the last few centuries for creating stunning displays of snowdrops right across the country, timely reminders to all of us that spring is on the way. As Alfred, Lord Tennyson wrote, 'Many many welcomes, February fair-maid'. And today, the number of people who make an annual pilgrimage to snowdrop gardens in the dark, cold days of February is extraordinary.

The Rococo Garden at Painswick, in Gloucestershire, has to open

several large fields to accommodate parking. Snowdrop Valley, near Wheddon Cross, on Exmoor operates a 'park and ride' system to prevent the narrow lanes from becoming clogged with traffic. Welford Park in the Lambourn Valley of Berkshire only opens its doors for a month or so in February, so visitors can witness wonderful carpets of snowdrops lining the river banks and flowing through the woods. Such events are repeated right across the country where few, if any, of these pilgrims in search of spring worry about the native status or otherwise of common snowdrops.

SNOWFLAKES — NATIVE OR ALIEN?

But if we can't claim the common snowdrop as a native, what about the two snowflakes? Summer snowflake is the more widespread species although, like snowdrops, remained undiscovered in the wild until the eighteenth century. Gerard knew it from gardens and considered it to be wild in Italy, which it certainly is. But it wasn't until the 1780s that the botanist and entomologist William Curtis found the first wild colonies along the Thames, between Greenwich and Woolwich. He later painted this species to include it in his beautifully illustrated *Flora Londinensis*. It was also found on the Wiltshire Avon, north of Salisbury and is now known from widely scattered but often dense populations throughout the British Isles.[13] It begins to look as if the same story as that of the snowdrop is unfolding. With the summer snowflake, however, the situation is a little more complicated.

Summer snowflake grows in abundance in wet woodlands by the River Thames at Withymead Nature Reserve, in Oxfordshire.

There are two subspecies of summer snowflake, *L. a. pulchellum* from the western Mediterranean and *L. a. aestivum* across the rest of its range. Both subspecies occur in Britain, though *L. a. pulchellum* is the one more frequently grown in gardens. As an adaptation to its native Mediterranean, it flowers in early April, two to three weeks earlier than *L. a. aestivalis*, which makes it a popular spring plant, despite its misleading common name. Any plants of the *pulchellum* subspecies found growing in the wild are definitely not native. So where does this leave the other subspecies, whose main range stretches from central and southern Europe across to northern Iran?

Elsewhere in northern Europe – in Germany, the Netherlands and Belgium – it is thought to be an introduced plant.[14] In Britain the situation is less clear. There are particularly dense populations along the

Thames, where William Curtis first found it in the wild, as well as along several of its tributaries. Along one such tributary, the River Loddon in Berkshire, they have been abundant for so long that the plant is often called the Loddon lily. Here they grow in suspiciously wild-looking conditions; tangled woodlands that are so wet underfoot it is easy to get a boot full of water while admiring the plants. Growing close to large rivers, the fruits and seeds of summer snowflakes are adapted to disperse by floating downstream, often for considerable distances. So they could have spread from cultivation further upstream. But some botanists now think these populations in south-central England are true natives.[15] I hope so. The sight of pendulous heads of glowing white flowers growing in tangled marshy woodland in places such as Withymead Nature Reserve (near South Stoke in Oxfordshire) or Rodbed Woods (near Medmenham in Buckinghamshire), as red kites swoop and whistle overhead, make for a memorable experience.

Richard Mabey describes how summer snowflake flowers were traditionally used in old May garlands in the village of Long Wittenham, on
the Thames in Oxfordshire, which could be taken as further evidence
of the plant being native in this area.[16] So it seems that *L. a. pulchellum*, wherever it is found, is a garden escape, as are plants of the other
subspecies outside the south–central area of England. Within this area,
however, the jury is still out. Perhaps some of the woodlands where it
is found really are inaccessible enough to have deterred early botanists
from exploring and discovering this otherwise conspicuous plant.

The summer snowflake also occurs in Ireland in widely scattered
colonies, some of which are also remote and inaccessible. One, on the
Dingle Peninsula of County Kerry, is at least a hundred miles from the
nearest main colonies in Cork and Limerick.[17] Just as there is a concentration of sites in south–central England, so too there is a similar
concentration in Ireland – around Limerick. In Ireland, though, some of
these colonies grow in reedbeds; the English colonies in contrast are all
in woodland. Summer snowflakes can survive in Irish reedbeds thanks to
the traditional way the beds are managed. The reeds are harvested early
in the year when they're cut about a foot above the ground, high enough
to spare the growing snowflake leaves. The snowflakes can then grow up
and flower, free from competition.[18]

In the case of snowflakes, the distinction between native and alien
matters – at least as regards the legal framework that supports conservation in the UK. If some populations of summer snowflake really *are* native, they would have to be considered 'Nationally Scarce' which would
trigger considerable conservation efforts on their behalf. The fact that
there are no such efforts shows that there is no real consensus yet as to
their status.[19]

Spring snowflakes in Britain, which flower from February to April,
are almost always escapes from cultivation. They are native to central
Europe, reaching as far as Belgium and to the Pyrenees. However, two
British populations, one in Somerset along the Doniford Stream, the
other in Dorset near Wootton Fitzpaine, are sometimes seen as native
because they are growing in sites relatively remote from gardens.

In fact, the Dorset site is only a kilometre or so (half a mile) from the
gardens of Wootton Fitzpaine Manor, but spring snowflakes are not such
effective river travellers as summer snowflakes. Their seeds, like those of
snowdrops, have elaiosomes – structures designed to attract ants. So,
unlike summer snowflakes, the seeds of spring snowflake are dispersed

by ants – in particular common red ants, *Myrmica rubra*, and cornfield ants, *Lasius alienus*,[20] and so are less likely than summer snowflakes to colonize remote riverbanks by floating down from distant upstream gardens. Nevertheless, most botanists now consider that even the plants in the Somerset and Dorset sites are garden escapees and not true natives.

But, whether native or not, the various snowdrop species enhance gardens and woodlands across the country. Together with the two snowflakes, they provide floral displays for much of the year. Autumn-flowering snowdrops are followed by the various spring-flowering species, which then overlap with spring snowflakes until these in turn are succeeded by summer snowflakes. But in many ways, the early spring species, like the common snowdrop, command the most respect as they break through frozen soil or even a covering of snow to let us know spring is round the corner.

SNOWDROPS: THRIVING IN THE COLD

Snowdrops have several adaptations that help them thrive in the cold months. They have hardened tips to their leaves, which help them break through frozen soil or snow, a trick that gives them their French vernacular name of *perce-neige* ('snow-piercer'). Their cells are packed with an antifreeze, preventing the growth of large ice crystals which would otherwise destroy the delicate cell membranes and kill the plant. Snowdrops have an almost uncanny ability to rise from apparently fatal cold. After a really hard frost the plants collapse and look as if they're not long for this world. Yet as soon as the temperature rises the plant picks itself up and carries on as normal, its cells undamaged thanks to the protection of its antifreeze. Snowdrop antifreeze is so effective, I've heard it said that snowdrop bulbs were used to de-ice tanks in the First World War.

Even young snowdrops are tough. Snowdrop seeds, like those of many woodland plants, germinate in autumn. But while the seedlings of plants like wild daffodils slow down during cold weather, those of snowdrops continue to grow, giving them a head start over other woodlanders.[21] In fact, the whole physiology of snowdrops seems attuned to cold weather. And that has resulted in a strange feature of their flowers.

Some plants that flower early in the year have adaptations to keep their flowers warm. Insects visit such warm flowers more frequently than others, to gain a brief respite from the chill air of early spring. The warmth of these flowers is as much a draw as their offerings of pollen and nectar. And after pollination, warmer flowers will speed the early development of the seeds. Wood anemone flowers track the sun like little radar dishes and the yellow centre of the flower is often over three degrees centigrade warmer than the air. Familiar daisies manage to keep the centre of their flowers more than seven degrees warmer.[22] The hanging bells of spring snowflakes, which open not much later than common snowdrops, are a full eleven degrees warmer than the cold March air.[23]

Drooping, bell-shaped flowers, like those of snowflakes, can trap heat rising from the ground. This is particularly effective in Arctic members of the heather family, like blue heath, *Phyllodoce caerulea*, a plant confined in Britain to a few cold mountaintops in Scotland.[24] Presumably spring snowflakes employ a similar trick to warm their flowers. So what about snowdrops that flower even earlier? Does the central cup, protected by the outer tepals, warm up in a similar manner?

A microscopic examination of snowdrop tepals shows that they are different from those of the closely related snowflakes. Snowdrop tepals have within them large cavities, filled with a kind of mucus, absent from snowflake petals. This has been interpreted, not unreasonably, as some kind of insulation to protect the flower from the cold or to retain trapped

Common snowdrops have been planted in churchyards for centuries.

heat.[25] Yet examine a snowdrop flower with an infrared camera that can accurately measure the temperature of different parts of the flower, and you'll get a surprise.

Snowdrop flowers are always much *cooler* than the surrounding air. In addition, the whole flower is the same temperature. Logic would suggest that the hanging cup formed by the inner tepals should trap rising warm air, or that the translucent, mucus-packed tepals should act like a miniature greenhouse by letting radiation in, then trapping it to warm the interior of the inner cup.[26] But the snowdrop defies this logic and stands in sharp contrast to snowflake flowers. This suggests two things. Firstly, snowdrops are simply geared up physiologically to work at lower temperatures and, secondly, that they are not as kind to their early season pollinators as many other flowers.

The emergence of snowdrops so early in the year means they've inevitably become associated with early spring festivals. They carpet the ground at Imbolc, on 1 February, a Celtic festival associated with Bride or Brighid, and are seen as a symbol of this Irish goddess of renewal and fertility. Given the non-native status of the common snowdrop in the British Isles, I don't know how long this association has stood or whether the association arose in ancient times in more southerly Celtic areas of Europe where the snowdrop is native. It would be interesting to find out.

After the arrival of Christianity in Britain, Imbolc became Candlemas, celebrated on 2 February. This festival arose from the Jewish tradition of the ritual purification of a woman forty days after giving birth. Candlemas is forty days after Christmas and thus is the Feast of the Purification of the Virgin Mary. And what better symbol of purification than the glowing flowers of snowdrops, blooming whiter than driven snow? On Candlemas Day young girls dressed in white carried garlands of snowdrops around their necks in procession to the church. The plants, which in many places are still called Candlemas bells, were then scattered on the altar.

Thanks to this symbolism, snowdrops have been planted in church-yards and around monasteries for many centuries. And I'm pleased to say that my mother, a gardening fanatic and perhaps the true source of my love of plants, has continued this tradition. She was a long-time parishioner of St Cuthbert's Church, Ormesby, a beautiful old building in tranquil surroundings on the southern outskirts of Middlesbrough, in an area otherwise much scarred by heavy industry. When visiting me in Bristol in the 1970s, she met with a fellow enthusiast, whose garden

Common snowdrops in
St Cuthbert's churchyard in
Ormesby, Middlesbrough.

was awash with spectacular snowdrops. Needless to say, she soon had an armful to take back to Middlesbrough, where she introduced them to the churchyard of St Cuthbert's. In the intervening decades they have thrived and spread. Today she is buried in this churchyard and in the cold, dark days of February her grave is surrounded by luminous white flowers. I think she would be more than content.

GALANTHOPHILIA

The first snowdrops to arrive in this country in the fifteenth or sixteenth century may well have done so in the hands of Italian monks. Many churchyards, like that at Ormesby, still have magnificent displays of snowdrops, as do some old monastic houses such as Fountains Abbey, not far away in North Yorkshire. In some places bunches of snowdrops are also brought into houses to purify them. In other places, though, this is considered unlucky. For some they are symbols of death rather than of a renewal of life. Because of their long association with churchyards, the Victorians considered that snowdrops grew closer to the dead than the living and an unopened flower looked uncomfortably like a corpse wrapped in its shroud. Bringing a single flower indoors was considered particularly unlucky.

But in their gardens Victorians grew snowdrops with great enthusiasm. The plants were slow to become popular after their introduction in the sixteenth century, but by the nineteenth century all that had changed. The Victorians were well known for a fervour bordering on mania when it came to collecting and growing certain groups of plants. Fortunes were spent acquiring rare ferns and orchids, among others.

At the beginning of the twentieth century, Edward Augustus Bowles, a self-taught botanist, gardener and botanical artist, coined the word 'galanthophiles' for those Victorians who collected snowdrop species and varieties with an obsessive zeal. Bowles called his contemporary snowdrop enthusiasts, of which he was one, 'neo-galanthophiles'. His last work, published posthumously in 1954, was a monograph of snowdrops and his passion for these plants is today commemorated in a variety of *G. plicatus* called 'E. A. Bowles'.

Galanthophilia declined after the Victorian era but has now returned with a vengeance. Today, snowdrop enthusiasts are even more passionate in their search for new and rare varieties than they were in Bowles's day, and they're proud to wear Bowles's label – galanthophiles. The tiniest change in the small green marks on the tepals is enough to send a true galanthophile into ecstasy. The extent of modern galanthophilia would probably have surprised even Bowles. In January 2011, £357 changed hands for a single plant of a new variation of *G. plicatus* 'E. A. Bowles' with no green marks at all, discovered in Bowles's own garden at Myddelton House, in the London Borough of Enfield. But that record didn't stand for long. Two months later, £360 was paid for a bulb of a variety of the common snowdrop (or possible a hybrid between *G. nivalis* and *G. plicatus*) called 'Green Tear', an admittedly beautiful plant with flowers suffused with green and etched with green lines.

A year later that record was smashed again when a single *G. woronowii* 'Elizabeth Harrison' sold for £725 on eBay. This plant, with yellow ovaries, was discovered in the garden of Elizabeth Harrison, the location of which, along with the identity of the buyer, was kept a closely guarded secret. Indeed, many serious galanthophiles keep their collections secret. Such is the enthusiasm for rare snowdrops that unscrupulous collectors think nothing of scaling garden walls in the dead of night to steal plants.

Thieves managed to steal a whole potful of 'Elizabeth Harrison' from a private garden that had opened to the public, while another pot, this time of 'Green Tear', disappeared from a nursery in Somerset. Snowdrop mania might be far more extreme today, but even Bowles was plagued by thieves. He took to numbering the snowdrops in his collection to avoid conspicuous name labels on his rarer specimens. After his death, some of his snowdrop collection was re-planted in 'Bowles Corner', in the RHS garden at Wisley, only for thieves to dig it up and make off with it.

Today some gardens tag their snowdrops, a practice started by the National Trust at Anglesey Abbey, Cambridgeshire, in a garden that has thrown up many rare varieties in the past. Other collectors make careful maps of their collections so they can quickly spot if any are missing. Even common snowdrops don't escape this unwelcome attention. Snowdrop rustlers from England have been known to cross the border into Scotland to dig up plants. This is big business. Some gangs even use JCBs to dig up lorry-loads of bulbs. One such load seized by police in Fife in 2003 was estimated to be worth £60,000. If they escape discovery, these gangs often make their way to Lincolnshire, a traditional bulb-growing area, where large quantities of bulbs for sale are less likely to attract unwanted attention.

On a more positive note, the growing obsession with snowdrops has now led to snowdrop festivals appearing up and down the country. Bowles's garden at Myddelton House hosts an event at the very start of the snowdrop season. And each year, a Galanthus Gala is held in different locations around the country which attracts enthusiasts from all over the world. At the same time many gardens open to show off their collections. One place that is always worth the pilgrimage is Colesbourne Park in Gloucestershire, which has been called 'England's best snowdrop garden'. It was started by the botanist Henry John Elwes after he brought back the plants that we now know as *G. elwesii* from Turkey in 1874. Other varieties were added and now some 250 grow there, often in spectacular displays. The garden, still under the care of the Elwes family, opens on each weekend through the snowdrop season.

With such a dedicated following it's hard to imagine anyone would have a bad word to say about a plant that so effectively cheers up a cold and grey day in late winter. But the early twentieth-century plant hunter Reginald Farrer was no fan. Farrer was, to say the least, eccentric. He collected plants from some of the most treacherous and remote places on the planet. And on occasions he would load his shotgun with seeds he'd collected on his travels and shoot them into the craggy cliff faces near his Yorkshire home. But he didn't have a good word to say about snowdrops. He wrote 'The snowdrop gives me chilblains, only to look at it... Was there ever such an icy, inhuman, bloodless flower, crystallized winter in three gleaming petals and a green-flecked cup?'[27] Clearly a confirmed galanthophobe.

SNOWDROPS AND CLIMATE CHANGE

Despite Farrer's views, the charm of snowdrops is undoubtedly their early appearance in the year. And in the modern world that appearance is getting earlier as climate change alters our weather patterns and seasonal temperatures. A long-term study at Kew Gardens in London suggests that the snowdrop season has advanced nearly a month in the last sixty years,[28] probably owing to warmer winters. A study in northern Germany, using twenty years' worth of data, has shown that snowdrop flowering is strongly tied to the average monthly air temperatures of January, February and March.[29] Using this relationship, it's likely that, with the carbon dioxide levels predicted for 2035, snowdrops will be flowering two weeks earlier still, and by 2085, a full month earlier. They will soon be plants of Christmas rather than Candlemas.

Another study, in sites across a number of locations in central Europe, painted a similar if more complicated picture. Between 1951 and 1995 there was a general tendency for snowdrops to flower earlier, though the advance in flowering date was only significant in about a quarter of the locations. But the early flowering trend in all locations was much more obvious in more recent years, from 1980 to 1995.[30]

Not surprisingly, snowdrops flower earlier in the heat islands created by modern cities, usually beating their rural cousins by about four days. But overall, rural snowdrops are advancing their flowering season faster than those in urban gardens. At the end of the twentieth century, urban snowdrops were advancing their flowering season by 13.9 days each decade, whilst rural snowdrops advanced by 15.3 days.[31] This is a faster advance than those kinds of plants that flower later in the season, so snowdrops are getting out of step with later spring plants. Meteorological data for central Europe suggests that between 1960 and 1990 the period from January to March has grown warmer, whilst April has become cooler, which would explain the snowdrop's more dramatic change in the start of its flowering.

SNOWDROPS AND SNOWFLAKES: NATURE'S PHARMACY

Gerard was one of the first to mention this 'early bulbous violet' in his famous *Herball*, a book that described the various uses of all the plants known to him. But his entry for snowdrops contains a curious note, saying that 'Touching the faculties of these bulbous Violets we have nothing to say, seeing that nothing is set downe hereof by the ancient writers, nor anything observed by the moderne'.[32] In other words, he knew of no traditional or contemporary medicinal uses for the plant, which is curious because we now know that snowdrops and snowflakes are both packed with chemicals that are proving very useful in modern medicine.

It's possible that he missed a reference to this plant by one of the more famous ancients, Homer. In *The Odyssey*, Homer describes how Odysseus's crew were poisoned by the nymph Circe, probably with something like stramonium, derived from the thorn apple, *Datura stramonium*. The god Hermes gave Odysseus an antidote to Circe's poison, from a plant

Common snowdrops carpet the woods of Welford Park in Berkshire in one of Britain's most spectacular displays.

which Homer said 'had a black root but milk-like flower. The gods call it Moly and it is difficult for mortal man to dig it up'.

The identity of moly has remained a mystery, but some scholars think that it might possibly have been a snowdrop. Homer's description of the milk-like flower certainly fits (after all, its Latin name, *Galanthus*, means milk-flower). But more importantly, its chemical effect in neutralizing the toxins from thorn apples fits well.[33] As we will see shortly, snowdrops are packed with exactly the right kind of chemicals to do just this.

But even if these properties were known to the Ancient Greeks, there doesn't seem to be much later evidence of snowdrops or snowflakes being used in folk medicine anywhere in their native range, even though countryfolk are usually very canny when it comes to the natural pharmacy on their doorsteps. It is possible, however, that those that knew about the value of these plants lived in the more remote stretches of the snowdrop's European range. For example, in the 1950s, while visiting an isolated village in the Carpathians, a Bulgarian scientist found a woman rubbing snowdrop leaves into her forehead to relieve nerve pain.[34]

Later, a Soviet scientist attending a conference in Prague in 1965 described how, while travelling in the Caucasus region, he'd come across a woman living in a remote village who was using extracts from the bulbs of the Caucasus snowdrop, *G. woronowii*, to treat the debilitating disease polio. The results were dramatic. Her patients made a full recovery, with no signs of the paralysis that normally afflicts sufferers.[35] So what was this miracle cure?

In 1947 a Soviet journal reported a previously unknown alkaloid in the common snowdrop. A few years later, a similar chemical was isolated from the Caucasian snowdrop. Later these alkaloids were also found in snowflakes, in even bigger quantities than in snowdrops, as well as in daffodils. In the early 1950s another Russian scientist showed that this chemical was something called an anti-acetylcholinesterase.[36] Acetylcholine is a neurotransmitter, carrying signals between nerve cells. It is broken down by an enzyme called acetylcholinesterase. The alkaloid from snowdrops and snowflakes is an anti-acetylcholinesterase – in other words it prevents the enzyme from breaking down the neurotransmitter, the very effect it would have needed to counteract Circe's poison in Homer's *Odyssey*.

That alkaloid is now called galanthamine and much of the research on its properties took place at the height of the Cold War, largely in the Soviet Union and Bulgaria, focused mainly on its effects in treating polio. It was also used in anaesthesiology, to reverse the effects of some anaesthetics. Galanthamine only attracted the interest of scientists in the West when it was realized that it could also alleviate the effects of Alzheimer's disease. Suddenly galanthamine was in demand, and its only commercial source was snowdrops – and particularly snowflakes – growing in south-east Europe.

Combined with their value as garden plants, the pressure on the wild populations of these plants soon became unsustainable. Turkey in particular is an important country for bulbous plants of all kinds, including fritillaries and crocuses as well as snowdrops, of which seven are endemic. In fact, Turkey has an astonishingly high rate of endemism – one in every three of its plants. But it exports 28,000 tons of plants for horticulture or medicine every year, including 30 million tubers or bulbs.[37] Many of these are orchids, whose roots are used to make salep,[*] a warm drink, or *maras dondurmasi*, a kind of ice cream. But around 8 million of those bulbs are snowdrops, worth around half a million dollars.[38]

In Bulgaria, following the pioneering work on drugs from snowdrops and snowflakes, the summer snowflake has been extensively exploited for its particularly high content of galanthamine. Between 1969 and 1970, 10–15 million tonnes of plants were harvested but that harvest soon fell to around 5 million tonnes a year as snowflakes grew scarcer. The summer snowflake is now considered endangered in Bulgaria.[39] Controls were put in place and commercial exploitation was allowed in only sixteen populations, though these populations represented a large proportion of summer snowflakes in Bulgaria.[40] After 1998 wild plants were no longer harvested for drugs, but only for genetic material to enhance cultivated stocks.

Snowflakes have been cultivated in Bulgaria since the 1980s, when the first plantation was set up near the town of Primorsko on the Black Sea coast.[41] And cultivated snowflakes have an advantage over wild ones. In cultivation, strains can be selected with particularly high levels of galanthamine. In the wild not all populations produce this alkaloid in high concentrations. Snowdrops and snowflakes produce a whole range of chemicals and the proportion of galanthamine can range from 0.2 per cent to 95 per cent. In Bulgaria summer snowflakes seem to

---

* Salep was also used to thicken a warm drink called saloop, which became very popular in England in the eighteenth and nineteenth centuries.

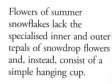

Flowers of summer snowflakes lack the specialised inner and outer tepals of snowdrop flowers and, instead, consist of a simple hanging cup.

be divided into different 'chemo-types', in different drainage systems. Along the Danube, for example, galanthamine levels are low, the plants here producing another chemical called homolycosine. But along rivers draining into the Black Sea, the snowflakes produce a high proportion of galanthamine.[42] The distribution of these chemo-types, each confined to different river catchments, also illustrates the importance of rivers in dispersing summer snowflakes.

Summer snowflakes are also threatened by loss of the wet woodlands that they thrive in. However, as their cultivation in Bulgaria has demonstrated, new populations are relatively easy to create. But attempts to re-plant populations in northern Italy showed that the snowflakes need to be planted densely in their new home if the population is to have any chance of maintaining itself. New populations don't produce many seeds if they are not planted densely enough.[43] It seems that a spectacular display of flowers is necessary to draw in pollinators, especially since summer snowflakes don't seem to produce any nectar as a reward. Snowdrops on the other hand produce a honey-scented nectar which can sweeten the air over large carpets on calm days. However, each individual flower doesn't produce much and they only release it once during the day, and indeed just once during the life of the flower.[44]

Autumn snowflake, an increasingly common garden plant which hasn't become naturalized in the wider countryside.

THE SNOWDROP'S INSECT PARTNERS

There aren't too many insects flying when the snowdrops are in bloom, though queen bumblebees may venture out. Bumblebees are more at home in cold weather than most insects and two species, *Bombus polaris* and *B. hyperboreus*, even occur above the Arctic Circle. Bumblebees can raise their body temperatures by shivering and their thick coat of hair insulates them, preventing heat loss. The queens from the previous season will have hibernated, safe from the worst of winter in an old mouse burrow or similar refuge, and emerge in the early spring to seek out a nest site. To be active this early in the year demands a lot of fuel, so early spring plants, even stingy ones like snowdrops, are a precious resource and for their part of the bargain, the few insects that are around to sample snowdrop nectar can affect pollination.

The snowdrop helps by providing conspicuous guides to the location of the nectar, particularly the green tips to the inner cup and green stripes lining the cup. As we've already seen, these reflect ultraviolet light very effectively, which makes them stand out to bees. Variations in these green markings entrance galanthophiles, but I wonder what effect such variations have on bumblebees or other pollinators?

If the pollinators fulfil their part of the bargain, the snowdrop will go on to produce seeds and to strike another bargain with insects. As mentioned earlier, the seeds of both snowdrops and spring snowflakes have structures called elaiosomes attached to their tips. These are packed with food that is particularly attractive to ants. To make use of this generous gift, the ants carry the whole seed back to their nests, where they proceed to remove the elaiosome.

In doing so, they may be giving the seed a better chance of germination. Snowdrop seeds are prone to fungal infections, particularly if the elaiosome is left intact. But once the ants have removed it, the seeds are less likely to be infected. And in taking the seeds underground, the ants have unintentionally sowed them in the perfect spot.[45] The snowdrop seed's physiology is geared up to take advantage of this kind of dispersal. Compared to another early spring plant, the wild daffodil, snowdrop seeds have different requirements for optimum germination.

The seeds of both snowdrops and daffodils need a warm summer temperature to break dormancy, so that they germinate in the cooler temperatures of autumn. But the germination of snowdrop seeds is better in darkness, while light levels have no effect on daffodil seeds. Daffodils are not ant-dispersed, so their seeds could end up anywhere, whereas, if all has gone according to plan, the snowdrop's seeds will be snug in the darkness of an ant's nest.[46]

Although it's hard to claim unequivocally that snowdrops or snowflakes are true natives of Britain, both have become part of our flora. Snowdrops in particular are both conspicuous and familiar even to those with no real interest in natural history or gardening. And, as Gerard noted, they are 'timely flow'ring', raising their heads when the festivities of Christmas are but a memory and the joys of spring still in the distant future. For that reason alone, they should be welcomed as members of our flora.

part

II

GRASSLANDS

Introduction

It's often fascinating to see the world through a different pair of eyes. A few years ago, I picked up an American friend from Heathrow Airport for her first visit to Britain. Shortly after joining the M4, heading west to my home in Bristol, she exclaimed in amazement that the land was so *green*. I've never thought of the M4 corridor as a showcase for Britain's green and pleasant land, especially at the start of February, but the further we went, the more my friend's astonishment grew. She'd lived in the spectacular forests of the southern Appalachians in North Carolina and in the dramatic canyonlands near Los Angeles as well as travelling widely across the United States, from the prairies and deserts to the sub-tropical forests of Florida, but by the time we got to the rolling hillsides of Wiltshire, she had fallen in love with the English countryside. Over the next few weeks I showed her scenery which, at least in my mind, was a more fitting example of the landscapes that had inspired poets and writers through the ages – the Wye Valley, North and South Devon, the Cotswolds. But I had to point out that the greenness that continued to strike her so forcefully was entirely artificial – the product of modern farming methods, and of tons of nitrogen fertilizers feeding grasslands sown with rye grass and clover. Green perhaps, but not pleasant.

Yet farming, for almost all of its history, from its origins in Neolithic times right up to the middle of the twentieth century, has created and supported rich and diverse landscapes – fields, meadows and pastures spangled with colourful wild flowers in glorious variety. Across Britain, grassy acres were painted sunshine yellow in spring and summer with buttercups and sheep-grazed downlands were dotted with pasque flowers at Easter, to be replaced with autumn-flowering gentians later in the year. Wetter grasslands glowed with the intense yellows of marsh marigolds or with the subtler pastel shades of cuckoo flower. Upland meadows were brilliant with globe flowers and wood cranesbill. And high mountain pastures were scattered with pink bird's-eye primroses, white mountain avens, multi-coloured mountain pansies, and with the intense blue stars of spring and alpine gentians. Even fields of crops, a grassland of sorts, were bright with corncockles and corn flowers, larkspurs and corn marigolds. In an old meadow, up to forty different kinds of wild flowers could be found in just a few square metres, compared to perhaps two to five in a modern sown and fertilized ley.[1]* But, curiously, many of these grassland plants were already present in the British Isles long before the first farmers made it here.

THE ORIGINAL GRASSLANDS

The presence of grassland plants in ancient history is betrayed by buried pollen grains, wrapped in a rot-resistant coat which is sculpted in such distinctive patterns that palaeobotanists can assign most of them to individual species.[2] And this is odd, since before humanity had an extensive impact the natural vegetation of almost all of Britain is generally assumed to have been woodland. But the presence of so many grassland species before widespread human settlement suggests that natural grasslands of some description must have existed alongside the forests.

Â Â Â Â The widely accepted view is that following the retreat of the ice sheets at the end of the last glaciation, some 10,000 years ago, most of Britain became cloaked in trees – the so-called 'wildwood' – though there were areas, such as exposed coastal clifftops and remote ledges on mountain crags along with dune slacks and salt marshes, that remained free of tree cover. Even within this great forest, grassy glades must have arisen as old trees toppled, allowing bright sunlight to reach the forest floor. But these pockets of grassland were small and short-lived. Seedling trees soon established themselves in these sunny clearings and eventually grew tall enough to close the breach in the canopy. Were such small and transient grasslands enough to maintain a diversity of grassland species? Or were larger natural grasslands more widespread than we used to believe?

Â Â Â Â Across Europe as a whole 18 per cent of its endemic plants are grassland species, which means there must have been substantial grasslands on which they could evolve. In Britain it's possible that parts of the

---

* A piece of land put down to grass or clover for one or a few seasons, in contrast to permanent pastures.

southern chalk grasslands are entirely natural and have never been tree-covered. The evidence comes from fossil snails, found beneath Neolithic monuments, that are largely characteristic of open, sunny grassland. This suggests that trees never colonized these areas in the wake of the retreating ice and might even explain the large concentration of Neolithic monuments here. Those early inhabitants of Britain picked these sites for their spectacular vistas.[3]

Some ecologists have also questioned our long-held vision of the wildwood as unending closed woodland. It wasn't trees, trees and more trees. Instead, they argue, large grazing animals were once abundant enough to have had a major impact on the forest by opening up much larger and longer-lasting clearings.[4] These animals included the aurochs, the wild ancestor of the domestic cow, extinct since the sixteenth century, and the tarpan, a wild horse that may have survived to the start of the twentieth century. Alongside these extinct large grazers were the more familiar native deer and wild boar, and in earlier times in Britain, in previous inter-glacials, these creatures were joined by European bison and even by elephants and hippos.

According to this new view, these animals created and extended openings in the wildwood, and maintained a kaleidoscopic mosaic of grasslands, scrub and forest, plenty of space for a grassland flora to flourish before farmers ever landed on our shores. Not everyone agrees with this

Hannah's Meadow, a Durham Wildlife Trust reserve in Teesdale in the northern Pennines.

scenario[5] and it's likely that the pattern of woodlands and grasslands in Britain was different from the rest of Europe, since tarpan disappeared from Britain long before the wildwood reached its full development, and bison did not recolonize Britain after the last glaciation. Of the really big grazing animals that trudged through the forests of Europe, in Britain only aurochs remained,* and could they alone have had a significant enough effect on the wildwood to create this mix of open and wooded ground? If not aurochs, there was one other species that, on its own, certainly could.

GRASSLANDS IN THE HUMAN LANDSCAPE AND IMAGINATION

Once humans arrived on Britain's shores, they began to fell the trees. Mesolithic hunter-gatherers probably began by clearing patches of forest around waterholes to make hunting easier, but may have begun more

Above: Muker Meadows National Nature Reserve in Swaledale, North Yorkshire.

Right: Eades Meadow, a Worcestershire Wildlife Trust reserve near Bromsgrove, has a spectacular display of green-winged orchids in early spring.

---

* As a point of pedantry, aurochsen is the plural of aurochs (like ox and oxen), though 'aurochs' as a plural is now widely used.

extensive forest clearances on areas underlain by thinner soils. However, once farming arrived the creation of grasslands accelerated. The advent of agriculture marks the start of the Neolithic period, about 6,000 years ago, an event often called the Neolithic Revolution, though this suggests a sudden arrival and spread of farming. In reality, farming took nearly 2,000 years to spread to all corners of the British Isles. Nevertheless, once agriculture arrived on these shores, woodland clearances began in earnest and a more familiar landscape slowly emerged. The work of felling trees to create fields was aided by the browsing and grazing of the sheep, goats, pigs and cattle kept by the first farmers and, as the Iron Age dawned, some 3,000 years ago, roughly half the landscape had been opened up, and the abundant pollen of grassland plants in soil samples from that time marked the spread of our now familiar grassland flora.

The exact nature of that flora depends both on where the grasslands are situated geographically and on how the grassland is managed, and to encapsulate this diversity, botanists have tried several different methods to classify grassland. The simplest and broadest classification is simply to follow their agricultural purpose – as meadow or pasture. Most people use these terms interchangeably, but they are two very distinct habitats that reflect the stark realities of the farming year. The biggest problem facing a livestock farmer is how to feed his animals throughout the whole year. In the warmer months, when grass grows vigorously, the herds can graze fresh grass in the pastures. But in winter grass growth slows or stops. So a farmer must also manage some of his fields for hay. In these meadows, grass is allowed to grow tall during the summer months and then cut, dried and stored to supply winter fodder. Successful livestock farming depended on just the right balance of pastures and meadows.

So there are two broad types of grasslands – pastures, which are grazed, and meadows, which are cut, two very different forms of management

that dictate the nature of the flora that's found in each habitat. However, the distinction between meadowland and pastureland is not quite as neat and straightforward as it sounds. Once cut, the grass in the meadow starts to grow again, at least until the cold weather settles in. So, in late summer and autumn, livestock can graze the 'aftermath' of the hay cut. And fields were often used as pastures in some years and as meadows in others. But where there was some continuity from year to year, these two forms of management created two very different floras. Pasture plants have rosettes of leaves that hug the ground to escape grazing mouths. Dandelions are good examples in lowland pastures and are often so successful that they turn these pastures yellow in the early spring. Many of the plants on sheep-grazed downland are similar. Stemless thistles, for example, have prickly rosettes that frequently pass unnoticed until sat on. In contrast, haymeadow species grow tall, to compete with tall-growing grasses. The hay cut is usually taken in mid to late summer, depending on season and weather, so most haymeadow plants have ample chance to flower and set seed in complete safety, whilst all those hungry mouths are firmly shut out of the meadow. Often, a much greater variety of plants thrive in haymeadows, and it's these colourful meadows that have been portrayed in poems and paintings of centuries past to evoke the idyll of a rural English summer.

Below: Lady's smock (or cuckooflower), a spring plant of damp meadows, flowers close to the time that the first cuckoos call.

Right: Marsh marigolds (or kingcups) colour the wetter patches of Hannah's Meadow in Teesdale, County Durham.

Shakespeare, Clare, Keats and a host of others have all captured the joy and glory of haymeadows in early summer:

> *When daisies pied and violets blue*
> *And lady-smocks all silver-white*
> *And cuckoo buds of yellow hue*
> *Do paint the meadows with delight*
> > William Shakespeare – *Love's Labours Lost, Act V, Scene II*

Writing in the first half of the nineteenth century, John Clare, the Northamptonshire 'peasant poet' was entranced by the flower-rich meadows that still covered much of the countryside.* In his poem 'Sport in the Meadows' he captures the essence of the meadows around his native village of Helpston as spring turns to summer:

> *Maytime is to the meadows coming in,*
> *And cowslip peeps have gotten eer so big,*
> *And water blobs and all their golden kin*
> *Crowd round the shallows by the striding brig.*
> *Daisies and buttercups and ladysmocks*
> *Are all abouten shining here and there,*
> *Nodding about their gold and yellow locks*
> *Like morts of folken flocking at a fair.*

---

* This description is engraved on a monument to Clare in Helspton, which is now in Cambridgeshire.

The farming landscape of varied grasslands was such an inspiration to Clare that the inscription on his memorial in Poets' Corner at Westminster Abbey reads 'Fields were the essence of the song'. In another poem, a sonnet, he described the flowers in a different kind of meadow.

> *I love to see the summer beaming forth*
> *And white wool sack clouds sailing to the north*
> *I love to see the wild flowers come again*
> *And mare blobs stain with gold the meadow drain*
> *And water lillies whiten on the floods*

'Mare blobs' is a wonderful name for marsh marigolds, large relatives of buttercups that grow in wet grasslands or in ditches. And though it wasn't his intention in this poem, Clare has highlighted a way to refine the classification of grasslands and add more detail, based on the finer points of how the meadow is managed.

TYPES OF GRASSLAND

Meadows fall into a number of different types, depending on how they are fertilized to produce a good crop of grass. Those meadows lying alongside rivers are flooded each year, and the silt dumped on them provides nutrients for the grasses and wildflowers in the following season. Flood meadows are those that flood naturally, while water meadows, like the famous examples along the Hampshire Avon, depend on irrigation channels and sluice gates for their life-giving silt. Shutting the sluice gates in the channels floods the meadow in a more controlled manner than is the case with flood meadows. And the ditches and channels are often stained gold, as John Clare observed, with mare blobs. Those meadows further from rivers were traditionally fertilized with the dung of the animals they would eventually feed. But the grass in water meadows, warmed over winter by water from chalk streams bubbling up from beneath the ground, got a head start in spring. This meant that water meadows were sometimes used as pastures instead of meadows.

So, the division of grasslands into meadows and pastures is a bit too simplistic – and too limiting. Technically, the high fells of the Pennines and the steep slopes of the Cotswolds are pastures, in most cases grazed by sheep (and rabbits). But they are different from each other in every way imaginable and also very different from the classic image of a pasture field, enclosed by hedges and full of contented cows. Upland pastures are wild and windswept places that feel remote from the hand of humanity, even though they are as much a product of agriculture as any other grassland. And in many places, upland pastures are now overgrazed by unsustainable numbers of sheep supported by ill-thought-out farming subsidies, creating a close-cropped bowling green of turf brightened by the occasional yellow flower of tormentil, *Potentilla erecta*. In the more mellow lowlands, the best chalk grasslands of the North and South Downs and the limestone grasslands of the Cotswolds grow tall each year with the flowering stems of upright brome, *Bromopsis erecta*, a grass characteristic of such grasslands and that clothes the slopes with a soft haze of feathery heads.

So another way to classify grasslands is to use these local variations, to focus on differences caused by the underlying rocks, by geography

Two contrasting types of limestone grassland. *Left:* The steep slopes of Rodborough Common in the Cotswolds, in Gloucestershire, are cut into younger and softer Jurassic limestone. *Right:* The upland grasslands of Widdybank Fell in Upper Teesdale overlie older and harder carboniferous limestone.

or by different forms of traditional management. For example, culm grasslands are found only on a rock formation called the Culm Measures in parts of Devon and Cornwall.[*] These are marshy, acidic grasslands with a rich diversity of plants. A scarce umbellifer, the whorled caraway, *Carum verticillatum*, is characteristic of these grasslands. Some fields are pink with the tattered-looking flowers of ragged robin, *Lychnis flos-cuculi*, others are dotted with saw-wort, *Serratula tinctoria*, meadow thistle, *Cirsium dissectum*, and devil's bit scabious, *Succisa pratensis*. This last plant is also important for being the foodplant of the rare marsh fritillary butterfly, so culm grasslands are one of this butterfly's strongholds in Britain. The caterpillars of the narrow-bordered bee hawkmoth also feed on devil's bit scabious, making culm grasslands as exciting to entomologists as they are to botanists. Rhos pastures, which are similar to culm grasslands, are found in South Wales and on Dartmoor and have a comparable assemblage of plants.[†]

Calaminarian grasslands form over soils that have high concentrations of heavy metals.[‡] These may be from past mining activities, for example

Left
Devil's bit scabious, a widespread grassland plant, particularly common on Culm grasslands in Devon.

Right: Harebell, also called bluebell in Scotland.
Far right: Meadow cranesbill.

---

[*] The Culm Measures are a thick sequence of rock strata that dates from the Carboniferous Period which outcrop in Devon and Cornwall.
[†] *Rhos* means moorland in Welsh and is found in many place names across Wales.
[‡] Calaminarian grasslands are named after the zinc violet, *Viola calaminaria*, which grows on zinc-rich soils in Europe. Calamine is a form of zinc ore.

for lead, silver or zinc, but calaminarian grasslands also form naturally on thin soils over rocks rich in heavy metals, such as serpentine. The heavy metals prevent scrub and tree growth, so these grasslands remain open without management and have a specialized flora that can cope with otherwise toxic concentrations of heavy metals. These include spring sandwort, *Minuartia verna*, and alpine pennycress, *Thlaspi coerulescens*, but thrift, *Armeria maritima*, normally associated with coastal sites, can also cope with these soils, as can sea campion, *Silene maritima*.

Another way to classify grasslands is simply by their altitude – lowland, upland and sub-montane. For example, lowland haymeadows, as we'll see shortly, are quite different from their upland counterparts. Botanists have also classified grasslands according to the soils on which they are growing – along a scale of basic (or alkaline) to acidic. As gardeners know well, many plants have distinct preferences for the base content of the soil and grow well only in a certain range. So, acidic grasslands have

a different range of plants from basic ones. In the middle of these two extremes, neutral grasslands, once widespread in the lowlands, had one of the richest assemblages of wild flowers.

All these classifications overlap, often in confusing ways, so, for example, many upland grasslands are on acidic soils – though not all. And none of these classifications truly reflect the sheer variety of grasslands found across Britain. Ecologists now turn to the National Vegetation Classification (NVC) (see page 12) which brings some measure of scientific rigour to the bewildering variety of habitats across Britain. In this system grasslands are broadly divided into mesotrophic grasslands (MG), covering a large range of 'typical' grasslands; calcicolous grasslands (CG), covering the grasslands of chalk and limestone; and montane/califugous grasslands (U), typical acid or upland grasslands. Each of these is broken down into smaller categories or communities, defined by its characteristic species. Each community is given a code and a tag of two of the most common species present. *MG5 Crested Dog's tail – Common Knapweed*, for example, is the way many lowland haymeadows are described according to the NVC. Each community can be further divided into sub-communities, such as *MG5a Meadow Vetchling sub-community*. This way, much more of the variety of British grasslands can be captured. Even so, it's only an approximation: every grassland is unique in its combination of location, soil, rainfall and management regime. The NVC is also an important conservation tool in that it allows us to take an inventory of our grasslands – an inventory that shows that the meadows that have inspired poets through the ages are now almost a thing of the past.

achair grassland at Traigh g, on the Isle of Lewis in the uter Hebrides.

THE DECLINE OF DIVERSITY

The farming landscape has always changed as it adapted to growing populations and responded to dramatic shifts in demographics spurred by events such as the Black Death and, much later, the Industrial Revolution. Various enclosure acts beginning in the second half of the eighteenth century also transformed the landscape as land passed from common use to private ownership. Private landowners then sought to maximize their profits by intensifying their farming methods. This contributed to a series of agricultural revolutions that had begun as early as the middle of the seventeenth century. But the pace of change began to accelerate further in the first half of the nineteenth century, with a move from tithe payments to monetary transactions. Tithes were originally a form of tax in kind – a tenth of a farm's produce given over to support the church and clergy. As land gradually passed from the church to private ownership tithes continued to be owed to the new landowners. In 1836 the Tithe Commutation Act required these tithes to be converted to a monetary payment – the tithe rent charge. Farming became part of the great capitalist enterprise. Around this time, a wide-ranging survey – the Tithe Survey – was carried out to list the areas subject to tithe payments. In many cases it also recorded the uses of the fields and so gives a detailed picture of the British countryside in the middle of the nineteenth century. And it seems that, despite all these changes, the landscape remained rich in wild flowers even as the twentieth century dawned, at least to judge from the writings of poets and naturalists from this period.

But within a few decades farming would undergo an even more radical transformation. The years following the Second World War saw a gear change as drastic in its impact as the original Neolithic farming revolution. The Second World War forced Britons to become self-reliant as supply lines from abroad were severed or curtailed by the German Navy. Every corner of cultivatable land became a precious resource, but

Right: Rough hawkbit seed head.

Below: Bird's-foot trefoil, abundant from the Hebrides to chalk downs of Kent in grasslands that haven't been dosed with nitrogenous fertilizers.

lowland meadows suffered more than most. Farmers often reserved the most productive ground for haymeadows since a nutritious crop of hay was vital for winter feed. But people can't eat hay, and vast acres of these flower-rich meadows were ploughed up for much-needed arable crops. Following the war, farming intensified further. Pastures were ploughed and re-seeded with high-yielding grasses, often mixed with clover and treated with herbicides to kill off competing wild flowers. These leys were also treated with nitrogenous fertilizers, which favoured the growth of the sown grasses at the expense of everything else. 'Improved' grasslands certainly improved productivity but at the expense of diversity – these grassy fields were as much monocultures as nearby fields of wheat or rape.

As the drive to maximize productivity swept across the British landscape, haymeadows also became outmoded. Improved grasslands can be cut for silage, fermented rather than dried, to provide more nutritious winter fodder. The farming revolution in the second half of the twentieth century saw the loss of a staggering 97 per cent of flower-rich grasslands. And with the flowers went all the insects that depended on them, from butterflies to bumblebees. Of our twenty-five species of bumblebees, three are now extinct and six have declined by around 80 per cent – a pattern repeated amongst many other groups of insects, some of which we depend on as crop pollinators.

Today, a view over that classic British scene of grassy fields rolling over hills and dales consists largely of 'improved' grassland. At first sight this looks like the very essence of our verdant countryside, but, as I stressed to my American friend, these fields are unnaturally green, coloured by liberal doses of nitrogen. And even a whiff of nitrogenous fertilizer is enough to exile many wild flowers. A whole group of plants, the legumes or pea flowers (Fabaceae) have adapted to thrive in nutrient-poor soils. These plants include the clovers and the bright-yellow bird's-foot trefoil, *Lotus corniculatus*, that grows into dazzling clumps on unimproved grassland. All of these plants have small nodules on their roots, packed with bacteria that can perform the neat biochemical trick of converting nitrogen gas in the atmosphere into a form that can be used by the plants. In essence, they have their own built-in nitrogenous fertilizer system, which gives them a competitive advantage in nutrient-poor soils, especially over the grasses. But once external sources of fertilizer are added to the soil, the legumes lose their competitive edge and disappear almost overnight.

Bird's-foot trefoil grows widely in unimproved meadows as well as on the downland slopes of chalk and limestone hills. It's the foodplant for the caterpillars of a number of butterflies, including the common blue, a jewel of unimproved grasslands. A superficially similar plant, the horseshoe vetch, *Hippocrepis comosa*, is restricted to the short turf of chalk and limestone grassland. It's the foodplant of two much rarer blue butterflies, the chalkhill and Adonis blues, the latter even brighter and more intense in colour than common blues. Horseshoe vetch is a more delicate plant than bird's-foot trefoil, and its flowers form a neat circular crown, making it a very elegant plant. A third yellow-flowered legume of chalk and limestone, the kidney vetch, *Anthyllis vulneraria*, is the foodplant of yet another blue butterfly, the small blue. It lays its eggs on the inflated flower bases of kidney vetch where they are often more conspicuous than the butterfly itself, which, as its name suggests, is tiny, and more brown than blue.

Chalk and limestone grasslands are found across wide areas of southern England, and there are fine examples in the Cotswolds and Chilterns, on the chalk of Wiltshire and on the North and South Downs. The best of these are moderately grazed, which keeps the turf short and open, providing plenty of opportunities for a range of wildflowers. These grasslands are formed over chalk or relatively soft limestones of Jurassic

Right: Spring crocus flower.

Far right: Naturalized spring crocuses at Inkpen Crocus Fie in Berkshire.

Overleaf: Spring crocuses provide an early nectar feast for bees.

age. Flower-rich limestone grasslands are also found on the Magnesian limestone, laid down in the earlier Permian period, and which now outcrops in a thin band running through Yorkshire and County Durham. Different grasslands grow on the even older and harder limestones of the Carboniferous Age in the Pennines, with smaller outcrops in the Scottish borders, and in north and south Wales and the south-west of England. The upland grasslands of the Pennines are also widely grazed by sheep, though by tougher varieties than on the southern hills.

GRASSLAND PLANTS

One family of plants spans all of these varied grasslands – the gentians (Gentianaceae). Included in this family are the centauries (*Centaurium* spp.) of which the delicate pink heads of common centaury, *C. erythraea*, are a common sight on many types of grasslands as well as in woodland glades and rides. Yellow-wort, *Blackstonia perfoliata*, is also common, producing heads of small yellow flowers on chalk and limestone grasslands. In addition, there are a number of species of gentians belonging to three groups, *Gentianella*, *Gentiana* and *Gentianopsis*, which range from fairly widespread species to those that are vanishingly rare. For me, gentians are real gems hidden away in many different kinds of grasslands, from the Scottish mountains to the chalk hills of Sussex. Often not easy to find, they always repay the effort. They count amongst their number a plant unique to Britain and they illustrate some fundamental concepts in

how such new species arise, so I've devoted Chapter 8 to these charming little plants.

Some grassland plants are easier to find than gentians. In spring and early summer, pastures and meadows turn sunshine yellow with buttercups (*Ranunculus* spp.). Buttercups give their name to a whole family of plants, the Ranunculaceae, which also includes many woodland species such as goldilocks, *R. auricomus*, monkshood, *Aconitum napellus*, and wood anemones, *Anemone nemorosa*. There are also numerous white-flowered buttercups – the water crowfoots – that are aquatic and hold their drifts of white flowers above the surface of rivers and lakes. But it is the yellow-flowered *Ranunculus* buttercups that are best known and that I explore in more detail in a separate chapter in this section.

Crocuses are familiar plants in gardens and parks up and down the country. These are true crocuses, belonging to the Iris family (Iridaceae) and not to be confused (though they frequently are) with the meadow saffron, *Colchicum autumnale*, which is often also called the autumn crocus. Two species of true crocuses have escaped from cultivation to become naturalized in unimproved grasslands. Although not native, they do form spectacular displays in some areas and as an early sign that spring is on the way, are, in my opinion, a very welcome sight. The spring crocus, *Crocus vernus*, has been growing in gardens from at least the start of the seventeenth century and by the second half of the eighteenth century was established in the wild. How they got there is the subject of a number of intriguing legends, an enigmatic side to their nature that only adds to their charm.

Dandelions are usually seen as noxious weeds but create stunning displays in early spring.

Overleaf:
Left: Dandelion seed heads are familiar as 'dandelion clock' to generations of children.
Right: Borne aloft on its parachute of feather hairs, a dandelion seed can be carried a long way by the wind.

Inkpen Crocus Field in Berkshire has a population of around 400,000 spring crocuses that local parish records show have been residents here for at least 200 years. The crocus field is part of a nature reserve, not because of the crocuses, which as old as they are, are still just naturalized plants, but because the fields are good examples of unimproved pasture. Even so, on a chilly March day, with bright patches of spring sunshine breaking through thunderous clouds and sweeping over these ancient pastures like a searchlight, the crocus display is stunning – the largest display of 'wild' crocuses in Britain.

These crocuses are natives of southern Europe and the Near East and local legend suggests that their corms were collected by crusading Knights Templar in the twelfth century and brought back home to produce a supply of the spice saffron. It's a nice idea: the Templars did own land in nearby Templeton, and saffron does indeed come from a crocus – but not this one. Saffron is the dried anthers of an autumn-flowering crocus, *C. sativus*. More likely, if less romantically, the spring crocuses here grew from garden rubbish dumped on the pasture a few hundred years ago.

There are several true crocuses that flower in the autumn, causing even greater confusion with the 'false' autumn crocus or meadow saffron (which is neither a crocus nor produces saffron). One of these, *C. nudiflorus*, has also naturalized itself, particularly in the north and west. They used to be so common in the flood meadows along the Trent in Nottinghamshire that they were picked and sold in bunches in Nottingham. More recently, it has been adopted as the county flower of Nottinghamshire. Like the spring crocuses at Inkpen, it is reputed to have arrived on these shores with returning crusaders, in this case the Knights of St John, who owned land right across the country. Again, the assumption is that they were brought back to provide saffron, and again it's the wrong species – though at least this one flowers in the autumn, at the same time as the true saffron crocus. But in this case, there may be an inkling of truth in the story. A study of autumn crocus sites in the Rochdale–Oldham area of Lancashire showed a degree of correlation with land held in the area by the Knights of St John.[6]

Along with buttercups and crocuses, dandelions, *Taraxacum* spp., are familiar plants, if only as persistent weeds in lawns and gardens. They

are so successful that they can invade pastures and turn them yellow in early spring, when they are a valuable early food source for bees. A few weeks later, when the dandelion's globular seed head has formed, these same pastures look like they're covered in a low-lying mist. It's such a common plant that most of us wouldn't give it a second glance. But dandelions present a real challenge to botanists. There are a lot of species of dandelion – an awful lot. In many places, dandelions produce their fluffy seed heads, familiar to generations of children as dandelion clocks, without the benefit of fertilization, a process called apomixis. So, as you blow on a dandelion seed head to tell the time, you are dispersing seeds that will produce plants that are identical to their parent – clones.

Slowly, mutations build up in these clones, so each ends up looking slightly different. Since each 'type' of dandelion breeds true and is isolated from all other types, it is, in essence, a separate species. Sometimes botanists refer to them as microspecies to reflect their special case. There are also a few species of dandelions that reproduce normally, by cross-pollination with different individuals. These true species sometimes hybridize and the hybrids then go on to reproduce by apomixis, so creating yet another microspecies.[7] At the last count, there were 250 species and microspecies of dandelions in this country and, if you knew

Right: The seed head of yellow rattle gives it its name. It rattles in the wind when the seeds are ripe.

Below: Wood cranesbill is a characteristic plant of northern haymeadows.

what you were looking for, you could find perhaps sixty kinds within a short walk from your house.

There can't be a plant more characteristic of grassland than the dandelion. It's found in abundance in traditional haymeadows, both in the lowlands and uplands, and grows on short-cropped downland and neglected roadside verges. Its seeds, drifting on the wind, can colonize recently cleared or disturbed ground and it doesn't take long for them to invade even the best-kept lawns. It's a plant that should be admired rather than despised.

In the following chapters, I shall look in more detail at several groups of plants associated at least in part with grasslands. I've already mentioned in passing gentians and buttercups. In addition, this section features orchids, primulas and fritillaries. Although many of our orchids are woodland species, the most conspicuous are those that live in grassland, where they sometimes grow in great profusion. As a group, orchids are both strange and intriguing, and the story of how they go about making more orchids is at times truly mind-boggling. Of our five species of *Primula*, three are characteristic of grassland. Of the other two, primroses frequently grow on grasslands as well as in woods, and oxlips, though now confined to woods in Britain, used to grow in large numbers in fields and meadows, and further east in Europe it is still a grassland plant. In their own way, primulas are just as mysterious as orchids. As we explore the curious phenomenon of heterostyly (the presence of different kinds of flower in the same species) we discover that despite centuries of ingenious research we still don't fully understand what makes even our most familiar wildflowers tick. Finally, snake's head fritillaries are only found in a few lowland haymeadows, plants as dependent on a long continuity of traditional management as any we've seen so far.

6

Buttercups

RANUNCULACEAE

BUTTERCUPS AND BUTTER

Most people can recognize a buttercup or at least have heard the name. Perhaps some of those people also realize that this name comes from their colour – that of the richest butter, with which these plants have had a long, if slightly surprising, association. I remember as a child holding a buttercup flower under people's chins to see if they liked butter. A bright golden reflection on the skin showed they did – though I don't ever recall finding anyone who didn't like butter – so bright are the petals. I didn't know it at the time, but that brightness is unique to buttercup flowers. Beneath the yellow pigment layer, the cells are arranged in such a way that they create two layers of air. The reflective properties of these layers are responsible for the intense yellow glow of buttercups and also serve to focus both visible and infrared light on to the centre of the flower. The flower acts like a parabolic reflector that warms the anthers and so speeds up pollen production, and further experiments showed that warmer pollen was more effective in pollination. The surface of the flower is also so smooth, it produces mirror-like reflections and the bright flash of a buttercup flower serves as a glowing beacon for pollinating insects. These insects also prefer warmer flowers since this helps keep their own temperature high, especially early in the year. So, as the scientists who recently discovered this noted, buttercups are primed for hot sex!

With less scientific rigour, some people have attributed the yellow colour of butter to buttercups or thought that cattle feeding in buttercup-yellow pastures would produce richer butter, which is odd, because buttercups contain some very unpleasant toxins. They produce a chemical called ranunculin, which makes the plants taste bitter and can even cause blistering.[1] If cattle do eat buttercups their milk yield is reduced, but the bitter taste of the plants usually ensures that cattle avoid feeding on buttercups at all. Even so, the link between buttercups and butter is so strong that buttercup leaves were sometimes rubbed on to the teats of milk cows in the belief that it would improve their butter.[2]

But these same people were well aware of the properties of ranunculin, even if they had no idea what it was. Extracts of buttercups were applied to the skin to deliberately cause blistering, which was thought to draw out the poisons that caused disease. In the Middle Ages, this cure was even tried on victims of the Black Death, though, of course, to no effect. I've also heard it said that in Europe beggars rubbed their skin with buttercups to make it blister and perhaps attract more sympathy. Yet despite the toxicity of ranunculin, buttercups have found their way into traditional medicine as a treatment for fever or rheumatism and as in many other cases discussed in this book, there's more than a grain of truth in this old folk wisdom. Ranunculin breaks down to another chemical, protoanemonin, which may indeed have some of the beneficial properties ascribed to buttercups. It may seem odd, given the buttercup's toxicity, that some of the best haymeadows that I've rambled through in search of photographs for this book are bright with buttercups. Fortunately, both ranunculin and protoanemonin break down quickly in dried plants, so by the time the hay is needed for winter feed it is no longer toxic to livestock.

THE COMMON BUTTERCUPS

The buttercup family (Ranunculaceae) consists of well over 2,000 species worldwide and about 600 of those are typical buttercups, *Ranunculus*. In Britain alone there are over twenty different kinds of these butter-cups, some difficult to differentiate without the aid of a lens and a bit of determination. There are three common buttercup species that cre-ate dazzling yellow fields in spring and early summer up and down the country; meadow buttercup, *R. acris*, creeping buttercup, *R. repens* and bulbous buttercup, *R. bulbosus*. They flower at different times, bulbous buttercups beginning first, usually in April, followed in turn by mead-ow buttercups and creeping buttercups. But all have a long flowering season, so it's possible to find them all in flower together. They can also all be found together in the same field, but since they have slightly dif-ferent ecological preferences, they don't always grow in the same part of the field. Bulbous buttercups are more tolerant of dry soils, so are best looked for at the top end of a sloping field, or marking out the tops of ridges in fields of ridge and furrow – the undulations that remain from ancient ploughing. In these drier soils, bulbous buttercups often wither away in the heat of summer, but they get their name from a bulbous corm at the base of the stem which enables the plant to hunker down and survive the worst of summer and the following winter. This bulb is also responsible for another common name for this plant – St Anthony's turnip – though packed as it is with ranunculin, I wouldn't recommend eating it.

Both meadow and creeping buttercups don't mind getting their feet wet and so thrive in flood and water meadows. The problem with waterlogging is that roots are starved of oxygen and suffocate. But in sodden soils, meadow and creeping buttercups produce air spaces in their roots – called aerenchyma – and they can use oxygen produced as a waste product of photosynthesis to fill these air spaces and allow their roots to breathe.[3] A less common species of buttercup, the celery-leaved buttercup, *R. sceleratus*, is so tolerant of waterlogging that it's usually found in wet mud by the sides of rivers rather than in grassland. It can even survive prolonged shallow floods by quickly extending its leaf stalks so its leaves emerge from the water – hence their celery-like appearance. It's just one more step to a life permanently in the water, the lifestyle adopted by the water crowfoots.

There are numerous kinds of water crowfoots in Britain, most found in clean rivers, where their finely divided underwater leaves form great banks that shelter small fish and invertebrates. Their white flowers are held just above the surface and one of the glories of wandering along a crystal-clear chalk stream in southern England is to come across swathes of these flowers displayed against the rippling silver water.

Fields yellow with buttercups are found right across the British Isles, from the machair of the Hebrides to southern lowland meadows.

GLOBEFLOWERS

In northern or upland meadows another kind of buttercup – the globe flower, *Trollius europaeus* – forms impressive displays. Below the high fells of the northern Pennines, with their gentians, violets and sandworts, the Yorkshire and Durham Dales are rightly famous for their traditional haymeadows, which have a very different character from those of the lowlands. Edged with dry-stone walls beyond which rolling moorland vistas stretch on forever, some have large populations of globe flowers, looking like giant buttercups with flowers that never quite open. Instead they form large yellow globes held atop tall stems. Like their southern counterparts, flower-rich northern haymeadows are now scarce and those that managed to escape the effects of modern farming are protected as nature reserves. Hannah's Meadow Nature Reserve in Baldersdale in Co. Durham is named after Hannah Hauxwell who lived at Low Birk Hatt Farm and farmed the harsh landscapes of the High Pennines for several decades in the middle and latter part of the twentieth century. Even as late as the 1980s, Hannah lived here with no electricity or running water,

managing the land as it had been for centuries, without resorting to artificial fertilizers or re-seeding.

In 1973, Yorkshire Television made a documentary called *Too Long a Winter*, featuring Hannah and her life at Low Birk Hatt. It's a wonderful piece of work, shot in a cinematic style, but most striking is the revelation that in the second half of the twentieth century, an hour's drive from the industrial centre of Middlesbrough, Hannah was living a life that would have been familiar to farmers centuries earlier. That continuity of traditional management means that Hannah's Meadow Nature Reserve is now a very special place. Damper patches are covered in cuckoo flowers, *Cardamine pratensis*, alive with green-veined white butterflies whose caterpillars feed on its leaves. The wettest patches are occupied by another large buttercup, the marsh marigold, *Caltha palustris*, which forms spectacular golden clumps. Further south, in Swaledale, Muker Meadows is another survivor from times past. Meadow and creeping buttercups flower here in profusion alongside plants more characteristic of northern haymeadows, like wood cranesbills, *Geranium sylvaticum*, lady's mantles, *Alchemilla* spp., melancholy thistles, *Cirsium heterophyllum*, and great burnet, *Sanguisorba officinalis*.

Right: Marsh marigolds grow in wet grassland or at the edge of ponds, streams and ditches.

Below: These buttercup yellow pastures in the North York Moors won't really turn butter yellow.

BUTTERCUPS OF FOREST AND STREAM

Buttercups are adaptable plants. Whilst the most familiar are found in grasslands, others are more at home in woodland. To find the goldilocks buttercup, *R. auricomus*, means searching in forests on base-rich soils where its yellow flowers on top of lanky stems glow in flecks of sunlight. Goldilocks buttercups produce seeds without the need for fertilization, a trick that they share with dandelions. So, like dandelions, each lineage of goldilocks buttercups has its own characteristics and since it can never cross with other lineages it is, strictly speaking, a separate species. By this reckoning, there are several hundred species of this buttercup in Britain alone. To differentiate between our more normal concept of a species and this somewhat overwhelming plethora of buttercups, botanists sometimes call such apomictic species 'agamospecies' or 'microspecies'.

Other buttercups are aquatic. The celery-leaved buttercup is half-way there, growing in wet ground around lakes and rivers, where it's joined by greater spearwort, *R. lingua*, lesser spearwort, *R. flammula* and the much rarer creeping spearwort, *R. reptans*. In fact, all the plants of this latter species in Britain may be hybrids between the true creeping spearwort found in mainland Europe and lesser spearwort. Rarer still, the adder's-tongue spearwort, *R. ophioglossifolius*, grows in just two sites in Gloucestershire. One is a small pond on Inglestone Common near

Wickwar, the other a flooded field corner at Badgeworth, near Chelten-
ham. Thanks to the presence of this extreme rarity, this otherwise unre-
markable patch of wet ground at Badgeworth has been turned into a nature reserve that, back in 1964, appeared in *The Guinness Book of Records*
as the world's smallest nature reserve. It was also Gloucestershire's first
nature reserve when, in 1933, its then owner handed it over to the Society
for the Promotion of Nature Reserves (the forerunner of today's Royal
Society of Wildlife Trusts). This long association of adder's-tongue spearwort with this particular corner of a grassy field means that the plant is
known to many botanists as the Badgeworth buttercup and they turn
up in droves each June, the only time the reserve opens its gates, to pay
homage to what is, I have to say, one of our least impressive buttercups.

RARE WEEDS

The felling of the wildwood didn't only create grasslands. Early farmers
also needed fields in which to grow their crops. Most of those crops –
wheat, barley, rye, oats – were, of course, grasses, but these 'grasslands'
provided very different challenges to wildflowers and were in many ways
much tougher places to make a living. Nevertheless, many plants rose to
those challenges and made a real success of forging a living among the
crops. The corn buttercup, *R. arvensis*, was once a common sight in arable
fields in many areas of Britain where it was joined by a colourful variety
of other plants – larkspur, cornflower, corn cockle, corn chamomile, field
cow-wheat, pheasant's eye. They are usually called weeds but I prefer to
see them as the ultimate opportunists. Of all these, the corn buttercup is
perhaps the least impressive, with its tiny yellow flowers. But wait until
those flowers fade and the seed heads form.

Corn buttercups are diminutive plants but their seed heads are
huge – nearly a centimetre (half an inch) long and covered in vicious-
looking spines. This is the most noticeable feature of corn buttercups
and responsible for their wide range of local names – hellweed, devil's
claw, devil-on-both-sides, devil-on-all-sides, devil's coach wheel and
devil's currycombs. They share this trait of large seeds with other
cornfield plants such as corncockle and it is one reason why these plants
are such successful arable weeds. Their seeds were hard to separate from
the similar-sized seeds of the crop, so were inadvertently re-sown every
year with the crop seeds. Unfortunately (for the buttercups if not for the

farmers), modern farming methods are better able to screen crop seeds and targeted herbicides have reduced once common crop weeds to the status of extreme rarity.

It would no doubt be a great surprise to a farmer from any time before the middle of the twentieth century to discover that today we have set up nature reserves to protect the plants he strove to eradicate, and now spend time and money to manage fields in ways that encourage all these weeds. The plant conservation charity, Plantlife, protects a number of rare arable weeds on their farm at Ranscombe in Kent, while clifftop fields near Pentire in Cornwall, carefully managed by the National Trust, turn yellow in summer with corn marigolds, *Chrysanthemum segetum*. At College Lake in Berkshire, the local wildlife trust farms a collection of fields which look more like flower beds than crops. A mid-summer walk around this reserve is both a joyous and sobering experience. Marbled white and meadow brown butterflies flit from sky-blue scabious heads to the flowers of corncockle, held on such tall stems they rise above the crops. Bright-red pheasant's eyes contrast with yellow corn marigolds, and hidden amongst the crop stems are the strange flowers of field cow-wheat and fumitory. These sights are reminders of a time when cornfields were as colourful as haymeadows and it's easy to imagine why farming landscapes inspired a great many poets, from Shakespeare to John Clare.

PASQUE FLOWERS

Perhaps the most intriguing member of the buttercup family is a plant of the short turf of the chalk and limestone downs of the southern half of England. The pasque flower, *Pulsatilla vulgaris*, produces large magenta flowers cradling a conspicuous bunch of bright yellow anthers. It's sometimes called Dane's blood in the belief that it is only found where Anglo-Saxons managed to spill the blood of Viking invaders. It shares this name, and its home on chalk and limestone, with the clustered bellflower, *Campanula glomerata*. The bellflower's clusters of large blue flowers are held on top of red stems that were said to be stained with the blood of Vikings buried beneath the ground. These peaceful downlands must have once been a scene of large-scale carnage! The pasque flower's less gory name reflects the fact that it flowers around Easter.

In Britain the pasque flower has a curious distribution, though one which probably has little to do with the exploits of Viking invaders.

verleaf: Pasque flower.

It is a plant of chalk and limestone grasslands, but noticeably absent from perfectly suitable grasslands on the North and South Downs, as well as those in Hampshire and on Salisbury Plain. The reasons for this remain a mystery.[4] Historically it occurred on the Magnesian limestone in northern England but disappeared from these grasslands as its habitat was lost to intensive agriculture. But there are no historical records of pasque flowers on those vast areas of chalk in the southern counties.

The historical records do show, however, that pasque flowers have been declining throughout their range for a long time, as continued agricultural improvements slowly claimed the nutrient-poor, short-grazed turf on shallow chalky soils that they need to survive. It has been claimed that the Parliamentary Enclosure Acts between 1750 and 1850 increased the rate at which these grasslands were ploughed up, as land moved from common to private ownership, and so hastened the demise of pasque flowers. However, the pattern of enclosures and subsequent land use was so complex it's hard to be certain.[5] But it *is* certain that the decline continued unabated and now pasque flowers grow only in isolated pockets, often in small and precarious populations.

Just as for our rarer gentians, these small populations suffer genetic problems that reduce the fitness of the plants and further hasten

Pasque flowers at Barnsley Warren, near Cirencester in Gloucestershire.

their decline. Pasque flowers have suffered a similar pattern of loss in Germany, where they used to be abundant on steppe-like grasslands. Genetic studies here have shown that small, isolated populations have less genetic diversity and are also drifting apart genetically as random mutations build up and spread quickly through each tiny population.[6] It's a well-recognized phenomenon, called genetic drift, and it can result in the rapid spread of deleterious mutations that may further speed the loss of pasque flowers.

Although many populations are small, it is still possible to find places that put on an impressive Easter flower parade. Fox Covert in Hertfordshire is home to around 60,000 pasque flowers and provides a glimpse of what many chalk or limestone grasslands in Britain must once have looked like. Beyond these shores, pasque flowers of several different species grow in profusion on the steppe grasslands of the *puszta* in Hungary. Some years ago I went to Budapest to record music for a wildlife series I was producing, but I only stayed in the studio for a short time – the call of the *puszta* was too strong. I rented a car and drove to Kiskunság National Park where I soon found impressive clumps of two other species of pasque flower, *P. pratensis* and *P. grandis*, scattered across the short windswept turf. It was there, standing in a chill early spring gale that swept unhindered across wide open plains, that I appreciated their alternative name of windflower.

Pasque flowers are just as attractive when they drop their petals and develop their seed heads. Each seed is crowned by a long, twisted, feathery filament and, clumped together on the seed head, they form a silvery crown that glows when the sun shines through it. When the seed falls on to damp ground, each filament absorbs water and straightens, which is said to propel the seed into the soil. I've not seen this happen with the pasque flowers that set seed in my garden, but then I've never sat and watched closely enough. However, the spiky awn (long projection from the seed) of the wild oat seed does exactly that. I've filmed the way these seeds gyrate and twist as the awn changes shape, powered by the absorption of water, until the seed screws itself safely into the earth.

Buttercups must be some of our most familiar wildflowers. Their glowing yellow heads grace pastures and meadows up and down the country or colour roadside verges and waste ground. Some might see them as weeds but in my mind, any flower that copes so well with our modern landscapes deserves nothing but admiration.

7

Fritillaries

LILIACEAE
FRITILLARIA MELEAGRIS

Fritillaries belong to the lily family and although other members of this family are covered in two other chapters, fritillaries have such an intriguing natural and cultural history that they deserve a chapter of their own. There are around 140 species of fritillaries growing all around the northern hemisphere, so it might seem disappointing that only one of them, the snake's head fritillary, *Fritillaria meleagris*, deigns to grow in this country. But this single species is both an iconic and enigmatic plant and where it grows, in a few lowland meadows, it often does so in many tens or hundreds of thousands of individuals, creating a haze of purple – one of our most spectacular wildflower displays.

Many of the other species of fritillaries grow in very different habitats from the snake's head. In both the Old and New Worlds they raise their delicate-looking bells in some harsh and inhospitable habitats. I've seen *F. graeca* growing on barren rocky slopes high in the mountains of Greece and Turkey, at a time when spring has barely made its presence felt. And I've found *F. pyrenaica* scattered over the dry slopes of the Pyrenees in northern Spain. Our fritillary, in contrast, is a plant of moist lowland meadows bordering rivers. Once such meadows were plentiful and, along with them, so was the snake's head.

But the agricultural landscape of Britain has been transformed over the last seventy years, starting with the 'Dig for Victory' campaign during the Second World War, when every corner of land was viewed with an eye for its potential to grow food. Lowland haymeadows, with their fertile soils, were soon ploughed and sown with crops to feed the beleaguered nation and as meadows became arable fields, so the fritillaries disappeared. Richard Mabey succinctly summarized the decline of the fritillary in his book *Flora Britannica*. Before the war, he said, the plant grew in twenty-seven counties in southern Britain, now it grows in twenty-seven meadows.[1] So those meadows where it does grow are now very precious places.

Right: Fritillaries at Magdalen College, Oxford.

Overleaf: The biggest displays of fritillaries are at North Meadow near Cricklade in Wiltshire.

FRITILLARY MEADOWS

One such fritillary meadow is at Clattinger Farm in Wiltshire, a place where I spend as many early spring days as I can. There are eleven glorious meadows here, covering 149 acres of the Thames watershed. Clattinger is unique. It is the only lowland farm in Britain that has never been soaked in agricultural chemicals and that long legacy of traditional management continues under its current owners, the Wiltshire Wildlife Trust. It is considered the finest example of an enclosed lowland meadow in the country so, not surprisingly, in 2013 Clattinger became one of the Prince of Wales' Coronation Meadows.

The idea of creating a series of Coronation Meadows, one for each county, to celebrate the sixtieth anniversary of the coronation of his mother, came to the Prince after reading Plantlife's 2012 report on the loss of wildflower habitats. In the sixty years since Elizabeth II came to the throne, wildflower-rich meadows have suffered some of the greatest losses of any wildflower habitat, so the Prince's initiative is certainly a timely one. In some counties wildflower-rich meadows will be created anew, by sowing seeds collected from old meadows and reinstating traditional forms of management. In others, existing flower-rich meadows will be protected and celebrated.

Clattinger carries the flag for Wiltshire – and a colourful flag it is. In spring some meadows here turn sunshine yellow, daubed with splashes of glowing purple as cowslips vie with green-winged orchids to attract early spring insects. Scattered in some of these meadows are occasional clumps of the nodding chequerboard flowers of snake's heads, but one meadow in particular is simply full of them. Perhaps 50,000 bells tremble in the wind, most of them the normal purple form, but amongst

them are some in gleaming virginal white.

Even in times past, when fritillaries were a more familiar sight, these plants were so notable that those fortunate enough to live close by fritillary meadows claimed them for their own. To the south of Clattinger lies the village of Minety and to the west, Oaksey. And each village claims its own special relationship with these charismatic blooms; hereabouts the snake's head fritillaries are either Minety bells or Oaksey lilies. The same theme is repeated elsewhere. Near Ford, in Buckinghamshire, fritillaries are frogcups, a name that has nothing to do with the local amphibians but is derived from a local corruption of the name of the village. And even beyond these shores, locals are proud of their fritillaries. They are as scarce in Sweden as they are here, but grow in some abundance in King's Meadow (*Kungsängen*) near Uppsala. Here they are called *kungsängslilja* – lilies of the King's Meadow.

In Britain fritillaries are celebrated with a profusion of other local names – chess flower, guinea-hen flower, leper lily (from the flower's resemblance to the bell once carried by lepers), Lazarus bell or chequered lily. And in many places the appearance of their blooms was also celebrated with fritillary days. On particular days fritillary fields were opened to the public and for donations of a few pennies to a local charity, the fritillaries could be gathered in armfuls. A few places still hold fritillary days, although the plant is now too scarce for those making the pilgrimage to pick any souvenirs.

Perhaps the best known is Ducklington's Fritillary Sunday. Ducklington is a small village on the River Windrush in Oxfordshire, and in the past many of the fields along this tributary of the Thames used to flood in winter. Then, fertilized by nothing but river silt, they were allowed to grow tall for hay. These are the perfect conditions for fritillaries, so the fields along the Windrush valley turned purple each spring. In the early decades of the twentieth century, fritillaries were so abundant they were shipped to the market at Covent Garden and sold by local children in the streets of Birmingham. But after the Second World War the water table was lowered, allowing the fields to be ploughed and planted with arable crops, mirroring the rapid decline of haymeadows across the rest of lowland Britain. One field, Ducklington Mead, survived. It was bought by the Peel family and is now leased to a farmer who manages it as a traditional haymeadow. Here, the fritillaries still bloom in abundance and on one Sunday a year, in mid- to late April, the field is opened to an admiring public.

Fritillary Sunday is organized by the local church, St Bartholomew's, and used, with the encouragement of the Peel family, as a means of raising church funds. The fritillary is also celebrated inside the church with a carving on the pulpit and delicate portraits on the stained-glass windows. In addition, the flowers adorn a range of the church's souvenir merchandise, from postcards to tea-towels, and the appeal of the flower extends well beyond its short flowering season. St Bartholomew's now offers Fritillary gift packs as Christmas presents.

It is to be hoped that Fritillary Sundays will continue long into the future. The deeds for the meadow are legally tied in such a way that if the Peel family do decide to sell, it can only be sold to the National Trust.

The other fritillary meadows are all similar fortuitous survivors of the great plough-up that then came under the protection of sympathetic owners and managers. The display at Iffley Meadow in Oxford is now in the care of the Berkshire, Buckinghamshire and Oxfordshire Wildlife Trust, whilst the fritillaries of Magdalen Meadow in Oxford fall under the aegis of the university college to which it belongs. Britain's most northerly fritillary colony, at Mottey Meadows in Staffordshire, is managed by English Nature as a national nature reserve. Here, too, there used to be a tradition of picking the plants on one Sunday in May and the villagers of nearby Wheaton Aston are just as proud of these plants

he end of a perfect spring day
North Meadow in Wiltshire.

as the people of Ducklington, Oaksey or Minety. In the village, there's a street named Fritillary Row and the flower appears on the badge of a local school.

NORTH MEADOW

The biggest display of all is now also protected as a national nature reserve, at North Meadow, between the Thames and the Churn near the small Wiltshire market town of Cricklade. This vast and ancient haymeadow is home to 80 per cent of the British population of fritillaries – around half a million plants. There's a much higher proportion of white fritillaries here than in the nearby display at Clattinger Farm. The main path through the display looks across the meadow to the south-west, so a crisp spring sunset is the perfect time to appreciate the scale of this spectacle. Backlit, the white fritillaries stand out like a galaxy of stars against the dark cloud of purple.

The North Meadow colony survived thanks to an institution that dates back to the Middle Ages – the Court Leet of Cricklade. Once, these manorial courts were responsible for local policing and for legislating and managing many other aspects of local life. Gradually their responsibilities were eroded as parish, shire and national institutions grew. The Court Leet of Cricklade still exists, one of only thirty-two left in England

Two Canada geese enjoy the display of fritillaries.

and Wales, though few of its original responsibilities remain. However, one key duty has survived – the appointment of a Hayward to manage the cutting and allocation of hay from North Meadow along with the grazing rights. So today Cricklade's Court Leet is mainly concerned with the management of North Meadow.

For at least 800 years North Meadow has been common land, managed by the manorial court. Thanks to this, in 1814, it escaped passing into private hands in the Inclosure Act of that year. Under the watchful eye of the Court Leet, the ancient patterns of grazing and hay-making persisted – and the fritillaries continued to thrive.

North Meadow is an example of Lammas Land. On 12 February each year all the grazing animals are removed from the meadow and the grass and other flowers allowed to grow. In summer this growth is then cut for hay. On 12 August (old Lammas Day) the commoners' stock, overseen by the Court Leet, is allowed back on to the meadow to graze through autumn and winter. The meadow plants can therefore grow throughout spring and early summer safe from hungry mouths, and they flower and set seed in profusion. This encourages not just fritillaries but a succession of other plants later in spring and summer.

This ancient form of management is critical to fritillary survival, a fact brought home to me on my annual pilgrimage to North Meadow in the spring of 2013. Out of half a million plants blooming the previous year, I saw barely a few dozen. And the meadow was a mess, covered in a rough thatch of flattened grasses. Wandering over the meadow, I saw a forlorn group of figures. They turned out to be representatives from Natural England and a farmer who owned one of the hay lots. We gathered in a circle to lament the situation. The summer of 2012 was particularly wet, they told me. I knew that only too well! I was out in most of it, trying to film and photograph orchids both for this book and for a TV documentary I was making. I recalled endless days huddled in waterproofs sipping lukewarm coffee as it was slowly diluted by the deluge until a brief respite allowed me to grab a few shots.

It was so wet that no one had been able to cut the hay on North Meadow and it now lay in a suffocating, decomposing and unwanted mulch. And the soil remained waterlogged for longer than is usual in most years. The fritillaries, it seems, decided to stay safely underground. They were all still there of course, even though individual fritillary bulbs don't persist from year to year. Instead, every year each fritillary makes a new bulb from food remaining in the old one together with additional food made by photosynthesis in its leaves. It does this even if it fails to show above ground, simply transferring material from the old bulb to a new one.[2] But it can't do this forever. Eventually it needs to produce leaves and make more food. So it wouldn't take many seasons of unfavourable conditions to eliminate the plants entirely. That year in North Meadow made it easy to see why, after more than half a century of unsuitable management of most of our lowland meadows, fritillaries are now so scarce.

North Meadow, like many of the fritillary meadows I've visited, has a timeless feel. The land management here has its roots in Saxon times, as does nearby Cricklade itself. A walled Saxon village was built here by Alfred the Great as a defence against the Danes. At the end of a sunny April day, with its promise of summer yet to come, a carpet of dandelions and fritillaries extends across the meadow towards the elegant village church, and you are left with the sense of a scene enduring and changeless. Yet that may be an illusion. Many botanists are uncertain as to whether the snake's head fritillary should really be part of this scene at all.

Inside a fritillary flower.

NATIVE OR ALIEN?

Is this charismatic plant really a native of Britain? Or are these spectacular sights of more recent origin? There's no doubt that the fritillary is a conspicuous plant, not only individually with its dramatic flowers, but also from its habit of growing in swarms of tens or hundreds of thousands. Yet the earliest generally accepted record of fritillaries in the wild dates to the first half of the eighteenth century.[3] It's hard to imagine that such colourful displays would have been missed by earlier botanists, but they weren't recorded until John Blackstone wrote to a friend in 1736 that the plant grew in a meadow near Haresfield in Middlesex and had been growing there for forty years. This meadow, later referred to as Maud's Meadow, was, for a while after its discovery, a well-known fritillary meadow, though the fritillaries there had all disappeared by the end of the eighteenth century. The local natural history society has attempted to reintroduce them to this historic site by planting 2,000 bulbs, but Maud's Meadow is clearly no longer to the liking of this exacting plant and the survival rate of these bulbs has been disappointing.

In contrast, the display of fritillaries at Magdalen College, Oxford, is still spectacular, yet the plant wasn't recorded here – a few hundred

metres from the oldest botanic garden in Britain – until 1785. Richard Mabey describes the incumbent professor of botany at the time in less than glowing terms. 'Humphrey Sibthorp [was] a man of such renowned indolence that he reputedly gave just one not very successful lecture in forty years.'[4] So perhaps Oxford's botanists were more inclined towards the comforts of their colleges than a chilly spring day on the local meadows. Or perhaps the fritillaries of Magdalen College were a late introduction, possibly from the nearby colonies around Ducklington.

In the eighteenth century rectors of the parish church at Ducklington were all presidents of Magdalen College, so it's quite possible that one of them took some of the bulbs from the fields around Ducklington back to his college and planted them in the meadow. But there are many who think all our fritillary colonies were similarly introduced.

Most fritillaries produce the typical checkerbox flower but a few plants display flowers of gleaming white.

In Sweden, the huge colony in the King's Meadow is generally agreed to have originated from a botanic garden in Uppsala established in 1665 by Olof Rudbeck.[5] The familiar garden flower Rudbeckia was named after him by his ex-student Carl Linnaeus. And in a nice touch of symmetry, Rudbeck's garden in Uppsala is today known as the Linnaean Garden. The fritillaries in nearby King's Meadow were first discovered in either 1742 or 1743 by a friend of Linnaeus. So wild colonies of fritillaries were discovered in Sweden and Britain at about the same time.

But fritillaries were well known in gardens from much earlier. The sixteenth-century herbalist John Gerard was familiar with it and called it the 'checkered daffodil' or the 'Ginny hen flower', from the resemblance of its chequered pattern to the spotted feathers of the guinea fowl. It doesn't seem to have had any particular medicinal value but was grown simply for its beauty. Gerard wrote: 'Of the faculties of these pleasant flowers there is nothing set downe in ancient or later writers, but are greatly esteemed for the beautifieng of our gardens, and the bosomes of the beautifull.'

It is hard to believe that such a spectacular plant, worthy to gild the bosoms of the beautiful and already familiar as an adornment to gardens, could have been missed as a wild native. Indolent professional botanists aside, there were a great many skilled amateur naturalists exploring the countryside between the sixteenth and eighteenth centuries who were most unlikely to have overlooked wild displays, especially those along the Thames Valley, so close to London. Yet in ancient meadows like North Meadow, whose history stretches back at least 800 years, the plant looks so much a part of the landscape that it's hard to believe it's not a native. So the riddle remains, perhaps adding to the charm of this singular plant.

Elsewhere in its range, there's no such puzzle. The snake's head fritillary certainly is native in Europe. It was first discovered in a field around 80 kilometres (50 miles) to the south of Paris[6] and its native range runs from central and southern Europe to western Siberia. Its original habitat here may well have been open forest, which explains why it does so well in gardens under deciduous trees, so long as they don't produce too much shade. A very similar-looking fritillary, *F. involucrata*,

still grows in such habitats today in the Alpes-Maritimes département of south-eastern France.

The snake's head fritillary grows in some abundance, also as an undoubted native, along the Rhine Valley. During the last Ice Age, when sea levels were much lower and Britain was joined to the rest of Europe, the Thames was a tributary of the Rhine. So it's easy to imagine that as the climate warmed, fritillaries could spread northwards, following the river valleys. Did they make it to the Thames before rising sea levels severed the connection between the Thames and the Rhine?

Whether native or not, the snake's head fritillary has certainly fitted itself into the ecology of lowland haymeadows in Britain. We've already seen that it's fussy about the management of the grasslands it inhabits. Traditional management for hay suits the snake's head well, but it's also choosy about soil conditions. It thrives in haymeadows that flood in winter, but it doesn't like soil that remains too wet, or which gets too dry.[7] In wet conditions, the plant sulks and either remains as a juvenile, non-flowering plant, or simply stays underground – as did most of the plants at North Meadow after the wet summer of 2012. In the right conditions, its growth cycle begins in August, just as stock is being returned to the traditional meadows. At this time of year, its bulb is deep underground, safe from grazing mouths, but it's stirring into life.

It produces roots that can contract and pull the bulb to the right depth in the soil. It's a neat trick that many bulbs can pull off, but fritillaries are particularly good at this. I grow a number of different species in tall pots, Long Toms, since many fritillaries like to be buried deeply. And if they don't like where I planted them, they will adjust their depth to suit themselves. Sometimes, when I come to re-pot after a few years, I have to search right at the base of the pot, occasionally under 20 centimetres of soil (8 in), to find them.

The snake's head seems happy at around 5–8 centimetres (2–3 in) either in my pots or below the surface of a haymeadow and by late summer the shoot reaches to just below the soil surface, then stops as the plant enters a period of dormancy over the winter. Now it's poised to thrust up stem and flower into the early spring air. Flowering in March or April, it has little competition from other, taller plants of the haymeadow, but its early appearance does give the fritillary a problem. It relies mainly on seed to reproduce and although it can self-pollinate, it's better for the plant to receive pollen from other, unrelated individuals. That means it has to rely on insects to move its pollen from plant to

A bee's eye view of a fritillary flower, showing the greenish nectaries radiating from the base of the flower.

plant and in the chilly spring weather, with frequent April showers, there aren't too many of those about.

FRITILLARY POLLINATORS

Spend any length of time in a fritillary meadow and you'll see a few bumblebees, often newly emerged queens, disappearing inside the hanging flowers. More detailed surveys have recorded solitary bees also visiting the flowers. Solitary bees pick up more pollen than bumblebees on each visit, but they forage widely among early spring flowers, so they aren't very reliable in carrying this pollen to another fritillary. Instead, it's the queen bumblebees that are the most efficient pollinators.[8] Over 80 per cent of visits to fritillary flowers were made by bumblebees and they are far more likely than solitary bees to visit another fritillary with their pollen load.[9] Furthermore, protected by a thick furry coat, they can remain active even at lower temperatures, so can keep up their pollination duties through capricious spring weather.

The fritillary pays for these pollination services by producing nectar rich in three different sugars (sucrose – the stuff you put in your coffee – fructose and glucose). The nectar also contains amino acids, vital for making proteins. It's produced by six nectaries that are easily visible if you peer into the flower. They appear as thin green strips about a centimetre long towards the base of the petals, set conspicuously against the chequered purple flowers. Nectar is a generous gift, expensive to make in terms of the plant's energy budget, so it needs to be used carefully. When the flower first opens, the solution is only 25 per cent sugar, but once the anthers split and the pollen is ready for pick-up, the fritillary cranks up both the volume of nectar and the sugar content, which now reaches 70 per cent.[10]

Growing in spectacular displays of hundreds of thousands might also be a strategy to help pollination. So many flowers so close together provide a huge volume of nectar at a time when a queen bumblebee is under a lot of pressure. Only queens survive the winter, so when spring comes, she's on her own. She must find a nest site and build a nest, complete with wax pots in which to rear her offspring. She must also provision this nest with both nectar and pollen to feed her growing larvae and until this new generation matures to become her workforce, she has to do all of this on her own, in unpredictable spring weather.

Half a million fritillaries all producing nectar and all within easy reach of each other is too good an opportunity for queen bumblebees to miss. Around 90 per cent of all the pollen on their bodies comes from fritillaries, which suggests bumblebee queens in fritillary meadows are very loyal to fritillaries, making them very effective pollinators.[11]

This successful partnership means a visit to a fritillary meadow later in the summer will reveal a fat seed pod perched atop each stem, stacked with three neat rows of flattened seeds, like plates piled on top of each other. Even so, fritillaries are well known for large and unpredictable swings in the number of flowers appearing each year. As we've already seen, bad weather in the previous year can have a dramatic effect, but this is not the whole story.

A ripe fritillary seed head has split to scatter the seeds.

These swings are largest on the wettest ground, where the fritillaries are at the edge of their tolerance, but all populations go up and down, with perhaps a fourfold difference over a four- to eight-year cycle. No one really knows what causes this. On the King's Meadow in Sweden these oscillations showed no relationship to any particular weather conditions or indeed any combination of weather variables. In any case, this was unlikely. Even in one geographical area the cycles in different meadows don't coincide – some populations are increasing whilst others, just a few kilometres away, are declining. It's just one more mystery associated with this unusual plant.

Its puzzling origins and strange appearance were well summed up by Vita Sackville-West. With her husband, Sir Harold Nicolson, she created the gardens at Sissinghurst Castle in Kent. She was also a poet and author and wrote an epic pastoral poem called *The Land* (1926), in which she describes the fritillary as 'Sullen and foreign looking… camping among the furze, staining the waste. With foreign colour, sulky-dark and quaint.'

And perhaps it really is foreign. We're still not certain. But that doesn't stop many people, myself included, making annual pilgrimages to the precious few remaining fritillary meadows to celebrate a very special plant.

8

Gentians

GENTIANACEAE

THE BRITISH SPECIES

In Britain, the gentian family contains a variety of centaury (*Centaurium*) species, with small but attractive pink flowers, and the widespread yellow-wort, *Blackstonia perfoliata*, with broad pale green leaves through which the stem passes – hence the name *perfoliata*, as the stem perforates the leaves. In addition, there is an assortment of plants referred to as gentians, the subjects of this chapter, which belong to three different genera, *Gentiana*, *Gentianella* and *Gentianopsis*. But just how many kinds of these gentians live in Britain is not such an easy question to answer, since there is a lot of confusion about the taxonomy of three of the members of the *Gentianella* group. The commonest species is the autumn felwort, *G. amarella*, but there are two rarer species, the early gentian, *G. anglica*, and the dune gentian, *G. uliginosa*, that can be hard to tell apart from each other and from autumn felwort – and as we'll see shortly may all be variations on a theme within a single species.[1] But the two remaining *Gentianella* species, the Chiltern gentian, *G. germanica*, and the field gentian, *G. campestris*, are easily distinguishable species.

There are also two species of *Gentiana* growing here. The spring gentian, *G. verna*, is confined in the British Isles to Teesdale in the northern Pennines and the Burren area of western Ireland. The alpine gentian, *G. nivalis*, is even more restricted and grows only on the high slopes of Ben Lawers in Perthshire. Rarest of all these plants is the fringed

Below: Ben Lawers in Perthshire is home to many rare mountain plants including alpine gentian.

Below right: Autumn felwort.

gentian, *G. ciliata*, which used to be classified amongst the gentianellas, but is now given its own genus, *Gentianopsis*. It grows in very low numbers on one site in the Chilterns.

GENTIANS IN A CHANGING LANDSCAPE

Autumn felwort, as its name suggests, flowers from late July through to early October and is a plant I associate with hot, dusty days in late summer on the steep grassy slopes of the Cotswold scarp. At this time of year the tall stems of upright brome grass, *Bromopsis erecta*, soften these slopes with a haze of feathery flower heads and the songs of stripe-winged and rufous grasshoppers, both species that prefer these limestone slopes, fill the air. Below the slopes, villages creep along a network of valleys and, built of honey-coloured Cotswold stone, seem as much part of the landscape as the flowery grasslands. Nestled among the wiry stems of upright brome are the flower heads of autumn felwort, appearing at their best when most other plants on these hot, dry slopes are looking a little the worse for wear. The most widespread of our gentians, autumn felwort grows up and down the country on chalk or limestone grasslands, as long as they are still managed traditionally and not fertilized by anything other than the dung of the animals grazing them.

The field gentian is easily distinguished from autumn felwort by the sepals enclosing the flower. Two of the field gentian's sepals are much larger and overlap the others, whilst the sepals of autumn felwort are all more or less the same size. Field gentians were once also widespread across Britain, though preferring more acid grasslands than the autumn felwort. But field gentians have largely disappeared from lowland England and are now found mainly in Scotland, Ireland and the uplands of northern England and Wales.

In fact, both species have declined during the twentieth century, and not just here in Britain but across much of their European ranges. In Sweden they have been lost from 88–98 per cent of their previous locations. Much of this loss was caused by a shift away from traditional management, though there are still declines even on sites where traditional management has continued, for reasons that are not obvious.[2] Thanks to their life cycle, the gentians are closely tied to the way grasslands have been managed over the centuries and none have taken kindly to recent changes.

Most British gentians are biennials or annuals that depend on seed to maintain their populations. They die after flowering once, and the seed doesn't persist in the soil as a seed bank that can ride out hard times.[3] They have to get everything right first time – pollination, seed germination and seedling establishment – with no second chances. This means that environmental conditions must remain optimal from year to year and as soon as they change, the gentians quickly disappear. Detailed studies of exactly what suits a field gentian have been carried out in Sweden, where traditional management of meadows is much the same as it was here – a cut in July followed by light grazing in the autumn. Cutting removes competition for these late-flowering plants, then late grazing opens up patches of turf that allows the seeds to germinate and the seedlings to establish themselves.[4]

The newer forms of meadow management entail grazing that is too intense for too long or a cut that comes too late or too early. In the case of a late cut the grass has grown too long by the time the gentians are ready to flower and in the second case, the gentian flowers are cut down before having a chance to flower. Even small changes result in a dramatic loss of plants.

Traditional forms of management have persisted for so long that evolution has fine-tuned gentians to the cycles of the farming year. Field gentians have adapted to traditional grazing regimes in several ways. There are two distinct types of field gentian, one that flowers early and one that flowers late. The early flowerers have finished the vital business of seed production before grazing starts. Late flowerers, rather than avoiding grazing, are more tolerant of it.[5] When grazed, or experimentally clipped, field gentians often produce more fruits than similar plants that are undamaged. Botanists call this 'over-compensation', and it's probably an evolutionary response to predictable damage.[6] If the gentian 'knows' that it's likely to get damaged at some point during its growth, it doesn't put much effort into the first few flowers and fruits since it's likely to lose them. If they get nibbled off the plant then it knows that, having grazed an area, grazers are unlikely to return, so it's safe to go all out and commit everything to flower and fruit production.

Likewise, some populations of autumn felwort, though not all, also over-compensate in response to light grazing. In these populations, plants that experimentally have around 10 per cent of their stems clipped go on to produce more fruits than unclipped plants. But heavier damage, where around 50 per cent of the plant was clipped, results in fewer fruits than are produced by undamaged plants.[7] It seems that these populations have adapted to the light grazing regime that has shaped their grassland homes for centuries, if not millennia.

GENTIANELLAS: EVOLUTION IN ACTION

Like the field gentian, autumn felwort also has early and late flowering variants, but in this country the early-flowering variety may have evolved into a separate species, endemic to the British Isles. Unlike most of our *Gentianellas*, early gentians flower in the first half of the year and so are now isolated from their late-flowering close relatives. The early gentian is sometimes called the English gentian, which underlines its endemism, although it is something of a misnomer as there are a few plants in Wales too. But Wales and England share mild and wet winters, probably the reason why an early-flowering form was able to evolve here – germinating

*eft: Field gentian. *Right*: Early or English) gentian.

in the autumn and growing big enough to flower in the first half of the year.[8] All the autumn-flowering gentians, on the other hand, germinate in the spring.

English gentians can be abundant in some places and one of the best places to find them is the chalk downs of the Isle of Wight. Surveys a couple of decades ago estimated that the Isle of Wight holds around four million plants, with a further one to two million in Wiltshire and Dorset, yet it's not at all common in the Cotswolds where I go each autumn to admire its parent species.[9] English gentians also vary dramatically in numbers from year to year on the same site. On one site, at Beachy Head in Sussex, 200,000 plants were reduced to just fifty in the following year. But such unpredictability adds to the joy of finding one of our few endemic plants, if it really is a distinct species.

Molecular studies can't distinguish between autumn felwort, dune gentians and early gentians, even though in these studies, both field gentian and Chiltern gentian are easily recognisable as perfectly distinct and well-defined species.[10] This raises the possibility that autumn felwort, dune gentians and early gentians are really all the same species, which varies according to the habitat it is growing in and the management regime that it has evolved to cope with. And as those management regimes change, the barriers that keep the forms separate may break down. There's evidence that, though largely separated by flowering time, there is some hybridization between autumn felwort and early gentians. Plants in Cornwall that were previously regarded as a sub-species of early gentian may in fact be just such hybrids.[11] In the future these three species may even merge back into one.

THE RARITIES

There's no such confusion over the Chiltern gentian, a spectacular species with much larger flowers than the others, and which, as its name suggests, is confined in this country to the Chilterns. It's the county flower of Buckinghamshire, but beyond this country it's widespread from France to the Balkans. Like the other species, it is dependent on traditional grassland management and has therefore lost ground right across its European range. As its remaining populations both shrink and grow more fragmented, Chiltern gentians suffer from genetic problems which mean that they produce less seed and that seed is also

hiltern gentian.

less viable. This is known as in-breeding depression and is a common problem for plants that are reduced to small, isolated populations. In a small population, genetic variability between plants is reduced, and since many plants don't do well when pollinated by genetically similar pollen, plants in small populations are on a slippery slope to extinction. But to make matters worse, Chiltern gentians also suffer from out-breeding depression. This means that gentians pollinated by plants from distant populations don't do well either. Plants pollinated by neighbours around 10 metres (33 ft) distant produce the most vigorous offspring.[12] Out-breeding depression may reflect a finely tuned genetic adaptation to local conditions. As we've seen, these gentians have evolved to fit specific management regimes, so such genetic fine-tuning might be expected. In this case, the arrival of genes from populations adapted to different local conditions gives rise to plants less able to cope with their own habitat. This suggests that plant conservationists, who often try to improve the genetic variety in small relict populations of rare plants by bringing in pollen from distant populations, would do well to exercise caution in this regard.

A world away from the chalky slopes of the Home Counties, the high fells of the northern Pennines are home to my favourite gentian species – the spring gentian. It has flowers of such an intense blue that they seem like fallen fragments of the vast sky that arches over these high fells. And it's only on the sunniest days that the gentians fully open their flowers. Spring gentians are confined to just two locations in the British Isles, both places to entrance any naturalist – the grasslands of Teesdale, along the upper reaches of the River Tees, and the Burren of western Ireland, facing into the wild Atlantic. Teesdale is home to many rarities, including the Teesdale violet, *Viola rupestris*, mountain avens, *Dryas octo-petala*, and the Teesdale sandwort, *Minuartia stricta*. These rarities grow on grasslands that overlay a form of carboniferous limestone called sugar limestone, named for its granular texture. Sugar limestone was formed by being baked shortly after it was laid down in a shallow carboniferous sea, some 300 million years ago. The intense heat required to create sugar limestone came from a huge intrusion of magma that today forms the Whin Sill. It outcrops lower down the Tees at High Force, where the river tumbles over a ledge of this resistant rock in one of England's biggest waterfalls. It then crosses County Durham and Northumberland and reappears on the coast, creating erosion-resistant mounds on which sit Bamburgh and Lindisfarne castles.

Above and right: Spring gentian

But in Upper Teesdale the legacy of the Whin Sill is the botanist's paradise of Widdybank and Cronkley Fells. Spring gentians aren't hard to find on Widdybank Fell in the short, sheep-grazed turf. They were first found here in 1797 by John Binks, who was apparently a lead miner from Middleton-in-Teesdale. This town was built on the abundance of lead ore in the vicinity, yet another legacy of the Whin Sill, and it became the north of England headquarters of the London Lead Company. The life of a lead miner was one of long, hard days so perhaps Binks was an official of the company, with more leisure time to explore the high fells further up the river. Spring gentians are locally called spring violets and the existence of a long-standing local name suggests they may have been known to the hill farmers before Binks introduced this plant to the botanical world. After all, it's hard to miss their bright-blue stars even on a day visit, so it's impossible to imagine that local shepherds wouldn't have admired its flowers as harbingers of spring in these bleak uplands. And if so, it's fitting that the spring gentian is now the county flower of Durham.

In western Ireland spring gentians also grow on carboniferous limestone, but here they do so at sea level. On the Burren of County Clare the bones of the landscape are laid bare in an area famous for its tracts of limestone pavement. Largely stripped of all soil, bare grey rocks roll down to the ocean, criss-crossed by deep fissures called grykes that divide the limestone into great slabs. All kinds of interesting ferns grow in the more humid air of the grykes, whilst mountain avens form drifts over areas of shallow soil. Neat tussocks of pink thrift find a foothold on bare rocks close to the sea and low-growing mats of wild thyme alternate with yellow mounds of bird's-foot trefoil. Here and there, red-flowered spikes of dark-red helleborines, *Epipactis atrorubens*, a kind of orchid, make a sharp contrast with the bare limestone. The whole area looks like a well-manicured rock garden, but one conceived on a vast scale.

In the rocky Burren landscape, spring gentians grow in those areas with enough soil to form short-turf grassland. They look slightly different from the Teesdale plants, which is, perhaps, not surprising.[13] Though both areas receive high rainfall, Upper Teesdale is cold and spring comes late. In contrast, the Burren is located in one of the mildest areas of the British Isles, warmed by its proximity to the Atlantic Ocean and the Gulf Stream. But both areas have extensive areas of short turf, critical for the survival of the spring gentian.

Spring gentian flowers are visited by bumblebees, though short-tongued species seem to have difficulty reaching the nectar at the bottom of the long, trumpet-shaped flower. Undaunted, these bees simply chew a hole at the base of the flower and steal the nectar, without pollinating the gentian. In Teesdale, many gentian flowers have such holes nibbled in them, but unlike other gentians, the spring gentian is longer-lived and can spread by sending out runners from which new rosettes pop up, so seed production is less critical.[14] And just as well. Detailed surveys of the gentians here have revealed that even if the gentians produce seed capsules they are likely to be nibbled off by sheep. These gentians have something of a love-hate relationship with the local sheep. They might lose flowers and seeds to them, but they need those nibbling mouths to crop the turf short otherwise they would be crowded out by more vigorous plants.

This delicate balance has been well illustrated by our other mountain gentian, the alpine gentian. This species has similar intense blue flowers but they are much smaller than those of the spring gentian. In Britain it grows only on Ben Lawers, which rises from the north side of Loch Tay in Perthshire, in the southern Scottish Highlands. Ben Lawers reaches over 1,200 metres (3,980 ft) in height and the gentians, along with other rare arctic–alpine plants, grow in a corrie near the summit, on areas of a rock called mica schist. Older than the carboniferous limestones

pine gentian.

of Teesdale and the Burren, these rocks too have been altered by heat. Near the summit of the mountain they support hanging gardens of plants like alpine forget-me-not, *Myosotis alpestris*, which has much larger sky-blue flowers than the more familiar forget-me-nots of the lowlands; rock speedwell, *Veronica fruticans*, also large-flowered; and alpine saxifrage, *Saxifraga nivalis*. It's a long and steep walk up to these gardens, but it's worth every step – a stupendous view and some of the rarest plants in the country.

Alpine gentians are found dotted amongst the turf and though smaller than spring gentians are not too hard to spot, as long as the sheep haven't found them first – because conservationists have noticed that many alpine gentian flowers are bitten off by sheep. So in an attempt to protect this species in its only British site, an area was fenced off in the late 1980s. Sure enough, alpine gentians grew bigger and better when sheep couldn't reach them, but after three years, the plants began to disappear as the turf grew thicker and more luxuriant.[15] Despite being on the sheep menu, alpine gentians need those same sheep to keep the grass and other vegetation clipped short. The fences were removed in the late 1990s and by 2006 the population of alpine gentians had begun to recover.[16]

Like the *Gentianella* species, alpine gentians depend on seed to maintain themselves, which is far from easy in the arctic climate at the top of Ben Lawers. The flowers only open in full sun, which, as any visitor to the Scottish Highlands will attest, is often in short supply up here. In dull weather the petals furl tightly together, which protects the pollen inside from torrential rain. Pollinators are also scarce at these altitudes, but the alpine gentians seem to get by. In other parts of their range, in higher mountains and in the Arctic, they are faced with even harsher climates yet still produce large quantities of seed that sometimes gets dispersed widely in the dung of grazing animals. This means they can pop up in unexpected places. They grow around the walls of farm buildings in Iceland and I was delighted to find a large population at Finse Station in south-western Norway.

Finse lies in the middle of the Hardanger Plateau – Hardangervidda – in Norway. Thanks to its altitude, Hardangervidda is a 2,500-square-kilometre (965-square-mile) chunk of the high Arctic transported to southern Norway, between Bergen and Oslo. It's home to a large herd of wild reindeer as well as to birds like golden eagles and gyr falcons.

Autumn felwort in late summer grasslands on the Cotswolds.

The Hardangervidda a remote area with no roads, though the plateau is crossed by the Bergen to Oslo railway line, which provides the best means of access. Alighting at Finse, it's a spectacular hike to Hardangerjøkulen, Norway's sixth-largest glacier. But before I'd gone two steps, I noticed the bright-blue flowers of alpine gentians growing amongst grass along the edge of the platform. After a long trek to see these plants at the top of Ben Lawers, here they were in great profusion a few yards from the station buffet.

Our final gentian is also the rarest. The fringed gentian was discovered near Wendover in Buckinghamshire in 1875 by Miss M. Williams. But when George Druce, botanist and sometime mayor of Oxford, was preparing *The Flora of Buckinghamshire*, he examined the dried specimen and declared it to be nothing more than a clustered bellflower, *Campanula glomerata*, another late-flowering plant of chalk grasslands. He wrote disdainfully that 'There must be some gross carelessness in such a record, as ciliata is not likely to occur in England.' But the carelessness was his and Druce's mistake was finally rectified in 1982 when fringed gentians were found again at the same site and added to the British list as a very rare native. There are old records in Wiltshire, from 1892, which were probably of another native population, now lost, and in Surrey (1910) where it was probably an introduction. But today, it is known from just one site at Coombe Hill, where in some years it doesn't flower at all. So for how long this plant will remain on the British list is an open question.

All the British gentians are intriguing plants – some, like autumn felwort, have an understated beauty, others, like Chiltern, spring and alpine gentians, are truly spectacular, the joy at finding them enhanced by their extreme rarity. Unfortunately, even our commoner species are now getting rarer, which is certainly no cause for joy. Like many grassland plants, they have suffered from the rapid intensification of farming following the Second World War and now have to face a climate that is changing more rapidly than at any time since the end of the Ice Age. This latter threat is certain to have a major impact not just on alpine gentians but on all our mountain plants and will likely effect lowland plants in ways we probably don't yet fully appreciate. Among the gentians, climate change combined with changing land management might see three fledgling species – autumn felwort, early gentian and dune gentian – fuse back into one interbreeding population. It's a sobering thought that our effects on the planet can even throw evolution into reverse.

9

Primulas

PRIMULACEAE

M ost people can recognize a primrose, with those primrose-yellow petals that appear at the first hint of spring, the perfect reflection of the pale sunlight at this early time of the year. In recent years, though, it's not unusual to find hedgerow primroses flowering over Christmas and primroses have now been recorded flowering in every month of the year. So these days the first rose – Prima Rosa – might just as well be called the last rose.

The primrose, *Primula vulgaris*, is one of five native species of *Primulas*, three of which, the cowslip, *P. veris*, and the oxlip, *P. elatior*, as well as the primrose itself, are large yellow-flowered species. The other two, the bird's-eye primrose, *P. farinosa*, and the Scottish primrose, *P. scotica*, are much daintier, pink-flowered species. All are (or were) plants of grasslands, although the primrose and oxlip are more characteristic of woodlands. Oxlips were once common in grassy places, at least in the small corner of England where they occur, creating displays to rival those of the best cowslip meadows. Now oxlips in Britain are largely confined to woodlands, although they still grow abundantly in grasslands further east in Europe. There are, however, still plenty of places in Britain where primroses grow in the open. Travel down almost any sunken Devon lane in spring and the high grassy verges are often yellow with primroses. Similar sights across the country have been a constant feature of spring for so long that they've been woven into folklore in widely popular songs like 'The Banks of Sweet Primroses'.[*] In the more humid climate of the West Country primroses are much less dependent on the shelter of woodlands and frequently found in grasslands. Even as far north as Scotland primroses often cascade down windblown cliffs, their pale yellow flowers harmonizing with the more intense hues of gorse, which also flowers at this time of year.

In the past, cowslips also grew in great abundance across Britain, perhaps once as common as buttercups, and similarly turned fields yellow in the spring. Their name comes from a less savoury association with grasslands – with pastures where cattle grazed. Farmers noticed that these plants were often more common around cow pats, or cow slups as they were once called. Like the banks of sweet primroses, cowslips were an integral part of rural culture and folklore. They were said to have sprung from the keys to heaven, dropped by St Peter – a fanciful

---

[*] Popular in the nineteenth century, though dating from earlier; the Road Folk Song Index lists 329 examples of this song.

reference to the bunch of flowers held on the top of each stem. Cowslips were strewn in front of spring brides along the path to the church and were woven into May garlands to celebrate Mayday as well as being ingredients of a potent country wine, which no doubt fuelled these rural revels. Plants of old established grasslands, cowslips were victims of the shift to more intensive farming, and they vanished from great tracts of the countryside. Today they are regaining some of that lost ground as they colonize unsprayed grassy roadsides and spread back into fields managed under more benign countryside stewardships schemes.

Like cowslips, the other two British primulas are only found in open grassland. Bird's-eye primroses in this country are either plants of high fell grasslands in the northern Pennines or of the short, rich turf growing on the magnesian limestone, a rock formation running up through Yorkshire and County Durham. To see Scottish primroses means a trip even further north, to the coastal grasslands of Caithness, Sutherland and Orkney, some of the most remote grasslands in the country.

In the past the epithet of 'first rose' was given to a wide range of spring flowers and it wasn't until the fifteenth century that the name was applied to the plant we now know as the primrose. But at this time the name 'primrose' was also applied to the cowslip, which was seen merely as a variety of primrose.[1] So what was *P. vulgaris* called before the 1400s? To add to the confusion, it may also have been called 'oxlip' since, like 'cowslip' and 'primrose', this is an old name and true oxlips, with a distribution restricted to a small area of eastern England, weren't finally recognized as a distinct species until the nineteenth century.

THE DISCOVERY OF OXLIPS

Where they do grow true oxlips often carpet woodland floors in great profusion. So it's a little surprising that it wasn't until 1660 that the Essex botanist John Ray described it as a distinct plant. Yet despite Ray's meticulous observations, confusion continued. Up to the second half of the nineteenth century, cowslips, oxlips and primroses were still seen by most naturalists and botanists as varieties of the same plant. No less an authority than Reverend Professor John Henslow, Regius Professor of Botany at Cambridge University, wrote in 1842:

Let a cowslip be highly manured, and its seeds sown in a shady,
moist aspect, and I suspect the chances are in favour of some
of them coming up as primroses or at least, as oxlips. I have
had several independent testimonies to the fact of cowslip roots
changing to primroses; and until proof, by direct experiment,
contradict the experiments of Mr Herbert and myself I cannot
help believing that the three species (as they are thought) and the
polyanthus, are merely races of one species.[2]

Some of this confusion is understandable. All three species hybridize and the primrose/cowslip hybrid bears some resemblance to an oxlip, so much so that it's still called the false oxlip. It would be left to a pupil of Henslow at Cambridge to clear up the confusion. In 1831 Henslow received an invitation to accompany a certain Captain Robert FitzRoy as a gentlemen companion on what was planned to be a two-year round-the-world survey voyage, on board HMS *Beagle*. Henslow's wife dissuaded him from going, so Henslow passed on the invitation to his pupil, Charles Darwin. The rest, as they say, is history.

After returning from what turned out to be a five-year voyage Darwin was already famous amongst naturalists and academics and corresponded with a great many of these people on subjects as diverse as primulas and pigeons. One such person was Henry Doubleday, another observant naturalist from Essex, who spent a lot of time around Bardfield in his home county, where oxlips grew in great quantities, both in woods and in meadows. Some of the meadows here must have been truly spectacular and were described at the time as turning yellow with oxlips in springtime. Doubleday was convinced that these plants were a separate species from either cowslips or primroses and sent specimens and a note to Darwin, dated 3 May 1860:

> *My Dear Sir*
> *I have read with real pleasure your very interesting work*
> *'On the Origin of Species' and I may, some day, send you a few*
> *remarks upon portions of it—*
> *My object in now writing is to say that I have tried a*
> *great many experiments upon the Primrose, Oxlip and Cowslip*
> *f1 [first generation cross] all of which tended to confirm my*
> *opinion that these three plants are distinct species – or what are*
> *called species in all our Botanical works – I never could raise a*

primrose from the seed of the Cowslip nor a Cowslip from the seed of the Primrose— The true Primula elatior or Oxlip with pale, drooping, scentless flowers appears to be a very local plant in Britain – but it grows in great profusion in swampy meadows at Bardfield in Essex. In wet winters these meadows are always flooded— The Primrose does not exist in the Parish of Bardfield although the woods and lanes there seem very favourable situation for it— The Cowslip is plentiful in the dry fields—

Twenty years since I brought a number of roots of Oxlips from Bardfield and planted them in my garden in a border under a north wall – they have grown luxuriantly there and seed profusely every year— Many thousands of seedlings have flowered and all have been similar to the original plants— There has not been a primrose or cowslip among them— [3]

Darwin's immediate reply to Doubleday has been lost, but nevertheless Darwin went on to study cowslips, primroses and oxlips in great detail and confirmed that the so-called common oxlip was in fact a hybrid between a primrose and a cowslip. However, he considered that

Doubleday's oxlip was, as Doubleday himself suspected and John Ray had figured out two centuries earlier, a distinct species, with a much more restricted distribution in Britain.[4]

The true oxlip is confined to a small patch of eastern England in an area of soils formed over the boulder clay where the counties of Cambridgeshire, Essex and Suffolk meet. But within this area it's certainly not a rare plant. It grows in many woodlands, sometimes in spectacular numbers.

Darwin called this plant the Bardfield oxlip, to distinguish it from the common (or false) oxlip, a singular honour as few plants in Britain carry a village name. And so the oxlip became the symbol of the village of Great Bardfield. It remains so today even though the 'Bardfield' part of its common name has been lost – as too have the oxlip carpets of Bardfield. Although they no longer grow in the parish in the profusion described by Doubleday, seeds have recently been collected from the few remaining plants and are being grown on in glasshouses at nearby Writtle College as part of the Great Bardfield Oxlip Project, which aims to restore this corner of Essex to its former glory.

HETEROSTYLY: ONE PLANT, TWO KINDS OF FLOWERS

Darwin's main interest in primulas was not in sorting out this centuries-old confusion, but in a peculiarity of their pollination system. The flowers of four of our primulas (the exception being the Scottish primrose) come in two distinct types called, when I was at school, 'pin-eyed' and 'thrum-eyed'. Pin-eyed flowers have a tall style which supports the stigma (the female part of the flower) high in the flower tube. The round head of the stigma, resembling the head of a pin, emerges from the centre of the flower tube. In thrum-eyed flowers the style is short and the wispy curls of the anthers (the pollen-producing male parts) poke out of the centre of the flower. Thrum was a term from the weaving industry. It was the fringe of the unwoven ends of a thread and the thrum-eyed flower has a similar untidy fringe at the centre of the flower.

In pin-eyed flowers, whilst the style is long, the filaments which support the anthers are short, so the anthers are buried deep in the flower tube. Conversely, in thrum-eyed flowers, in which the anthers are long, the style is short and so it's the stigma that's buried in the flower tube. Today they are most often referred to as short-styled and long-styled flowers, which is indeed how Darwin referred to them in a more obvious if less poetic description.

These different flower types had been known since the late sixteenth century,[5] some 300 years before Darwin became interested in them, though it was always assumed to be simply some form of normal variation between flowers. But Darwin's incisive and logical mind soon realized that there must be more to it than this. He already knew that this form of variation, which is called 'heterostyly' (Greek for 'different styles'), is not restricted to primulas, and we now know that some form of heterostyly occurs in twenty-eight different families of plants.[6] Darwin studied many of these, giving him material for one of the last books he wrote, *The Different Forms of Flowers on Plants of the Same Species* (1877).[7] Despite the variety of flowers that show heterostyly, large sections of this book were devoted to the British primulas, which are still the classic examples of heterostyly and which of course were convenient for Darwin to study both in the wild and in his garden.

This puzzle fascinated Darwin and piecing together evidence for the reasons behind it gave him, he confessed, as much pleasure as any of his other meticulous studies. And it also started an area of study that is still yielding fruits today. The value of his studies was certainly recognized at the time. In a tribute to Darwin published a year after his death, Alfred Russel Wallace (the co-discoverer of the mechanism of natural selection) saw it as important in eulogizing the great man's life to include a detailed summary of this book.[8] So what did Darwin make of this puzzle?

clip: the two cutaways – pin
d thrum.

He had already spent a great deal of time studying orchids and the devious methods they use to increase the likelihood of cross-pollination (see pages 206–310). It seemed to him that here was another mechanism for the same end. He observed that each individual plant has flowers of only one type and furthermore the stigma in long-styled flowers occupied the same relative position in the flower as the anthers in short-styled flowers, exposed at the mouth of the flower tube. And vice versa, the stigma and anthers are more or less in the same position, deep in the flower tube, in short-styled and long-styled flowers respectively. This exercise in three-dimensional flower geometry is a little confusing but hopefully the photographs above and to the left will make it a little clearer.

If a pollinator probes primula flowers, Darwin reasoned, it will pick up pollen in two places on its body, corresponding to the different positions of the anthers in long- and short-styled flowers. And as it continues to probe other flowers for nectar, pollen picked up from long-styled flowers will be in the right place to pollinate the stigma of short-styled flowers. And of course, the reverse is also true: pollen picked up from short-styled flowers, with anthers at the top of the flower tube, will be in the perfect place to pollinate the long-styled stigma, also emerging from the top of the flower tube. In other words, long-styled flowers can only pollinate short-styled flowers and vice versa, so favouring fertilization by an unrelated plant – exactly what a plant wants. In many plants out-crossing like this produces more vigorous offspring. It is a winningly simple and persuasive account of primula pollination. But there's a lot more to this than meets the eye.

Darwin also showed that if a long-styled flower was artificially cross-pollinated with another long-styled flower the plant produced only a few seeds. And artificially cross-pollinating short-styled flowers resulted in virtually no seed at all. So it's clearly not just the different arrangement of anthers and styles that prevents similar flowers from pollinating and fertilizing each other. Research over the following 150 years showed that although Darwin was – in some ways – more or less right, the story of primula pollination is far more complex and intriguing than he could have ever imagined.

Darwin studied these flowers in microscopic detail and realized that the position of the stigmas and anthers wasn't the only difference between the two types of flowers. We now know that there are six differences between long- and short-styled flowers, including the differences in style and anther length. In addition, long-styled stigmas are covered in long papillae, whilst those on the short-styled stigma are short. Long-styled flowers produce small pollen grains whilst those of short-styled flowers are much larger. The cells that make up the long style are much longer than those that make up the short style and the shape of the stigma is different, being domed in long-styled flowers and flattened in short-styled ones.[9]

These differences seem to be responsible for the incompatibility of same-flower crosses that Darwin documented through several different mechanisms. Long-styled pollen rarely sticks to a long-styled stigma, though if it does it can germinate. But the growing pollen tube, which normally extends down through the style to reach the egg cells, can't penetrate through the long papillae. Short-styled pollen landing on short-styled flowers rarely germinates at all, though it can be made to do so in artificially high humidity, suggesting that in nature it needs the long papillae of long-styled flowers to create high enough humidity levels to trigger germination. On the other hand, the germination of pollen from long-styled flowers is not so dependent on humidity.[10]

The blocking of same-flower pollen can also occur in the specialized tissue of the style[11] and in addition the anthers may also coat the pollen grains with a distinct chemical signal that allows the stigma to recognize the right and wrong sorts of pollen. So the prevention of same-flower crosses is controlled in several different ways apart from the different positions of stigmas and anthers.

And that means there's a big puzzle here. If there are other ways of ensuring cross-pollination that are distinct from the reciprocal arrangement of stigmas and anthers, what's the point of having two forms of flowers, especially since, as we'll discover shortly, there are some big disadvantages to heterostyly? And it might not even be that effective. While some modern studies suggest that Darwin was right and that heterostyly *does* make cross-pollination more likely, other studies suggest the opposite. Often large amounts of incompatible pollen are found on the stigmas of both kinds of flowers. Since this kind of arrangement has arisen independently in twenty-eight different families of plants, often with remarkable similarity, it must be doing something important. But, despite 150 years of research following Darwin's pioneering studies, we're still not entirely sure what that is.

Perhaps the principle function of heterostyly is to prevent self-pollination, with its associated problems of in-breeding, by physically separating the anthers from the stigma. If so, then its effectiveness differs between flower types. Most of the wrong sort of pollen grains on long-styled stigmas come from self-pollination.[12] It might seem that it should be the short-styled flowers, with their anthers held above the stigma, that would be more prone to self-pollination, as pollen can simply drop from the anthers on to the stigma. But this doesn't take into account the behaviour of pollinating insects. The exposed long-styled stigma inevitably comes into contact with all parts of a visiting insect's body and, as the insect withdraws its tongue, it will often rub off the pollen it's just picked up from the anthers of the same flower.[13] So heterostyly isn't that effective in preventing self-pollination.

Another suggestion is that rather than being a mechanism for promoting out-crossing, or at least limiting self-pollination, heterostyly is a mechanism to stop interference between the processes of pollen pick-up by a pollinator and pollen deposition.[14] This may also reduce the wastage of valuable pollen grains that end up on incompatible stigmas.[15]

And heterostyly does seem to confer other advantages. Recent detailed surveys of heterostylous plants have shown that in the long run heterostylous families of plants show a greater diversification of species. This effect comes from reduced levels of extinction within the group rather than rapid speciation, perhaps because heterostyly reduces the deleterious effects of in-breeding.[16]

Yet heterostyly comes with a serious health warning. In most populations long-styled plants and short-styled plants exist in roughly the same numbers and that means only half the local population is available for pollination. And it gets worse. In this country both cowslips and primroses are still fairly widespread and in places exist in large populations. But elsewhere in Europe the situation is not so rosy. In Belgium, for example, both species have shown rapid decline over recent years and remaining populations are often small. And having two incompatible types of plants means that these small populations are effectively just half their apparent size when it comes to the ability to find a mate and reproduce.

And in really small populations the proportion of long-style to short-style plants changes from 50:50. The smaller the population, the greater the impact of occasional chance events. So the unlucky destruction of a few short-styled plants in a tiny population might mean their extinction in that area.

It's also easier for random genetic changes to become established in such small populations (a process known as genetic drift). Together these changes can mean that, by pure chance, numbers of one form of the plant can be reduced in comparison to the other and that's exactly what has happened in the smallest populations in Belgium.[17] When one form outnumbers the other by more than 3:1 the reproductive success of that population falls. So small populations of heterostylous plants may be particularly vulnerable to extinction. Evolution, though, has found an intriguing way out of this dead end – the somewhat drastic solution of getting rid of heterostyly altogether.

Primroses are abundant on the open cliffs of St Abb's Head, Berwickshire.

Understanding how natural selection can do that depends on understanding the genetics behind heterostylous flowers, something that was unknown in Darwin's day. Indeed, it is one of the triumphs of Darwin's and Wallace's theory that when genetics was finally understood, it meshed perfectly with their theory of natural selection.

Darwin's and Wallace's theory depended on inherited characters being passed down the generations, though neither man had any idea of the mechanisms of such inheritance and some of Darwin's suggestions were well wide of the mark. DNA, the stuff we now know to be responsible,

might have been discovered eight years before Darwin published his work on primulas,* but its structure and significance had to wait first until 1944, when Oswald Avery and his colleagues demonstrated the role of DNA in inheritance, and then further until 1953, when Watson and Crick discovered the famous double helix structure of DNA. And it was later still that we gained understanding of exactly how genes work and how they are passed from generation to generation with the variations necessary to provide the raw material for natural selection.

We've already seen that apart from style and anther length there are several differences between long- and short-styled flowers. In total there are three genes responsible for controlling all these features and they sit very close together on the chromosome. Since they effectively work as one gene they are sometimes treated as one 'supergene'. Chromosomes exist in matched pairs, so each plant has two copies of the supergene. The supergene for short-styled flowers is dominant to the one for long-styled flowers (which is consequently called 'recessive'). It's as if the short-style supergene trumps the long-style one. So to produce long-style flowers, each chromosome must have identical copies of the recessive long-style supergene. On the other hand, short-style plants need only one copy of the dominant short-style supergene. They may well have a copy of the long-style supergene on the other chromosome of the pair but its effects are masked by the dominant gene and the flowers develop into short-styled ones.

Darwin was aware that variation in characteristics down the generations was a vital ingredient in his theory – so much so that he generally referred to his idea as 'descent with modification', though he had little idea how that variation was generated. One way, we now know, is during sexual reproduction, when the chromosomes of each matched pair swap bits along their length. Like the heterostyly supergene, genes can exist in two or more forms, each producing different characters, so swapping like this mixes up the different forms of each gene on each chromosome. Only one of each chromosome of the pair is passed on from each parent to their offspring, but thanks to this swapping it carries a combination of characters different from the parent's chromosomes.

But the closer together the genes sit the less likely they'll be separated

---

* In 1869 the Swiss scientist Friedrich Miescher isolated nucleic acids from the nuclei of white blood cells, paving the way for the identification of DNA as the carrier of genetic inheritance.

as the chromosomes swap bits along their length. The individual genes controlling flower type sit very close together, which is why the supergene works almost as a single gene. But just occasionally the molecular scissors that chop up the chromosomes manage to separate the individual elements of the supergene and recombine them.

In this way, a single flower might develop a long-styled stigma and short-styled anthers. In such a case, both anthers and stigma sit at the top of the flower tube, close enough to ensure self-pollination. And since the anthers are producing short-style pollen, it is perfectly compatible when it lands on the nearby long-style stigma.

This recombination of characters must be a rare chance event but it does happen. A few populations of primroses with such self-fertile flowers were discovered back in 1940, growing in the Chilterns and in Somerset and North Devon.[18] Since then more populations have been found in these areas.[19] In such places these plants (called homostyles) exist in mixed populations with normal long- and short-styled plants, though they often outnumber them. Homostyle populations have also been reported in Ireland, from Ballymaice in County Dublin.[20]

And the fact that all three forms exist together is more than a little curious. Homostyles are capable of self-fertilization and not surprisingly they frequently produce much more seed than heterostyles, since pollination with plenty of pollen grains is pretty much guaranteed. And homostyles can dispense with the services of pollinating insects, which in any case are often in short supply early in the year. In one set of experiments, homostyles and heterostyles were caged with and without insects. Homostyles set seed, and plenty of it, irrespective of whether they shared their cage with insects. On the other hand, heterostyles failed to set any seed in the absence of insects.[21]

So, in a mixed population homostyles should outcompete heterostyles by virtue of producing more seed, gradually replacing them. However, when those populations found in 1940 were surveyed again forty years later, no change in the proportion of homostyles to heterostyles was found to have taken place. Yet again a simple and elegant story turns out to be far more complex in reality. Somehow homostyle plants must have disadvantages that balance their advantages.

It's been suggested that since both stigma and anthers are exposed at the top of the flower tube, it's easier for slugs and snails to completely sterilize the flower by rasping away at both male and female parts.[22] And seed pods laden with numerous seeds might be targeted by hungry rodents more frequently than the less tempting seed pods of heterostyles. Yet detailed studies showed no difference in flower damage or seed predation between heterostyles and homostyles.[23]

But when these populations were looked at over a number of years, some differences did appear. In one year, as expected, self-fertilizing homostyles produced the most seed, but in another year, short-styled flowers out-produced both long-styled flowers and homostyles.[24] The differences seem to be down to the number of pollinators available to the heterostyles. Wet springs with few pollinators hand the advantage to self-fertilizing homostyles but in a year with plenty of active pollinators buzzing about, the advantage might swing to the heterostyles.[25]

The sheer number of seeds is not the whole story, however. Plants have limited resources, so those that produce lots of seed can only afford to make small ones. If enough pollen arrives to fertilize only a few seeds, then the plant can at least afford to make its seeds bigger by packing them with more food resources for the embryo. And not surprisingly, bigger seeds with better-provisioned embryos germinate and survive better.

Although the heterostyles need insects to reproduce, some botanists have suggested that, paradoxically, it's the poor pollinator years that give the heterostyles an advantage over the homostyles, by allowing them to produce fewer, larger seeds that will be more likely to grow into mature plants. In this scenario, variation in the abundance of pollinating insects from year to year creates a dynamic equilibrium. If this variable ever changes such that the advantage regularly lies with one system, then that system should come to dominate. And there's one kind of habitat where that has happened.

Scottish primrose near Dunnet Head, Caithness.

BIRD'S-EYE AND SCOTTISH PRIMROSES

So far we've said little about our two small pink-flowered primulas, the bird's-eye and Scottish primroses, though I have already alluded to the fact that the Scottish primrose is the odd one out. Like primroses, cowslips and oxlips, the bird's-eye primrose has long- and short-styled flowers, but the Scottish primrose is a homostyle – and it's a homostyle everywhere it grows. Although some genetic studies suggest that at least in theory a few long-styled plants could be produced, none have been found.[26]

To see this tiny but beautiful plant you'll have to travel to the north coast of Scotland or to Orkney – and that's its entire world distribution. The Scottish primrose is more Scottish than white heather or thistles. And it's perhaps the hardest of the British primulas to find, not because its intense mauve flowers don't stand out in the short turf, but because it grows on clifftop grasslands, along a spectacular coastline packed with distractions. Guillemots, razorbills and puffins arc out over the ocean from ledges and burrows below, fulmars soar on stiff wings and overhead both great and Arctic skuas cruise above these seabird cities looking for birds returning to breeding ledges with food for chicks. Like a fighter plane, a skua stoops on a heavily laden bird and pursues it, the skua following every twist and turn of its victim until in desperation the auk or gull drops its catch, which the skua deftly catches before it has even dropped a few feet.

Scottish primroses also grow in the rich grasslands that form behind coastal dunes. These are the 'machair' grasslands that develop on windblown sands and which are some of the most beautiful places in the country to explore. The most famous examples are on the western fringes

Below left and right: Bird's-eye primroses on Widdybank Fell in Teesdale, County Durham.

of the Outer Hebrides, particularly the Uists and Benbecula, where Atlantic gales have created vast areas of sandy flats. But there are some lesser-known, though no less spectacular, examples along Scotland's northern coast. Behind the dunes fringing Dunnet Bay is a magnificent expanse of machair – now a Coronation Meadow for Caithness (see page 221) – and here the distractions are botanical. Common twayblades grow in drifts, glowing a particularly intense shade of green when illuminated by an occasional shaft of sunlight. Banks of yellow kidney vetch spill over the drier patches whilst the deep-purple spikes of northern marsh orchids colour the wetter hollows. Your eye darts from the porcelain-white flowers of grass of Parnassus to the elegant lines of butterwort flowers held delicately above bright-green rosettes of insect-trapping leaves – from carpets of eyebrights to almost hidden frog orchids. And amongst all this are the delicate mauve flowers of the Scottish primrose.

It's closely related to the bird's-eye primrose, which itself is only found, in Britain at least, on the high fells of the northern Pennines and along the coast of north-east England, particularly on the Magnesian limestone of County Durham, home to many rare or intriguing plants. But the two species differ in their number of chromosomes.

Bird's-eye primrose has two sets of chromosomes, the normal condition. The Scottish primrose however has six sets. Plants frequently evolve new species by polyploidy, by doubling, tripling, quadrupling, or more, their basic complement of chromosomes. The Scottish primrose seems to have arisen from the bird's-eye primrose by tripling its chromosome number.[27, 28] Polyploidy also seems to confer hardiness on plants, and the more copies of the basic chromosome set, the hardier the plants seem to be (though there are other factors at work apart from the chromosome number).[29]

Globally, the ancestral bird's-eye primrose is the most widespread of any primrose species, growing across Europe and Asia to the shores of the north Pacific, south to the Altai and Tian Shan Mountains. It grows from sea level in County Durham to well over 5,000 metres (16,000 ft) in the Himalayas. And across this vast range, it seems to have given rise to several new species, by multiplying its basic chromosome number. And these hardier descendants were able to move further north still, to occupy land close to Ice Age glaciers. Seeds of the Scottish primrose have been found in Ice Age deposits in Cambridgeshire, which at the time would have put it close to the edge of the ice sheet itself.[30]

Other species probably had similar origins. *P. scandinavica*, which has four times the basic number of chromosomes, grows in the mountains of Scandinavia and *P. stricta*, which has seven times the number, is one of the hardiest of all species, growing in the high Arctic of Canada and Greenland. But all these species face a problem. Insects are few and far between in these harsh climates.

Fortunately, polyploidy gives them another advantage. It increases the rate at which chromosomes swap segments during sexual reproduction and therefore greatly increases the chances of producing a self-fertile homostyle flower. Being independent of pollinators is a huge advantage in these tough habitats.

Unlike the homostyle primroses in balmy Somerset, the Scottish primrose evolved and still lives in much harsher places where insect pollinators are often scarce. In these conditions heterostyles are easily outcompeted and the whole population switches to homostyly. Genetic studies suggest that polyploidy has arisen separately five times in this group of primulas and in four of those cases the plants have also switched to homostyly, which suggests a strong link between polyploidy and homostyly, creating hardy plants that don't need insects for pollination and so are ideally suited to colonize harsh northern or high altitude climates.

That said, the Scottish primrose is something of a wimp compared to related Arctic species. Its population falls dramatically after a sequence of hard winters, though after a run of mild winters it can spread and occasionally colonize habitats inland from its current strictly coastal distribution.[31] In fact, in times past there were a few permanent inland colonies, though these have long since disappeared with the decline of traditional land management. And it doesn't like hot summers either, which makes this fussy Scottish endemic something of a conservation problem.[32] It's virtually impossible to grow in cultivation and south of its usual haunts (which means virtually the whole of Britain) it rarely lives more than a couple of years, even though in the wild plants can live for thirty years. Perhaps that's why earlier botanists wrongly saw this plant as a biennial.[33]

It grows only in short, tightly grazed turf within sight and sound of the ocean and depends on traditional crofting methods for its survival. Where conditions are right there can be tens of thousands of plants, though 'improvements' to farming methods over the last few decades have meant that many such large populations have been lost.[34] Even in those remaining good sites, such as at Yesnaby on Orkney Mainland (one of the most studied populations of this plant) and even in good years, only around 20 per cent of the plants flower, usually only the largest and best-established ones. Since it can self-pollinate, a low density of flowering plants shouldn't necessarily affect seed set on individual healthy plants. Nevertheless, it seems that only in the best years can this species produce enough seed to maintain its population.[35]

Occasionally hoverflies visit the flowers, so where there are plenty of plants growing together there is a chance of cross-pollination. Such occasional out-crossing might produce genetically fitter individuals, and perhaps these 'super-fit' primroses form that small percentage of plants that flower and set seed.[36] But overall, individuals in all populations don't show much genetic diversity, perhaps because a single founding plant builds up the population largely by self-pollination, creating a genetically uniform swathe of plants. It may also be because the plants are all closely adapted to the same very particular habitat.[37] In either case, low genetic variability limits the plants' ability to respond to changes.

There is already evidence that this charming little plant is facing problems from climate change, but it may well have done so since the end of the Ice Age. During the Ice Age it occurred much more widely across Britain before retreating to its current position. Now, living where it does in the far north of Britain, it has nowhere else to go.

The related bird's-eye primrose is neither so restricted nor so fussy. In Britain it grows in two very different kinds of place: on the high fells of the Pennines and on lowland grasslands along the coast of north-east England; though in both cases it needs high levels of moisture in the soil. There are a few records of plants growing on dry banks or dry pastures,[38] but in my experience I always get wet knees while photographing this plant.

It grows in some abundance in the botanical hotspot of Widdybank Fell in upper Teesdale. Here its pink stars dot the grassland at the edge of streams or flushes, whilst on drier ground, drifts of mountain pansies, *Viola lutea*, look like swarms of tiny butterflies flying over the grass. And scattered around are the impossibly blue flowers of spring gentians, *Gentiana verna*. Add to that the occasional sight of merlins cruising over the hills and the plaintive songs and calls of golden plovers and it's easy to lose a whole day wandering over these fells.

The bird's-eye primrose, *P. farinosa*, gives its name to a whole group of primulas – the farinose primulas. 'Farina' is Latin for flour and refers to the whitish covering of the leaves. This is largely composed of a substance belonging to a family of chemicals called flavones, which often form pigment molecules. Flavones are responsible, among other examples, for the brown and orange colours in meadow and hedge browns and other butterflies in the same family. Pigments work by reflecting some wavelengths of light (giving them their colour) and absorbing others. Flavones are particularly good at absorbing ultraviolet radiation, which can be very damaging at high altitudes where higher levels can penetrate the thinner atmosphere. It may well be that the farina on the leaves of bird's-eye and other high-altitude primulas serves as a sunscreen to prevent damage by ultraviolet radiation, as has been suggested for other Alpine plants.[39]

It takes over an hour's drive from Widdybank Fell to reach populations of bird's-eye primrose growing at sea level near the coast of County Durham. These low-altitude plants still have a farina over their leaves, but they do look different. They have lighter green leaves rather than the grey-green leaves of the Pennine plants. They also differ in flowering time, the high-altitude plants flowering earlier. This may seem a little odd, since the northern Pennine climate is a lot colder than the coastal limestones of County Durham. However, the growing season at high altitudes is a lot shorter than in the lowlands. In this part of the world it's shortened by a full ten days for every 80 metres (262 ft) climbed.[40] So the Pennine plants can't afford to hang around; they need an early start. Some botanists think that these differences are enough to see the Pennine and coastal plants as different races of bird's-eye primrose.

In fact, this is a very variable plant right across its whole global range, though much of that variety is not genetic but merely due to growing in different conditions. However, in one population at least, growing on the Baltic island of Öland, flowering time seems to be genetically controlled.[41] And elsewhere in its range there are other genetic differences between different populations.

In the Alps, populations growing above 1,750 metres (5,740 ft) are distinct from those growing below that height. The two groups of plants are separated by forests growing at the tree line, with those populations above the tree line being genetically much more diverse. And like the populations on the Pennines and the Durham coast, they too differ in the time they flower.[42] Whether the two British populations belong to different genetic races is open to discussion, but in any case, even in its restricted range in Britain we can glimpse the variability of this plant that has allowed it to spawn so many new species.

Such a wide range of variability is common in plants with large ranges, as different sub-populations adapt to different conditions. And in the past such sub-populations of bird's-eye primroses became isolated then re-mixed as glaciers and ice sheets advanced and retreated during the Ice Age, creating ample opportunity for the birth of new species.

As if the presence of two different kinds of flowers in these primulas wasn't confusing enough, the bird's-eye primrose also varies as to whether it has a long or short flower stalk, at least in some populations. It's been well studied on the Swedish island of Öland in the Baltic, where these two distinct kinds of plants are clearly present.[43] Yet on the mainland bird's-eye primroses don't vary in this way. In Britain a variety with a short or non-existent stem has been recorded on Cronkley Fell in Upper Teesdale but no systematic studies have been done here.

Where they do exist, the two forms behave differently. The tall flowers, held above the surrounding vegetation, are more easily found by insects and generally these plants set more seed.[44] But curiously, the short-stemmed form even sets less seed when it is hand-pollinated and pollen is therefore no longer a limiting factor. So there must be more deep-seated differences between the two forms than just how conspicuous the flowers are. If the long-stemmed form is so much better at setting seed why doesn't it out-compete the short-stemmed one? Just as with the continued coexistence of homostylous and heterostylous primrose plants in Somerset and the Chilterns, there must be some disadvantage that offsets the long-stemmed form's greater seed-producing capabilities.

The seeds of bird's-eye primroses are eaten by moth caterpillars, in particular by a tiny moth called *Falseuncaria ruficiliana*. If the long-stemmed form is more conspicuous to pollinators it will probably also be more conspicuous to such seed predators. And long-stemmed plants are also more likely to be eaten by bigger predators – by grazing cows, for example.[45] So depending on the density of predators both large and small, the advantage swings from long-stemmed to short-stemmed forms, in the long term maintaining a balance between the two types. These effects vary from place to place and therefore so too does the proportion of short-stemmed plants in each population. It can vary from 3 to 74 per cent,[46] reflecting these different pressures in different places.

HYBRIDS

The natural history of our primulas is further complicated by their ability to hybridize. Cowslip, primrose and oxlip can all hybridize with each other, though with varying degrees of success. A number of different factors affect the ability of these different species to cross, but an obvious one is that the two parent species must occur close enough to each other such that pollinators can carry pollen from one to the other. In fact, all three of our yellow-flowered primroses have different ecological preferences which limits contact between them and therefore the likelihood of hybridization.

Oxlips are plants of central Europe, used to cold winters. In Britain they grow only in a small area of Suffolk, Essex and Cambridgeshire, the part of Britain with the most continental climate. Here they are further restricted to soils of chalky boulder clay.[47] They are not so restricted in Europe and generally they become more common the further east you travel.[48] The primrose, on the other hand, is a plant of western

Above: False oxlip flowers are halfway between those of their parents, a cowslip and a primrose.

Right: This false oxlip plant ha flowered in Lower Woods, South Gloucestershire, for ma consecutive years.

Europe, with its milder winters. In northern Europe, at least, primroses get scarcer as you travel east. Poland, for example, is home to some of the most spectacular forests remaining in Europe, yet primroses are rare plants.

Amongst these three species the oxlips are also the most tolerant to waterlogged soils. Primroses are the next most tolerant, followed by cowslips. Conversely, cowslips are the most drought tolerant.[49] Cowslips, therefore, are more usually found on dry open hillsides or meadows. Both primroses and oxlips grow in woodlands, but in the centre of the area where oxlips are common there are very few primroses, probably owing to its more continental climate. And even where they share a wood they usually grow in different places: the primrose preferring moist but not waterlogged soils whilst the oxlip is happy in soils that get very waterlogged in spring.

But even though the opportunities for hybridization are limited, it does happen. Oxlips and primroses produce a hybrid called *P. x digenea*, and at one time it was feared that such hybridization with primroses might be wiping out pure oxlips from their small range in Britain. This idea was first raised by Miller Christy in 1897, when he presented a paper

on oxlips and primroses in which he considered the 'modest and retiring Oxlip is, in this country at least, being gradually hybridized out of existence by the more aggressive Primrose'.[50] Only a few years after the oxlip was finally recognized as a distinct species its long-term survival in Britain was being questioned.

Although many aspects of Christy's paper would later be proved right, his gloomy prediction about the fate of oxlips now, happily, seems unfounded. In Knapwell Wood in Cambridgeshire, for example, in the 1930s, Henry and Doris Meyer found both primroses and oxlips. When they returned in 1947 they found that it was primroses that had decreased in abundance.[51] In the 1960s the woodland ecologist Oliver Rackham visited these woods to find primroses had vanished entirely.[52] A similar pattern was evident across many of the woods where both primroses and oxlips occurred. Oxlips had declined to some extent, but primroses far more so.

So oxlips don't seem to be in danger of being overwhelmed by primroses. Instead, the observed decline in oxlips has been due to loss of habitat. All the glorious oxlip meadows, such as those described by Henry Doubleday in his letters to Darwin, have been destroyed. Oxlips also fare badly in hot dry summers, and they suffer where they are heavily grazed by fallow deer. The long, hot summer of 1976, for example, reduced oxlip numbers drastically, though where they were protected from grazing they were able to make a good recovery.

Despite the changing fortunes of oxlips, in those areas in which they co-habit with primroses it is primroses that have declined more severely, at least up to the 1990s when Oliver Rackham collated observations made over many decades.[53] He thinks the primrose decline is down to a number of factors, all interacting in complex ways. One reason is undoubtedly our changing climate. There always has been a conspicuous hole in the otherwise ubiquitous distribution of primroses in parts of Cambridgeshire, a reflection of the plant's preference for an Atlantic rather than continental climate. This hole is generally filled with oxlips. It's only around the edges of the hole that oxlips and primroses occur together, though here the primroses must be on the edge of their comfort zone. Any change in climate towards a more continental one, the kind of effect expected from climate change, will favour oxlips over primroses.

One factor that Rackham doesn't consider important is the hybridization suggested by Miller Christy. Yet there is a twist in this tale. The hybrid *P. x digenea* hasn't really shown any dramatic increase and more importantly it doesn't seem to cross-breed with pure oxlips. Such back-crossing is the way in which primrose genes could slowly infiltrate themselves into the oxlip population, gradually diluting pure oxlip genes. At least that's what it looks like if you try to spot these backcrosses by their physical appearance, by a mixture of oxlip and primrose characters in one plant. This was the only way of recording backcrosses until fairly recently. But now, with the emergence of molecular studies, a new story is emerging. These techniques can reveal primrose genes invisible to field botanists and show that some primrose genes are present in a proportion of the oxlips where the two species occur together.[54]

Those oxlips shown by molecular analysis to contain some primrose genes are very variable, some being recognisable in the field, but many others being indistinguishable from pure oxlips. Clearly the degree of back-crossing has been underestimated, but does that mean Miller Christy was right after all? Probably not. There is no loss of fertility or seed production within this population of tainted oxlips when compared to woods with only pure oxlips, so it is unlikely that this is a major threat to the continued existence of oxlips in this country, certainly not in comparison to climatic effects or changes in woodland management.

Other factors affect the ability of primulas to hybridize – including the existence of the two forms of flowers in each species that we've already looked at in detail and which are thought to promote out-crossing. We've seen that the two forms of flowers are structured such that the anthers and stigmas overlap in relative position between the two different forms. Recently this matching of relative positions of reproductive organs has also been compared between primroses, oxlips and cowslips.[55] As might be expected, there is much less overlap in the positions of the reproductive organs within the same form (short- or long-styled) of flowers of different species. But this too varies. There is very little overlap between oxlips and primroses, a small though variable amount of overlap between cowslips and oxlips and most overlap between primroses and cowslips. This may well affect the ability of certain species pairs to hybridize. The relatively close match between cowslips and primroses suggests hybridization

low left: Pink primroses are casionally found in the wild, obably as a result of cross-llination with other bspecies or varieties from ewhere that are commonly own in gardens.

low right: Across their wide nge primroses come in a wide riety of colours but pale llow is the typical flower lour in the British Isles.

verleaf: Common primrose, *imula vulgaris* subspp. eboldii.

between this pair of species will be the easiest and indeed their hybrid, the false oxlip, is the most commonly found.

In Lower Woods Nature Reserve in Gloucestershire, I know of several spectacular clumps of false oxlips. This ancient woodland has wide grassy rides (locally called 'trenches') running through it which have a diverse grassland flora, including numerous cowslips. In the woodland on either side of the rides there are plenty of primroses and the proximity of the two parent species ensures a good chance of hybridization. These hybrids are long-lived, perhaps because they exhibit 'hybrid vigour', a common biological phenomenon in which hybrids show increased fitness. Each spring I wander along Horton Great Trench, the largest of the grassy paths through Lower Woods which once, in the seventeenth century, was the main road from Wotton-under-Edge to Bristol, to photograph a particularly large false oxlip. I have photographs dating back fifteen years and the plant was large and mature even then, so I have no idea how old it really is. False oxlips, which have primrose-like flowers held in a cowslip-like head of multiple flowers, are very attractive plants, so I have no plans to stop photographing this particular plant just yet.

Ecological and structural differences affect the likelihood of pollen from one species reaching the stigmas of another. But pollination is only the start of the story. For a hybrid to succeed it must germinate and grow and here too some hybrids do better than others. After pollination a primula's ovules must be fertilized just as is the case for animal eggs, by the joining together of two nuclei each containing one set of chromosomes to create the 'normal' cell nucleus with two sets of chromosomes. The cell can then go on to divide and produce an embryo. But the act of fertilization is a little more complicated in plants than it is in animals.

The pollen grain is actually a tiny organism, with several nuclei each containing one set of chromosomes. If pollination is successful, the pollen grain germinates and sends a long tube down the length of the style, the stalk that connects the stigma to the plant's ovary, often much deeper in the flower. Each pollen grain penetrates the ovary and releases its tiny nuclei. If one finds an egg cell, it fuses and combines its single set of chromosomes with those in the egg nucleus. But there are other cells nearby, which have the full complement of two sets of chromosomes (at least in the case of cowslips, primroses and oxlips). A pollen nucleus will also fuse with one of these to create a cell with three sets of chromosomes. Rather than dividing to create a multi-celled embryo, this cell grows into the endosperm, a tissue packed full of nutrients which will feed the growing embryo. This is the stuff we eat when we dine on large seeds such peas and beans; if you look carefully on your dinner plate you'll find a tiny pea embryo nestling between the two parts of the endosperm. Since its job is to feed the embryo, the rate of growth of the endosperm is matched to that of the embryo. The seeds of oxlips, primroses and cowslips develop at different speeds and that gives some hybrids a problem. For example, oxlip seeds develop slowly, whereas cowslip seeds develop much more quickly. So, if an oxlip provides the eggs (the seed parent) and a cowslip provides the pollen, the embryo will be half oxlip and half cowslip, but the endosperm will be two-thirds oxlip. This means that the endosperm grows at the oxlip speed, much slower than the developing half-and-half embryo. So part way through its development the embryo will starve and the seed will fail.

Similarly, in the more familiar primrose–cowslip cross, the embryo will fail if the primrose is the seed parent. False oxlips can only arise when a cowslip is the seed parent and the pollen comes from a primrose. So it matters which way the cross happens. Combined with the structural differences in the flowers of each species and the plants' ecological requirements it's a wonder any hybrids exist at all. Yet a quick look around your local garden centre says otherwise – row upon row of multicoloured varieties of garden primulas, all of them hybrids. The popular polyanthus probably originated as a primrose–cowslip cross before being further bred and 'refined'. These hybrids can also be further crossed with oxlips to create a triple hybrid called *P. x marbeckii*. This hybrid has occasionally been found in West Suffolk and Cambridgeshire, possibly as a natural triple hybrid or perhaps more likely from pollen arriving in an oxlip wood from nearby garden polyanthus.[56]

A walk in the woods might sometimes reveal a pink primrose, especially if you are walking in West Wales. Even without hybridization primroses vary in colour across their large range. The subspecies *P. vulgaris balearica* (in the mountains of Mallorca) and *P. v. atlantica* (in Algeria and Morocco) have white flowers, whilst *P. v. rubra* (in south-east Europe and Turkey) has red or purple flowers. The most spectacular, *P. v. heterochroma*, from the shores of the Caspian, comes in a veritable rainbow of colours, including purple, red, violet, white or the more familiar yellow. These subspecies have also been used in garden crosses to add more colour, and it's likely that the pink primroses of Wales have received pollen from one of these garden varieties.

SEEDS OF CHANGE

short-styled (or thrum-eyed) cowslip flower.

After pollination by the right sort of pollen and the successful growth of the embryo, the plant is then faced with the problem of dispersing its seeds. Primroses produce a structure on their seeds called an elaiosome – an organ filled with nutritious oils and fats as an inducement to ants to carry off the seeds. Often they bite off the elaiosome, but leave the seed some distance from the parent plant. However, like much else to do with these plants, the theory seems better than the practice. In one study, ants removed only 17 per cent of the seeds,[57] whilst in another the figure was only 22 per cent.[58] Rodents did a lot better, collecting around 70 per cent of the seeds. Ants generally only moved the seeds a few metres at best. Rodents carried their harvested seed capsules further, so may be the more effective dispersers of primrose seed. They store around a third of their harvest, so it's not unusual to find clumps of young plants around rodent burrows.[59] Ants, though, do their bit, and it's sometimes possible to find clumps of plants around ant nests too.

Oxlip and cowslip seeds don't produce elaiosomes, so must rely on wind for dispersal. Seed dispersal in oxlips has been measured and not surprisingly found to be very poor.[60] In fact, it may be in the interests of oxlips and primroses to limit the dispersal of their seeds. Seedling survival is generally low, but often those that germinate near their parents do better, probably because the local soil conditions suit them – otherwise their parents wouldn't be growing there in the first place.[61] Modelling the growth of primrose populations on a computer lends supports to this idea. In a virtual woodland long-distance dispersers were more likely to end up in dense woodland, conditions inimical to primrose seedlings.[62] So short-range dispersal is probably a safer bet.

Primrose seedlings do best in open, well-lit conditions, different from the optimum habitat of their parents in more closed woodland. This makes primroses, along with oxlips, ideally suited to life in coppiced woodland. In traditional coppices the understorey, usually hazel, was cut off at ground level and left to re-sprout over the following decades, their multiple stems providing valuable poles for building and fencing or for making charcoal. A scattering of larger trees (standards) was left to provide shelter for the growing shrubs. Different blocks of woodland were felled at different times, so in a large coppiced woodland there were always patches in different stages of growth.

Primrose seedlings germinated in newly cleared areas, then the maturing woodland provided humidity and shelter for the older plants. When these plants set seed there was always a newly cleared area nearby to provide a nursery for their seedlings. The growth and flowering of both primroses and oxlips declines as the woodland grows thicker, but under traditional management it's never too long before the woodland is opened up again to create the perfect conditions. In the years following coppicing there is often a dazzling display of woodland flowers. The decline in this form of traditional management has meant a decline not just of primroses[63] and oxlips[64] but of many woodland plants. And with the departure of the plants, many once familiar woodland insects that depend on these plants for food have disappeared also.

The caterpillars of the Duke of Burgundy fritillary, *Hamearis lucina*, feed on the leaves of primroses or cowslips, but only those in a particular condition. They prefer lush, vigorous plants with large leaves.

In woodlands primroses reach this condition in the year or two after coppicing. So the Duke of Burgundy is usually absent in coppiced sections of the wood the year immediately after coppicing but becomes common for two to three years after that. After five years have passed the primroses are too shaded. They are weaker plants and unattractive to this demanding little butterfly. So the decline of coppicing has seen a dramatic fall in the population of the little Duke.

The Duke of Burgundy also feeds on cowslips growing on scrubby grassland. Again it prefers vigorous plants. Cowslip seedlings establish well in open ground, such as that created by cows when they trample the grasslands to mud during the winter. Before these plants are once again swamped by grasses and other taller plants, they reach the perfect condition for Duke of Burgundy fritillaries. So in both woodland and scrub, managing these sites for healthy primroses and cowslips also boosts numbers of this rare butterfly.

We might have only five species of native primulas but their intriguing natural history has kept botanists busy since the days of Charles Darwin; and puzzles remain over many aspects of the lives of these plants. And that's the real beauty of nature. It was the humble primrose that first opened my eyes to the fact that there was a lot more joy in nature than just ticking off those animals or plants that you've seen. As a schoolboy I was an avid birdwatcher, bug hunter and reptile collector and then my biology teacher introduced the class to the intriguing existence of the pin-eyed and thrum-eyed flowers of primroses. Until that point I'd seen natural history and biology as two separate subjects – one to enjoy, the other to endure.

But the next time I was wandering through the spring woodlands fringing the North Yorkshire Moors, close to my childhood home, I took time out from looking for dippers and adders and peered closely into the flowers of primroses. Yes, it was true. Some plants had pin-eyed flowers, some thrum-eyed. Astounding! Biology clearly happened outside the classroom. And what was true for primroses was almost certainly true for the rest of biology. Suddenly there was even more fascination in nature, just as Darwin had discovered when he admitted that he'd enjoyed his studies of primulas as much as anything else he'd done.

IO

Orchids

ORCHIDACEAE

As far as I'm concerned all plants have their own particular beauty and fascination, but I know I'm not alone in thinking that there's something extra special about the orchid family. Perhaps it's those outrageously colourful and extravagant blooms of tropical hybrids, bred for instant impact. For the more discerning, it might be those rare and exotic species growing hidden in remote tracts of tropical swamps or rainforests. Or perhaps it's the exuberant diversity of this family of plants, a feature that was hammered home to me with striking clarity while I was shooting a film on orchids in 2013. I had travelled to the rainforests cloaking the slopes of Mount Kinabalu in Borneo, reputed to be one of the world's hotspots for orchids. And it didn't disappoint. There were orchids everywhere – trees draped with so many, in bewildering variety, that it looked as if their weight would break the branches. A local botanist who'd been clambering over Kinabalu for decades told me there are close on 900 species on this one mountain alone. I left with my head spinning from such overwhelming diversity.

Our mere fifty-two or so British species might seem a little under-whelming in comparison, but that's far from the truth.[1, 2] They possess just as much mystique as their tropical relatives – a touch of the exotic on our downs, in our woodlands and increasingly along our roadside verges. And anyone who shares this enthusiasm for these special plants is in good company. After completing *On the Origin of Species* (1859), Charles Darwin's next book was entirely devoted to orchids, and full of wonderfully detailed studies that supported his insights into evolution by natural selection that he'd outlined in the *Origin*.[3] And more than that, his work on orchids expanded his ideas on how evolution might work and won over more of his contemporaries, who were initially scep-tical of the mechanisms he presented in the *Origin*.[4] The American bot-anist Asa Gray (1810–88) perhaps best summarized the importance of Darwin's orchid book. Gray had a mind that was open to evidence-based science but he was also a staunch believer that nature's marvels displayed the hand of a creator God. Yet of Darwin's orchid work, he wrote '[had] the orchid book appeared before the *Origin* the author would have been canonized not anathemised by the natural theologians.' Orchids helped consolidate the single most important idea in biology.

I've been fascinated by orchids for as long as I can remember and, over the years, the more time I spent looking for them and reading about them, the more I realized that this fascination boils down to three aspects of orchid natural history; the alluring rarity of some orchids, the sheer number of orchid species – and sex, which has driven the evolution of spectacular and complex flowers. This family of plants illustrates evolution in action in ways undreamed of by Darwin.

THE POLLINATION GAME I – HONEST ORCHIDS

Darwin was drawn to the close study of orchids byt the way the many strange and varied ways in which they go about making more orchids, particularly the lengths they go to in achieving cross-pollination. He wrote:

> In my examination of orchids, hardly any fact has struck me so much as the endless diversity of structure for gaining the very same end, namely the fertilization of one flower by another.

And he soon discovered that orchids are different from most other plants in that they pack all their pollen into two (or more in some tropical genera) distinct structures called pollinaria. Each pollinarium consists of a cohesive mass of pollen (the pollinium) and a stalk or caudicle at the base of which is a sticky pad of glue (the viscidium). These structures are easily seen in the bee orchid, *Ophrys apifera*, for example, where they

mmon twayblades and
en-winged orchids.

dangle like two tiny yellow sausages in the centre of a fresh flower.

Orchids have, in essence, put all their eggs into one basket – or at least all their pollen into two pollinia, which is almost as bad. It gives them a major problem. A pollinating insect can pick up all the pollen produced by that flower in a single visit and if it doesn't visit another orchid of the same species then all of that flower's pollen is lost. The opposite extreme is adopted by plants like grasses. They produce vast amounts of dust-like pollen which the wind blows everywhere (including into our sensitized nostrils). It's down to chance whether a pollen grain finds a receptive stigma of the right species. But grasses release so much pollen that a few grains are almost certain to find their way to other flowers of the same species. An orchid can't afford to leave anything to chance. It must ensure as best it can that its precious pollinaria get to another flower of the right species and that means, as many other plants have done, enlisting the help of animals.

A single flower of a lizard orchid shows the extremes to which orchids can modify th petals, especially the lip.

The first hurdle for any plant to overcome is persuading animals to act as go-betweens. In most plants this is done by displaying brightly coloured petals or sepals to advertise a reward of sugar-rich nectar and encourage willing volunteers. As a visiting insect helps itself to nectar, it is dusted in pollen from the anthers. With a bit of luck it will eventually visit another flower of the same species, dusted with enough pollen to allow the insect to effect pollination. This is an honest transaction. Insects are rewarded for their help, either with sugary nectar for instant energy or by keeping some of the protein-rich pollen load. Female bees, for example, collect nectar for flight fuel and pollen to feed their growing larvae.

Some orchids, like the common twayblade, *Neottia ovata*, adopt this honest system, though their advertising budget seems a little tight. The common twayblade is as different from those flamboyant tropical orchids as it's possible to be. It has a spike of small, green and very inconspicuous flowers – or at least inconspicuous to us. Spend some time lying on your belly with your nose pressed up close to one of these fairly common orchids and you'll see a whole array of insect visitors that seem to have no difficulty finding the flowers.

While lying on your belly, you might also notice the characteristic structure of orchid flowers. Orchids have several peculiarities in their genetic code that allows individual petals and sepals to evolve in entirely separate ways. The existence of this so-called 'orchid code' has allowed orchid flowers to develop an array of forms more varied – and often

more bizarre – than other families of plants.[5] In particular, the lower petal – the lip – has taken on all manner of shapes and textures. The twayblade's lip is a long, tongue-like structure, forked at the bottom. Running down the centre, there's a groove that glistens in the sunlight. Touch it and you'll find it's sticky. The flower produces nectar, which then simply oozes down the grooved lip.

The even more inconspicuous lesser twayblade, *N. cordata*, and the bird's nest orchid, *N. nidus-avis*, belonging to the same genus, all more or less do the same thing and all have many and varied insect visitors.

Small insects land on the lip (one of its functions is simply as a landing platform) and then work their way along it, sucking up the nectar as they go. Like a trail of breadcrumbs, the nectar leads the insect into the centre of the twayblade flower where it bumps into the pollinaria. At the base of each pollinarium is a blob of quick-setting glue, and as the insect triggers sensitive hairs around the pollinarium's base, the glue packet explodes and attaches the pollinaria to the insect. For small bugs, like ichneumon wasps, the pollinaria may be nearly the same size as the insect and the surprise explosion is more than enough to send the insect on its way, fuelled by the twayblade's sugary offering, hopefully, to find another twayblade.

Any flower with accessible nectar attracts a wide range of insects. In the case of the *Neottia* orchids this includes small flies, ichneumon wasps and small beetles. But there is no guarantee that, with lots of different kinds of plants producing equally attractive nectar, these insects will ever visit another orchid of the right species. And if they don't, all that pollen is wasted. On top of that, such a handy source of nectar also attracts insects that aren't such good pollinators. I once watched a thick-legged flower beetle, nearly the same size as the orchid flower, guzzling nectar from flower after flower along the spike, seemingly oblivious as more and more pollinaria were glued to its head. Eventually, it had pollinaria stuck on top of pollinaria, extending out from its head like bright yellow antlers. Finally, its strange ornaments began to impede its nectar guzzling, but the beetle was big enough simply to rip off the pollinaria with its front legs, dropping them to the floor. Again, all the pollen from each of the flowers it had visited was wasted.

Yet twayblades are common and widely distributed, so the system, which looks a bit hit-and-miss to our eyes, seems to work well for the orchid. Presumably the sheer number of visiting insects increases the chances of successful cross-pollination.

Even so, some orchids have evolved to attract a more exclusive and loyal clientele – by making the nectar harder to reach. Our two butterfly orchids (the greater, *Platanthera chlorantha*, and the lesser, *P. bifolia*) and the fragrant orchid (now split into three closely related *Gymnadenia* species – see page 335) have long, thin tubes or spurs a centimetre or two long, extending from the back of the flower. They only produce nectar towards the tip of this spur, so only long-tongued insects like butterflies and moths can reach it. And since such insects have a more exclusive supply of nectar, free from competition from other insects, it makes sense for them to favour these orchids over other plants – which is just what the orchid wants.

The two species of butterfly orchids produce their nectar in the evenings, so their name is something of a misnomer. Instead they attract long-tongued moths and I always feel that one of their older names – 'white angel' – is not only more accurate but far more evocative. Their pale flowers do seem to shine with an unearthly glow at dusk, presumably making them conspicuous to moths as darkness falls.

Greater butterfly orchids.

The best way to tell the lesser butterfly and greater butterfly orchids apart is to compare their pollinaria: in the case of the lesser they lie parallel in the flower; in that of the greater they splay outwards towards the bottom. But the two species are also said to differ in the length of their spurs, the lesser butterfly orchid having a shorter spur. This, so the story goes, is a neat trick to avoid cross-pollination. The different-length spurs attract different moths, with shorter-tongued moths favouring lesser butterfly orchids. Indeed, the greater butterfly orchid is said to have evolved from the lesser by a mutation that increased spur length, thus attracting different pollinators and effectively isolating the long- and short-spurred forms as the different species we see today.[6]

Darwin was well aware that such intimate adaptations lent great support to his theory of evolution by natural selection. It was why he was always excited by the arrival of new specimens, although none more so than a species of comet orchid that he received from Madagascar. In a letter to his friend, the botanist Joseph Hooker, he wrote:

> have just received such a Box full from Mr Bateman with the astounding Angræcum sesquipedalia with a nectary a foot long— Good Heavens what insect can suck it.

The nectary that Darwin referred to is a flower spur similar in structure to those of the butterfly orchids but far longer. It is such a strange flower that it piqued Darwin's curiosity and as I read his words, I too found it hard to imagine the reason behind such an extreme feature. So I tracked down an orchid enthusiast who grew this same species and he promised to call me should his precious specimen flower. Several months later the call came through and I was soon ringing the doorbell of a very ordinary-looking house on a council estate in Gloucester. Several greenhouses were squeezed into the small garden, each crammed with an astounding diversity of orchids. And there, occupying pride of place on the central stage of one greenhouse was a flowering comet orchid. It was easy to see how it acquired its common name as its huge spur tailed out behind the flower. I also understood Darwin's puzzlement. An insect would need an unbelievably long tongue to reach the nectar reward. Darwin knew that some of the longest-tongued insects in Britain are hawkmoths, but none came close to being able to reach the comet orchid's nectar. After examining his specimen, he wrote:

> It is, however, surprising that any insect should be able to reach the nectar: our English sphinxes [hawkmoths] have probosces

as long as their bodies; but in Madagascar there must be moths
with probosces capable of extension to a length of between ten
and eleven inches.[7]

And he was right. Many years after his death, just such a moth was discovered, a subspecies of Morgan's sphinx moth, *Xanthopan morgani praedicta*, its subspecific name honouring Darwin's bold yet accurate prediction. For my orchid film I knew I had to include this extraordinary story, so I contacted scientists working with this orchid species in Madagascar. After many sleepless and uncomfortable nights in the rainforest, with remote cameras trained on flowering comet orchids, they captured a scene that would have made Darwin weep with joy. A Morgan's sphinx moth approached the flower and unfurled an impossibly long tongue. Somehow it had complete control over a hair-thin, 30-centimetre-long (12 in) tongue. It hovered in front of the flower and delicately inserted the tip of its tongue into the flower, then flew forwards, sliding its tongue to the bottom of the spur. The scientists who recorded this were just as excited as Darwin would have been. They leapt for joy when they replayed the video footage. Morgan's sphinx moth is the only pollinator of this kind of comet orchid, the two species so closely co-adapted that they are now dependent on each other, bound together by their extreme adaptations.

Lesser butterfly orchid.

But the story is not so clear cut with butterfly orchids. A meticulous survey of the two species in 2008 showed spur length in both species changes with latitude.[8] In addition, if a flower is removed the flower above it on the stalk will grow a bigger lower lip, suggesting that some aspects of flower size also depend on what resources the plant can make available to each flower.[9] And, although the story has it that the different spur lengths attract different moths, there must be some crossover, since hybrids exist between the two species (although some apparent hybrids may simply be aberrant forms of one or other of the species). Detailed field observations also confound armchair theorizing. Quite a few different kinds of moths have been identified pollinating these orchids, so the neat idea of very specific pollinators co-adapted to each species in the manner of the Madagascan comet orchid probably needs rethinking.

However, as we've already noted, the arrangement of the pollinaria is diagnostically different in these two species, and that means that they generally end up attached to different places on a visiting moth – on its proboscis in the case of the lesser butterfly orchid and on the eyes in

the case of the greater. That might help to isolate the two species. But it's equally possible that these two orchids may not even be different species at all. Despite the reasonably consistent differences in the way the pollinaria are arranged, it's very difficult to tell the two of them apart at the molecular level. This lack of genetic difference indicates that there must still be a lot of mixing of genes between the two 'species', again suggesting that their pollinators are not all that faithful to each kind of orchid. So perhaps we should see the lesser and greater butterfly orchids as one and the same species.[10] When similar ideas were put forward in the nineteenth century, long before genetic analysis was ever dreamed of, Darwin could not have disagreed more forcefully:

> *The two forms differ in a large number of characters, not to mention general aspect and the stations inhabited... these two forms certainly differ from one another more than do most species belonging to the same genus.*

For the time being, the current crop of field guides agree with Darwin. Perhaps in our two butterfly orchids we are witnessing the early steps in the evolution of a new species. An almost imperceptible genetic change has changed the arrangement of the pollinaria, perhaps enough of a difference to begin to isolate the two kinds, allowing more substantial differences in their genetics to evolve and so create a greater divergence as time passes.[11]

Darwin worked out many of the intricate mechanisms employed by orchids in their attempts to get pollinaria from one flower to another, but even he didn't guess at some of the most extraordinary adaptations. And one reason for this was that he flatly refused to believe that some orchids could be deceitful.

THE POLLINATION GAME II — DECEITFUL ORCHIDS

Many decades before Darwin's work a German scientist, Christian Sprengel (1750–1816), in a snappily titled book, *The Secret of Nature Discovered in the Form and Fertilization of Flowers*, put forward the notion that many orchid flowers don't give their pollinators a reward of nectar at all. His ground-breaking work was largely ignored or ridiculed by his contemporaries. Much later, Darwin would praise Sprengel's meticulous studies, but he too simply refused to believe that some orchids didn't provide nectar for their pollinators. Insects, he assumed, were far too smart to fall for 'so gigantic an imposture'.[12] And surely he has a point? Since many pollen-eating insects, when presented with pollen that is packed tightly into pollinia, seem to find the prospect unappetizing, why on Earth would they bother to visit nectarless orchid flowers? There just isn't anything in it for them.

But this time Darwin was wrong. We now know that a great many plants have flowers that don't produce nectar. However, it is the orchids who have embraced this strategy in a big way. Nectarless flowers have evolved in 7,500 species of plants in 32 different families but, of this number, fully 6,500 species belong to just one family – the Orchids.[13] And the only way such flowers can attract insects is by deception.

That deception can take many forms. The strange-looking tongue orchids, *Serapias*, seem to attract their pollinators by presenting them with an inviting opening in the centre of the flower that looks like a burrow. One species of tongue orchid, the small-flowered tongue orchid, *S. parviflora*, may be a newly colonizing native in Britain (see pages 314–15), but several other species occur further south in Europe. Observations on the long-lipped tongue orchid, *S. vomeracea*, in Israel, suggest that this species provides an overnight shelter for its pollinating bees. In late afternoon female solitary bees usually take shelter in their nest holes for

A display of sword-leaved helleborines at Chappetts Copse in Hampshire.

the night, but since the males don't make their own holes, they have to make do with old beetle holes or similar nooks and crannies. And many of them crawl into the flowers of this tongue orchid. Although the 'hole' looks enticing from the outside, it's blocked on the inside by the orchid's reproductive structures, making it uncomfortable for the bee. So the males move from flower to flower to find one where they can settle down for the night, and in doing so move pollinaria between flowers. Eventually, as night falls, they make do with squeezing into the flower as best they can. The orchid provides no nectar or edible pollen, but it does reward the bee with central heating. In the morning, the flower traps heat like a miniature greenhouse, warming the sleeping bees so they can make an early start.[14]

Orchids have evolved some very ingenious ways to deceive insects. The sword-leaved helleborine, *Cephalanthera longifolia*, is a widespread plant, occurring in Scotland and Wales as well as in England, but its populations are scattered and often very small, so it's not always easy to find. The only exception that I know is at Chappetts Copse in Hampshire, where several thousand sword-leaved helleborines grow in a spectacular display. A close look inside its tubular white flowers will reveal a bright-yellow mass of filaments. This is not the plant's pollen but the yellow colour and texture seems to mimic the appearance of soft, powdery pollen, a draw particularly for female bees looking for pollen to feed their growing brood.[15]

The much commoner white helleborine, *C. damasonium*, is likewise often an elusive plant. I usually see it in beechwoods on lime-rich soils, especially near clearings or along the edges. Beechwoods on the Downs, the Chilterns and Cotswolds are all good places to look. The porcelain-white flowers of this orchid barely open, but again if you part the petals you'll see a dusting of what looks like pollen on the inside. However, the white helleborine is largely self-pollinated, which rather goes against the idea that the yellow dusting in the flowers of this species is a pollen-mimic evolved to attract insects. But insects sometimes visit the flowers of the white helleborine and may assist the orchid in its reproduction by triggering the pollinia to attach to the nearby stigma.

Darwin observed these two helleborine species closely and occasionally found that the yellow filaments had been nibbled, suggesting that they might indeed fool bees. However, David Roubik, a contemporary expert on tropical bees, who has spent many long hours observing stingless bees in Panama, has never seen any of them try to gather 'false pollen' from

Left: The yellow crumbly texture inside a sword-leaved helleborine flower may be 'false pollen' serving as a lure to female bees.

Above: Sword-leaved helleborine.

the wide array of supposedly pollen-deceptive orchids in these diverse rainforests.[16] So whether this yellow powdery texture really is a deceit on the part of the orchid is still open to question.

The third and by far the rarest of our *Cephalanthera* orchids has taken a different approach. The red helleborine, *C. rubra*, is also a dweller in beechwoods, at least in this country. In Spain and France I've seen tall and robust flower spikes of this species growing like weeds along roadside verges, but here in England it is confined to just three woodland sites: Workman's Wood in Gloucestershire, Windsor Hill in Buckinghamshire and Hawkley Warren in Hampshire. These sites were all once closely guarded secrets though since they are now easily found on the internet, I don't feel like I'm breaking any confidences in naming them. In all these places it sometimes fails to flower at all. And when it does flower it is often less than imposing. I've seen it in bloom in Workman's Wood where it produced far fewer flowers than the impressive spikes in continental Europe, characteristic of a plant struggling on the edge of its geographical range.

When it does flower here, its main pollinators are now people. Trying not to leave anything to chance, conservationists hand-pollinate any red helleborines that bloom, a tactic that seems to work. In the ten years up to 2007, prior to hand-pollination, the Buckinghamshire plants produced just one mature seed pod, but with a helping hand, four seed pods were produced in 2007 alone. The red helleborine now has the most efficient and loyal pollinator possible, though even the most ardent of Darwinian evolutionists would not suggest that this is what nature intended! However, the truth is even stranger.

In Britain red helleborine flowers are visited mainly by one particular kind of bee, *Chelostoma campanularum*, though not by females as might be expected if these orchids were, as has been suggested for their cousins, using false pollen as a lure. Instead it's the males of *C. campanularum* that enter the flowers. As implied by their scientific name, female *C. campanularum* collect their pollen from bellflowers, *Campanula* spp., and males visit those same bellflowers to find females. So, somehow, male bees seem to be confusing bellflowers and red helleborines. To our eyes, although the flowers are of vaguely similar shapes, they are distinctly different in colour, but bees don't see the world in the same way we do. They are sensitive to ultraviolet wavelengths and seen in this light, bellflowers and red helleborines do look very similar. The red helleborine is a mimic of the bellflower and male *Chelostoma* bees are fooled into entering red helleborine flowers in their search for mates.[17]

But how effective is this method of pollination if the Buckinghamshire helleborines only managed to set one seed pod in ten years until humans stepped in? In Europe those more robust spikes of red helleborines draw in many more kinds of bees among which are two other species of *Chelostoma*, including the much bigger *C. nigricornis*, and this latter species seems to be the most effective pollinator. *C. campanularum* is just too small to pick up the helleborine's pollinaria effectively.[18] Unfortunately, *C. nigricornis* doesn't occur in Britain, which explains the poor seed set and is perhaps one reason why red helleborines struggle to survive here.

Elsewhere in Europe this form of deceit seems to be successful. And, in addition, the red helleborine has found a way of forming a more exclusive relationship with just a few kinds of bees, greatly increasing the chances that its pollinators will carry its pollinaria to other red helleborines (or, of course, to bellflowers, in which case the pollinia will be wasted).

Most flowering plants use generalist pollinators and are visited by lots of different species. Because they produce large quantities of loose pollen they are less worried (in an evolutionary sense) about their pollinators being faithful. But the deceptive orchids, with their precious pollinaria, have developed more intimate relationships with a smaller number of insects which hopefully will prove more faithful to each species of orchid.[19] The most effective way of bringing this about is by sexual deception, of the sort practised by red helleborines. Other species, however, found even more fiendish ways to fool insects looking for love.

THE POLLINATION GAME III — SEXUAL DECEIT

The bee orchids, *Ophrys*, have developed sexual deceit to a fine art. One of these, the early spider-orchid, *O. sphegodes*, has been studied intensively and has revealed an incredible intricacy wrought by natural selection. Had he known about what this group of orchids get up to, Darwin would have been impressed.

Early spider-orchids grow like weeds in parts of continental Europe. Around the Mediterranean they grow in lush clumps, each tall spike bearing ten or more individual flowers. Despite their striking appearance, they are responsible for more personal disappointments than any other

orchid. There are many *Ophrys* species around the Mediterranean, including some rare kinds confined to very small areas. I've travelled around many Mediterranean countries in search of these scarce *Ophrys* and I've lost count of the number of times I've found an apparently unfamiliar *Ophrys* on some remote, garrigue-covered hillside, only to have the thrill of discovery evaporate as I look more closely and discover it is yet another variation on the broad theme of *O. sphegodes*.

In Britain the situation is reversed and the thrill undiminished by finding an early spider. They are not at all common in this country, scattered across a few sites in the south. In the past the best place to see them in any numbers was on the cliffs of Dorset's Isle of Purbeck, around Durlston Head and west towards Dancing Ledges. And this is still an undeniably beautiful place to photograph them. But their most impressive stronghold is now on a site that is essentially an industrial landscape.

Early spider orchid.

In 1988 work began in earnest on the Channel Tunnel in Kent (after many abortive attempts dating back to the nineteenth century). Those digging from the British side found themselves with nearly 5 million cubic metres of excavated chalk needing a new home. Even as early as 1843 a chalk platform had been created at the base of Dover's famous white cliffs to provide a route for the Dover to Folkestone railway. During earlier attempts to dig a channel tunnel in the 1870s and 1880s, the dumping of chalk spoil had led to this platform being extended. In the 1980s it was chosen as the most suitable site to dump the chalk from the latest excavations under the Channel. Thus did Samphire Hoe, the newest part of Kent, come into being. And shortly after its creation, early spider-orchids moved in from the adjacent cliffs.

Now several thousand early spiders grow in the thin chalky soil, the largest British colony, some nearly reaching the stature of their Mediterranean cousins. And all these orchids are pollinated by a single kind of bee – a mining bee, *Andrena nigroaenea* (although recent research in Italy has demonstrated that early spider-orchids there are more frequently visited by another *Andrena, A. bimaculata*).[20]

Andrena belongs to the often-overlooked majority of bees, the solitary bees, who, as their name suggests, don't form large social colonies like honeybees or bumblebees. For her nest, a female *Andrena* digs a tunnel in sandy soil, off which she constructs several side chambers, each one waterproofed with a secretion from a gland (Dufour's gland) in her abdomen and then stocked with pollen and a single egg. Mining bees often form buzzing colonies of thousands of individuals, but don't let this fool you into thinking they are social. The right consistency of soil is critical for successful tunnel-digging, so suitable areas often attract large numbers of bees. However, they are all working alone, labouring on their own nests and provisioning for their own offspring. Once all the chambers are stocked with pollen and an egg, the female bee seals the nest and that's the last contact she'll have with her offspring.

After hatching, the larva grows in solitary confinement, slowly munching its way through the pollen mass until it is fully grown. It then pupates and, shortly afterwards, the adult bee emerges. Each bee sits tight in its cell through the cold winter months and in the early spring begins to dig its way out, just as the early spider-orchids are beginning to flower.

Once on the surface, male and female bees need to find each other. The most common form of long-distance communication amongst insects is chemical – pheromones released by the female that drift on the wind. So potent are these chemicals that only a few molecules will trigger sensors on a male's antennae and send it flying upwind, tracking the pheromone to its source.

There are around sixty-five species of *Andrena* bees in the UK, some of them so similar that it requires a microscopic examination of their genitalia to distinguish them. The bees themselves also need a way to tell each other apart and, without the option of a microscope, they do it by smell. The pheromone released by a female is actually a concoction of several dozen chemicals, each of which can trigger a response in a male's antennae. But this cocktail of chemicals is different in different species, giving males a foolproof way of distinguishing species that to our eyes are virtually identical. Well, almost foolproof.

A male *A. nigroaenea* following a pheromone plume of the correct cocktail for his species might well find himself landing on the seductively hairy lip of an early spider-orchid. A recent analysis has shown that early spider-orchids produce twenty-four different chemicals, all of which trigger a reaction in male bees[21] and which are a close match for the chemical mix released by females. The males are so convinced that they often attempt to copulate with the flower and, in their frenzy, they pick up the orchid's pollinaria. Botanists and entomologists call this 'pseudo-copulation'; bees call it a waste of time.

Orchids have become so good at fooling insects that it creates a major problem for their hapless victims. After all, a male bee needs to spend his short, precious life mating with females of his own species, not orchid flowers. Surely natural selection would have found a way to equip the male bee with the ability to tell the difference between the two? But the orchid is exploiting another aspect of bee biology.

The chemical communication system of all solitary bees is so effective that it doesn't take long for a virgin female to be discovered. In those species that do nest in loose colonies, the females are quickly pounced on by so many males that you can watch balls of bees rolling over the ground. Somewhere in the middle of this mass, a lucky male might well be engaging the complex lock-and-key mechanisms of his genitalia, always assuming the female hasn't been killed by the violent attentions of so many over-ardent males – which is not a rare occurrence.

Clearly a male bee can't take the time to consider his options, to sample the chemical mix more carefully. In evolutionary terms, he has no choice but to pounce immediately on anything that is giving off the

Right: Frog orchid on the Hebridean machair at Uig Bay on the Isle of Lewis.

Below right: Marsh helleborine at Max Bog, near Bristol.

right signals. If it smells about right and feels about right – go for it! And, also in evolutionary terms, the early spider-orchid 'knows' this. But, just as Darwin believed, insects aren't that stupid. The male bees eventually spot that they've been duped. And they rarely get fooled twice, so only very few male bees will visit a second early spider-orchid and deliver the pollinaria.

Compared to nectar-producing orchids such as twayblades and butterfly orchids, the fiendishly complex system followed by the many sexually deceptive species seems somewhat inefficient. Fruit set (the number of flowers that go on to produce fruits) in deceptive orchids is very poor when compared to their more generous, nectar-producing relatives.[22] Originally, the first orchids to evolve were probably nectarless, but if simply producing nectar can increase fruit set so much, why haven't all orchids evolved a nectar reward?

Producing nectar does have a cost to the plant, though not always that much. It varies from 3 per cent to 37 per cent of the plant's daily energy budget, depending on how long a flower lasts. Longer-lived flowers, like those of many orchids, must keep producing nectar for longer, so increasing the cost to the plant.[23] And any nectar left after the flower is fertilized is often absorbed, which also suggests that it represents a significant outlay of energy for the plant. So the cost of producing nectar might be one reason for evolving an alternative strategy of deception. Yet many other plants produce copious quantities of nectar, so there must be other reasons why so many orchids rely on deception.

Insects spend much less time on orchids that offer no reward. This should hardly come as a surprise, but it was confirmed in a simple yet very informative experiment, in which nectar was added to the normally nectarless flowers of green-winged orchids, *Anacamptis morio*. The green-winged orchid relies mainly on bumblebees for pollination and after artificial nectar was added to the flowers the length of bee visits increased from an average of 10 seconds to more than a minute.[24] And these longer visits seem to increase the chances of self-pollination. As the bee spends more time probing around each flower spike, it increases the chances it will pick up and then deposit pollinaria on the same plant.[25] In orchids that normally out-cross,* self-pollination produces much poorer quality seed. Even pollen from orchids in the immediate vicinity, which are likely to be related, produces poorer seed.[26]

---

* i.e., allow themselves to be fertilized by an unrelated individual.

So one effect of deception is to encourage insects to spend less time on each plant, which may in turn promote out-crossing. In addition, insects initially probe nectarless flowers more deeply, as if they can't believe that there really is no nectar reward on offer. In doing so, there is more chance of their picking up the pollinaria. This effect has been demonstrated in the giant orchid, *Himantoglossum robertianum*, a European relative of the lizard orchid, *H. hircinum*, a species that occurs sporadically around southern Britain. If nectar is added to this normally nectarless orchid, bees probe less vigorously and so pick up fewer pollinaria.[27] So perhaps deception also helps to ensure pollinaria are picked up effectively.

And sexual deception in particular seems to have other advantages that help account for its widespread adoption amongst orchid-kind. Orchids that offer a nectar reward have the highest pollination efficiency, defined as the proportion of flowers that have had pollen removed compared to those that actually get pollinated. Nectarless, food-deceptive orchids fall far behind in comparison, but sexually deceptive orchids are almost

A specimen of the sawfly orchid turned up in Dorset in 2014, possibly a natural colonist but more likely a human introduction.

as efficient as rewarding species.[28] This might explain why some of the original nectarless, food-deceptive orchids switched to sexual deception rather than the more obvious trick of offering an expensive nectar reward.

Deception also seems to help maintain genetic diversity in populations. For reasons that aren't entirely clear, the pollinators of deceptive orchids seem to travel further, carrying pollen to more distant populations. So again, switching from food deception to sexual deception makes evolutionary sense. An orchid can increase its pollination efficiency yet keep high rates of gene flow between populations.[29]

We've already seen that a key feature of sexual deception is that the orchid is tuned into only a few species of pollinator – or even just a single one – probably a reason why pollination efficiency is high in such species. But these pollinators also seem to be more careful go-betweens. Sexually deceptive orchids don't suffer from as much pollen-loss as food deceptive species. This means they can make do with fewer flowers than food deceptive species – another big energy saving in a switch to sexual

Below left: Bee orchid.

Below right: Green-winged orchid.

deception.[30] All these subtle advantages help explain the prevalence of sex and lies in orchids, despite the apparently poorer fruit set in those orchids adopting this strategy. But even this may be an illusion.

Recently, a particularly dedicated team of botanists decided to count the number of seeds produced by each orchid flower spike in species with different pollination strategies. This is no mean undertaking – orchid seeds are like dust and produced in prodigious quantities. But the effort was worth it. They found that although deceptive orchids produce fewer fruits than rewarding ones, each seed capsule contains far more seeds. So, in the end, the total number of seeds produced by deceitful orchids is not that different from rewarding ones. And they still have all the other advantages outlined above over honest and food-deceptive orchids.[31]

Sexual deception is very species-specific and once an orchid has set off down that evolutionary route, it can delve ever deeper into its pollinator's world. It can crack more of the bee's code. In bees such as *Andrena*, females release a post-copulatory pheromone as soon as they have been mated.[32] This chemical is produced by the female's Dufour's gland, the same gland that becomes active after mating to produce the lining of her nest cells. This chemical tells male bees not to bother her as she is now fully engaged in the task of nest-building and will vigorously reject any further attempts to mate. And early spider-orchids do exactly the same thing.

Above right: Pyramidal orchid.

Below right: Southern marsh orchid.

Once a flower has been fertilized, the orchid doesn't want bees to waste their time visiting it, when other flowers on the same spike may still be in need of their services. So the orchid produces a close mimic of the female bee's 'leave-me-alone' pheromone.[33] Thanks to this chemical, two-thirds of bees quickly leave any pollinated flower to visit a second flower on the plant, which may still require pollinaria pick-up or delivery.[34]

Once a bee has picked up pollinaria from a plant, it's better from the orchid's point of view if the bee flies to another plant rather than self-pollinating the orchid it has just visited. And some *Ophrys* species have evolved yet another way of exploiting a bee's behaviour to this end. Close observations on a species from Crete with very dramatically marked flowers, *O. heldreichii*, showed that its pollinating bees, male *Eucera berlandi*, in their eagerness to be first to a female, flew straight on to the flower with no hesitation. But once they worked out they'd been duped, they spent up to a minute hovering in front of the flower. It's likely that they were memorizing the distinctive lip pattern in order to avoid being fooled again. Since all the lip patterns on an individual plant are identical, that means the bee will not land on other flowers of the same plant, so the plant avoids self-pollination. But the lip patterns vary between individual plants of this species, patterns that the unfortunate male bee hasn't yet memorized and that therefore remain seductively attractive to him.[35] Such adaptations are so complex and intricate that they defy belief. And indeed some orchid biologists don't believe them. After all, they argue, how discriminating can these male bees really be if they'll try to mate with your finger as long as it is coated with an appropriate mix of chemicals? I've tried it – and they do!

But from the orchid's point of view, sexual deceit seems to have many advantages over the food deceit of nectarless orchids. The transfer of pollen to the stigmas of the right species seems to be more efficient in sexually deceitful species. Overall, the reproductive success (in terms of numbers of seeds produced) of both types is about the same, yet thanks to more efficient pollen transfer, sexually deceitful *Ophrys* species can make do with many fewer flowers. Food-deceitful orchids have to produce a conspicuous floral display to draw in pollinators, which, in species like green-winged orchids creates an irresistible draw, both to would-be pollinators and to naturalists as well. Even though they save energy by not producing nectar, food-deceitful species are still making a considerable energetic investment, which sexually deceitful species can avoid.[36, 37]

But picking up the pollinaria is only part of the story. To complete the process of pollination and fertilization the pollinaria not only have to get to another plant of the right species, but also have to make contact with the female parts of the flower. And that involves another ingenious adaptation, which was worked out by Charles Darwin himself.

The first orchids that Darwin worked on were early purple orchids, *Orchis mascula*. One of my favourite places to spend the lengthening days of spring is a large area of ancient woodland, Lower Woods, not far from my home in Bristol. In amongst the coppiced hazel stumps are many tall and stately spikes of early purples, so one spring I decided to repeat some of Darwin's meticulous observations. Just as Darwin had done, I gently poked a pencil into a recently opened early purple flower and when I withdrew it, two pollinia, mounted on their short stalks, like little lollipops, were glued to the tip – just as they would be to the tongue of a probing insect.

After about twenty seconds, the lollipops began to bend forward, through nearly 90 degrees. The motion took only about ten seconds and I felt an unexpected elation sitting on the forest floor watching this, much as Darwin must have done 150 years previously. Darwin showed that this bending is simply due to the stalk drying out and can be reversed if it is carefully wetted,[38] but he also worked out the evolutionary reason behind this curious trick.

The bending motion brings the pollinia into the right alignment to contact the stigma. In their original upright arrangement, the pollinia are in the wrong position to be attached to the stigma and can't effect pollination. But Darwin realized that the clever bit is the delay in bending, which gives the insect time to finish feeding on that flower spike and leave to find another, so avoiding self-pollination.

However, insects spend significantly different amounts of time on different orchids. As we've already seen, insects spend longer on orchid flowers that have nectar and the bending time of the stalk reflects this, taking longer in those orchids that produce nectar. In this way, the pollinia won't be re-aligned to intercept the stigma until after the insect has eaten its fill and left the flower. As I spent a few happy hours poking pencils into orchid flowers, I couldn't help but admire the ingenuity both of natural selection and of Darwin's explanation of the delayed re-alignment of the pollinaria. But this may not be as clever as it appears at first sight. Recent genetic studies show that in reality out-crossing orchids suffer from considerable degrees of in-breeding. In other words, despite the delayed bending, insects must frequently carry the pollinaria only as far as another flower higher on the same stem.

Above: Early purple orchid.

Right: Violet helleborines can b[e] found in the dark recesses of late summer woodland.

SEEDS LIKE DUST

When an insect carrying pollinaria lands on a receptive flower it delivers a vast number of pollen grains. In many other kinds of flowers often only a few grains of pollen remain attached to the insect when it arrives at a receptive flower, and certainly the amount of pollen it brings varies tremendously. It takes one pollen grain to fertilize each seed, so if an insect brings only a few pollen grains, only a few seeds can be produced. But the orchid's pollinium guarantees that there will be no shortage of pollen once pollination happens. Such a large supply of pollen can fertilize huge numbers of seeds. This is the big advantage of packing pollen into a pollinium and orchids are not the only plants to have come up with this strategy. But producing seeds in this number means that each seed can only be very small.

Because orchid seeds are so tiny, it's often assumed that they can be carried long distances on the wind, allowing orchids to disperse widely. And for some this seems to be the case. Military orchids, *Orchis militaris*, are confined to just three wild locations in Britain: two in the Chilterns and one in Suffolk.[39] But all three populations are genetically distinct, suggesting independent colonization of each site by seeds blown over from Europe.[40] Conversely, the genetic similarity of lady's slipper orchids across vast areas, from the Pyrenees to Scandinavia, also suggests that seeds can be transported long distances, essentially connecting up plants across this whole area into one single population.[41]

The curious distribution of the Irish lady's-tresses, *Spiranthes roman-zoffiana*, may also be a result of long-distance seed dispersal. It's really a North American plant, but also grows in scattered colonies in the Inner and Outer Hebrides, with a few sites on the Scottish mainland, and in sizeable colonies in western Ireland. These are its only European outposts. A few other species, such as the pipewort, *Eriocaulon aquat-icum*, a curious grass-like plant with button-shaped flower heads, have a similar distribution. In the case of Irish lady's-tresses, it was said that its distribution in Scotland matched that of the favoured wintering areas of Greenland white-fronted geese, which nest in Greenland and Canada. Could migrating geese have brought these plants? It's an often-heard theory, but almost certainly wrong.

A closer look at the orchid's distribution in Ireland and Scotland shows that many populations, particularly in Ireland, are well away from traditional wintering areas of these geese. And the geese nest in the high Arctic, well north of the orchid's North American range. In addition, Irish lady's-tresses used to occur in a small colony in Devon, where not even the boldest Greenland white-fronts venture. It's far more likely that seeds were blown on the prevailing westerlies. In its European haunts Irish lady's-tresses don't produce much seed but in North America three-quarters of the plants set seed. And new colonies of Irish lady's-tresses keep being discovered on our side of the Atlantic, suggesting that seed may be arriving here on the wind all the time.[42] But not all orchids possess such prodigious powers of seed dispersal.

The lady orchid, *O. purpurea*, is a speciality of the woodlands of Kent, though it does occur in a few other locations in southern Britain. I try to make a spring or summer pilgrimage to Kent each year, since it is such a wonderful county for orchids. And exploring the county's rich orchid flora is made all the more special because Darwin's home, Down

Lady orchid.

House, around which he made so many of his meticulous observations of these plants, is also situated here. The early spider-orchids of Samphire Hoe are always worth a visit in April. Later in the year, the even rarer late spider-orchid, *O. fuciflora*, blooms on the downs above Wye and Folkestone. Man orchids, *O. anthropophora*, and monkey orchids, *O. simia*, along with a host of commoner species, also add to the county's appeal for orchid-lovers, but for me it's the tall and elegant spikes of lady orchids blooming in the green-suffused shade of Kent's woodlands that make a perfect orchid-hunting day.

More pragmatically, when botanists looked at the genetic make-up of seedlings around mature lady orchids they found that they were all closely related, suggesting that seed dispersal is generally limited to just a few metres around each plant.[43] Most of the seeds of green-winged orchids, *A. morio*, and *Dactylorhiza majalis*, a European species of marsh orchid, seem to fall no more than a metre (3 ft) away from the parent plant, while the seeds of the tiny late-flowering autumn lady's-tresses, *Spiranthes spiralis*, travel only 15 centimetres (6 in) or so.[44]

These observations seem counter-intuitive, given the dust-like seeds of orchids, but by now we should have learned to accept nothing at face value in this family of plants. And this new knowledge is critically important for orchid conservationists. In projects designed to boost seed set, conservationists often resort to hand-pollination, but the message now must be – don't hand-pollinate with close neighbours, as they are likely to be close relatives.

ORCHID COLONISTS

Although most seed might fall close to the parent plant, in theory it takes only a small number of seeds to travel further to establish a new outpost. And since orchids produce seeds by the thousand, there is a good chance that at least a few will arrive in unexpected places.

It's possible that the small-flowered tongue orchid, *S. parviflora*, arrived on our shores like this. In 1989 two specimens of this species were found on a clifftop in Cornwall, after which they continued to flower on and off in following years. Seed was collected from these plants and the resulting seedlings planted out around the original colonists to bolster what some botanists considered the vanguard of a new species of orchid to Britain.[45] The nearest colonies lie just 175 kilometres (110 miles) away

across the Channel, on grassy islands off the coast of Brittany, so not too far for the dust-like seeds to blow on the prevailing winds. But others doubt that the Cornish plants arrived naturally.

Three other species of tongue orchids have also been found occasionally in Britain. A greater tongue orchid, *S. lingua*, found in south Devon in 1998, was thought to be a subspecies that occurs naturally in Algeria. That area of Devon is one that sometimes experiences 'red rain', coloured by dust blown up from the Sahara, so again some suggested that this could have been a natural colonization event,[46] though most now think this plant arrived with human help. More recently, a colony of eighty greater tongue orchids was discovered in Essex. Again, the origin of these plants is unknown, though planting by humans is suspected. The same is true for two other tongue orchids that have turned up. A heart-flowered tongue orchid, *S. cordigera*, appeared in 1996 in a chalk quarry in Kent, suspiciously close to specimens growing in the garden of a hardy-orchid enthusiast. There is also a much older record, from 1918, of the scarce tongue orchid, *S. neglecta*, in a cornfield in the Isle of Wight. The consensus is that, with the possible exception of the small-flowered tongue orchid on that Cornish clifftop, the others were all deliberate introductions.

Nevertheless, new surprises continue to pop up every now and then. In 2014 a single sawfly orchid, *Ophrys tenthredinifera*, was discovered growing in Dorset, a long way from its Mediterranean home. Some botanists have speculated that the orchid had been blown right across Europe by winds associated with more frequent high-pressure systems caused by climate change.[47] But as with the tongue orchids, other botanists question whether the sawfly orchid actually made it here under its own steam. Orchids attract some very passionate and dedicated – some would say obsessive – enthusiasts, who occasionally plant out non-native orchids or scatter seed. The late Francis Rose was a well-respected botanist and author of some excellent field guides. But he had a propensity for scattering Mediterranean orchid seeds around his home in Surrey, much to the consternation of other local botanists.

Closer to the sawfly orchid's Dorset home is Belmont House in Lyme Regis, once home to the writer John Fowles, another orchidophile with a penchant for *Ophrys* species. Both sombre bee orchids, *O. fusca*, and woodcock orchids, *O. scolopax*, grew naturalized in his garden, and though I don't know that he planted sawfly orchids, his garden certainly shows that introduced Mediterranean *Ophrys* species thrive in the Dorset climate. But it's certainly possible that the sawfly orchid is a new colonist. As average temperatures in Britain rise, a number of new animals and plants have made a natural appearance in the UK in recent years and have begun to spread. With their tiny seeds, we might expect orchids to be amongst the first pioneers of our twenty-first century flora and fauna.

FUNGAL PARTNERSHIPS AND THE PROBLEMS OF ORCHID CONSERVATION

But the tiny size of orchid seeds also creates a major problem. These seeds are too small to contain any food reserves to fuel the growing seedling until it can grow green leaves and make its own food by photosynthesis. So orchids have had to find another way of feeding themselves when they first germinate, one that involves yet another intimate partnership, this time with soil fungi.

Fungi are truly ubiquitous. The more you look, the more you find.

Everyone is familiar with the above-ground fruiting bodies of fungi – toadstools and mushrooms, puffballs and brackets, but these are just the tips of a fungal iceberg. In the main, fungi exist as tiny threads, hyphae, that form a massive network running throughout the soil. Fungi live by breaking down organic matter found in the upper layers of the soil but often form intimate relationships with plant roots, from herbs to trees, exchanging nutrients for mutual benefit. The plants receive vital minerals like phosphates from the fungi and in return the fungi take up nutrients from the plant, made by photosynthesis. All the plants in a forest are connected up by fungal threads in what German forester Peter Wohlleben has described as the wood-wide web![48]

When an orchid seed falls into the soil, it is penetrated by fungal threads, from which the orchid steals nutrients, allowing it to germinate and produce a protocorm, a seedling structure unique to orchids. This protocorm grows root-like structures called rhizoids that allow more fungal threads to penetrate the cells. Inside the orchid's cells the fungal hyphae form coiled structures, called pelotons, which the orchid digests to provide the food it needs to grow into a more conventional-looking seedling. In this way, the fungus supplies the orchid seedling with food until it has grown large enough to produce green leaves and make its own food. Even then, in most orchids the fungal relationship persists, supplementing the orchid's own food production by photosynthesis. This elegant solution to the problem of minute seeds has one flaw, however: orchids can only form their one-sided relationship with a small number of species of fungi. And if it happens that the right fungi are not present in the soil where the seed falls, it simply can't germinate.

In the past this quirk of orchid biology has made them very difficult to grow in cultivation and has created major headaches for orchid conservationists trying to grow plants for re-introduction schemes. The lady's slipper orchid, *Cypripedium calceolus*, is one of our rarest and certainly one of our most spectacular orchids – so spectacular that it was targeted by gardeners and plant traders from the eighteenth century on through to the Victorian era when there was a craze for collecting and growing orchids. These enthusiasts dug up any specimens they could find, which meant just about all of them. The wild population of *C. calceolus* was eventually reduced to just one plant in the Yorkshire Dales, its location a closely guarded secret to prevent it too ending up in someone's garden. Its whereabouts may have been unknown to human predators, but not to the local slugs. In order to prevent damage from this

quarter, this last wild plant used to be smeared in soot, a final indignity for such a magnificent plant.

It's a great pity that these orchids are now so rare in Britain. In the eastern forests of North America a closely related species grows abundantly on some sites and only serves to emphasize what we are missing. In a virtually unknown reserve, the G. R. Thompson Wildlife Management Area, along the Appalachian Trail in Virginia, I've found clump after clump of the yellow lady's slipper, *C. parviflorum*, growing up through carpets of large-flowered trilliums, *Trillium grandiflorum*. And in the drier pinewoods along the eastern coastal plain, the equally spectacular pink lady's slipper, *C. acaule*, is perhaps even more abundant. These plants are so extravagant, so tropical-looking, that no matter how many I see, each one still stops me in astonishment. And our own *C. calceolus* grows in some abundance in Scandinavian woodlands and on

Lady's slipper orchid reintroduced to Gait Barrows National Nature Reserve in Lancashire.

Baltic islands, occasionally in carpets, its exotic blooms looking even more out of place in these northern forests.

But soon we should once again be able to enjoy this spectacular plant in Britain, thanks to intensive research at the Royal Botanic Gardens in Kew, where botanists have cracked the problems of germinating orchids in cultivation. Margaret Ramsey, who has been working on the problems of growing lady's slippers in cultivation for many years, now has a room full of them, ranging from tiny fuzzy white blobs – the newly germinated protocorms[*] – to luxuriant green masses, growing out of transparent jelly in glass jars. When I visited her at Kew, surrounded by row upon row of jars of orchids from all over the world, she explained that the lady's slipper was one of the hardest nuts to crack, not least because the fungus partner proved impossible to find.[49]

But orchid seed can also be germinated in agar jelly so long as just the right mixture of nutrients and vitamins are provided to replace those normally supplied by the fungus. The question is – what is just the right mixture? This technique of orchid growing (known as sterile culture) is more like alchemy than science. In the end it was the Swedish paediatrician (and orchid grower), Svante Malmgren, who eventually came up with perhaps the best mixture to satisfy the fussy orchid: it was based on an intravenous nutrient solution for premature babies – good, he said, for small patients, whether human or orchid.

Intensive work on culture and reintroduction programs for British and European orchids began in earnest with the Sainsbury Orchid Project in 1983 with financial support from Sir Robert and Lady Sainsbury.[50] By 1989 the project was able to begin planting out lady's slipper seedlings in sites previously occupied by these orchids. The first of these reintroduced plants, at Ingleton in Yorkshire, flowered in 2000. The eventual aim is to restore the lady's slipper to its pre-Victorian abundance, a time we should all look forward to with great anticipation.

Most of the re-introduction sites are still kept secret, with the notable exception of Gait Barrow National Nature Reserve in Lancashire. It makes sense to open a single site for visitors to admire this spectacular plant, as it makes it less likely that people will be tempted to trample over other sites that are less well wardened. This strategy works for several of our rarest plants and animals: another successful example of its

---

[*] An embryonic plant, consisting of a tuberous mass of cells with root-like rhizoids that link up with the fungal hyphae.

implementation is the 'public' site at Collard Hill in Somerset, where visitors can see large blue butterflies. I've filmed the yellow lady's slipper at Gait Barrow, where one spectacularly large and floriferous plant grows decorously at the base of a limestone boulder. As we set up our cameras, the warden remarked that we might well be pointing our lenses at the most photographed plant in the country.

Many orchids maintain their relationship with root fungi, even when fully grown, though usually this becomes more of an equal partner-ship.[51] Creeping lady's tresses, *Goodyera repens*, is an orchid of Scottish pinewoods, though there are good populations in the Cumbrian pine forests of Whinfell as well as a peculiarly isolated population in Norfolk, now presumed to have been introduced accidentally with imported pine trees. Like other orchids, this species needs a fungal partner in order to germinate and, even after it grows, it maintains its fungal connections and obtains its phosphorus and nitrogen through this route. But as it produces green leaves and begins to photosynthesize, the flow of carbon reverses. Now, the fungus obtains some of its carbon from the orchid. A relationship that began as one-sided in favour of the orchid becomes truly symbiotic.[52] In the longer term both fungus and orchid benefit, though the incentive, if any, for the fungus at the seed germination stage is still not at all understood.

Some orchids remain entirely dependent on fungi throughout their whole lives. A good example is the bird's-nest orchid, *N. nidus-avis*. It gets its name from a nest-like tangle of roots, which are intimately bound up with fungi belonging to a group known as the sebacinoid fungi. Bird's-nest orchids have no chlorophyll, but instead are a pale, somewhat sickly colour, almost the same hue as the fallen beech leaves through which they grow, which makes them hard to spot. One trick is to lie flat on the ground and scan the forest floor from orchid height. This works because in the dense shade of beechwoods, it's too dark for most normal green plants to grow, so the spikes of bird's-nest orchids stand out on the open forest floor. Lying prone like this in a beech forest is not only a good way to spot them, but also an excellent way to appreciate how the bird's-nest orchid's use of soil fungi has enabled it to thrive in an environment where few other plants can.

Green plants get their minerals from the soil and carbon from carbon dioxide in the air, then use the power of sunlight, harnessed by the green pigment chlorophyll, to combine these to make organic material. Bird's-nest orchids, on the other hand, get everything they need through their

rd's nest orchid.

fungal connections. The exact physiology of this relationship has proved quite hard to study, but it now seems that the minerals the orchid needs come from organic material in the soil, digested by the fungus, while the carbon compounds come ultimately from the forest trees, to which the fungus is also connected.

Lying there on the forest floor will give you a new perspective on woodlands, both literally and ecologically. A fungal plumbing system connects the trees into a single physiological entity through which nutrients can be exchanged. This system even allows trees to communicate with each other in ways we are just beginning to understand.[53] And there in front of you, decked in the hues of fallen leaves, a bird's-nest orchid is cheating on the system. This ruse has freed the orchid from the direct need for light. It can grow in the deep gloom of beech forests with virtually no competition from other herbaceous plants. Through the fungal threads, the bird's-nest orchid has a direct link to the canopy of the beech trees bathed in sunlight high overhead. In a sense, the bird's-nest orchid does have leaves; they just happen to belong to the trees.

There is a far rarer orchid that plays the same trick. The ghost orchid, *Epigogium aphyllum*, is without doubt the rarest British orchid; so rare it was declared extinct in 2005 after having been last sighted in a Buckinghamshire woodland in 1986. The plant conservation charity Plantlife used the official extinction of this plant to issue *The Ghost Orchid Declaration*, part of a campaign to prevent further extinctions of plants in Britain. But, just days after a big press launch, a single tiny ghost orchid unapologetically turned up again after an absence of twenty-three years, this time in a woodland in Herefordshire. This is typical behaviour for this elusive orchid. Obtaining all its food from its fungal partner, it can live underground for many years with no need to expose itself to botanists. For this reason, to see a ghost orchid in Britain is the holy grail of most orchid hunters.

Because they depend entirely on fungi for their food, these orchids are called myco-heterotrophs. And a third British orchid has a similar lifestyle – the coralroot orchid, *Corallorhiza trifida*. The coralroots are really a North American group of orchids; ten species occur there. Only *C. trifida* has extended its range to the Old World. All of the American species seem to be true myco-heterotrophs, though recent research has shown that the situation in *C. trifida* is more complicated.[54] Although leafless, like ghost and bird's nest orchids, coralroot orchids do have some chlorophyll in their stems and flowers. And chemical analysis has confirmed that they only get about three-quarters of their carbon via their fungal connections and only about a half of their nitrogen through this route.

Part of the allure of orchids is their rarity and unpredictability, a large part of which is down to the distribution of their fungal partners. The fungi that orchids need don't occur everywhere, though we still know very little about the finer-scale preferences of these organisms. One of the nearest places to my home to find bird's-nest orchids in abundance is at Buckholt Wood in Gloucestershire, part of the Cotswold Commons and Beechwoods National Nature Reserve running along the scarp slope of the Cotswold Hills. Here there are patches where thirty or forty spikes occur in just a few tens of square metres. Yet I can walk across great stretches of identical-looking forest floor without seeing a single plant. Then, suddenly, I spot another spike and dozens more resolve themselves in the gloom. Presumably this patchiness is related to the distribution of the right fungi. These orchids need at least two different fungi in the soil before they can grow – one to germinate the seed and another to maintain the mature plant.

Logic dictates that if orchids are growing in a particular patch of woodland, the right fungi must be present. So, not surprisingly, experimental packets of bird's-nest orchid seeds germinate and grow more successfully if planted near existing orchid patches.[55] Perhaps this is the reason why orchid seed doesn't seem to disperse far, and why orchid seedlings are so often found near their parents. Those seeds that don't travel far have a much greater chance of landing amongst a patch of the right fungus, which allows them to germinate and grow successfully.

Recent work on calcareous grassland confirms that the patchy distribution of three common orchid species, chalk-fragrant, green-winged and early purple orchids, reflected a similar patchy distribution of communities of fungi that are thought to be important to each of these orchids.[56]

A large part of orchid natural history, not least the rarity and extreme unpredictability of some species, has been shaped by the peculiar biology of orchid pollination and by the consequences of their having such tiny seeds. These characteristics certainly add to the attractions of orchids, but they also give conservationists a serious headache. Species like the ghost orchid are notorious for living for extended periods underground, invisible to botanists. Other rare species, such as the red helleborine, may also disappear underground for long stretches, especially if their appearances above ground trigger the unwanted attentions of deer or slugs. They don't make things easy for those who would cherish them, yet orchids have a long history of coming back from the brink.

EXPANDING AND CONTRACTING RANGES

When Angus Webster wrote *British Orchids*[57] in 1898, military orchids, *O. militaris*, were common enough for him to include notes on how to cultivate them in gardens. But by the early years of the twentieth century they were growing ever more scarce. In 1925 C. B. Tahourdin wrote in *Native Orchids of Britain* that the military orchid was 'now so rare that only a few privileged persons know where, if at all, it can be found'.[58] Indeed, it was soon presumed extinct in Britain. Then, in 1947, J. E. (Ted) Lousley took his family on a now famous picnic (at least amongst botanists) in the Chilterns. He describes the incident in *Wildflowers of Chalk and Limestone*, a classic in Collins' *New Naturalist* series, and a story that certainly whetted my appetite for flower hunting when I first devoured this book in my youth.

> *In a way it was just luck. The excursion was intended as a picnic, so I had left my usual apparatus at home and took only my note-book. But I selected our stopping places on the chalk with some care, and naturally wandered off to see what I could find. To my delight I stumbled on the orchid just coming into flower.*

Above and right:
Military orchid.

Lousley kept the location of his picnic a closely guarded secret, but later botanists stumbled on what was presumed to be the site: Homefield Wood near Hambleden in Buckinghamshire, which is now managed by the Berkshire, Buckinghamshire and Oxfordshire Wildlife Trust. Thanks to careful management, in May the spectacular flowers of military orchids grow in abundance across the rough grassy slopes. Return in late summer and the seed heads of the military orchids are still standing, but the colour is provided by Chiltern gentians, another scarce flower that thrives on this excellent nature reserve.

A parallel story can be told of the monkey orchid, *O. simia*, which at one time was thought to be merely a variety of the military orchid. The monkey orchid wasn't lost entirely from this country, but by 1950 it was reduced to just one site in Oxfordshire, where in some years just one plant flowered. Yet both military and monkey orchids have made good recoveries.

Eventually, military orchids were discovered at three sites: two in the Chilterns and one in Suffolk. But after their discovery these populations began to decline drastically. To combat the decline of military orchids, botanists germinated their seeds and grew them on in cultivation and later the seedlings were planted out in new sites to extend the orchid's range. Despite such efforts, these introductions did not fare well, with few plants surviving. However, in 2000 twelve tubers from mature plants growing at Homefield Wood were transplanted to a nearby National Trust site and these plants have done much better.[59] Despite the mixed fortunes of these attempts to help the military orchid, numbers of plants at the original sites began to increase, and considerably so in the last decade.

Monkey orchids have also increased recently as its grassland sites are managed more sympathetically, but possibly also owing to climate change. There is some evidence from studies of monkey orchids in Holland that cold weather when the plants first appear above ground in January or February can be lethal,[60] so milder winters in recent years might be responsible for better survival rates and an increase in population. It is

Below left: Monkey orchid at Park Gate Down in Kent.

Below: 'Lonkey' orchid, a hybr[i] between monkey orchid and lady orchid at Hartslock nature reserve in Oxfordshire.

just as likely, though, that appropriate management at the sites of both these species has been responsible, but it's hard to be certain. Thanks to the peculiarities of orchid biology, the time it takes for the plant to develop from germination to a mature flowering plant is so long that it's not easy to make correlations between particular management practices and the eventual success or otherwise of mature plants.

One of the easiest places to admire monkey orchids is at Hartslock, another nature reserve managed by the Berkshire, Buckinghamshire and Oxfordshire Wildlife Trust. Its slopes overlook the Thames near Goring, a view that encompasses classic scenery of southern England. But the best displays of orchids here are now not the original monkey orchids but a more vigorous hybrid with the lady orchid, so-called 'lonkey orchids'. These hybrids have conservationists scratching their heads. There are small colonies of lady orchids in the Chilterns, but genetic studies show that the Hartslock ladies are distinct from these orchids, and indeed from those in Kent. Instead, they seem to be most similar to populations much further south, around the Mediterranean.[61]

It's possible that their tiny seeds could have blown here naturally or they could have been carried here by humans. We've already seen cases of misguided enthusiasts doing just that elsewhere, scattering seeds of both native and non-native orchids, though no one has owned up to doing this at Hartslock. The lady orchids were first seen in 1999 and the first hybrids recorded in 2006. Since then the number of hybrids has increased exponentially, and they now form an impressive display, since the hybrids are much larger than the monkey orchids, bearing a closer resemblance to lady orchids.

It's likely that not only will the number of hybrids at Hartslock carry on increasing, but they will also cross with their parents, diluting the genomes of the original monkey orchids. This situation has caused orchid biologist Richard Bateman to raise some interesting and challenging questions. I had the pleasure of working with Richard while making my orchid film a few years back. As we discussed the scope of the film, usually over a pint or two in his local pub, he raised many areas of current controversy in the world of orchids, including the existence of Hartslock's lonkey orchids. An understandable reaction from conservationists is to remove the hybrids to protect the integrity of the monkey orchids – especially if the lady orchids were human introductions. But Richard points out that Hartslock's monkey orchids are pretty weedy specimens. He suspects that this is because collectors in the past favoured the more robust specimens for their herbarium sheets, imposing a kind of unnatural selection on the population that meant only feeble specimens survived. In addition, since the population of monkey orchids fell to such low levels in the middle of the twentieth century, they have passed through a genetic bottleneck. In other words, today's populations derive from very few or even single individuals, which inevitably means that genetic variation in these populations is very low.

So perhaps an injection of genes from more robust lady orchids, as the vigorous hybrids cross-pollinate with true monkey orchids, would help redress the situation. These orchids (monkey, lady, military and several other European species) are all closely related and in many places in Europe, where they are much commoner, they hybridize naturally and very freely. As we will see, orchids frequently form new species by hybridization, so, especially if the lady orchids arrived at Hartslock naturally, we could simply be watching evolution in action.

Lizard orchid.

The situation is a highly complex one, and there are no easy answers, but it's vital that people like Richard Bateman make us question our assumptions.[62] Very often, conservation becomes preservation as we try to maintain some kind of status quo, some idealized state that for whatever reason we see as 'natural'. Yet by preserving the genetic identity of Hartslock's monkey orchids, we might be preserving a state of affairs which, far from being 'natural', was brought about by our Victorian forebears.

The recent spread of lizard orchids, *Himantoglossum hircinum*, highlights other factors at play in the fall and rise of orchid populations. As a student in the 1970s, I had to make a pilgrimage from Bristol to Kent to see good numbers of these spectacular plants growing in the rough of a golf course near Sandwich. It was a long and, for a student, expensive journey, but one made all the more worthwhile by my being able to pay homage to the equally scarce clove-scented broomrape, *Orobanche caryophyllacea*, growing at the same site. Now there are plenty of lizard orchids growing just fifteen minutes away from my home in Bristol, on the much less peaceful site of a busy road verge – though at least I don't have to avoid flying golf balls or angry golfers.

The lizard orchid gets its English name from the resemblance of their extraordinary flowers to a long-tailed lizard scampering up the stem. Its specific name – *hircinum* – however, means 'goat', a reference to the smell of the flowers, which is readily detectable even when competing with roadside fumes. But just how powerful this scent is was brought home to me when I had cause to carry a couple of potted lizard orchids in my car over a long distance.

While making the film on orchids that took me to the slopes of Mount Kinabalu in Borneo, I also needed to film lizard orchid flowers in carefully controlled studio conditions back in Bristol. I had obtained cultivated specimens from an orchid grower and drove them back to Bristol on a warm summer's day, with the plants in full flower. I knew the derivation of its Latin name and was familiar with the distinctive aroma of lizard orchids from photographing them in the field. Slowly but surely, the car filled with the cloying scent of goat. I then made the mistake of stopping for an energizing infusion of caffeine at a service station, where I had no option but to leave the car in a sunny car park. When I returned to the car after just half an hour, I couldn't believe the stench that had built up – it was more powerful than any herd of goats I've ever smelled. And it stuck to everything – my car smelled of goat for weeks afterwards, giving rise to no small number of witty (and not so witty) observations from passengers. The French have it right: for them this is *orchis bouc* – the billy-goat orchid.

Lizard orchid populations in Britain have had something of a roller-coaster ride since they were first discovered. Back in the nineteenth century they were largely confined to Kent, then underwent an expansion of both range and population size in the early decades of the twentieth century, a time when military and monkey orchids were declining rapidly. In 1927 the Welsh botanist Eleanor Vachell found lizard orchids on the dunes near Burnham on the Bristol Channel, a much closer trip from Bristol. But this was followed by a sharp decline in numbers, though, strangely, not in range, between the 1950s and the 1990s, necessitating my long excursions to Kent in the 1970s. Their most recent nadir has been followed by an increase in numbers again over the last few decades.[63] A careful analysis of the large population at Sandwich suggests that in this case changing climate may well be responsible. The pattern of population decline and expansion correlates well with the incidence of rainfall, the plants seeming to need at least two wet growing seasons before setting good seed.

Taken together with today's impressive roadside displays of fragrant, pyramidal and common spotted orchids these stories might suggest that all is rosy in the orchid garden, but there is no room for complacency. Overall, the range of many orchid species has declined during the twentieth century,[64] and the orchids' quirks of biology and ecology leave them potentially at risk.

We have already seen that the number of seed capsules produced is significantly lower in nectarless orchids and a few botanists have speculated that this feature of deceitful orchids might be linked to rarity, or vulnerability to local extinction. One of the first to suggest this was Charles Darwin after making detailed observations of the lady orchids of Kent. He wrote: '…the suspicion naturally arises that Ophrys fusca [= Orchis purpurea] is so rare a species in Britain from not being sufficiently attractive to insects, and to its not producing a sufficiency of seed.'[65] However, despite the obvious logic of this statement, a detailed study of the patterns of orchid decline in Holland and Belgium suggests that there is no difference in vulnerability between nectarless, deceitful orchids and honest, rewarding species[66] – and we now know that this shouldn't be a surprise. More recent studies have shown that nectarless orchids, though producing fewer seed pods, produce similar total amounts of seed to rewarding ones, so it's unlikely that they would be any more vulnerable to extinction. Instead, the main threat seems to be the old enemy, continued habitat loss, not helped by climate change. Yet, as scarce as some of its individual species are, the orchid family has an extraordinary abundance of species.

ENDLESS FORMS MOST WONDERFUL

When asked what could be inferred about the mind of the Creator from a study of his works, the biologist J. B. S. Haldane is reputed to have replied 'an inordinate fondness for beetles'. Whether he actually uttered these words is debateable, but the sentiment is incontrovertible. With a minimum of 350,000 species already described, beetles are far and away the most diverse group of insects. Had the same question been asked of a botanist, the answer might well have been 'an inordinate fondness for orchids'.

Orchids can't match the sheer evolutionary exuberance of beetles, but amongst plants, orchids are often claimed to be the most numerous family. Estimates for the number of species vary wildly – as they do for beetles and most other groups of organisms – but the number probably lies between 15,000 and 30,000 species. Robert Dressler suggests a figure of 19,500,[67] which actually puts orchids in second place behind the daisy family (Asteraceae) with 23,000 species. Whatever the number, the Orchidaceae is undeniably a rich family of plants.

Not so long ago this was seen as all the more remarkable since the

orchid family was thought relatively new in evolutionary terms. Most   Burnt orchid.
flowering plant families diversified during the Cretaceous period,
between 145 and 65 million years ago. This was a time when insects were
also rapidly diversifying and since the two groups are intimately tied
together through pollination, the blossoming of these two groups was
linked by a mutually stimulated process of co-evolution.

Orchids were thought not to have evolved until the Eocene (56–33.9
million years ago), long after the main co-evolutionary radiation of
flowering plants and insects. But recently several finds of fossil orchid
pollen attached to insects trapped in amber have pushed the origin of
orchids further and further back. In 2007, in the Dominican Republic,
a bee carrying orchid pollen was found trapped in amber that dates to
the Miocene, some 15–20 million years ago.[68] Then, in 2017 a small gnat,
with attached pollinaria, was recovered from Baltic amber, dated to 40–
55 million years ago.[69] Using such fossils to help calibrate a molecular
clock, it is now thought that modern orchids must have first arisen

sometime in the late Cretaceous, perhaps 76–84 million years ago.[70] The original ancestral orchid could be considerably older. It looks as though orchid history is longer than was previously supposed and their diversity therefore less surprising, though no less impressive.

However, the story is far from over. Some groups of orchids are clearly still busy diversifying, which makes their classification extremely difficult. But taxonomy, the study of classification, has recently received a boost from new molecular techniques which allow us to look directly at the genetic make-up of organisms. This has given us a radical new view of relationships within the orchid family.

Speciation requires reproductive isolation – some kind of barrier that prevents the free flow of genes across the whole population. Such a restriction of gene flow allows the separate parts of the population to build up genetic differences which, when they become great enough, create two new species. Factors that isolate some members of a population and begin to shape them into a new species are many and various. We've already seen some of them in the mechanics of pollination, but a number of other factors are also at play. A walk over some of southern England's chalk downlands at the right time of the year might reveal the white and umber spikes of the burnt orchid, *Neotinia ustulata*. But what *is* the right time of year? There are two distinct populations – an early-flowering form (May/June) and a late-flowering form (July). There is no real physical difference between these plants, though they usually occur on different sites, leading to the suggestion that differing long-term patterns of grazing might be responsible. At one site, though, at Willingdon Down in East Sussex, both forms grow in the same place.[71]

Whatever the reason, such a shift in flowering time could isolate some populations of plants, preventing the free flow of genes across the whole population. In the future this might mean that the two sub-populations could evolve in different ways. This may or may not happen in the case of burnt orchids, but it serves to illustrate how one kind of event – a shift in timing – might kick-start speciation.

Another trigger for speciation is ecological separation. The fen orchid, *Liparis loeselii*, is a small and inconspicuous species that occurs in dune slacks in South Wales and open fens in Norfolk. In this case the two forms of the plant do look a little different and are described as varieties (*ovata* and *loeselii* respectively) of the same species. However, these two forms occur more widely beyond their limited distribution in the UK. Specimens that look very similar to the Welsh dune form occur in similar habitats in northern France, while specimens that are closer to the fen variety in Norfolk occur elsewhere in France. Molecular genetics also allies these northern French orchids with the Welsh ones and the remaining French ones with the East Anglian orchids.[72] However, because the genetic make-up of the two varieties is distinct, gene flow between *L. l. ovata* and *L. l. oeselii* must be restricted in some way, otherwise the distinction would blur through cross-pollination. In this case, if that restriction persists we could be witnessing the start of a split into two separate species. This restricted gene flow is not too surprising, since the two varieties occupy very different habitats, which keeps them geographically distinct – an ecological barrier that allows each variety to go its own separate way.

Advances in molecular genetics have revolutionized our understanding of orchid relationships. I'm sure I'm not the only naturalist of my generation to have turned the pages of recent publications with dismay, as Latin names learned with a retentive young brain now have to be re-learned by a more reluctant memory. In many cases species have switched from one genus to another as molecular analysis has clarified relationships, and occasionally one species has become several.

This has happened with the fragrant orchid, in which recent molecular analysis has revealed the presence of three perfectly good species. Today our orchid flora is enriched by the presence of the chalk fragrant orchid, *Gymnadenia conopsea* (the original single species thought to inhabit the UK), the marsh fragrant orchid, *G. densiflora*, and the heath fragrant orchid, *G. borealis*.[73] All three orchids can be told apart by subtle differences between their flowers, but, like the two fen orchid varieties, they also have different ecological preferences, as their new common names imply.[74] These orchids also have different peak flowering periods.

These variations in peak flowering time may be driven by their pollinators. Fragrant orchids are honest, nectar-producing species that attract butterflies and moths. Active at dusk and during the night, moths can't bask in the sun to raise their temperature for flight, so they have to rely on burning fuel to remain active. It therefore makes sense for them to minimize their flight distances between flowers to conserve energy. This may promote in-breeding amongst fragrant orchids, since near neighbours are likely to be related. Genetic analysis does suggest such in-breeding amongst populations of fragrant orchids,[75] which in turn could eventually create genetically distinct populations, a precursor to further speciation.

The relationship between orchids and their pollinators is thought to be a major factor in driving speciation, particularly amongst those groups – like the bee orchids, *Ophrys* spp. – that have evolved exclusive relationships with particular species of insects. These relationships require very precise chemical communication such that only a small change in chemistry could produce a change in pollinators. As the insect pollinators have themselves evolved and split into new species, so the chemicals used by females to attract males have changed slightly, preventing cross-breeding. More closely related species are more recently separated and their pheromones therefore more similar. If a small change occurs in the chemicals produced by an orchid flower, causing it to become attractive to a different species of bee, it is likely that it will be a species closely related to its original pollinator. If switching pollinators can drive the formation of new species, the pattern of evolution in the orchids should reflect that of the bees. In a study of Australian orchids pollinated by thynnine wasps, researchers found that the family tree of the wasps was indeed mirrored by that of the orchids, suggesting speciation by this route.[76]

Chalk fragrant orchid. The nectar filling the basal half of the spur is clearly visible.

Amongst the *Ophrys* orchids of Europe it looks as though their recent rapid diversification was similarly driven by switches to new pollinators.

Initially they relied on wasps for pollination, but a switch to bees of the genus *Eucera* followed by further switches to *Andrena* bees, independently in two separate lines, fuelled the rapid evolution of new species.[77] And this process may still be happening.

The fly orchid, *O. insectifera*, is a small, inconspicuous *Ophrys* of lime-rich grassland and scrub in the southern half of Britain. In some ways it is one of the more convincing visual mimics of an insect, with a shiny blue patch in the centre of the lip that has the same reflectance as the closed wings of an insect. It is pollinated by a small wasp, *Argogorytes*, and, like other *Ophrys* species, uses chemical mimicry as well as visual mimicry to fool male wasps into trying to mate with the flower. However, chemical analysis of the scents used by fly orchids collected in France and Sweden has revealed three distinct types, one of which attracts two species of the usual *Argogorytes* wasp and one of which seems more attractive to *Andrena* bees. The third type attracted neither bees nor wasps.[78] Perhaps, as is now accepted with fragrant orchids, there are three separate species lurking under the guise of 'fly orchid' – or, if not now, then at some point in the near evolutionary future.

Each kind of sexually deceptive orchid has evolved an intimate relationship with just one or more likely a few related species of insects, which should limit pollen from one species ending up in the flower of another. However, this system clearly isn't perfect and hybrids between different *Ophrys* species are often found. The hybrid between two European species, *O. arachnitiformis* and *O. lupercalis*, has the interesting property of producing an 'intermediate' scent, different from either of its parents, which just happens to attract different pollinators.[79] So, in the space of just one generation, by acquiring a different species of pollinator, such hybrids are reproductively isolated, a pre-requisite for new species formation. Now it is clear why there is such confusion over the classification of *Ophrys* orchids and why different authors claim such vastly divergent estimates for the number of species. Although some recognise over 350 European species, others think there are only nine, consisting of a bewildering array of 'microspecies' and 'mesospecies' delimited by adaptations to different groups of pollinators.[80]

The bee orchids are not the only group of orchids to bewilder taxonomists and field naturalists alike. And in these other groups it is again the process of hybridization and the subsequent 'fixation' of some hybrids as distinct species that is responsible. The problem is that this process is happening all the time. This is well illustrated by a particularly

Fly orchid.

vexing group, *Dactylorhiza*. This group of orchids, which includes the various marsh orchids, common spotted, *D. fucshii*, and heath spotted, *D. maculata*, can provide enough of a challenge here in Britain, but we have it easy compared to the rest of Europe.

Estimates for the number of species in Europe and North Africa range from six to sixty-one. Species such as heath spotted and common spotted, which are relatively easy to tell apart in this country, grade seamlessly into each other elsewhere in their range. To simplify a fiendishly complicated story, let's start with two 'normal' species, the common spotted orchid and the early marsh orchid, *D. incarnata*. By normal, I mean that each has the customary set of paired chromosomes (known as homologous pairs, derived from the Greek for 'same', since each chromosome of the pair is the same), one of the pair coming from each parent, just as is the case with you and me – a state known as the diploid condition. During reproduction, each member of the chromosome pair separates as the reproductive cells form, with the result that both male and female cells end up with only half the diploid set. The actual choreography is far more complex than that, but the end result is the same – a sex cell with just one of each of the original chromosome pair. When these cells fuse to create a new embryo, each contributes a chromosome to make up the diploid pair again.

These two orchids, early marsh and common spotted, along with heath spotted orchids are, in essence, the parents of the rest of this confusing group. They frequently hybridize to produce a baffling range of intermediates. If two different species (with different chromosomes) hybridize, the resulting fertilized cell should be in big trouble. The slightly different chromosomes from each parent won't match up properly to form pairs – a situation that, in most animals, renders the hybrid sterile. Indeed, this has formed part of the definition of a species. Animals that belong to the same species produce fertile offspring and those that can't are deemed to belong to separate species. But plants confuse the issue.

These orchid hybrids simply double up all their chromosomes. They end up with twice the number of their parents (in other words they have four homologous chromosomes – a condition known as tetraploid) but at least each chromosome now has a matched partner, which means the plant is capable of reproducing. And *Dactylorhiza* orchids have been doing this for millennia.

The older hybridizations have had time to establish themselves as distinct species. *D. elata and D. majalis* are two of the oldest of these 'hybrid species'. Neither occurs in Britain, though it used to be thought that *D. majalis* was a British native. *D. elata* and *D. majalis* probably evolved in southern Europe during the time that northern Europe was sealed beneath the ice caps of the last glaciation. After the ice melted, *Dactylorhiza* orchids could move north and continue the process of generating new species through hybridization. Among others, these younger, northern 'hybrid' species include, in Britain, the widespread southern marsh orchid, *D. praetermissa*, and northern marsh orchid, *D. purpurella* (derived from early marsh and common spotted crosses), and the Irish marsh orchid, *D. kerryensis*, derived from an early marsh and heath spotted cross.[81]

But the exact status of various populations and 'species' of these tetraploid orchids has, to say the least, been fluid over the last few decades. Botanizing in the Western Isles of Scotland using an older field guide, you might be excited to find a western marsh orchid, *D. majalis*. A more recent field guide might excite you further. Your find has been upgraded to its own endemic species, the Hebridean marsh orchid, *D. ebudensis*. Western marsh orchids in Ireland were also elevated to a new species, endemic to Ireland, the Irish marsh orchid. Other populations of supposed western marsh orchids in Scotland were, however, relegated to a subspecies of the widespread northern marsh orchid. This fine state

*Below left and right:
Common spotted orchid.*

of affairs lasted until 2013, when, with his colleagues, Richard Bateman carried out a definitive study in an attempt to clarify the confusing relationships between all these orchids.[82] So, in a plot with more twists and turns than a soap opera, here is the latest thinking.

Irish marsh orchids get to keep their exalted status as an endemic species, but, after reaching the heady heights of a species endemic to a few Hebridean islands, the Hebridean marsh orchid has been relegated to a form of another marsh orchid species, Pugsley's marsh orchid, *D. traunsteinerioides*, which itself has not been immune to changes of fortune. In your older field guide, this latter species occurred widely across Britain and Ireland. But where its ranks were swelled by the addition of plants from the Hebrides, it lost out in a major way in the south of its range. Below a line from the Wash to Bristol, Pugsley's marsh orchids are now thought to be a variety of the widespread southern marsh orchid.

I've photographed many of these orchids, back in the days when photography meant taking slides. Unfortunately, Fuji never considered *Dactylorhiza* taxonomy when they designed their slide mounts. There's not enough room on my oldest slides to accommodate all the crossings-out as I've tried to keep pace with a group of plants in which our knowledge is evolving as rapidly as they are. And we're probably not finished yet!

All of these crosses involved the early marsh orchid and because the early marsh orchid itself comes in five different forms, they have generated a variety of different-looking new species. Two of its subspecies, the cream-flowered *D. incarnata ochroleuca* and the deep pink *D. incarnata cruenta*, with its heavily spotted leaves, have very restricted ranges in Britain, but the other three are more widespread. In many locations, two or more of these forms occur together. A recent molecular study of plants from Norway and Sweden has shown that, though these forms appear genetically distinct to greater or lesser degrees, some gene flow persists between them.[83] Nevertheless, they are presumably distinct enough to create a range of different hybrids with common or heath spotted orchids.

Above: Early marsh orchid.

Right: Northern marsh orchid.
Overleaf: A single flower of a southern marsh orchid.

SELF-POLLINATION

The other common way that orchids have diversified is by adopting self-pollination. Although for many species self-pollination produces poorer-quality seed, a great number of orchids seem to have got around

these genetic limitations. In these orchids the pollinia either just crumble and fall on to the receptive stigma or the flower fails to produce glue, making it easier for the pollinaria to detach and drop on to the stigma. Such orchids gain a great advantage in that pollination is guaranteed and they often set seed in large quantities. But each plant is genetically isolated; no pollen from genetically different individuals contributes to the seeds. So any mutations don't become diluted by out-crossing. On the contrary – assuming they don't disadvantage the plant – they will be preserved in the genetically isolated line, in essence creating an instant new species as the population carrying that mutation builds up.

Several of our orchids self-pollinate – for example, bee orchids, *O. apifera* and white helleborines, *C. damasonium*. But it is amongst a different group of helleborines, the *Epipactis* helleborines, that self-pollinating species have proliferated, creating a confusing bouquet of similar-looking species that confounded botanists until molecular techniques enabled their relationships to be clarified. Under such chemical scrutiny the number of European species of *Epipactis* rose from twenty-six to fifty-six in just six years, although the very latest research (unpublished at the time of writing) suggests that twenty-six might be nearer the final truth.

We in Britain have several 'normal' out-crossing *Epipactis* helleborines – violet helleborine, *E. purpurea*, dark-red helleborine, *E. atrorubens*, marsh helleborine, *E. palustris*, and the broad-leaved helleborine, *E. helleborine*. Broad-leaved helleborines are pollinated by social wasps, the kind of wasps that spoil late summer picnics. I also often see hoverflies visiting broad-leaved helleborines, though how effective they are as pollinators I don't know.

Often, the wasps that visit broad-leaved helleborines seem a bit wobbly on their feet. That's because the nectar of this species can have a high alcohol content, perhaps the reason why they are so attractive to wasps on warm, lazy summer afternoons. The alcohol is produced by fermentation of the sugar-rich nectar by bacteria and fungi that may well have arrived on the feet of previous visiting wasps. So in a sense this concoction is a wasp home-brew and, to judge by the wasps' behaviour, as lethally potent as some of the stuff I've unwisely tried over the years. But there may be good reasons why this helleborine laces its nectar with alcohol. The wasps hang around the flowers for longer, like drunkards hanging around a bar, and this might increase the chances of their picking up the orchid's pollen.

In addition to out-crossing species like the broad-leaved helleborine, we have a number of self-pollinating species: narrow-lipped, *E. leptochila*; green-flowered, *E. phyllanthes*; dune, *E. dunensis*; Lindisfarne, *E. sancta*; and Tyne, *E. tynensis*. All these species seem to have arisen as separate self-fertilizing lines from the out-crossing broad-leaved helleborine, with the possible exception of the Tyne helleborine, which may have arisen as a further mutation from the dune helleborine and is probably best seen as a variety of that species. The Lindisfarne helleborine also remains enigmatic. It is confined to a small area of dunes on the Northumbrian island of Lindisfarne, and the few hundred plants that grow here seem to represent the entire world population. Its genetics have been examined and it shows significant differences from narrow-lipped helleborines, but has similarities to dune helleborines, so it's not clear whether it arose by mutation from the narrow-lipped helleborine or whether it is better seen as a subspecies of dune helleborine.[84]

And if this isn't confusing enough, it's now clear that it's not just mutations in the genes that control speciation – because there's more to chromosomes than DNA. A range of proteins serves to activate, deactivate or modify the expression of the genes themselves, and since they are physically attached to the chromosomes, these chemical switches can also be inherited by subsequent generations. In one group of tetraploid *Dactylorhiza* orchids, which hail from very different environments, this 'epigenetic' material differed between the species and was probably responsible for some of the different ecological tolerances of each of these species.[85]

This is yet another illustration of how complicated the evolutionary biology of orchids is and how much hard (and expensive) work in genetic analysis is needed to unpick this particularly bushy part of the tree of life. There is clearly a lot still to do to produce a definitive family tree of these confusing groups of orchids. And some of the self-pollinating species also come in numerous distinct varieties, not distinct enough to qualify as full species, but further confusing the picture. As with other groups of orchids, we must remember that what we see today is just a snapshot of evolution in action.

Charles Darwin finished his *Origin of Species* with a reminder that we need to observe all of nature through the lens of evolution:

Below: White helleborine.

Below right: Dark red helleborine.

It is interesting to contemplate an entangled bank, clothed with many plants of many kinds, with birds singing on the bushes, with various insects flitting about, and with worms crawling through the damp earth, and to reflect that these elaborately constructed forms, so different from each other, and dependent upon each other in so complex a manner, have all been produced by laws acting around us... There is grandeur in this view of life, with its several powers, having been originally breathed into a few forms or into one; and that, whilst this planet has gone cycling on according to the fixed law of gravity, from so simple a beginning endless forms most beautiful and most wonderful have been, and are being, evolved.

Some think that the tangled bank to which Darwin referred was in reality Downe Bank, near Darwin's home, one of his favourite orchid hunting spots. It's still rich in orchids and is now under the care of the Kent Wildlife Trust. Wandering over its diverse turf and pondering its displays of orchids with Darwin's final paragraph in mind, I can't help but think that the last line of the *Origin of Species* is particularly appropriate for the orchid family: endless forms most beautiful and most wonderful indeed.

part

III

OPEN GROUND

Introduction

The groups of plants featured in this section have a significant presence in the variety of naturally open habitats found around the British Isles. The grasslands of Section II are, of course, also conspicuously open habitats. However, today's grasslands were largely created by felling the wildwood – they are human landscapes. While there were, without doubt, wholly natural glades and grasslands within the wildwood, just how extensive these areas were is still a matter of intriguing, and occasionally heated debate amongst ecologists. But even so, most of the grasslands in Britain today have their origins with our farming forebears. In this section I focus on habitats that have always remained open without our help, which really means mountaintops above the tree line and coastal fringes.

SAND AND SHINGLE

Around our extensive coastline are sandy and shingle beaches, saltmarshes and grassy or heathy patches on the ledges of cliff faces and on clifftops. All of these places have never been shaded by trees and all have been colonized by a wide range of plants, some highly specialized for life in these exposed habitats. Such open ground forms one of the three major sections of the National Vegetation Classification that I outlined in the Introduction to Section I. Some maritime heaths, where trees are pruned by wind and exposure, may also be natural, though most of our extensive inland areas of lowland heath and upland moor are the result of forest clearances over the millennia.

Since nature seems to do its damnedest to confound our best efforts to squeeze it into neat boxes of classification, some naturally open habitats grade imperceptibly into human landscapes. The felling of forests has extended mountaintop grasslands below the natural tree line, and maritime heaths close to the coast transition inland into heaths created by the felling of woodland. In the interests of completeness, this chapter will stray into these places from time to time.

Most of these habitats have remained open because they are tough places to make a living – too tough for trees to grow. Exposed high mountaintops are not for the faint-hearted in the plant world. And even at sea level the going gets tough. A sandy beach, while idyllic for us, is just as inhospitable to plant life as those freezing, windswept peaks. Its large grains of sand retain no water, there's little in the way of organic material to supply nutrients and its surface is continually on the move, driven before the wind. But when the wind speed drops below about 16 kilometres an hour (10 miles an hour), blown sand grains can begin to pile up into dunes. If the supply of sand from the beach is limited, the dune gradually migrates inland as wind picks up grains on the windward side and drops them again on the lee. With a more plentiful supply of new sand, another dune begins to form in front of the first, creating parallel lines of dunes along some stretches of the coast. Protected to some extent by new dunes on the seaward side, or having migrated a

Dunes stabilized by marram grass along the northern shore of the Tees estuary.

little way inland and now out of the worst of the wind, the surface of the older dunes begins to stabilize and that's all the invitation that some plants need.

Lyme grass, *Leymus arenarius*, spreads by extending long stolons, stems that grow horizontally below the surface of the sand. At intervals along their length (at swellings known as nodes) these stems send down roots and push up another tuft of leaves. Both leaves and roots trap sand and further stabilize the dune. Lyme grass grows rapidly – fast enough to keep pace with the continued growth of the dune as new sand is blown in. But if this accretion rate becomes too great, the lyme grass is buried alive. Even so, all is not lost. Marram grass, *Ammophila arenaria*, is bigger, tougher and faster-growing and takes over on dunes growing at greater rates, again helping to stabilize the surface. Eventually grasses and sedges stabilize the sand surface enough for other plants to gain a roothold, though these later pioneers still need to cope with shifting sand, drought, lack of nutrients and salt spray.

Sea bindweed, *Calystegia soldanella*, with its glorious flowers of confectionary-pink and white, hugs the ground. Sea sandwort, *Honckenya peploides*, grows into large mounds. Sea holly, *Eryngium maritimum*, forms spiky clumps so spectacular that many of its relatives, along with their hybrids (known to gardeners as eryngos) are grown for their architectural appeal. Mounds of searocket, *Cakile maritima*, covered in delicate pinkish-purple flowers are joined by elegant spurges – sea spurge, *Euphorbia maritima* and Portland spurge, *E. portlandica*. All these plants are often separated by large areas of bare sand, so this stage in the dune's life is called the 'yellow dune' phase. At this stage, such dunes remind me of a themed minimalist garden that might gain an award at a flower show. They are entrancing places to explore, with new gems over every ridge, but best admired from afar. The sand is still unconsolidated, and the plants' existence is already precarious. Trampling over these dunes soon causes erosion and makes life even tougher for these pioneer species.

There's a synergy amongst these plants – a kind of positive feedback – that speeds up the consolidation of the dunes. A study in Canada, where sea sandwort also grows, showed that its large clumps trapped the seeds of the New World version of lyme grass, *Leymus mollis*, and subsequent lyme grass seedlings found it easier to establish a foothold amongst these clumps than on the open sand, before sending their stolons out into the bare dune.[1] Sea sandwort, though important in dune ecology, has an understated beauty. Its neatly stacked, slightly fleshy leaves descend in size up the short stem, which is crowned by small and inconspicuous flowers. They might not look much compared to nearby clumps of pink searocket but they hide an intriguing secret. Like many other plants, some individuals bear male flowers, others female flowers, a condition referred to by botanists and gardeners as 'dioecious', except that sea sandwort flowers are not that simple. Male flowers, though largely concerned with producing pollen, can still produce a few seeds. And the sex ratio of the offspring from male and female flowers differs. Male flowers produce offspring with a ratio of three males to every female. Female flowers, on the other hand, produce male and females in equal numbers. This odd situation is known as 'sub-dioecious' and is seen as a step on the road to the more widespread dioecious condition.[2] So sea sandwort is just as important to evolutionary botany as it is to helping create these dune gardens.

Eventually the dune surface becomes stable enough for less adventurous plants to colonize. They clothe the whole dune and below them the sand surface is covered with a growth of lichens and mosses. Since bare sand is no longer visible, the stage is called the 'grey dune' phase. Organic matter builds up to form a thin soil, further reducing erosion, and the dune is well on the way to becoming a grassland, with many of the plants familiar from such places. This narrow fringe of natural grassland grades inland into grazing lands created by humans. A very special case of dune grassland on this boundary between natural and man-made habitats occurs around the Western Isles of Scotland and to a lesser extent along Scotland's north coast. This is the machair that we visited in the previous section, formed on shell sand blown inland by Atlantic winds. It's home to a wonderful variety of plants and echoes to the rasping calls of corncrakes and the deep hum of great yellow bumblebees. It's a truly magical place to explore in the *Simmer Dim*, the protracted period of twilight when late evening light illuminates drifts of northern marsh and early marsh orchids, along with the most robust and fleshy spikes of the normally modest frog orchid. In damper patches the veined white flowers of grass of Parnassus, *Parnassia palustris*, are held upwards towards the heavens as if in supplication to the gods of the mountain in Greece after which it is named. But those flowers, like cups of the finest porcelain, are a sure sign that this plant is not a grass – it belongs to a family called the Celastraceae, to which, rather unexpectedly, the shrub spindle, *Euonymus europaeus*, also belongs. It's a testament to the structural flexibility of plants that a hedgerow or

A few plants can cope with the tough life on a shingle bank such as that at Slapton Ley in Devon. *Above:* Viper's bugloss. *Right:* Sea bindweed.

Overleaf: Bloody cranesbill.

woodland shrub and a tiny grassland herb can belong to the same family. Grass of Parnassus is said to have acquired its misleading name because in Ancient Greece, cattle grazing the slopes of Mount Parnassus acquired a taste for this plant, making it an honorary grass, at least in the minds of the local farmers.

In some places around the coast, sand is replaced by shingle, which in many ways is an even tougher place to make a living. Yet it, too, is colonized by plants, many the same as dune colonists, others more specific to shingle. There are several particularly impressive banks of shingle in the UK. Chesil Beach, in Dorset, is 29 kilometres long (18 miles), 200 metres (656 ft) wide and reaches 50 metres (165 ft) in height. It's also one of the most exhausting places I've ever walked, feet slipping and rolling over loose cobbles as I searched for shingle plants.

The currents that created this place also graded the pebbles in size from one end to the other and it's said that local fishermen can land anywhere along this beach at night and know exactly where they are just by the size of the pebbles. Other substantial shingle beaches have developed at Slapton Sands in Devon, Cemlyn Bay in Anglesey and Scolt Head in north Norfolk.

The tiring walk along the shingle is rewarded by discovering those toughest of plants that can cope with life in loose pebbles. Sea kale, *Crambe maritima*, is related to cabbage and looks similar, but is not to be confused with the true wild cabbage, *Brassica oleracea*, which was the ancestor of cultivated cabbage, along with sprouts, cauliflower, kale, broccoli and a host of other varieties that have been pushed around the dinner plate by generations of children. Wild cabbage also grows around the coast of Britain but more usually on cliff ledges and clifftop grasslands. However, despite being

tough enough to survive in loose shingle, sea kale was also eaten. Those living near shingle beaches used to heap up pebbles around the plants to blanch them before harvest. And by the eighteenth century it was also cultivated in gardens, a time when it became popular enough to be served to the Prince Regent (later George IV) on those occasions that he visited Brighton's Royal Pavilion. Its popularity even stretched across the Atlantic and sea kale found a place in Thomas Jefferson's *Garden Book*, published in 1809, in which he kept records of plants he grew in his gardens at Monticello.[3]

One of the most impressive plants of shingle banks is the yellow-horned poppy, related to the red poppies of crop fields but with a large bright yellow flower. The 'horn' is a long, twisting seed pod that forms after the flower is dropped. It's a spectacular enough plant to have drawn the attention of Robert Bridges, Poet Laureate from 1913 to 1930, who encapsulated the tough life faced by yellow-horned poppies when compared to field poppies:

A poppy grows upon the shore,
Bursts her twin cups in summer late:
Her leaves are glaucus-green and hoar,
Her petals yellow, delicate.
She has no lovers like the red,
That dances with the noble corn:
Her blossoms on the waves are shed,
Where she stands shivering and forlorn.[4]

Another attractive plant of shingle, the oyster plant, *Mertensia maritima*, is now mostly confined to northern shingle banks. It used to be more widespread, but populations in the south of Britain have declined as those further north expanded. Its seeds can survive several weeks in sea water, which allow it to colonize new areas of shingle. As a pioneer species, it's also well equipped to colonize waste earth and rocks dumped at the coast.[5] Its seeds need a period of low temperature to germinate, so floating in cold sea water on their way to a new home primes the seeds for germination once they wash ashore.

On the sheltered lee side of shingle banks, shrubby sea-blite, *Suaeda vera*, grows into low bushes. In places it's even managed to colonize sea walls, though its shrubby growth makes inspections of vital sea defences rather difficult. But the plant is tough enough to withstand an occasional flailing to expose the wall for long enough to check its integrity. And

within a year the shrubby sea-blite is almost back to its former size.[6] That kind of resilience is a prerequisite for any plant growing in such exposed places.

SALTMARSHES

Sea heath, *Frankenia laevis*, and sea purslane, *Halimione portulacoides*, often grow on shingle but can also be found on saltmarshes, another naturally open landscape around the coast. Sea heath is a scarce plant but sea purslane can blanket large areas of ground with its fleshy leaves. Saltmarshes form in more sheltered areas where mud or fine sand is deposited. A few resilient plants can colonize any mud that's left uncovered for long enough between the tides and then, as they trap more mud and silt, they build up the level of the marsh, allowing other plants to colonize. Eventually salt-tolerant grasses join the community, which becomes marshy grassland, often grazed, and which therefore again grades into man-made grasslands inland.

This whole process depends on those first saltmarsh pioneers, plants that are faced with nothing but bare, salty mud. One of these pioneers is glasswort, *Salicornia* spp., which is undaunted by periodic submersion in seawater and roots happily growing in waterlogged mud where there's little oxygen. This little plant is a key player in saltmarsh creation, but it has other uses. Glasswort gets its name from the fact that when it is burned it yields soda ash, an important ingredient in glass-making. It is also edible and when in season, frequently turns up in shops and supermarkets, where it is usually called samphire. After cooking, its fleshy green stems taste a little like asparagus, though a lot more salty. A related plant on the west coast of Canada, where it is also eaten, is known as beach asparagus.

Glasswort is not the only coastal plant to have a gourmet following. Sea kale is still popular in some circles and the oyster plant gets its name from the fact that its leaves taste like oysters. Those fleshy grey-green leaves of sea purslane that blanket large tracts of saltmarsh are also edible, though almost too salty if eaten raw. However, a brief steaming reduces the saltiness, making them more palatable and the plant is very popular with those seeking the epicurean delights of our wild flowers.

Cord grass, *Spartina* spp., is another important early colonist, helping to consolidate the forming marsh, but some kinds of cord grass are now so vigorous and so effective at invading muddy ground that they are swamping the other plants, and their impenetrable leaves and roots are causing problems for wading birds that feed in saltmarshes. This disturbing development can be traced back to 1870, in Southampton Water, where an entirely new kind of cord grass popped up, as if from nowhere. But an explanation for this surprising event was soon discovered. In this area our well-behaved native species, small cord grass, *S. maritima*, found itself growing alongside a species introduced from North America, *S. alterniflora*. The North American plant probably arrived as seeds in ballast from ships arriving at Southampton, perhaps four decades earlier. But by 1870 the two plants had hybridized, as many plants are wont to do, and produced a sterile hybrid, Townsend's cord grass, *S.x townsendii*.[7]

Then, in 1879, another form of cord grass was discovered in the same area, common cord grass, *S. anglica*, a plant that has only ever been found in England. It was later worked out that this species arose by a doubling of the chromosomes of Townsend's cord grass, another common trick amongst plants, which produces an instant new species.[8] These new cord grasses proved to be vigorous colonizers of bare mud, and spread quickly. *S. anglica* was seized on as an ideal plant to transplant around the country in order to stabilize muddy coasts and river banks. Unfortunately, it turned out to be too good at its job and became an invasive species, threatening the saltmarsh habitats it should have been helping to create. Having planted it, conservationists now found themselves trying to control it. Thankfully, in a number of areas, common cord grass has recently suffered from a form of natural die-back, alleviating the threat at least in some places.

HEATH AND BOG

Exposure to wind and weather also creates open grasslands on clifftops and on the wider ledges. The windswept turf is often bright with a great variety of plants. Several kinds of orchids grow in abundance and, around the south-west coast, the tiny blue flowers of spring squill, *Scilla verna*, look like miniature bluebells, falling in drifts down grassy steps to the sea. Even more localized, wild asparagus, *Asparagus prostratus*, is found

Thrift grows on saltmarshes, clifftop grasslands and high mountains.

on just a few spots around the south-west coast. These plants and their relatives are dealt with more fully in Chapter 14. A second community of plants, maritime heath, also grows on exposed areas around the coast. Here the dominant plants are heathers, *Erica* spp., but they're joined in places by sea plantain, *Plantago maritima*, thrift, *Armeria maritima*, and sea campion, *Silene maritima*.

One special example of maritime heath juts out into the English Channel from the tip of Cornwall's southernmost coast – the Lizard. Amongst the heathers here is a very special one – Cornish heath, *Erica vagans*, a plant that likes growing close to the mild influence of the Atlantic. In the UK it's found only on the Lizard, but outside this country it also grows in the Atlantic climates of western France and Spain. It's a particularly beautiful heather with large sprays of pale pink flowers, reputedly because it was blessed by Joseph of Arimathea. Joseph supposedly visited Britain 2,000 years ago, landing first in Cornwall, where he spent the night on a comfortable bed of Cornish heather. He's also said to have travelled north to Glastonbury, where he planted his staff in the ground on Wearyall Hill. Here it grew into the Holy Thorn, a form of common hawthorn, *Crataegus monogyna* 'Biflora', which flowers both at Christmas and then again at the more normal time in spring. It still grows on the slopes of Wearyall Hill in Glastonbury though it was badly damaged by vandals in 2010.

Parts of the maritime heath of the Lizard, along with a few other patches of coastal heath around the country, are probably natural[9] but the Lizard heath extends inland across the peninsula, into heathland created and maintained by humans. This place is famous for a number of extreme rarities apart from Cornish heath, and many of these grow in the bare areas created by old trackways across the heath, so are more dependent on open ground made by humans than that made by nature.

There are other areas of heathland scattered across Britain, in both uplands and lowlands, resulting from ancient clearances of trees. They're often rich in both plants and animals that have depended on the long cultural history of heathlands, wastes where heather or gorse could be cut for bedding or fodder but otherwise left as wild lands. Unfortunately, the cultural value of heathlands has declined and many, particularly in the lowlands of Dorset, Hampshire and Surrey, have been lost to our modern culture – in the form of new housing developments. In the uplands, vast tracts of moorland are now managed by burning to create a heather monoculture which boosts red grouse numbers, the basis of

Red valerian growing on the rich clifftop grasslands of Berry Point National Nature Reserve in Devon.

Overleaf: Cottongrass growing in a valley bog on the Mendip Hills in Somerset.

highly lucrative shoots for the privileged classes. Though one native species benefits from such management (at least until it is peppered with lead shot), the variety of life suffers, a situation only made worse by both legal and illegal control of predators.

Some areas of heathlands are so heavily waterlogged they've become bogs. Here, a thick layer of wet peat has created some of our most fascinating habitats, in which exploration is spiced up by the constant danger of disappearing up to your waist (or worse) in foul-smelling water. In the west and in higher areas, where more rain falls than evaporates, blanket bogs develop and cover vast tracts of land. The excess rain washes iron through the soil and this builds up into a hard and impermeable iron pan below the surface which then causes waterlogging. Sphagnum mosses thrive in these sodden soils and their dead remains, which can only partially decompose in acid, oxygen-starved wet conditions, build up a layer of peat, cutting off nutrients from the soil below. So bogs are characterized both by extreme waterlogging and a severe lack of nutrients. Bogs can also form in valleys and on plains where drainage is impeded in some way. In the latter case, a dome of peat builds up and, since peat is like a sponge, it remains waterlogged even though the bog is raised above the general lie of the land. For this reason these places are called raised bogs. In a few of the wettest places in Britain some of

these bogs may have developed naturally rather than after the clearance of trees.[9]

Some of the richest lowland bogs are found in Dorset and the New Forest in Hampshire. On some, a layer of peat has built up over water, thick enough to support a person's weight – just about. But as you walk on it, the ground sways sickeningly beneath your feet, which is why such places are called 'quaking bogs'. And there's always the thought that if you step on a thinner patch of peat, you might disappear beneath the bog. But you have to venture out on to this treacherous ground if you want to find some of the real gems of this sodden world. Bog orchids, *Hammarbya paludosa*, are tiny and green, almost impossible to spot in the sphagnum moss and it might not seem worth taking the risk to see such an unimpressive plant, but there are giants here too. The large marsh grasshopper, *Stethophyma grossum*, is Britain's biggest grasshopper and one of the most strikingly coloured. It's only found on a few of these southern bogs, usually in the wettest places. After a hot summer's day spent squelching through New Forest bogs to photograph bog orchids and large marsh grasshoppers, it takes a long time for the distinctive aroma of 'bog' to vanish from clothes and skin.

Blanket bog covers vast tracts of Sutherland's flow country.

MOUNTAINTOPS

The windswept peaks of our tallest mountains seem like a long way from the hot and steamy bogs of Dorset or the chiselled coastline of the Lizard peninsula but they're also naturally open ground. Above around 600 metres (1,970 ft) (depending on location) trees are no longer able to grow. In countries less heavily impacted by humans the natural tree line is not a sharp demarcation but instead, trees become more stunted and more scattered, creating a delightful natural bonsai garden called the Krummholz zone. In Britain, forest clearances or, conversely, commercial plantations mean there are very few places where we can see such a natural tree line.

Entering the exposed world above the tree line, we might first be struck by plants familiar from open coastal habitats. Thrift, *Armeria maritima*, turns sea cliffs bright pink with its tightly bunched flower clusters and it grows in impressive drifts over saltmarshes. One of my favourite places to appreciate such carpets of pink is along the shores of Lindisfarne in Northumberland. On the sheltered side of the island facing the Northumberland coast, thrift covers many acres. However, thrift seems just as happy perched on high mountains, though up here it doesn't create such spectacular displays. This strange distribution pattern shouldn't be too surprising. Thrift has evolved to cope with extreme exposure, whether at sea level or hundreds of metres up a mountain. Likewise, mountain avens, *Dryas octopetala*, and roseroot, *Rhodiola rosea*, can both be found at sea level and at high altitude. And I've seen the diminutive and charming moschatel, *Adoxa moschatellina*, also called 'townhall clock' from its tiny green flowers arranged around the faces of a cube, in my favourite local woods near Bristol and high up on the slopes of Ben Lawers in Scotland. But some families of plants are more characteristic of these high places. Some kinds of saxifrages, *Saxifraga* spp., are at home in the lowlands, for example meadow saxifrage, *S. granulata*, an attractive if often overlooked plant of unimproved meadows and grasslands. But most of our saxifrages require a bit of strenuous,

Glen Coe.

and occasionally nerve-wracking, climbing to appreciate – and a few of these are now vanishingly rare. I will explore this hardy group of mountain plants in more detail in Chapter 12. The next chapter looks at carnivorous plants that are all confined to open bogs, and the following chapters feature the alliums and some of the lilies that favour the open ground of coastal or inland cliffs and coastal grasslands.

II

Butterworts,
Bladderworts
& Sundews

LENTIBULARIACEAE
DROSERACEAE

T o live in a bog means coping with both extreme waterlogging and very few nutrients, which is why one group of plants do particularly well here – carnivorous plants. They're happy in the wettest of conditions and get the nutrients they need for growth by catching and digesting insects.[1] It's such a successful trick that, around the world, many plants from a wide range of different families have evolved an insect-eating habit. Even in Britain, our carnivorous plants belong to three unrelated families, united in their strategy of catching and digesting insects to obtain the nutrients they can't get from the soil. But the mechanisms they use to do this vary from family to family and even within one family. The three families of carnivores that lurk in Britain's bogs are represented by the native sundews, *Drosera* spp. (Droseraceae), and butterworts, *Pinguicula* spp. (Lentibulareaceae), along with the purple pitcher plant, *Sarracenia purpurea* (Sarraceniaceae) introduced from North America but thriving in several places in the British Isles. A fourth group of carnivorous plants, the bladderworts, belong to the same family as butterworts but are aquatic.[2] Their leaves and traps grow underwater, although their flowers are held above the surface.

The simplest way to catch insects is to use a sticky trap, the same idea we invented with flypaper, and the plants that use this trick are often called flypaper traps. Usually, the trap takes the form of sticky hairs and as botanists have looked more thoroughly at a greater range of plants, a surprising number have turned out to have flypaper traps – even the humble tomato is a killer.[3] Plants evolved sticky hairs on leaves and stems to discourage leaf-eating insects, although smaller insects often get stuck and die. Catchflies, *Lychnis* spp., get their name from the fact that their stems and leaves are often covered in tiny dead insects. But to qualify as a true carnivore, a plant must also digest the insect and make use of the nutrients released – and some plants have found very ingenious ways to exploit this food source.

While making a film on carnivorous plants, I came across one very curious example of this ingenuity – a South African plant, locally called the flycatcher bush, *Roridula gorgonias*. This bush grows tufts of leaves covered in dense, sticky hairs that make it look a little like a giant sundew, although it is completely unrelated. The glue on the hairs is a kind of resin that makes it much stickier than the mucous blobs of true sundews, and the flycatcher bush can catch very large flies. However, it can't digest them, at least not without help. When you look closely at this plant, you'll discover that it is covered in small bugs who skip around the leaves paying no heed at all to the resinous traps. They are a kind of assassin bug, *Pameridea roridulae*, which lives only on this plant. The bugs soon track down any insect trapped on the leaves and, as is the way of assassin bugs, they pierce their victim with stiletto mouthparts and inject toxins that quickly kill and then begin to digest the trapped insect. The bug can now suck up a nutritious broth of partially digested fly, and what comes out of the other end of the bug is a ready-made plant fertilizer, easily absorbed by the flycatcher bush. Because it needs the help of *Pameridea*, the flycatcher bush is sometimes called a proto-carnivorous plant but it is a good illustration of how true flypaper carnivores, like sundews, may have evolved.

SUNDEWS

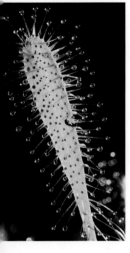

The three species of sundews living in Britain are easily told apart by the shape of their leaves. The most frequent is the round-leaved or common sundew, *D. rotundifolia*, which has small, round leaves. The greater or English sundew, *D. anglica*, has elongated leaves, while the oblong-leaved sundew, *D. intermedia*, has more oval leaves, intermediate between the first two as suggested by its Latin name. Oblong-leaved sundews often grow in bog pools, their leaves rising above the surface of the dark, peat-stained water in a bejewelled carpet. All three trap insects on the glandular hairs that cover the leaves, each hair topped with a blob of sticky mucus. For a long time it was assumed that these sticky leaves, like those possessed by many other plants, were there simply for protection, since no one could quite bring themselves to believe in a plant that caught and ate animals. One of those that thought the idea of a carnivorous plant was an abomination was the Swedish botanist Carl Linnaeus, the originator of the binomial system of nami-ng plants and animals (see page 50). Linnaeus developed a classification system that gave all the species he knew a place in the natural order, a structure he assumed reflected the mind of God. And in that divine order there surely could be no place for meat-eating plants. In a letter dated 16 October 1768, he wrote that the idea of an insect-eating plant was 'against the order of nature as willed by God'. Backed by the authority of Genesis 1, 29–30, he was convinced that plants had been created to sustain animals and people and not the other way around. Anyone who thought otherwise was therefore guilty of blasphemy.

English sundew.

Overleaf: Oblong-leaved sundew.

Nearly a century later, Charles Darwin, no stranger himself to accusations of blasphemy, straightened out this woolly thinking. He became fascinated by these plants and showed beyond doubt that they really were carnivores, getting nutrition by digesting their victims. He described them as the 'most wonderful plants in the world' and devoted a whole book to them, *Insectivorous Plants*, published in 1875.[4] When an insect is trapped on some of the sticky hairs, adjacent hairs quickly bend towards it, which traps the insect even more securely. The leaf then curls up around its victim making escape impossible, and also bringing more digestive glands on the leaf surface to bear on its meal. Darwin experimented by drop-

ping different substances on the leaves and watched their reaction. He found that only certain substances caused the leaf to react. Stones and glass beads had no effect, but an insect, a piece of meat or even a spot of urine caused the leaf to furl. In 1850 he wrote to his friend the botanist Joseph Hooker, director of the Royal Botanic Gardens at Kew, in great excitement: 'The leaves are first rate chemists & can distinguish even an incredibly small quantity of any nitrogenised substance from non-nitrogenised substances.' Darwin became so fascinated by these extraordinary little plants that his wife, Emma, wrote in the same year to Mary Lyell,[*] 'at present he is treating *Drosera* just like a living creature, and I suppose he hopes in the end in proving it to be an animal'.

A few years ago I repeated these experiments for my carnivorous plants film, though I chickened out of trying the urine option. We shot the sundew's reaction in timelapse, which made the results even more

---

* Mary Lyell was a geologist, but as often happened in the Victorian era, she was eclipsed by her husband Charles Lyell, a geologist whose ideas greatly influenced Darwin, and who became a regular correspondent

eft and above:
Common butterwort.

bove right: Alpine butterwort.

obvious. Only substances containing nitrogen interested these plants. Darwin later went on to show that this nitrogen ended up inside the plant's tissues, making them true carnivores. But the idea that plants could really be carnivorous was still seen as heretical by many botanists of Darwin's day and just as he had been with his even more radical ideas on the origins of species, he was worried about publishing his results. In the November of 1860 he wrote to Charles Lyell: 'I will and must finish my Drosera MS [manuscript], which will take me a week, for, at this moment, I care more about *Drosera* than the origin of all the species in the world. But I will not publish on *Drosera* till next year, for I am frightened and astounded by my results.' Darwin didn't publish his book *Insectivorous Plants* for another fifteen years.

Sundews are very effective flypapers and I've often found large dragonflies, such as keeled skimmers, *Orthetrum coerulescens*, or black darters, *Sympetrum danae*, both powerful fliers, stuck fast on their leaves. But a few insects have managed to turn the tables on the sundew. The caterpillar of the plume moth *Trichoptilus paludum* feeds on the leaves of common sundew without any obvious adaptations to avoid becoming a meal itself.[5] It seems simply to be very careful about where it puts its feet. Plume moths have discovered this unusual source of food elsewhere in the world too. In North America another species, *Buckleria parvulus*, has been found feeding on the pink sundew, *D. capillaris*. *Buckleria* adds insult to injury by supplementing its diet with any insects that the leaf has already trapped. It then feeds directly on the blobs of mucus like clearing a minefield, and when the plant is disarmed the caterpillar can feast on the leaf without worry.[6]

Emma Darwin may have been amused by the thought that her husband saw sundews as little animals, but in a way, Charles Darwin was right, as I discovered when I visited the laboratory of David Jennings at the University of South Florida in Tampa. He was curious about whether sundews really were like animals, at least to the extent that they competed with other animals for prey. Around the university are swampy forests which in places are carpeted with pink sundews, and scattered between them are silken mats made by funnel-web wolf spiders, *Sosippus floridanus*. Both sundews and spiders catch similar insects, although the spiders do so in a more dramatic manner. They are frighteningly fast. If a small insect walks on to the silken mat, the spider dashes out of its lair at the edge of the web at such a speed that it's just a blur. The insect doesn't know what's hit it. When insect prey gets scarce, David found that these spiders build bigger webs to increase their chances of catching a meal. But the bigger the webs, the less well-nourished the local sundews are. The spiders are depriving the sundews of prey, although this competition works in both directions. When there are fewer insects around, the spiders build their webs further from the sundew patches, presumably to ensure that any insect that does wander along will end up on a web rather than a sundew.[7] In Britain it's not unusual to find the lairs of wolf spiders around patches of common sundews and I wonder whether a similar relationship exists here. For a pink sundew, catching an insect doesn't necessarily mean it has won the competition with animals. I have discovered oak toads hanging around sundew patches and if a sundew caught a large insect, a toad quickly stole it. Obviously, toad tongues must be stickier than sundew leaves, since as soon as a toad shot out its tongue and hit the trapped insect, it was able to haul the insect off the sundew leaf.

When sundews flower they produce a gracefully curved spike of flowers that open sequentially along the stem. These flowers are dependent on insects for pollination, which presents the plants with an obvious conundrum – how does it avoid trapping and killing potential pollinators? In many species the flower spike is very tall for such a small plant, a fact that has led some botanists to suggest that sundews are keeping insects attracted to the flowers at a safe distance from the lethal traps. However, this obvious solution to the plant's dilemma doesn't seem to be the case. Some kinds of sundews have much shorter flower stalks but botanists could find no difference between long- and short-stalked species in the number of potential pollinators killed on the traps. Instead, tall flower spikes have evolved in some species of sundew to raise their flowers above the herbage and make them more obvious to pollinators.[8, 9]

BUTTERWORTS AND BLADDERWORTS

There are also three species of butterworts growing in Britain: common butterwort, *P. vulgaris*, large-flowered butterwort, *P. grandiflora* and pale butterwort, *P. lusitanica*. As a native plant, large-flowered butterwort is restricted to south-west Ireland, but it has been naturalized in a few places around the UK. A fourth species, Alpine butterwort, *P. alpina*, used to occur in Scotland, possibly a native, possibly introduced, but is now extinct. They all have a rosette of bright-green leaves with the edges partially furled inwards along their length like a half-finished roll-up cigarette. At first sight these leaves don't look like sticky traps, but a closer look reveals short hairs or tentacles, much smaller than those of sundews yet each with a blob of mucus on the tip, and a scattering of

Large-flowered butterwort.

stalkless, or sessile, glands across the leaf surface. They can occasionally catch remarkably large prey though most of their victims are small and their empty husks often litter the surface of the leaves. Once an insect is caught, glands at the base of the tentacles release digestive enzymes which coat the prey. Then the sessile glands release more enzymes and the fate of the victim is sealed. Near the site where the prey was trapped, leaf cells also lose their internal pressure, forming a dip in the leaf into which the prey sinks, wrapping it in more digestive glands. The leaf margins can also roll inwards, though only slowly, and the purpose of this seems more to retain the leaf's secretions and the products of digestion than to further ensnare the prey, as is the case with the sundews.

Britain is also home to seven species of bladderworts, *Utricularia* spp., that grow underwater though they thrust their spectacular yellow flowers into the air above. They're not so easy to tell apart, and all have the same kind of trap, the bladder that gives them their name. These bladders grow on the underwater leaves and have a lid at one end. The plant actively pumps water out of the bladder, reducing the internal pressure and bending the sides of the bladder inwards. When a small creature touches a trigger hair on the bladder, the lid pops open, the sides flip back out and water rushes in. Anything in the vicinity of the trap when it fires stands no chance of escape. The trap deforms and sucks in water in less than a millisecond, making it one of the fastest plant movements ever recorded.[10] Once the prey is sucked inside, the lid then slams closed, sealing the prey inside where it is slowly digested.

A bladderwort trap is such an elaborate structure that it raises the question of how it evolved. Bladderworts belong to the same family as butterworts and although the traps of the two groups look and work in entirely different ways, butterwort-like leaves in the common ancestor of butterworts and bladderworts could feasibly give rise to bladderwort traps. Butterwort leaves are often rolled inwards along their length which both contains their prey and the products of digestion. The ancestral bladderwort may then have rolled up its leaves further to form a tube, with digestive glands lining the inside. Some means of pumping water through the tube would have increased the trap's efficiency and if the entrance to the tube became blocked, the cellular pumps driving the current could then serve to reduce water pressure on the inside of the sealed structure.

THE NATURALIZED PURPLE PITCHER

Elsewhere in the world, carnivorous plants have evolved another kind of trap to catch prey, pitfall traps or pitchers. Several unrelated families have come up with variations on this theme. In South-east Asia I've found the giant pitchers of *Nepenthes rajah*, one of the largest of the Old World pitcher plants (Nepenthaceae), hanging from the tips of the leaves and big enough to trap the occasional unwary rodent. In North America a different family (Sarraceniaceae) has hit on a similar trick. These pitcher plants, *Sarracenia* spp., grow upright pitchers formed from modified leaves. The pitchers are not as large as those of some of the Old World *Nepenthes*, but what they lack in size they more than make up for by sometimes growing in great profusion in marshes and bogs. One of the most entrancing days I've ever spent was on a small private nature reserve in Alabama which was carpeted with white-topped pitchers, *N. leuco-phylla*. The pitchers of these plants are tall and thin, reaching up half a metre (20 in), dark green but strikingly topped with bright white etched with a filigree of dark lines. The plants covered hundreds of square metres, in my opinion one of the world's most spectacular botanical displays. A lid angled over the pitcher stops it from overflowing with rainwater. The underside of the lid has a slippery surface but also secretes nectar – a honey trap to draw in victims. Preoccupied with feasting on this free lunch they are likely to lose their footing and tumble into the pitcher below. And over this stunning display, the air was alive with insects, including several kinds of large swallowtails, far too big to fall into the trap, yet happily feasting on the copious supplies of nectar.

One of these New World pitchers, the purple pitcher plant, *S. purpurea*, reaches north into Canada where it thrives in cold northern bogs. This species has been introduced into several

Naturalized purple pitcher plants from North America are thriving in Wareham Forest, in Dorset.

places around the British Isles, where it also does well in our similar climate. Several populations were established in Ireland and there were another twenty sites across the UK where it also grew. Today only eleven of those sites survive, the largest being in the Solway wetlands in northern Cumbria. I've waded out across the bog at Wareham Forest in Dorset to see another population that also seems to be doing well. The large clumps of its fat purple pitchers seem as much at home here as the native sundews that sparkle around the bog pools close by.

The pitchers are filled with liquid which drowns the plant's victims and which in some species also contains digestive enzymes to break down the prey. But on closer examination, these pitchers turn out to be far more than just traps. Armed with a bulb baster from a local kitchen store (normally used to suck up juices from around a roasting joint to baste it), I spent a day in the swampy pinelands in coastal North Carolina, sucking out the contents of purple pitcher plants and examining them in a small aquarium. As expected, there were plenty of decomposing insects in this foul-smelling broth, a testament to the effectiveness of these traps, but there were also lots of living ones, particularly mosquito larvae. These traps are like little ponds, whole ecosystems inside each

Below: Purple pitcher plant.
Right: Each pitcher is home to variety of mosquito larvae, including these predatory ones belonging to the genus *Toxorhynchites*.

pitcher, and the purple pitcher depends on this for its survival. The pitchers of this species produce no digestive enzymes. Instead, it relies on several kinds of mosquito larvae to break down and digest its prey. The plant can then absorb nutrients in the excretions of the mosquito larvae, in much the same way that the flycatcher bush in South Africa depends on the droppings of its symbiotic bugs.

Just as the *Pameridea* bug is only found on flycatcher bushes, so two species of mosquito larvae are entirely confined to the little ponds created by purple pitcher plants. The pitcher plant midge, *Metriocnemus knabi*, lives in the upper part of the pitcher and the pitcher plant mosquito, *Wyeomyia smithii*, lives deeper below it. Together they form a processing chain which eventually supplies the pitcher plant with nutrients. Midge larvae feed by chewing away at whole carcasses, breaking them into smaller pieces which are rapidly colonized by bacteria. In the deeper layers, the mosquito larvae feed by filtering small particles and bacteria from the water and depend on the rain of particles from above created by feeding midge larvae.[11] To complicate matters further, on my day of draining pitcher plants of their fluid, I also extracted the larvae of a predatory mosquito, *Toxorhynchites* spp., a huge, sausage-shaped beast that sucks up smaller larvae as if it were eating spaghetti. I have yet to take my bulb baster out on to the bogs inhabited by naturalized colonies of purple pitchers in Britain, but I presume that the introduction of this plant into the British Isles also meant the introduction of several foreign species of mosquito.

After travelling the world and across the British Isles in search of carnivorous plants, I share Darwin's enthusiasm for these groups of plants. He called them 'the most wonderful plants in the world'[12] a description that became ever more applicable as Victorian explorers discovered ever more strange and bizarre carnivorous plants in remote corners of the world. These discoveries only helped fuel the Victorian fascination with Gothic horror, especially when tales of trees that trapped and ate people filtered back to Victorian Britain. This tale, of course, proved fictitious,[13] but, as so often with natural history, the truth is often far stranger than fiction.

12

Saxifrages

SAXIFRAGACAE

If any family of plants epitomize the open spaces of high mountain-tops or remote corries and cliffs it must be the saxifrages, *Saxifraga* spp. Their name means stone-breaker, an apparently appropriate epithet for these hardy colonists of open ground as they send their roots deep into crevices on bare rock faces. The true origin of their name, however, is rather disappointingly a reference to the supposed medicinal properties of some species; it refers to their use in breaking up kidney stones. And even this is unlikely to be true. The name 'saxifrage' originates in the first century AD, with the Greek herbalist Dioscorides, who wrote a five-volume treatise on the medicinal properties of plants. *De Materia Medica* was read and widely accepted for 1,500 years and his ideas were incorporated into medieval herbals. Since most kinds of saxifrages in Britain grow in remote mountains, the only saxifrage illustrated in sixteenth-century British herbals is the meadow saxifrage, *S. granulata*, a plant of lowland meadows. One of the guiding philosophies of early herbalists was the *Doctrine of Signatures* – the idea that God had thoughtfully placed clues to a plant's medicinal uses in the shape, colour and texture of leaves, roots and flowers. Meadow saxifrage has stone-like bulbils (reproductive structures) within its rosette of leaves and those leaves are kidney-shaped, a clear indication of its efficacy in treating kidney stones and a further vindication of Dioscorides' ideas. Modern research has, however, failed to find any such properties.

Below: Meadow saxifrage
Right: Purple saxifrage.

Charles Darwin also developed an interest in this genus. He thought that saxifrages were closely related to the sticky-leaved carnivorous sundews that had fascinated him for so many years. He realized that some saxifrages, such as the rue-leaved saxifrage, *S. tridactylites*, and the kidney saxifrage, *S. hirsuta*, also have sticky leaves, and he wondered whether these plants were on the evolutionary path to carnivory. He was wrong about the close relationship between sundews and saxifrages, but in thinking more widely about carnivory in plants, he was far ahead of his time.

Recent work has shown that a surprising number of plants, including cinquefoils, *Potentilla* spp., and geraniums, *Geranium* spp., are capable of both catching and digesting insect prey.[1] I don't know of any similar work on saxifrages but given the widespread ability to make use of nutrients from decomposing insects, it wouldn't come as a great surprise if Darwin was right in his speculations about the sticky-leaved saxifrages. And, though not related to sundews, molecular analyses have recently shown that saxifrages are indeed allied to a carnivorous plant – a pitcher plant, the Albany pitcher, found only in the far south-western corner of Australia.[2] Perhaps Darwin was not too far off the mark after all.

SAXIFRAGES OF MOOR AND MOUNTAIN

Hunting out our native saxifrages is the perfect excuse to head out into some of the wildest landscapes remaining in Britain, their appeal made all the more alluring by the extreme rarity of some species, although one of the more widespread of these mountain species is also one of the most beautiful. Despite living in harsh climes, the purple saxifrage, *S. oppositifolia*, flowers early, its trailing stems growing into mats covered

in large purple flowers that open in March or April, just as the snow is melting. It's a tough little plant that, in Greenland, is part of some of the most northerly plant communities in the whole world. In Britain it's characteristically a plant of rugged mountain slopes but it grows at sea level on the Isle of Lewis in the Hebrides and at Cape Wrath in the far north-west corner of Scotland. There are few insects in the cold climates where it grows, so the flowers are self-pollinated and they trap what heat there is to speed seed development in the short growing season.

There are two yellow-flowered saxifrages growing in Britain, the commonest being the yellow mountain saxifrage, *S. aizoides*. But curiously, although this species occurs as far south as Cumbria and the north Pennines, it is absent from the mountains of North Wales. Much scarcer, the marsh saxifrage, *S. hirculus*, has declined markedly over the last century both in Britain and across Europe.[3] A plant of base-rich mires and flushes, it once grew in both lowlands and uplands. Today it is confined to high-altitude sites in a few scattered locations in Scotland and in its stronghold in a small area of the northern Pennines, where there are several thriving colonies along a 50-kilometre-stretch (32 miles) from Cross Fell to Stainmore.[4] It also grows in some abundance in wet runnels alongside the track leading to the summit of Ben Lawers. However, it may grow in many more sites than we think. Sometimes, when sheep are removed from an area in the uplands, marsh saxifrage flowers suddenly appear, often in some profusion. Several new sites have been discovered in this way, where sheep grazing must have prevented

Below: Mossy saxifrage.
Right: Drooping saxifrage.

the plants from flowering. But it's no good trying to encourage marsh saxifrages by excluding grazers. Without grazing, other plants grow rank and soon out-compete the saxifrages. Marsh saxifrages exist in a delicate balance with the sheep that share their montane home.

Mossy saxifrage, *S. hypnoides*, grows along stream sides where it's almost invisible amongst clumps of moss until it opens its mat of white flowers. In the south, it grows in Cheddar Gorge in Somerset but is commoner, and much easier to find, further north. Starry saxifrage, *S. stellaris*, puts up a single spike of white starry flowers from a glossy rosette of leaves. It too grows along mountain streams and on wet rock ledges and, as befits this hardy group of plants, has been found growing higher than any other British plant, at 1,340 metres (4,400 ft) on Ben Nevis.[5] It's not uncommon in mountains in the north and west of the UK but a similar species, the Alpine saxifrage, *S. nivalis*, is much scarcer and confined mainly to Scottish mountains, with a few populations in Cumbria and Snowdonia. These latter populations are probably close to their tolerance for the balmy south and set much less seed than the Scottish plants. On Ben Lawers it reaches over 1,200 metres (3,980 ft) and there are records from 1,300 metres (4,300 ft) in the Cairngorms, not much short of the record-holding starry saxifrage.

HIGH MOUNTAIN SAXIFRAGES

Many saxifrage species reach high up into the mountains, but there are three truly montane saxifrages in Britain: Highland saxifrage, *S. rivularis*, tufted saxifrage, *S. cespitosa*, and drooping saxifrage, *S. cernua*. The commonest, though it's by no means abundant, is the Highland saxifrage, confined to a scattering of Scottish mountains. It seems to relish cold and grows close to sites where snow lies late, so is usually found on northern or north-easterly slopes where it's more than happy to have its roots bathed in cold meltwater. The drooping saxifrage has a similar predilection for late-lying snow, to the extent that one of its sites is sometimes still snow-covered even after mid summer's day.[6] After such a late start, there's little time to flower and often drooping saxifrages don't bother. Instead they produce small bulbils along the flower stalk that drop off and grow into new plants. Since these are genetically identical to their parents, patches of drooping saxifrage are often made up from clones. They're only known from Ben Lawers, parts of Glen Coe and a few colonies on and around Ben Nevis. Yet despite its rarity, plants are still stolen from the wild by criminal collectors.[7] I'll never condone the uprooting of any wild plants, but at least I can understand why unscrupulous enthusiasts are drawn to exotic-looking specimens such as orchids. Those responsible for digging up these saxifrages must be obsessive in the extreme, however, since drooping saxifrages, usually shy to flower at all, are hardly the most spectacular of British plants.

The third of this trilogy of extreme plants, tufted saxifrage, was one of the first plants to recolonize Britain in the wake of the retreating ice. At the height of the Ice Age it grew in the Lea Valley in north London, close to the southern edge of the ice sheet, and as the Ice Age ended it occupied ground further and further north as new land was slowly revealed by the melting ice. Pollen analysis shows it was the first plant to colonize Cwm Idwal in Snowdonia, where a small colony still hangs on.[8] Otherwise it now grows in just a handful of Scottish sites.[9] In 2014 it was discovered on Trotternish Ridge on Skye, a site so inaccessible it needs a rope climb to find it. So it's entirely possible that the plant is commoner than we think, simply growing out of sight of all but the most intrepid of botanists.

Right: Alpine saxifrage.
Below: Starry saxifrage.

But tufted saxifrage is struggling in its Welsh home, which is the most southerly site for this species in north-west Europe (it occurs a little further south in the Urals and in North America). And its fight to survive at the southern edge of its range hasn't been helped by collectors who removed plants during the nineteenth century. Back in the late 1970s a good friend of mine, David Parker, made a detailed study of this and related saxifrages. When David started his work in Cwm Idwal there were just two clumps of tufted saxifrage left and one of those died in the long, hot summer of 1976.

David propagated seeds from these plants at Liverpool University's Botanic Gardens at Ness. In 1978, 325 plants were given new homes in Cwm Idwal but even these struggled to survive and by 2014 only one plant from the original introductions was left. By 2016 this had grown to five plants and now two of the nine original introduction sites support a few plants and some plants have managed to recolonize the site lost in 1976, so tufted saxifrages are just about hanging on in Snowdonia. This far south, mild winters and hot, dry summers are a real problem[10] so climate change could finally spell the end for these plants, whose ancestors were first to arrive in the great bowl of Cwm Idwal after the ice retreated. But in the long term, the tufted saxifrages on Snowdon might well be doomed; a tragedy made all the more poignant because these plants have had such a long history here and consequently are genetically distinct from other populations. And other snow-loving, cold-weather species will have similar problems in the years to come. Many of our mountain plants have gradually retreated to the very tops of the highest mountains over the last twelve millennia as our climate warmed naturally, seeking the cold, harsh conditions in which they thrive. Now, with further warming fuelled by humanity, they have nowhere else to go but extinct.

LUSITANIAN SAXIFRAGES

Many people are familiar with a much commoner saxifrage – London pride, *S. x urbium*. This is a garden hybrid, frequently used as a ground-cover plant in those hard-to-fill dry, shady places, which rewards the gardener with a constellation of starry white flowers in late spring. This hybrid was known from the seventeenth century but before 1700 the accolade of London pride was given to the plant we now call sweet William. I have no idea what the saxifrage did at that time to deserve its new name, but later it becomes easier to see why Londoners might take pride in this plant. Its ability to grow in neglected or dry, barren places meant that it rapidly colonized the rubble of bombed-out houses in the aftermath of the Blitz. It became a symbol of the resilience of Londoners in the face of nightly bombing raids and Noel Coward even wrote a popular song about the plant, called 'London Pride'.

Although London pride is widely naturalized, one of its parents is a true native, at least in Ireland. St Patrick's cabbage, *S. spathularis*, grows in south-west and western Ireland, mainly in counties Galway, Kerry, Cork and Waterford. Thanks to this Irish heritage, London pride is also sometimes called St Patrick's cabbage and less frequently prattling Parnell, which may also have Irish origins. I presume the Parnell is

Rosy saxifrage.

Charles Stewart Parnell, who became a leader in the Irish nationalist movement in the late nineteenth century. The other parent is *S. umbrosa*, another popular garden plant which is confusingly often called London pride too. A better name is Pyrenean saxifrage, since this is where it is a wild native.

The true St Patrick's cabbage, *S. spathularis*, favours areas of extremely high rainfall, which is certainly the case in the south-west corner of Ireland where it grows. Elsewhere, it grows only in the Iberian Peninsula, a strangely disjunct distribution that it shares with a number of plants and animals in south-west Ireland. They make up the *Lusitanian Flora and Fauna*, and they remain an enigma. The puzzle is why they occur in the Iberian Peninsula but not in western France or England, where suitable habitat often exists, and then crop up again in south-western Ireland.

Did they survive as a relict population in this corner of Ireland during the height of the last Ice Age while they were obliterated from other parts of their range in the north? Or did they somehow disperse from the Iberian Peninsula to Ireland after the ice retreated? Sea levels were much lower at the end of the last glaciation, which means that the shape of western Europe's coastline was unrecognisably different from today, and perhaps at that time the distribution of Lusitanian plants and animals was just as different. They may have been more widely spread around the western fringes of Europe until rising sea levels drowned part of their home. But there is still no widely accepted answer to this mystery.

There are more than a dozen other plants with this same distribution, including a tree, the strawberry tree, *Arbutus unedo*. These plants are joined by Lusitanian animals such as the Kerry spotted slug, *Geomalacus maculosus*, which, like St Patrick's cabbage, needs high rainfall and humidity. I once made a trip to Killarney National Park just to find this slug, which may seem a little eccentric to some. But it is a particularly handsome slug with a history as mysterious as the Lusitanian flora, and I was delighted to find specimens in several places in the fairytale oakwoods above Killarney and on the slopes of MacGillycuddy's Reeks, a mountain chain in Kerry with a name you just want to keep saying over and over. There is also another saxifrage to add to this list of Lusitanian animals and plants – the kidney saxifrage, *S. hirsuta*.

Kidney saxifrages are much rarer than St Patrick's cabbages in south-west Ireland, where they are restricted to counties Cork and Kerry, though in the Iberian Peninsula this is reversed, and kidney saxifrages are by far the more widespread species. In Iberia their ranges don't overlap much, but where they do, these two species hybridize and produce a plant called *S. x polita*. Their ranges overlap much more in Ireland, and in Kerry and Cork the hybrids are common. The extent of hybridization is worrying Irish conservationists. Genetic analysis of the kidney saxifrages in Kerry and Cork show that most have been infiltrated to some extent by the genes of St Patrick's cabbage as the hybrids breed with their parents. This is called back-crossing and although it is a natural phenomenon, the genetic purity of the parent species becomes a concern when one or both parents exist in small populations or live in a restricted area. Kidney saxifrage genes have also penetrated the St Patrick's cabbage population, but to a lesser extent and since St Patrick's cabbage lives in lots of places beyond the range of the kidney saxifrage, the genetic integrity of the Irish populations is under no real threat.

A third scarce saxifrage can also occasionally be found in the Kerry mountains, the Irish saxifrage, *S. rosacea*, although it is easier to find in the rocky landscapes of the Burren in County Clare. Like many saxifrages, it favours the open ground of cliff ledges, scree slopes and rock gullies. It isn't really one of the true Lusitanian saxifrages since it used to occur in the mountains of North Wales as well, where it was last recorded in 1978.[11] There are also old records purporting to be of native plants from Scotland but today these are usually regarded with suspicion.[12] The Irish saxifrage has also declined in its Irish sites over the last century, although this may be as much to do with under-recording in recent years as to do with a real decline and it can also be confused with the much commoner mossy saxifrage, which doesn't help with revealing the true picture. Growing on the bare limestone pavements of the Burren, sometimes only a few hundred metres from the sea, the tight clumps of Irish saxifrages covered in white flowers look like they should be winning medals at alpine flower shows. Yet they are only one of the special plants in this botanic hotspot on the west coast of Ireland.

The last saxifrages to mention are much more widespread. The rue-leaved saxifrage, *S. tridactylites*, is common in Britain, particularly in chalky and limestone areas where, amongst mosses and stonecrops, it helps create miniature rock gardens on dry stone walls. It also grows in open turf and exposed rocky outcrops and is increasingly common in a variety of more recent man-made habitats. These intrepid colonists are slightly different genetically from plants growing in wilder places, a pointer to an increasingly recognized phenomenon of 'unnatural selection'.[13] Our impact on the natural world extends to the most basic processes of evolution, often in surprising ways. Snakes in Australia are evolving smaller mouths following the arrival of cane toads from South America. These toads are highly toxic to Australia's native fauna, so snakes with mouths too small to eat a toad are now more successful and the trait has spread through the population. Cliff swallows in the US nesting under busy freeway bridges have evolved shorter tails, which gives them extra manoeuvrability and enough agility to avoid onrushing trucks. It's not clear what effect the genetic differences are having in rue-leaved saxifrage, but it ranks alongside the ever-growing number of examples illustrating unnatural selection.

The meadow saxifrage, *S. granulata*, as its name implies, is a plant of damp meadows and old grasslands. Its sprays of white flowers would once have been a common sight but agricultural intensification and the increasing use of broad-spectrum herbicides has reduced meadow saxifrage populations dramatically in recent years. Even so, it still occurs across England, Scotland and Wales, although absent from south-west England and north-west Scotland. It is also rare in Ireland, where it is confined to a couple of sites in County Dublin.

Meadow saxifrages are pollinated by a wide variety of insects despite not offering a very generous nectar reward. Instead, all the meadow saxifrages flower at the same time and over a short period, briefly spangling grasslands with their white stars. This spectacular display attracts the attention of insects from far and wide and overwhelms other flowers in the meadow. But meadow saxifrages are not entirely dependent on insects. They can spread very effectively by means of a mass of bulbils produced among their leaves. As we saw at the start of this chapter, these stone-like bulbils might well have been responsible for giving this whole group of plants their name of 'stone-breakers', but their real purpose is not to signify medicinal uses of the plant. They serve to propagate meadow saxifrages rapidly and to help them colonize new places. They are easily stuck to the muddy feet of grazing cattle and can be carried far afield from the parent plants to start a new colony.

Meadow saxifrages flower in the spring and by the summer have died back to nothing. Their bulbils, however, persist and germinate in the autumn to grow into a flowering plant by the next spring, so if grasslands are managed sympathetically, meadow saxifrages can soon recolonize lost ground. This saxifrage of lowland grasslands is a beautiful plant, sometimes growing in glorious displays, but it is the meadow saxifrage's high mountain cousins that appeal to me. There's nothing more satisfying than a strenuous hike through mountain scenery when it is rewarded by the discovery of these hardy plants. A tight constellation of white flowers draws attention to a starry saxifrage growing on top of a mossy boulder in a crystal mountain stream. Squelch through sodden moss where a shallower gradient causes the stream to spread and slow, and the bright-yellow flower clusters of yellow marsh saxifrage stand out from clumps of rushes. A scramble over tumbled boulders on the mountain slopes reveals a natural rock garden where the colourful mats of purple saxifrage grow tight to the contours of the rocks. They might not literally be 'stone-breakers' but they are completely at home amongst hard, stony landscapes of mountain and fell.

13

Alliums

AMARYLLIDACEAE

Alliums are well known to gardeners as dramatic architectural plants. The star of Persia, *A. christophii*, carries huge globes of starry lilac flowers on tall stems. *A. aflatunense*, a native of Kazakhstan and Kyrgyzstan sports smaller, though still substantial, heads of purple flowers and is often grown en masse to create colourful beds of texture and colour. The flowering onion, *A. schubertii*, looks like an explosion frozen in time, with an open head of flowers through which longer flower stalks erupt. For this reason, it is sometimes called the firework allium. Our native and naturalized alliums, though not all so large, have a similar architectural beauty and have the advantage of often growing in spectacular scenery. Rosy garlic, *A. roseum*, with its delicate pink starburst of flowers, and round-headed leek, *A. sphaerocephalon*, perch on precipitous cliff faces of inland gorges and wild leek, *A. ampeloprasum*, grows on rocky coasts in the south-west of Britain. Some are so successful at colonizing open ground they've become weeds of arable fields, with bulbs buried deep beyond the reach of the plough. And the three-cornered leek, *A.triquetrum*, an invasive if rather attractive alien, is capable of colonizing tarmac and paving stones if there is as much as a small crack to gain a roothold.

All alliums are green factories, manufacturing a vast range of chemicals which imbue the plants with their typical smell and taste of garlic, and have been used for millennia for their medicinal properties. Modern science has vindicated many of these old folk remedies, making alliums a valuable source of modern medicines. Apart from their value as ornamental and medicinal plants, *Allium* is an important genus for another reason. It includes three very familiar plants; garlic, *A. sativum*, onion, *A. cepa* and leek, *A. porrum*, all of which have escaped into the wild from kitchen gardens in various places up and down the country. Most people will also be familiar with chives, *A. schoenoprasum*, which is probably a genuine native in a few localities on thin soils over limestone rocks, but it has also escaped cultivation and occurs more widely across the countryside.

When the great Swedish botanist and classifier of life Carl Linnaeus first described the alliums in his *Species Plantarum* in 1753, he recognized just thirty species. Today there are at least 750 described species,[1] perhaps as many as 800.[2] In Europe as a whole there are some 110 species, though stepping across the Bosphorus into Asia, Turkey alone has 141 species. This riot of alliums makes our dozen or so commonly found species seem eminently manageable. Turkey is especially rich in species because it lies

Three-cornered leek.

in the middle of one of the two main centres of distribution for alliums. The first stretches from the Mediterranean Basin through Turkey and across to Central Asia, whilst the second is in western North America. Alliums therefore are virtually all plants of the northern hemisphere, at least as natives, with the curious exception of *A. dregeanum*, which grows in South Africa. However, thanks to their food, medicinal and ornamental value, alliums have now been spread widely across both hemispheres.

In addition to these domesticated food plants, many wild alliums can also be eaten. The three-cornered leek has a much more delicate flavour than garlic, extolled by several international chefs. But some may be a little too potent. Writing in his famous *Herball* of 1633 John Gerard says of wild garlic: 'leaves may very well be eaten in April and May with butter, of such as are of a strong constitution, and labouring men'. Not the highest recommendation!

Because of their food value, as well as their medicinal value, alliums from continental Europe have been brought to Britain for many centuries and introduced so widely that only around half the alliums found growing wild today are true natives. We have five or six natives (botanists are still split on the status of one extremely rare species) and another six or so alien species that are frequently found in the wild. The standard British *Flora* lists twenty-three species, though many of the non-natives are not widely naturalised.[3] However, alliums from across the world are now so popular as garden plants that many more species could easily be found naturalized close to gardens.

Our true natives are ramsons, or wild garlic, *A. ursinum*, a woodland species covered in Chapter 2; crow garlic or wild onion, *A. vineale*; field garlic, *A. oleraceum*; sand leek, *A. scorodoprasum*; wild chives, *A. schoenoprasum*; and possibly round-headed leek, *A. sphaerocephalon*. However, British sand leeks, which grow most commonly in a band from the Humber to the Solway Firth and in eastern Scotland, are sometimes thought to be plants derived in horticulture from a southern European sub-species of sand leek. We'll see shortly that classifying alliums is not for the faint-hearted.

The two most widespread species are crow garlic and field garlic, which have often been confused. Indeed, field garlic was often referred to as crow garlic in the past. The most widespread naturalized species are three-cornered leek, *A. triquetrum*; few-flowered garlic, *A. paradoxum*; keeled garlic, *A. carinatum*; and wild leek, *A. ampeloprasum*. In some places, honey garlic, *A. siculum*, sometimes called *Nectaroscordum siculum*, especially in garden centres, also seems quite happy growing wild.

WILD LEEKS

Many of the widely naturalized species are often found around the sites of old settlements – a clue to their origins here. That's particularly true of perhaps our most spectacular allium, *A. ampeloprasum*. Two varieties occur here, the rarest being var. *ampeloprasum*, the wild leek, which grows to an impressive 1.8 metres (6 ft) tall, with a tennis ball-sized head of around 500 flowers. It's widely regarded as the ancestor of the familiar leek, as well as the kurrat, a Middle Eastern version of the leek, in which it's the leaves rather than the swollen leaf bases that are eaten.[4]

The wild leek grows in only a few sites in the south-west of Britain. It's a native of the Mediterranean region where it's particularly common in vineyards – indeed 'ampeloprasum' means 'vine leek' in Ancient Greek. But here in Britain it's generally only found close to ancient settlements.

It grows on two tiny islets, Steep Holm and Flat Holm, in the

Wild leek in bud.

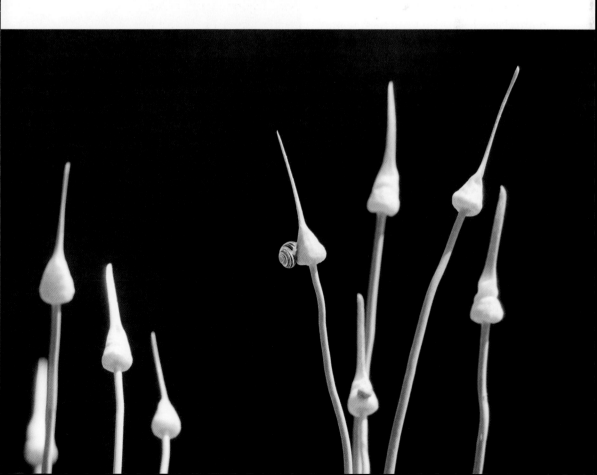

Bristol Channel. Back in the twelfth century, Steep Holm was the site of an Augustinian priory. The monks inhabiting this isolated rock were well aware of the useful properties of many plants and doubtless planted the wild leek along with several other unusual plants that still grow on the island. Five hundred years later wild leek was so abundant on this island that it merited a comment in the 1625 account book of the Manor of Norton Beauchamp, to which Steep Holm belonged at the time. It was one of the dominant plants on the island and was eaten in great quantities by the local rabbits. These rabbits were an important source of meat for the manor in the seventeenth century, but unfortunately the wild leeks so 'tainted the rabbits that they were not worth eating'.

Wild leek has declined on both islands since then and now there are perhaps just a few hundred plants on each island. Nevertheless, since Flat Holm is now

Babington's leek.

officially part of Cardiff, the wild leek, progenitor of the botanical emblem of Wales, has been enthusiastically adopted as the county flower. More recently a small colony of wild leeks was discovered further west, at South Stack in Pembrokeshire. Contrary to the long-term declines on the islands in the Bristol Channel, the plants here seem to be increasing. In 2002, when the plants were first seen, there were just sixteen flowers but by 2013 that had risen to eighty-three flower heads.

The wild leek has also done well after introductions much further afield. It grows widely in many eastern states of the US, where it's often called the Yorktown onion. The Battle of Yorktown (1781) sealed the victory of the American Continental Army over the British and more or less marked the end of the American Revolutionary War. Legend has it that the seeds of the Yorktown onion came from Europe during this time – maybe with the French troops that assisted the American forces – mixed in with crop seeds or fodder. Perhaps because it's a reminder of the birth of the American nation, it's illegal to pick the plant in York County, Virginia, even though it's a non-native and, as we'll see shortly, some of its close relatives have become hated weeds in the United States.

Back in Britain, a second variety of *Allium ampeloprasum* is more widespread, at least in the south-west of England, growing in open woods, railway embankments, roadsides and along the coast.[5] This is Babington's leek,* var. *babingtonii*, a plant that also grows in a few places along the west coast of Ireland and on the Aran Islands, at the mouth of Galway Bay. Babington's leek looks very different from the wild leek. It still grows to an impressive height and produces a large spherical flower head, but the individual flowers are all sterile. A few individual flowers grow long stalks and produce smaller secondary flower heads on top, making it a much more untidy-looking plant than var. *ampeloprasum*. Yet other flowers fail to develop properly at all and instead produce bulbils – tiny bulbs that can be seen at the base of the normal flower stalks.[6]

As they swell, the bulbils grow heavy, until eventually the tall stem topples over and the bulbils germinate around the fallen head to produce a clump of plants. Because they are produced asexually, these new plants will be exact replicas of the parent plant. That genetic similarity might limit the ability of Babington's leek to adapt to new circumstances, but at least it's not dependent on pollinators and so can produce large numbers of offspring whatever the vagaries of the weather.

The wild leek, on the other hand, relies on sex and seed for reproduction. Since the seed is likely to have been fertilized by pollen from a different plant, the wild leek's seeds will all be genetically different from their parents, but the amount of seed it produces is limited by the activity of pollinators. These are two contrasting strategies, each with advantages and disadvantages. But each variety of *A. ampeloprasum* is stuck with its own particular method – Babington's leek never produces seed, whilst the wild leek never produces bulbils. One other variety of this intriguing plant, var. *bulbiferum*, grows widely in Guernsey and has the best of both worlds, producing both bulbils and fertile flowers on the same head, a strategy adopted by several other species of allium, as we'll see later. Var. *bulbiferum* also has a third reproductive strategy. It produces a mass of daughter bulbs underground.

---

* Named after Charles Cardale Babington (1808–95), a botanist and contemporary of Charles Darwin.

The strategy adopted by Babington's leek means that it can only ever produce clones of itself, but a really surprising discovery was made back in 2001 when the genomes of Babington's leeks from across its entire range in the south-west of Britain were compared. It turns out that the whole population in this country is genetically identical – it's all the same clone![7] It's highly unusual for a single clone to be so widespread. The infamous Japanese knotweed is another example, as is the star of Bethlehem, *Gagea spathacea*, discussed in Chapter 14,[8] but Babington's leek has a few other surprises.

Babington's leek occurs in a much wider variety of habitats than the wild leek, which is confined to places where competition is not too intense. Even around its native range in the Mediterranean, the wild leek is not a strong competitor and prefers habitats kept clear of other rank vegetation – such as the vineyards after which it is named. And this is a bit of a puzzle. Usually, plants with a bigger genetic variation can cope with a bigger range of habitats, whilst a narrow genetic base confines a plant to an equally narrow range of options. Yet, because of its clonal reproduction, Babington's leek has a much smaller genetic variation than wild leek. So why is Babington's leek so much more catholic in its choice of habitats? No one really knows.

Its history in this country is just as enigmatic. The earliest records of plants that could be Babington's leek come from the 1830s, where they seemed to have been confined to old orchards in Cornwall[9] – habitats not dissimilar in structure to vineyards. Later records continue to describe this as a plant of old orchards, until a sudden rapid expansion that, by 1909, saw Babington's leeks occupying a much broader range of habitats. A closer look at the genetics of Babington's leek may give some clues as to why it behaved like this.

There are many examples scattered throughout the pages of this book of the phenomenon that botanists call polyploidy (see, especially, Foreword, page 13, and pages 269–70). This refers to the ability of plants to multiply up their chromosomes to two, three, four or more times the basic number during reproduction. This can sometimes result in a distinct plant that can't interbreed with its parental type – an instant new species. Sometimes polyploidy makes it difficult for the new plant to reproduce sexually, but it can still reproduce vegetatively, producing clones of a new asexual species.

Polyploidy is so frequent an occurrence in plants that it's a major mechanism for the evolution of new species. Babington's leek is a

Right: Rosy garlic.

Overleaf: Culinary leek.

hexaploid; that is, it has six copies of each chromosome. The wild leek, on the other hand, is a tetraploid, having just four copies. Often (though by no means always), plants with higher levels of polyploidy are more robust or can survive harsher conditions. Babington's leek is certainly one of the few plants in south-west Britain that is actively growing above ground during winter and early spring – betraying its origins as a Mediterranean plant. It may simply be that such polyploid plants have more genetic material – more DNA – so can produce larger quantities of proteins such as enzymes that drive the processes of life. Perhaps the switch to hexaploidy in Babington's leek happened fairly recently, allowing its sudden emergence from Cornish orchards and enabling it to live in a wider variety of places than wild leek.

However, the story becomes more intriguing still. *A. ampeloprasum* belongs to a somewhat confusing group of very similar alliums which includes *A. iranicum*, *A. polyanthum* and *A. atroviolaceum*. Sometimes *A. iranicum*, for example, is seen as just another variety *of A. ampeloprasum* and sometimes all the varieties of *A. ampeloprasum* are given full species status. The confusion also extends to the English names of this group of alliums. As well as wild leek, var. *ampeloprasum* is sometimes called elephant garlic and sometimes great-headed garlic, both fitting names given its impressive stature.[10] But sometimes 'great-headed garlic' refers to other plants, such as *A. iranicum* and *A. polyanthum*.[11]

Traditionally, botanists were restricted to examining the physical features of plants to try to work out the relationships between them. This was how Carl Linnaeus began to sort the natural world into some semblance of order in his *Species Plantarum*, but this can lead the unwary botanist up the garden path. Some plants, such as the marsh orchids (see Chapter 10) have always been particularly troublesome and what constitutes a 'species' changes continually. Just look back through a range of field guides published at different times and you'll see what I mean.

But today we have sophisticated techniques that allow us look directly at the genetic code of a plant. In theory, at least, this should provide us with a more definitive family tree. As these techniques grow ever more refined and quicker to implement, botanists are able to examine more and more plants. The resulting family trees often contain surprises that would not be revealed by more traditional approaches.

Looking at the family trees based on recent genetic studies, var. *babingtonii* is related to other hexaploid (x6) and octoploid (x8) plants, including *A. commutatum and A. bourgeaui*, but separate from all the tetraploid (x4) versions of *A. ampeloprasum* that were examined.[12] Perhaps this helps explain the differences between the two 'varieties' living

Below: Culinary leek.
Right: The Avon Gorge in Bristol, home to many kinds of native and alien alliums.

in south-west Britain – they may be less closely related than is usually assumed. It's possible that they should even be seen as separate species.

Some of the familiar culinary alliums are also tetraploid and the same study showed that all these tetraploid vegetables sit together in a single group, suggesting that they all derive from the same ancestor. We've already met the leek and the kurrat, but the group also includes bulbous leek and pearl onions, the latter named from its tiny spherical bulbs. It's usually said that culinary leeks were derived from the tetraploid wild leek, but these genetic studies suggest something different. Molecular evidence puts culinary leeks closer to two other species of allium, *A. iranicum* and *A. atroviolaceum*, casting doubt on the wild leek's credentials as the progenitor of the culinary leek.[13] Perhaps the good people of Cardiff would like to reconsider their choice of county flower.

The south-west of Britain is particularly rich

in alien alliums. The three-cornered leek is a highly invasive though attractive species that, in places, carpets the ground in early spring with elegant, drooping white flowers, a little reminiscent of white bluebells. It was introduced into cultivation in Britain in 1752 from its western Mediterranean home and began to appear in the wild on Cornish hedge banks in the 1860s. By the 1930s it had reached Devon and has continued to spread since. It's so invasive that it's now illegal to plant this species in the wild. Like the wild leek, it too has been introduced far and wide. In Australia it's called onion weed and local authorities struggle to control its spread. However, three-cornered leek is edible, with a delicate garlic flavour. All parts can be eaten, some with more flavour, some with less. So Australians are being encouraged to eat three-cornered leeks as an act of public duty – eat 'em to beat 'em.

ALLIUMS IN THE AVON GORGE

Perhaps the best place in the south-west to see alliums, both native and alien, is in the Avon Gorge in Bristol. Here, the River Avon has cut a steep-sided gorge through carboniferous limestone and created both a spectacular landscape and a botanical hotspot. Spanned by Brunel's iconic Clifton Suspension Bridge, the gorge falls away in steep limestone cliffs on the Bristol side while the slightly gentler slopes on the opposite side are cloaked in trees that make up Leigh Woods – a national nature reserve. Despite its proximity to a bustling city, both woods and cliffs are home to many rare plants, some found only here. The gorge has an ever-increasing number of rare and endemic whitebeam trees, *Sorbus* spp., as new ones are discovered all the time. These trees have arisen here through a complex history of hybridization between more widespread species. At the other end of the scale, Bristol rock cress, *Arabis scabra*, grows as an inconspicuous flattened rosette on some of the cliff ledges. It too is only found naturally in Britain in the Avon Gorge, though it has been introduced to a few other locations in the past; however, it appears to have died out in these places. Recent searches by the Somerset Rare Plant Group have failed to find any remaining plants.

The special flora of the Avon Gorge has been known for a long time. The rock cress, for example, was discovered in 1686. Over a hundred years before that, William Turner discovered the first of the gorge rarities, the honewort, *Trinia glauca*, in 1562. Turner, from Pembroke College, Cambridge, was probably Britain's first true naturalist, making careful studies of birds and plants in particular. He also wrote a very early herbal, listing the properties of many species of plants, both wild and domestic. And thanks to Turner's writings, the Avon Gorge was on the botanical map right from the beginning.

John Gerard came here in 1597 and left another description of honewort, the roots of which he said were good to eat. In his footsteps came John Parkinson, John Goodyer, Thomas Johnson, even Sir Joseph Banks. The visitors' list reads like a 'Who's Who' of Britain's most famous botanists through the ages. The gorge is only about half an hour's walk from my home in Bristol, so I too am a frequent visitor, if somewhat humbled by the giants of botany who explored this place before me.

There's always something to see – if not rare and interesting plants, then perhaps a flock of hawfinches cracking seeds or ravens dancing on the wind. Trapdoor spiders lurk in the undergrowth and, overhead, peregrines scythe through the sky. Most visitors to the gorge are more than satisfied with nature's display – but not a certain G. H. Wollaston, a teacher at nearby Clifton College. In 1897 he collected the bulbs of several allium species whilst visiting Sicily and then scattered them around the top of St Vincent's Rocks and Observatory Hill, close to the suspension bridge, to 'enhance' nature's efforts.[14]

One of these was the rosy garlic, *A. roseum*, an attractive species with a spray of pretty pink flowers that grows abundantly in dry open spaces around the Mediterranean. The sunny cliffs of the gorge were a close enough match to its Sicilian home for rosy garlic to establish itself in a few places. Low numbers were reported in the early 1900s, after which they spread slowly. In 1972 several hundred plants were counted,[15] though they were still confined to just a few rocks. But by the 1990s the plants were present in their thousands and much more widely distributed.[16]

Some of the gorge's special plants are perched on precarious ledges high above the river and you need nerves of steel to get close to them. But the rosy garlic display can now be viewed from the path that winds along the edge of the gorge, passing conveniently parked ice-cream vans en route. At the top of the gorge, with the spectacular backdrop of the Clifton Suspension Bridge, there are also impressive displays of Sicilian honey garlic, *A. siculum*, again courtesy of Mr Wollaston. Its large flower heads are made up of a cascade of about thirty long-stalked flowers, another allium that resembles a firework caught in mid-explosion.

Like the rosy garlic, this species was slow to spread. It was first seen on St Vincent's Rocks in 1906, but remained in low numbers, more or less confined to the site of its original introduction.[17] Now its red and orange flowers, glistening with nectar on the inside, are abundant and hum with honeybees and bumblebees, making this the perfect place to finish your ice cream.

The other alien garlics in the Avon Gorge have followed a similar history. The keeled garlic, *A. carinatum*, comes from the meadows, heaths and scrublands of Europe and is widely naturalized throughout Britain. In the gorge it was first noticed in 1904. In 1972 there were still only a few hundred plants on St Vincent's Rocks, though by then thousands were growing on Observatory Hill. Today there are tens of thousands of plants and they have spread across the gorge to Leigh Woods. Another alien, the few-flowered garlic, *A. paradoxum*, is also spreading through this national nature reserve.

In amongst this invasion of alien alliums is one species that is perhaps a very rare native – the Bristol onion or round-headed leek, *A. sphaerocephalon*. The Avon Gorge is its only mainland site, though it does also grow at St Aubin's Bay in Jersey. It was first seen in the gorge in 1847, apparently in two places over a kilometre apart, long before Wollaston's experiments in enhancing the local flora. In the late nineteenth century, James White, who later compiled *The Bristol Flora*,[18] found around twenty flower heads on a ledge of St Vincent's Rocks and by 1933, several hundred flowering plants were known, ranging right down the cliffside almost to the road at the bottom.[19] In the 1970s 4,500 plants were counted,[20] but this spread hides a more complex history.

The round-headed leek is on the edge of its range here. It thrives in a dry Mediterranean climate so does well on the exposed rocks of the gorge in hot, dry summers. The count of 4,500 plants followed the exceptionally hot and dry summer of 1976. It struggles to cope with

Round-headed leek (or Bristol onion); its only mainland site in Britain is along the Avon Gorge in Bristol.

our all too frequent cool and wet summers. After the particularly wet summer of 1988, for example, only twenty-nine flowering plants were found.[21] In the past it has also suffered from outbreaks of onion rust[22] and in 1995 was severely affected when the suspension bridge, above one of its strongholds, was cleaned by shot-blasting with copper slag. Ever since its discovery its globular flower heads have also been picked, at least in its more accessible sites. At the end of the nineteenth century James White mentioned that it 'suffered from the pranks of scrambling boys who, in attempting to gather the flowering heads, pull up the root and all from the thin loose soil'.[23] This still happens, though when the picker smells the pungent aroma of garlic they usually discard their bouquet. Doubtless several other garlic species have been spread around the gorge in a similar way.

But the round-headed leek struggles to cope with some of the alien invaders. The keeled garlic produces a dense mass of bulbs that lie close to the surface and therefore tend to smother the round-headed leek. Several of the gorge's special plants are similarly threatened by other invasive alliums. As rosy garlic spread, it began to smother autumn squill, *Scilla autumnalis*, a tiny, late-flowering relative of the bluebell. The situation became so serious that in the 1970s botanist Clive Lovatt could find no more than a handful of plants. Where they had once been abundant

Round-headed leek.

they now grew in just three widely separated patches, which prompted Clive Lovatt to collect all the seed he could. The seed was germinated and grown in cultivation at the University of Bristol's Botanic Gardens, which, at the time, was conveniently located across the gorge in Leigh Woods. Once mature, the plants were established back on the cliffs, some close to their original haunts and others in new places.

The only way to prevent keeled garlic from out-competing the round-headed leek is to pull up the offending aliens by hand – a very intensive way of safeguarding this particular gorge rarity. And not everyone agrees that the round-headed leek *is* a true native. As we've seen, most of the gorge's rarities were discovered hundreds of years ago. The discovery of the round-headed leek in 1847 is, therefore, suspiciously late. How could such a conspicuous plant, that grows to a metre (3 ft) in height, topped with a red flower head not far short of the size of a golf ball, be missed by so many eminent botanists?

The naturalist and botanist Peter Marren, for one, doubts that the round-headed leek is a native.[24] He suspects that some Victorian enthusiast saw the newly constructed suspension bridge as the perfect place to launch bulbs of the round-headed leek on to the otherwise inaccessible ledges of St Vincent's Rocks below. Well before the exploits of G. H. Wollaston, there seems to have been a long tradition amongst the populace of Bristol of scattering seeds and bulbs of garden plants around the gorge and the surrounding Clifton Down. In compiling his *Bristol Flora*, James White was aware of this – a practice he describes as 'painting the lily and gilding refined gold'.

On the other hand, it's possible that until recently the round-headed leek was confined to the most inaccessible parts of the gorge by past land use and so missed by botanists. In the medieval period, the Downs (flat, open grasslands running alongside the gorge on the Bristol side) were common land and heavily grazed – sometimes over-grazed – by sheep. So many nibbling mouths could have easily grazed down any accessible leaves of the round-headed leek. By 1847 the commoners of Clifton Down no longer exercised their grazing rights and by the last quarter of the nineteenth century only a few hundred sheep grazed the downs. Grazing finally ceased in 1925.[25] Reduced numbers of sheep may have allowed the round-headed leek to spread more widely. Certainly, the timing of its discovery fits with the relaxation of grazing. Furthermore, in many years round-headed leek doesn't flower abundantly and when it does it is easily confused with crow garlic, ample reasons why it may have

Keeled garlic.

endured in the Avon Gorge as an undiscovered native for so long. Clive Lovatt, who has pieced together the history of the round-headed leek in the Avon Gorge from old records and manuscripts, tells me that he is now convinced that, for all these reasons, it is a genuine native. From his painstaking detective work, he also told me that it looks like the first records for this plant came from Sea Walls, a long way downstream from the Clifton Suspension Bridge, which casts doubt on its origins as bulbs launched from the bridge. We may never know whether the round-headed leek is a true native or not, but surely a little mystery only adds to the charm of this spectacular and rare allium.

ALLIUMS AS MEDICINE

Whether the round-headed leek is native or not, the Avon Gorge remains a hotspot for alien alliums, in many cases introduced to beautify its rocky slopes. But alien alliums were also widely introduced across the country for their medicinal value. This valuable property of alliums has been known for millennia. In the Codex Ebers (sometimes called the Ebers Papyrus), an ancient Egyptian medical text dating back to 1550 BC, alliums are prescribed for heart problems, headaches, tumours, bites and worms.[26] More than a thousand years later, Hippocrates and Herodotus extolled the virtues of alliums to the ancient Greek world.[27] Hippocrates, known as the father of Western medicine, prescribed garlic for respiratory problems, parasites, poor digestion and fatigue. Apparently, athletes in the original Olympic Games in Ancient Greece were even given garlic before competing – presumably less fuss was made back then about performance-enhancing drugs!

In the Middle Ages Benedictine monks used common garlic to prevent diseases spreading and, as we've already seen, wild leek on the island of Steep Holm probably owes its existence there to the Augustinian priory. The monks, though, may not have used garlic themselves. At the time it was also seen as an aphrodisiac, so not recommended for those who had taken vows of chastity.

In the second half of the nineteenth century, the pioneering French microbiologist Louis Pasteur showed that this ancient wisdom was well founded. He demonstrated that extracts of alliums had anti-microbial properties. During the First World War they were applied to wounds to prevent gangrene and in the Second World War extracts of allium were so widely used on the Eastern Front that they became known as Russian penicillin.

In 1944 the American organic chemist Chester Cavallito discovered that the medically active agent was a chemical called allicin, one of a family of organic molecules that contain sulphur and that are also responsible for the flavour and smell of alliums. These compounds have strong antioxidant properties, which seem to be the basis of most of their medicinal effects. Garlic is still widely taken for its therapeutic properties today and modern medicine has shown that it contains a whole variety of these organo-sulphur compounds, which do indeed have many of the effects described over the last 3,500 years, from anti-cancer to anti-microbial activity.

In the last 100 years some 1,200 papers have been written on the therapeutic properties of culinary garlic and onion, but now interest is spreading to wild species. Where wild alliums abound they are often used in folk medicine, pointing to possible uses in modern medicine. In areas where it is more common, round-headed leek has many such uses. In Spain, Italy and Ukraine it is eaten, either raw or cooked, while around Lake Baikal in Russia it is even used as a moth repellent.[28] Modern research has identified around ninety different compounds in oil extracted from this plant and many of them show strong antioxidant and antimicrobial properties.

Rosy garlic might be a problem alien here, and it is certainly hard to get rid of in the Avon Gorge, but in Tunisia – where it is a native and is collected for medicinal use to treat headaches and rheumatism[29] – it is under threat. Modern analyses have identified nineteen compounds in its essential oil, some at much higher concentrations than found in the widely used common garlic. Who knows what useful chemicals await discovery in alliums other than the familiar garlic, onion and leek? Plants are extraordinary chemical factories, producing complex organic compounds, the manufacture of which would defeat the best organic chemists. And all done in an environmentally friendly way, powered only by the sun. But to reap this harvest effectively means paying careful attention to the taxonomy of alliums. Rosy garlic, for example, has several distinct varieties and one, var. *odoratissima*, found only in North Africa, produces useful compounds not found in either common garlic or other varieties of rosy garlic.[30]

POLYPLOIDY: INSTANT EVOLUTION

But unpicking the taxonomy of alliums is no small task as each species can be very variable, presenting the bewildered botanist with a confusing array of forms, subspecies and varieties. That's because, as we've already seen with wild and Babington's leeks, alliums can multiply up their basic number of chromosomes to many different levels, which is not just of interest to lab-bound geneticists. This trick allows alliums to behave in different ways and adapt to different circumstances. So understanding the secrets hidden in the nucleus at the centre of each allium cell is crucial for field botanists trying to get an accurate picture of the ecological range or invasive potential of different alliums.

In the basic condition – as it is for most animals as well – the chromosomes in each cell exist in pairs, one derived from each of the parents. Since there are two of each chromosome, these organisms are called *di*ploids. Polyploidy, in which there can be three copies of each chromosome (triploid), four, (tetraploid), five (pentaploid) and on up to much higher levels, is very common in plants, though much less so in animals. In humans, triploid embryos, where perhaps two sperm fused with a single egg, usually die. Though, curiously, some of our cells, such as some in the liver and in muscles, become polyploid during normal development. Amongst our fellow vertebrates, a few fish and amphibians are entirely polyploid. Indeed, some fish have as many as 400 chromosomes. A few invertebrates are also polyploid, but plants have really embraced polyploidy in a big way. Estimates vary widely, but somewhere between 30 per cent and 80 per cent of plants are polyploid.[31]

Allium species may differ from each other in their level of polyploidy, but even within a single species there may be diploid, triploid or tetraploid forms and the degree of polyploidy can make a big difference in where they can live. In its native Mediterranean range, diploid rosy garlics all occur in natural communities, whereas polyploids are found in man-made habitats.[32] I've already mentioned that polyploids often occupy broader ecological ranges or tougher places than their diploid relatives, perhaps because polyploids have more copies of each gene. This means that they can make larger quantities of proteins, which allows them to cope with tougher conditions. But they may also have more biochemical flexibility than diploids. Since they have multiple copies of each gene, some copies can carry on making the original proteins, while others are free to evolve in new directions, and produce different proteins, allowing polyploids to occupy a wider variety of places. This may also explain why some varieties of alliums produce some useful medicinal chemicals that others don't.

Honey garlic.

All of this should also make plants with higher ploidy levels more competitive. However, the competitive differences between different ploidy levels is not always obvious. Tetraploid, pentaploid and hexaploid plants of field garlic grown in experimental conditions showed no differences in their competitive abilities.[33] Even so, polyploid plants are often more robust. Sand leeks, for example, have a triploid form which grows much taller than its diploid form.[34] The ploidy level of alliums can also influence flower colour. In field garlic, tetraploid plants tend to have whitish flowers, whilst pentaploids have reddish flowers.[35]

Whatever the complex ways in which it dictates ecology, polyploidy has certainly played a central role in plant evolution. It's possible, for example, for a diploid plant to give rise to a tetraploid plant in one step, simply by missing a chromosome segregation stage when a cell divides. If this new plant can't breed with the rest of its diploid population or occupies a different habitat, it ends up being declared a new species. And this may be the origins of our common field garlic, which belongs to a very confusing group of alliums centred on the pale garlic or Mediterranean onion, *A. paniculatum*. From an evolutionary standpoint, this is a very young group, still rapidly evolving – hence the confusion surrounding it. Field garlic may have originally arisen from the pale garlic by such a single genetic 'mistake', producing four of each chromosome. In fact, there are two widely separated populations of tetraploid field garlic across its world range, suggesting that this speciation event may have happened twice. This calls into question what we mean by a species. 'Field garlic' may have arisen twice, in two separate places, in which case it should really be seen as two species.[36] And then, to confuse things yet more, field garlic went on to multiply its chromosomes further on several later occasions. It now exists in six different ploidy levels, from three to eight times the original diploid number of pale garlic.[37]

Some of these higher levels may also have arisen independently in different locations.[38] Hexaploid field garlics have been found in Spain, Austria and the Czech Republic, but they are only really common in the latter. Here they have recently expanded their range into man-made habitats, suggesting that these hexaploids may have arisen here in the recent past. If you feel confused after the last few paragraphs, you are not alone. We like to think of species as discrete and recognisable categories, but in many ways the species 'field garlic' has no such meaning. Our tidy minds might like neat boxes in which to file species, but it's not the way nature works – especially in groups that are evolving rapidly through polyploidy.

Since the pale garlic group is obviously still actively evolving, it's hardly surprising that some of these speciation events are quite recent – as seems to be the case with the hexaploid version of field garlic. It differs from the others in having a higher maximum rate of photosynthesis.[39] This is probably an adaptation to living in more open habitats and its distribution suggests that this innovation arose quite recently. This may be parallel to the case of the hexaploid Babington's leek, which we met earlier and which may have arisen as recently as the early nineteenth century, allowing it to colonize habitats beyond the Cornish orchards where it was first described.

Although often complicated, the broad patterns of distribution of the different ploidy levels do sometimes correlate with the differing ecologies of each type. But not all of the observed patterns can be explained like this. Since the different types can arise independently and at different times, some aspects of the distribution pattern must also relate to the histories of these plants since the end of the last Ice Age. As the ice retreated 10,000 years ago, much of Europe was left as a botanical *tabula rasa* – cold steppes occupied by a few hardy species. But a bigger variety of plants soon began to recolonize the continent from refuges in the south-west and south-east and those that were quickest off the mark were able to establish themselves most effectively.

Smaller genomes, like those of diploids, helped the invasion front move quickly across the still challenging terrain of cold steppes. Such small genomes take less energy to replicate and often these plants produce smaller seeds, which can disperse further. Once these diploid populations had established themselves, different ploidy levels arose here and there, allowing the plants to fine-tune themselves to new environments, including those created by humans as we began to transform the landscape as thoroughly as the ice had done earlier.[40]

Ploidy levels also have effects on how alliums reproduce. Some ploidy levels, especially with odd numbers of chromosomes, make it hard for plants to reproduce sexually. Instead they have to resort to reproducing asexually – making clones of themselves. We've already encountered the three main ways in which alliums make more alliums, in the example offered by the different varieties of *A. ampeloprasum*.

They can reproduce sexually by producing seeds, or they can reproduce asexually by producing bulbils on the flowering stem or offset bulbs below ground. The latter come in two varieties – soft, which usually begin growth quickly, and hard, which can remain dormant for some time. Most intriguing is the balance between producing seeds and bulbils.

Some alliums rely entirely on one strategy; others adopt a mixed approach. The three-cornered leek produces a profusion of seeds which are dispersed by ants – very effectively, to judge by how invasive this species is when introduced outside of its normal range. In other species, like *A.*

ampeloprasum, some plants adopt the seed strategy, others produce bulbils and yet others mix and match as appropriate. Each of these different types is usually described as a genetic variety: in the case of *A. ampeloprasum*, as vars. *ampeloprasum*, *babingtonii* and *bulbiferum* respectively. The same is true for keeled garlic, *A. carinatum*, in which var. *carinatum* produces bulbils, while var. *pulchellum* (meaning 'beautiful') produces flowers and seeds. Likewise, rosy garlic has been divided into varieties, var. *roseum* and var. *bulbiferum*, depending on whether the plants produce seeds or bulbils. But it's not that simple… it rarely is with alliums.

Some rosy garlics produce a few seeds amongst their bulbils and, more importantly, one 'var.' can switch to another when conditions change.[41] Clearly, these plants are not true genetic varieties, merely plants that can change their reproductive strategy as needs arise. Although ploidy levels or other genetic differences do seem to play some role in dictating reproductive strategy, these are clearly not the only factors at play. These other factors are best unpicked in our two commonest native alliums, crow garlic and field garlic, which have been studied in great detail over the years.

Field garlic.

FIELD GARLIC AND CROW GARLIC

In the past these two species have been confused – not an unusual state of affairs amongst alliums in general. Today *A. oleraceum* is called field garlic and *A. vineale* crow garlic. But in many old herbals *A. oleraceum* was often called crow garlic. Even the great Linnaeus seems to have been confused. He may have been looking at the wrong plant when he described crow garlic in his *Species Plantarum*.[42] Not a great start in trying to understand the differences and similarities of these two plants.

Despite the confusion of earlier botanists, the two plants are fairly easy to identify. Crow garlic has only one bract at the base of the flower head, while field garlic has two, and they are much longer than the

flower head, unlike the short single bract of crow garlic. They also differ somewhat in the details of their ecology. Both do well in the open, but field garlic can tolerate much more shade. As the level of shade increases, crow garlic soon stops flowering and instead grows bigger leaves; its strategy is to build up reserves in its bulb as fast as it can. Its long-term survival is its priority, in the hope that the habitat may eventually open up again, allowing it to reproduce once more. Field garlic, on the other hand, continues to flower in partial shade. In full shade, crow garlic ceases to grow at all, whilst field garlic, though slow, can still grow.[43]

Like many other alliums, crow and field garlic can adopt different strategies for reproduction. Sometimes the flower head is made up entirely of flowers, sometimes entirely of bulbils and sometimes bulbils and flowers share the flower head in varying proportions.[44] Even the plants with all bulbils are quite attractive as these start off a deep maroon colour. Often the bulbils germinate on the plant, creating an untidy green hair-do.

So the question is – what controls these strategies? Is it simply down to the habitat the plant finds itself in, or do different strategies really represent genetic varieties? And if so, do the differing levels of polyploidy play a role? There do not seem to be any broad ecological differences between plants adopting different forms of reproduction, so the finger of suspicion points at some form of genetic determination.[45]

For field garlic, ploidy level does seem to have some effect on the reproductive strategy. With increasing degrees of polyploidy, flower number (and mass) falls and reproduction by bulbils becomes more important.[46] However, all levels of polyploids produce some seeds, though often just three or less per head. Ploidy level also affects bulbil production. Tetraploids produce more (but lighter-weight) bulbils, while bulbils from pentaploids have a higher germination frequency.[47] Germination of seeds from all types doesn't differ.

Although the degree of polyploidy seems to be implicated, it's clearly not enough on its own to explain the field garlic's choice of reproductive strategy. And if that's not complicated enough, we also need to include the third strategy, producing daughter bulblets underground. To explore this further, we need to switch the story from field garlic to crow garlic – and look again at the advantages and disadvantages of each strategy.

In many plants seeds are an insurance policy against hard times. They can remain dormant in the soil, awaiting favourable conditions before germinating. Bulbils that don't germinate immediately usually

just rot. But in crow garlic, seeds are only viable for around a year (as are its bulbils) – not a long-term survival strategy. Underground bulblets, on the other hand, can remain dormant for up to five years.[48] It's the underground bulblets, therefore, that are the plant's long-term insurance policy.

Crow garlic often exists in patches that all have a very similar genetic structure, in part because its underground daughter bulblets are an important part of its reproductive strategy. But underground bulbs can't disperse far, or colonize new areas. In most cases, plants rely on lighter seeds, atop stems held high in the air, for dispersal. And certainly crow garlic seeds can disperse around half a metre (20 in) – which represents a rapid march when added up across many generations, and therefore a good reason to produce seeds as well as underground bulblets. But it turns out that the aerial bulbils, though heavier than seeds, also disperse to similar distances.[49] So once again we are led to the question of why both seeds and bulbils exist above ground.

Above and left: Crow garlic.

One answer may yet involve the plant's various insurance strategies. Bulbils germinate very rapidly, sometimes even before they've fallen from the flower head. Seeds germinate the following spring. So the plant may be hedging its bets against either a poor autumn or poor spring. But even this doesn't seem to be the whole story.

Across most of its large range crow garlic seems to rely on asexual reproduction – to judge from detailed studies of the genetics of plants in different regions.[50] Crow garlic is a successful weed in agricultural areas and rapid asexual reproduction by both bulblets and bulbils is undoubtedly a major factor in its success in these areas. However, some sexual reproduction by seed does take place, especially in the south of its range around the Mediterranean. On the other hand, in Britain, in the north of its range, sexual reproduction is very rare.

The evolutionary biologist John Maynard Smith (1920–2004) once said that the evolution of sex is the hardest problem in evolutionary biology. That's because, in evolutionary terms, sex is an extremely bad idea. Maynard Smith saw a twofold cost to sex. Firstly, sex involves the production of both males and females. If a female reproduced asexually, each of her offspring could go on to produce their own offspring, and so on. Producing males as well as females effectively halves the number of offspring that can go on and produce more offspring. Secondly, because sex involves the fusion of genetic material from both parents, each is only passing on half its genes. Natural selection should favour the evolution of those individuals that pass on more of their genes – so it should favour asexual reproduction over sexual reproduction on both of these accounts.

Over most of its range, crow garlic does seem to favour asexual reproduction. And bulbils do better than seeds for other reasons. They are clones of their parents and grow much better when surrounded by fellow clone members. This is probably due to their interactions with fungi in the soil that provide the plant with minerals in return for sugars produced by the plant during photosynthesis. Many plants live in such intimate association with fungi, each fine-tuned to the others' needs. For that reason, generations of plants growing in one place will have become genetically closely adapted to the local fungi. So clones produced by bulbils will automatically also be well-adapted to the local conditions.[51]

Bulbils do particularly well in comparison to seeds when the plants are crowded close together. Under these conditions food is in short supply and so a close relationship with symbiotic fungi is all the more important.[52] But what happens when a less friendly fungus turns up? Pathogenic fungi can be lethal if they can get past the plant's defences. Their ability to do this also depends on how well attuned the pathogens are to the plant's genetics. If a pathogen turns up with the right genetic kit to get round a crow garlic's defences, it can wreak havoc on the entire population, since they are all more or less identical. And this is where sex comes in.

Sex generates variety. And variety can stop a parasite in its tracks. In fact, parasites may have played a significant role in the evolution of sex in both animals and plants. This idea became known as the Red Queen hypothesis. This idea was originally proposed by evolutionary biologist Leigh Van Valen (1935–2010) who named it after the Red Queen's race in *Through the Looking Glass* by Lewis Carroll, in which Alice had to keep running just to stay in one place. In a similar way, sex has to continually generate variety just to stay one step ahead of parasites.

Asexual reproduction serves crow garlic well in most circumstances, but it can't give up sex entirely. When pathogens are around, it can switch to sexual reproduction until it has outpaced them, at which time it can switch back to more efficient asexual reproduction – until once again its pathogen catches up. It's a finely balanced dynamic equilibrium; at times favouring one strategy and at times the other – a very common reason for such variability in nature.[53]

And certainly there is great variability in the quantity of either seeds or bulbils produced by crow garlic, both within and between populations and from year to year. But not all this variation can be explained by the hypothesis outlined above. Environmental factors also play a role in generating the complex patterns we've been examining.

Seed production needs pollinators. In the case of field garlic, these are largely wasps. Field garlic has pale-pink or green flowers with dark-brown veins, typical of wasp-pollinated flowers,[54] but in addition to wasps, bumblebees and flies also carry out pollination duties for field garlic.[55, 56] In all cases, more favourable seasons produce more pollinators and years with plenty of pollinators probably favour sexual reproduction.[57] Other environmental factors also effect the production of flowers. As we've seen, field garlic is more tolerant of shade than crow garlic and whilst field garlic can flower in shade, crow garlic can't.[58]

Apart from these environmental factors, there are also historical factors to consider in the balance between seeds and bulbils. Since sex generates variety, seeds are more likely to be able to colonize new areas, where some will have a combination of genes that suits whatever novel environment in which they might find themselves. Once established,

Wild chives.

these plants can then switch to asexual reproduction to quickly fill the space. So sex helped the plants colonize new areas, particularly after the Ice Age, when new opportunities opened up in northern Europe. But later ecological changes then favoured bulbil production. Those changes were wrought by humans – by the spread of agriculture. Bulbils are about the same size and weight as wheat seeds, so were hard to exclude from the harvested crop and were re-sown with wheat seeds into fertile ground the following spring. So the asexual forms of field and crow garlic spread with agriculture and became pernicious weeds – another reason why bulbil-producing plants are so common in many parts of their range.

INVASIVE ALLIUMS

Even in areas where it's a native, crow garlic can become a weed. It behaves itself in northern Scandinavia, where it is more of a maritime plant, but in the south it has been regarded as a weed for some time, causing Carl Linnaeus to complain that it was so common that it tainted milk from pastures where it grew.[59] In Britain it doesn't seem to have become a problem until the early twentieth century and here it's a more serious weed on heavier clay soils.[60]

But crow garlic has become much more of a problem where it has spread beyond its native range. It arrived in the United States, where it's called Jamestown grass, probably sometime in the seventeenth or eighteenth century. Jamestown, on the James River, which flows into Chesapeake Bay, was England's first permanent colony in the US. It was established in 1607, a decade and a half before the more famous Pilgrim Fathers landed at Plymouth in Massachusetts. However, it's more likely that Jamestown grass arrived much later, either with Welsh colonists to Pennsylvania or in grain shipments from France.[61] In any case it quickly became a noxious and hated weed.

Crow garlic is a particular problem in states from Massachusetts to Georgia, where it coats rollers used on crop fields with a sticky mess. It also thrives in pastures. Although some reports suggest cattle avoid the plant,[62] Linnaeus's complaints about tainted milk suggest they don't. In fact, in places in the US it also taints the beef and in large enough quantities may even be lethal to cattle. Cattle deaths in Indiana, for example, have been blamed on crow garlic.[63]

Crow garlic has also reached Australia, New Zealand and Chile, where it again causes problems. In some ways it's surprising that it has become such a weed since it doesn't do well in competition with crops. Crow garlic plants grow much more slowly when growing with wheat than when growing on their own.[64] And ploughing often buries the bulbs deeply. Plants growing from bulbs buried more than 10 centimetres (4 in) deep produce fewer bulbils and if they are buried deeply enough, the bulbs can't grow at all.[65] In such cases the bulbs go dormant for a year and wait until the plough brings them closer to the surface. And as we've seen, daughter bulbs can go dormant for five or six years. That, after all, is their job – to wait out the bad times. Even in good conditions, only around one-fifth to one-third of these daughter bulbs germinate in their first year.[66] And so crow garlic persists in the crop.

Crow garlic is undoubtedly the worst weed amongst its kin, but other alliums cause a few problems. Babington's leek has also been introduced into North America, though it's generally not a problem, except in Arkansas. It has also become a weed in parts of Australia. Rosy garlic causes problems for native plants in the Avon Gorge, but in parts of its range some varieties have also become agricultural weeds.[67] And three-cornered garlic is so invasive that it can dominate hedgerows, woodlands or pastures – and does so in parts of Britain's south-west. Here its colonies are so densely packed that it outcompetes other spring plants such as primroses and violets. On my regular walk to and from my workplace in Bristol, I pass several urban gardens that are also a solid blanket of three-cornered leeks, briefly spectacular in March when they create dense stands of white flowers. And I have to admire their tenacity. Stretching beyond these gardens for perhaps a hundred metres (110 yards) in all directions, three-cornered leeks line the streets, their abundant seeds having found a home where old stone walls meet the tarmac of pavements.

Alliums are a mixed blessing. They have provided us with several important food plants, along with flavouring for countless dishes. They also provide a whole range of medicines. Dramatic architectural varieties have been bred for the garden and are popular in flower arrangements. Yet some have become pernicious weeds, their distinctive flavour tainting milk, beef and even rabbit meat. But in all cases they have posed some intriguing questions for botanists and naturalists and the answers to these reveal some deep truths about the biological world.

14

Lilies of Open Ground

LILIACEAE
ASPARAGACEAE
TOFIELDIACEAE
NARTHECIACEAE

We began our exploration of some of Britain's best-loved wildflowers with a group of woodland species that were united by the fact that they all used to be part of the lily family. We end with a similar group, although in this case they are predominantly plants of open ground. The lily family once contained 4,500 species in 300 genera but modern molecular analyses have reduced this to just 705 species in 15 genera. In Britain, those genera remaining in this shrunken lily family are *Fritillaria*, *Gagea*, *Lloydia*, *Lilium*, and *Tulipa*. I've given our only (possibly) native fritillary, the snake's head, its own chapter (Chapter 7). In this chapter, I'm going to explore the natural history of *Gagea*, *Lloydia* (recently included within *Gagea*) and *Tulipa*. Only three species of *Gagea* are natives of Britain, the yellow star of Bethlehem, *G. lutea*, a scarce woodland plant, and the Radnor lily, *G. bohemica*, one of our great rarities, found at only one site in Britain, atop Stanner Rocks on the Welsh border. The Snowdon lily, *Gagea serotina*, previously *Lloydia serotina*, is another great rarity, found in Britain only on rocky outcrops around Snowdon.

I might be flying in the face of the latest science, but I'm also including some of the erstwhile lilies in this chapter, since that's where they live in my favourite and well-thumbed field guide, *Collins Flower Guide*,[1] and therefore also in my mind. Some of these are now not just in other families, but in different orders, showing what a mixed bag the old lily family was. These include wild asparagus, *Asparagus prostratus*, two species of squill, *Scilla* spp., native and naturalized grape hyacinths, *Muscari* spp., Scottish asphodel, *Tofieldia pusilla*, and the bog asphodel, *Narthecium ossifragum*. Several native and naturalized species of star of Bethlehem, *Ornithogalum* spp., also grow in Britain. Despite having identical common names, these plants are not related to the *Gagea* species mentioned above, which are still part of the lily family. *Ornithogalum* now resides in the asparagus family.

THE GAGEAS

Most members of the lily family, past and present, are attractive plants, though some, such as the Scottish asphodel or the yellow star of Bethlehem, take a bit of finding and then a close approach on hands and knees to appreciate their charm. And some are extremely rare in Britain, which always adds to their allure. One of the hardest to see, at least in close up, must be the Snowdon lily. It survives only in Britain on inaccessible cliffs around Snowdon where even the boldest of sheep can't reach it. In fact, it's so hard to spot in its remote crevices, even in flower, that credit must go to Edward Lhwyd, the plant's discoverer in the seventeenth century. Somehow he managed to find this plant even though it wasn't flowering at the time.

Lhwyd's discovery was described by John Ray in 1690, in his *Synopsis Methodica Stirpium Britannicarum* ('Synopsis of British Plants'), which was the nearest thing to a field guide to British plants in the seventeenth century. Ray was perhaps the first in that great English tradition of parson-naturalists and he contributed some important ideas to the emerging study of taxonomy a generation before Linnaeus. It was Ray who first came up with the concept of a biological species and Linnaeus would later gain most of his knowledge of the British flora from Ray's *Synopsis*. But Ray wasn't entirely sure how to classify the plant that Lhwyd had found. In 1696, Lhywd managed to find a specimen in flower and Ray thought it might be a species of *Ornithogalum* or perhaps even a new genus. Since it turned out to be the latter, it seemed fitting that the new genus, *Lloydia*, commemorated Lhwyd's sharp eyes. Unfortunately, modern science has been less kind to Lhwyd. Genetic analysis suggests that *Lloydia serotina* should really be *Gagea serotina*.

There are several distinct populations of this plant around the Snowdon massif – at Cwm Idwal, Ysgolion Duon, Cwm Glas and Cwm Brwynog – all on slopes that face north- or north-east, shaded from the sun and sheltered from wet south-westerlies, but kept moist by frequent mists.[2] Yet, as inaccessible as its favoured ledges and crevices are, one site was nearly destroyed by bulb collectors in the 1940s. In that light, it made sense that earlier botanists, like Owen Rowlands (1742–1819) of Blaen y nant, kept their knowledge of the whereabouts of the Snowdon lily a closely guarded secret. Rowlands only divulged the locations he knew on his deathbed.[3]

The Snowdon lily might be vanishingly rare in this country, but it is found widely around the world, so widely, in fact, that it is the world's most widespread lily. I've never seen the plant in its Snowdon fortress, but I have found it in the Rocky Mountains of North America and it's also found widely throughout the Alps and northern Asia.[4] Given its wide range, it's easy to think that from a global perspective the tiny population in North Wales is of no real conservation importance. However, the Welsh plants are genetically distinct, not just from those

Overleaf: Naturalized grape hyacinths.

distant populations in the Rockies, but from the much nearer plants in the Alps. Even the different populations around Snowdon are distinct. This suggests that the Welsh plants have been isolated for some time. They may well have endured the Ice Age on these remote crags rather than following most of our flora in retreat before the advancing ice sheets, only to recolonize our islands from refuges in Europe 10,000 years ago when the ice finally relented. So conserving these tiny Welsh populations is an important part of preserving the genetic diversity of this species.[5]

In 1965 botanists thought that the prospects for the Snowdon lily in Britain had improved considerably with the discovery of a new population on Stanner Rocks in Radnorshire. The botanist R. F. O. Kemp uncovered a withered bulb amongst moss specimens he'd been collecting from this outcrop of base-rich volcanic rocks in the Welsh borders. He tentatively identified it as the Snowdon lily, adding to a substantial list of rarities already known from this site. His record stood for nearly a decade until another botanist, Ray Woods, returned to the site in 1974. Though still early in the season, he found one faded white flower and a lot of withered leaves. The plant clearly flowered much earlier in the year than Snowdon lilies. And he could see that the leaves were covered in short hairs, unlike the leaves of the Snowdon lily, which are hairless. That's the kind of thing to excite a botanist. He realized that this plant must belong to the closely related genus *Gagea*, and if so it had to be a species new to the British Isles.

Kemp's earlier confusion is understandable. As I've mentioned, modern genetic studies consider *Lloydia* to be so closely related to *Gagea* that the two really belong together in this latter genus.[6] But the discovery of a new species of *Gagea* was far more exciting than merely extending the range of Snowdon lilies in Britain. Woods returned a year later, in mid-January, trying to catch this mystery plant in flower. He was rewarded with one fresh flower – bright yellow rather than white. Searching through European flora he thought the plant might be the appropriately named early star of Bethlehem, *G. bohemica*. In 1978 Woods met *Gagea* expert E. M. Rix at Stanner Rocks, where they found twenty-five plants in flower amidst many thousands of non-flowering plants. They confirmed its identity, after which the plant became known in Britain as the Radnor lily.[7]

Both of these plants illustrate the curious phenomenon of what might be called 'parochial nomenclature'. The 'Snowdon' lily occurs right around the northern hemisphere, where it is usually called mountain spiderwort (in Welsh it is called 'y bryfedog', which also translates as spiderwort) or, in North America, the common alplily. And the 'Radnor' lily is widespread across Europe, where 'early star of Bethlehem' is a far better description of this plant. There are plenty of other examples of 'parochial nomenclature' amongst both plants and animals, from Essex skippers and Camberwell beauties to Deptford Pinks, indications of the pioneering roles of British naturalists through the ages, but which don't reflect the broader distribution and ecology of these species beyond Britain. For me, seeing our wildflowers in this broader context always seems so much more satisfying.

In Europe the Radnor lily has a wider range than most other *Gagea* species. And across this range it is a highly variable species which differs according to local environmental conditions and ploidy level.[8] The Welsh plants, for example, are pentaploids – they have five copies of each chromosome. Elsewhere, Radnor lilies range from plants that are diploid (having one pair of chromosomes – the 'normal' condition) to hexaploids (having six of each chromosome).

Reflecting this genetic variability, Radnor lilies vary widely in height, flower size and ecology.[9] In some parts of their range they grow in base-rich rocks, as at Stanner Rocks. But in a few places, including Moravia and Bohemia in the Czech Republic, they seem happy on acidic rocks.[10] The plants look and behave so differently that they are sometimes divided up into different species, with *G. bohemica* itself as a plant of the dry grasslands of south and central Europe, *G. saxatilis* on dry rocky outcrops from Germany in the north to Portugal in the west and Sicily in the south, and *G. szovitzii* in dry stony slopes in south Ukraine, Russia and eastern Romania.[11] But whatever their appearance and ecology suggests, genetic studies indicate that these plants are probably all just one highly variable species.[12]

Across their broad range, Radnor lilies show that John Ray's definition of species – a neat box into which all similar individuals clearly fit – is not so easy to apply in practice. In the first volume of his *Historia Plantarum*, published in 1686, he was the first to attempt a biological definition of a species when he wrote:

> *…no surer criterion for determining species has occurred to me than the distinguishing features that perpetuate themselves in propagation from seed. Thus, no matter what variations occur in the individuals or the species, if they spring from the seed of*

one and the same plant, they are accidental variations and not such as to distinguish a species… Animals likewise that differ specifically preserve their distinct species permanently; one species never springs from the seed of another nor vice versa.[13]

Long before evolution was understood, Ray considered species to be immutable – permanently fixed in space and time. We now know that species change through time and the biological definition of a species has been refined accordingly. Even so, we still tend to think of species as neat boxes. But time and again through the pages of this book, we've found that nature is much more fluid, especially in groups of plants that are evolving rapidly. And as we'll see shortly, Radnor lilies, and indeed their whole genus, are doing just that.

All across their range Radnor lilies seem happiest in open, hot and sunny locations, like those around the Mediterranean or in the continental climate of central and eastern Europe. In north-west Europe, for example, in much of France and at Stanner Rocks, the plants can only grow on warm south-, south-east- or south-west-facing slopes. Stanner Rocks is particularly suitable because it lies in the lee of the Black Mountains in Wales, which intercept the frequent south-westerly winds in this part of the world. The mountains create a phenomenon called a lee wave, which results in a small cloud-free area at a certain distance downwind, in this case corresponding to the location of Stanner Rocks. Members of the Herefordshire Gliding Club often fly in this area and confirm that such a gap in the clouds is very common over Stanner Rocks.[14]

The Radnor lily shares its home with a number of other plants which are also more at home in the dry and sunny continental climate of central and southern Europe and are therefore rare in our wet and cloudy corner of the continent. These include the spiked speedwell, *Veronica spicata*, and the sticky catchfly, *Lychnis viscaria*. However, the remains of ancient pollen discovered in scattered areas across Britain suggest that these latter plants were once more widespread in the wake of the retreating ice at the end of the last Ice Age. At this time climatic conditions in Britain were more continental. These plants probably colonized Britain from the continent as conditions became suitable and then became confined to those few locations that suited them as the climate changed to a wetter, cloudier one. No ancient pollen from the Radnor lily has ever been found in the UK. And the genetics of the Radnor lily suggest that it survived at least the last Ice Age, and possibly others, perched on Stanner Rocks, just as the Snowdon lily did in its lofty home in North Wales, rather than recolonizing these islands more recently from the south.

Our remaining native species of *Gagea*, the yellow star of Bethlehem, shuns such exposed rocks and craggy mountainsides. It's a plant of lowland forests and so is certainly the easiest of its genus to find, though it still takes some looking for. Its populations are often small and widely scattered in damp woods or along hedgerows and riverbanks. And it is frequently very shy in flowering, particularly in shady places. Its leaves look a little like those of bluebells, with which it sometimes grows, though they can be told apart on very close inspection – by their hooded tips. It often flowers early, though nowhere near as early as the Radnor lily. On the few sites I know in my area of the south-west it's often at its best by early or mid-April – a loose cluster of starry yellow flowers that seem to glow in the early spring sunshine.

Just across the Channel there are several other similar-looking plants, the most widespread being *G. pratensis*, confusingly also sometimes called the yellow star of Bethlehem. But that's not the only source of confusion with these plants. As I mentioned above, this genus is evolving

Yellow star of Bethlehem.

rapidly, and in a number of different ways. One common way for plants to spawn new species is by polyploidy. For example, G. *lutea* has six copies of each chromosome whilst G. *pratensis* has five.[15] In the past, these plants must have arisen from a species with just the normal single pair of each chromosome (diploid). The most primitive members of the genus, plants like G. *graeca* and G. *trinervia*, which are restricted to the Mediterranean, are indeed diploids, as this scheme suggests.[16] The nearest relative of these 'basal' *Gagea* species seems to be the Snowdon lily, which has the same number of chromosomes (twelve pairs), thought to be the original number of chromosome pairs in the most primitive members of this particular branch of the lily family – a branch that also includes two other closely related genera, tulips, *Tulipa*, and dog-tooth violets, *Erythronium*.[17] At some point in their history some *Gagea* species ended up with multiple copies of their chromosomes which allowed evolution in the group to speed up and the number of species to proliferate. According to some, there are perhaps 280 species of *Gagea* worldwide, making it the largest genus in the lily family.[18] But polyploidy is not the only reason for such a large number of species.

New *Gagea* species also arise by hybridization, which brings us back to our own yellow star of Bethlehem, G. *lutea*. Several new species seem to have arisen in Europe when G. *lutea* crossed with its near relative, G. *pratensis*. This latter species looks very similar to G. *lutea*, but grows in more open habitats (indeed, it is sometimes called the meadow gagea). G. *pratensis* is widespread across Europe, though it hasn't made it across the Channel to Britain, which is a pity, since, like our native yellow star of Bethlehem, it has a wonderfully understated beauty. In some areas of Europe both species are attractive enough to be frequently planted together in churchyards, which further increases the likelihood of hybridization.[19]

Hybrids often end up with odd numbers of chromosomes, which interferes with the production of sex cells, making such hybrids sterile. But no matter – *Gagea* can reproduce asexually, an ability that is neatly illustrated by G. *spathacea*, a species that grows alongside G. *lutea* in woodlands in Europe. G. *spathacea* is a more robust plant than G. *lutea*, with larger leaves, although otherwise very similar. Despite the fact that it grows widely across Europe as far north as Scandinavia, and is more common in Germany, its English name is Belgian gagea.

G. *lutea* has six copies of each chromosome, whereas G. *spathacea* has nine, the odd number causing a malfunction in meiosis, the process of cell division that creates the sex cells. Consequently *G. lutea* reproduces largely by seed whereas *G. spathacea* produces asexual bulbils and rarely bothers to flower at all.[20] Asexual species can only ever produce clones of themselves, but that doesn't seem to have limited the success of *G. spathacea*. Right across its range, *G. spathacea* plants are all virtually identical – a single megaclone that has spread from its origin, probably as a hybrid, 1,500 kilometres (932 miles) from Sweden in the north to Italy in the south.[21]

The Radnor lilies perched on Stanner Rocks also produce no seed, but this may have as much to do with being on the edge of their range as with the fact that they have an odd number of chromosome copies (five in the British plants). That's why so few of the Welsh plants flower – probably only around 1 per cent – and why Rix and Woods found so few flowers amongst thousands of non-flowering plants. Further south they flower more freely and produce at least some seed.[22]

Radnor lilies grow in poor soils where a lack of nutrients also seems to play a part in sterility. Species typical of rocky soils, like Radnor lilies or golden gageas, *G. chrysantha*, an Italian species, flower much less frequently than species of richer soils.[23] Snowdon lilies also grow in poor soils and are similarly restricted by lack of nutrients. Flowering and seed production take a lot of energy. In the Alps, only about 15 per cent of Snowdon lilies flower and in all cases, they only ever produce a single flower on each plant. Some plants are hermaphrodite (with flowers that produce both pollen and seed), others are male (with flowers producing only pollen). And this is intriguing.

Gardeners will be familiar with some plants that have two sexes, just like animals, any individual plant producing only male or female flowers. We'll meet one such plant, the wild asparagus, later in this chapter. This is an adaptation to out-crossing – fertilization by an unrelated plant – which usually produces more vigorous offspring. About 6 per cent of all flowering plants fall into this category (dioecious). Most other plants produce either hermaphrodite flowers or male and female flowers on the same plant. To have some plants in a population that are male and some that are hermaphrodite is very unusual, though not so unusual that botanists haven't given it a name – androdioecy.

On theoretical grounds, androdioecy shouldn't exist. For natural selection to maintain this mixed population, each type of plant must leave equal numbers of offspring (to have 'equal fitness', in the jargon of evolutionary biologists). Hermaphrodite plants can leave their genetic legacy in the next generation both by producing pollen and by producing seeds from pollinated ovules. That means male plants in a mixed population of hermaphrodites and males must pollinate twice as many ovules as hermaphrodite plants to make up for their lack of ability to produce seeds, otherwise they leave fewer of their genes in the next generation than their hermaphrodite neighbours. In such a case natural selection would favour hermaphrodites and 'male-only' plants would disappear. Experiments show that male plants do not pollinate more ovules than hermaphrodites so androdioecy shouldn't exist – at least not as a stable reproductive strategy. But it turns out that Snowdon lilies are not breaking the biological rule book. Apparent androdioecy in this species is more likely down to the tough conditions these plants live in.

Producing pollen requires a lot less energy than producing seeds. Experiments with Snowdon lilies in which individual plants were followed through several seasons showed that after producing seed in one year, the plant needed some time off. In the following year it would either not flower at all or produce a male flower. So there aren't really separate male and hermaphrodite plants. Instead, the production of male flowers is a lower-cost way of staying in the reproductive game until the plant can build up enough reserves to produce seeds again.[24]

The Scottish asphodel, *Tofieldia pusilla*, is another plant of poor soils. Like the Snowdon lily, it is found right around the northern hemisphere, across the northern United States and Canada (where it's called the Scotch false asphodel), Greenland and Iceland and throughout much of Arctic Europe and Asia along with mountain ranges further south. As a plant adapted to poor soils, it is very slow growing. It's also an evergreen, since it can't afford to grow new leaves each year.[25]

Those species growing in poor soil also suffer from competition with other kinds of plants, which again limits seed production. At least in the south of its range, the Radnor lily flowers much more frequently and sets more seed when it makes up at least three-quarters of the ground cover where it's growing and competition with other, more vigorous species is therefore reduced. And, of course, flowering so early means there are few pollinators around in any case, so further limiting seed set.

Though not as early as Radnor lilies, most *Gagea* species are flowers of early spring and those relying on seed for reproduction have to time their flowering to coincide with early flying insects that provide pollination services. How much seed they produce depends on whether spring comes early or late, though not in the way that might be expected. A warm start to the year doesn't necessarily mean a good year for the yellow star of Bethlehem. This plant spans the whole of Eurasia, at home in woodlands from the Cotswolds, where I am familiar with it, to Japan. In Japan it is largely pollinated by bees, in particular solitary bees of the genus *Halictus*. In warm years, when spring comes early, the yellow star of Bethlehem also flowers earlier. The year 2002, when Japan had the warmest spring for forty years, offered an extreme case. All the spring flowers bloomed between seven and seventeen days earlier than usual. But, despite the longer spell of warm weather, the yellow star of Bethlehem set very little seed. Other spring flowers, which were pollinated by flies, weren't affected in the same way. Similar studies in the US show the same results; bee-pollinated species do poorly in warm springs.

It seems that bees and flowers measure time in different ways. Plants keep a running total of warm days (technically 'accumulated temperature days') and flower after a certain number of warm days. Bees, on the other hand, simply respond to the local maximum temperature at the site where they are hibernating. The net result is that in a warmer spring, the number of warm days quickly adds up to trigger yellow star of Bethlehem to flower, even though the maximum temperature reached on each day isn't high enough to wake the bees.[26] This has huge implications for such plants as climate change begins to advance the arrival of spring. Bee-pollinated plants will likely suffer from poor seed set as they lose synchrony with their pollinators.

But yellow star of Bethlehem has a few tricks to help offset these problems. Early in the season, even a normal one, flies are often the only pollinators around and they can pollinate yellow star of Bethlehem, if not very effectively. And unlike Snowdon lily, yellow star of Bethlehem has a loose spray of flowers which open sequentially, so that, hopefully, some flowers will be open during the peak bee season.[27] Yellow star of Bethlehem is one of a whole suite of woodland flowers that grow and flower before leaf-burst in the canopy shuts out the light. They're called spring ephemerals, which is not just a botanical term but a very evocative phrase as well; for me it always conjures up the transient nature of the very start of spring when the world is poised between winter and the full flush of spring. It's a time when the first fresh green shoots pierce the iron-grey floor of winter woodland. But blink and this borderland between winter and spring is gone. Everything has turned green and spring is well on the way to becoming summer.

And timing is everything for the yellow star of Bethlehem. It needs all the light it can get. The number of seeds produced is much higher in plants growing on the edge of woodland, so even when the trees are bare, light is a limiting factor in the depths of the wood. And when the canopy begins to open seed set falls off rapidly.[28] But yellow star of Bethlehem has one final trick. The yellow petals are backed by green bracts that, like leaves, can photosynthesize. All the sugars synthesized by the bracts are transported to the flower to speed fruit development before the light is cut off. Fruit growth depends almost entirely on this floral photosynthesis. Removing the leaves has little effect on fruit and seed development, whereas removing the bracts results in stunted and under-developed fruits.[29]

BOG ASPHODELS

Those species growing in open habitats don't face the problem of sunlight being stolen by the opening tree canopy. And apart from rocky mountain crags and exposed clifftops, mires and bogs are usually too wet for trees to gain a roothold. In such soggy places, the ground is sometimes carpeted with the sulphur-yellow flowers of bog asphodel, *Narthecium ossifragum*. In the past this plant was often called the bastard asphodel. This is how it was known to William Withering (1741–99), an influential English botanist and geologist. In 1776 he published *The Botanical Arrangement of*

Bog asphodels grow in abundanc in wet moorlands and heathland

all the Vegetables Naturally Growing in Great Britain, an early British *Flora* which followed the newly established Linnaean system of classification. But Withering removed all the explicit sexual overtones of Linnaeus's work (see Chapter 1, pages 52–3). He produced this bowdlerized version of Linnaeus, as he explains in his introduction, to allow the book to be used without causing embarrassment, particularly by women. In this work, the plant we know most commonly today as bog asphodel is referred to as either bastard asphodel or Lancashire asphodel. The latter name dates back at least to the sixteenth century because the plant was (and still is) widespread across the wet moors of Lancashire. Across the border in rival Yorkshire, the one county unlikely to adopt the name Lancashire asphodel, it was known as 'moor-golds', perhaps the most evocative and descriptive name for the plant. In a few places it was called 'maiden's hair', since it could be used as a blond dye for hair or cloth. However, bog asphodel is perhaps the most appropriate name since it seems happiest in the most sodden ground.

Although many of our bogs were created by the clearance of trees, in some of the wettest areas of Britain, this habitat may be entirely natural. Here, the annual rainfall is so high and the ground so wet that trees cannot survive. Bog asphodel, on the other hand, thrives with inundated roots and when battered by frequent torrential downpours. It might even depend on rain for pollination. Rain pollination, in which water droplets help to move pollen from the stamens to the stigma, has been

described for several plants in high rainfall areas, though it is not easy to prove. But in some telling experiments during a rare dry spell in the Faeroes, Danish scientists discovered that only those bog asphodels that were drenched with a watering can were able to produce seed pods.[30] If any plant could take advantage of high rainfall like this, I feel it would be the bog asphodel, a plant that epitomizes the very wettest of our landscapes.

As pretty as it is, bog asphodel also has a reputation for being poisonous. Its specific name – *ossifragum* – means 'bone-breaker' and comes from a belief that sheep grazing on bog asphodel developed brittle bones. Withering records this belief in his *Botanical Arrangement* where he wrote, 'This plant is supposed to soften the bones of animals that eat it but this opinion wants confirmation. Cows and Horses eat it. Sheep and swine refuse it.' Withering was right in questioning this belief. In fact, bog asphodel's reputation as a bone-breaker is more likely because it grows in acid mires, low in calcium ions, and it's a lack of this mineral, vital for bone growth, that causes brittle bones. But bog asphodels do contain compounds that are toxic to some livestock. While sheep (and rabbits for that matter) nibble on bog asphodel with no apparent ill effects, cattle do seem to suffer. About a quarter of the cattle grazing on one mire with bog asphodel lost condition and eventually most of these cows died.[31] Similar cases of poisoning are reported from time to time, often resulting in severe kidney damage and death.[32]

Bog asphodel flowers are attractive in close-up, with their orange anthers.

On wet moorland, especially where the ground water is flowing slowly, bog asphodels can be extremely abundant, their spikes of yellow flowers and contrasting brick-red anthers putting on quite a display. In Sweden they sometimes form a monoculture over sizeable areas but unfortunately in Britain, even on the best sites, they never achieve anything like this spectacle.[33, 34] And today they are struggling to survive on many sites. Like the sphagnum mosses among which they grow, they are very sensitive to the nitrogen and sulphur pollution that is now so all-pervasive. This has caused the extinction of some sphagnum mosses in upland Britain and a reduction in numbers of bog asphodels. Nitrogen in particular allows more competitive plants like grasses to gain the upper hand, changing wet heaths into grasslands dominated by purple moor grass, *Molinia caerulea*, and wavy hair grass, *Deschampsia flexuosa*, to the total exclusion of bog asphodel.[35]

WILD ASPARAGUS

Like some bogs, exposed coastal cliffs are also sites that remain open without human help and are home to a number of the erstwhile lilies, including the rare wild asparagus, *Asparagus prostratus*. The familiar cultivated asparagus is *A. officinalis* and in the past wild asparagus was regarded as merely a subspecies of this, *A. o. prostratus*, distinguished from the cultivated asparagus, with its upright stems, by the prostrate stems of the wild form. However, genetic studies show that they are in reality two distinct species.[36] And wild asparagus in Britain is a rare plant, growing within sight and sound of the sea, but only on around twenty-eight sites in the south and west. Nine of these sites have fewer than ten plants and only three have more than a hundred plants. Making its status in Britain even more precarious is the fact that wild asparagus has separate male and female plants, so halving the effective population size and making each and every plant precious.

In 1997 a single female plant was discovered on Portland in Dorset. The nearest male plant was hundreds of miles away, and the only pollinators that can work over that kind of distance are botanists. Pollen from male plants in Cornwall was brought to this lone female, which obligingly produced forty-four berries containing ninety-two seeds. The seeds were grown on in cultivation and two years later, sixty young plants were planted out in two groups, one at the east end of Chesil Beach and the other near the lighthouse on Portland Bill. Five years later, fifty-five plants were still going strong and on the verge of flowering, so hopefully this kind of last-ditch intervention will prove successful.[37]

It used to be thought that cultivated asparagus derived from wild asparagus, though that probably isn't the case. Wild asparagus is a western European plant, native to Britain, Ireland, Spain, France, Germany and the Netherlands. Cultivated asparagus, on the other hand, seems to be of eastern European or west Asian origin. The first guide to growing asparagus that we know of was written in AD 65 by the Roman agricultural author Columella, but before that the Greeks also grew it. Its name probably derives from a word in an old Iranian language – it comes from 'spargea', meaning 'shoot'.[38] It seems to have been brought to the Rhine Valley around 1212 by Crusaders and since then has been widely naturalized, obscuring its original distribution.

Cultivated asparagus has been intensively bred since the days of Columella, but most modern varieties seem to derive from a Dutch

Seed head of spiked star of Bethlehem.

variety called Violet Dutch, which means cultivated asparagus today has a narrow genetic base.[39] However, there are around 150 species of *Asparagus* worldwide, ranging from woody shrubs and vines to the more familiar-looking herbs. The spears of several species of wild asparagus, for example *A. horridus* and *A. acutifolius*, are also collected for food around the Mediterranean so genes from these wild plants could be used to improve cultivated varieties, giving an added incentive to conserve wild asparagus species.

BATH ASPARAGUS

In the past the inhabitants of the Georgian city of Bath enjoyed their own version of asparagus, though 'Bath asparagus' is not really an asparagus at all. It's actually another plant called star of Bethlehem, though unrelated to the *Gagea* 'stars of Bethlehem'. The alternative English name for Bath asparagus is spiked star of Bethlehem, *Ornithogalum pyrenaicum*. The largest populations of this plant in Britain occur around Bath and nearby Keynsham. Here the plant puts up a spectacular 1-metre-high (3 ft) flower spike. Local inhabitants collected the unopened inflorescences, which bear a passing resemblance to true asparagus, for food. I'm not sure how long this local delicacy has been served up, but Collinson, in his *History of Somersetshire*, published in 1791, described these flowers for sale in Bath market. And according to two Keynsham residents, interviewed

by David Hill, co-author of the *Biological Flora* for this species, Bath asparagus was still eaten regularly up to 1939.[40] Even in the 1980s and 1990s, flowers from some of the biggest displays mysteriously disappeared, presumably to be served up somewhere with butter.

Elsewhere, spiked star of Bethlehem is found in Wiltshire and Gloucestershire and the plant is also native in Bedfordshire and in Ashridge Wood in Berkshire. It has been introduced into Shropshire, Surrey and Suffolk. In western and central Europe its distribution pattern is similar to that in Britain; a scarce plant, growing in scattered populations. But it's much more common in parts of the Balkan area.[41] It also grows as far south as Morocco and in central and eastern Russia and the Caucasus and Crimean regions where it grows on steppe grasslands and even

survives amongst crops in arable fields. In Britain it grows mostly in hedgerows and woodlands. It is less frequently found in open fields unless sheltered by bracken or brambles, but in Europe it seems happy in meadows and open grasslands in mountainous areas.[42]

Spiked star of Bethlehem is probably on the edge of its range in Britain, its distribution limited by summer temperature. It also struggles to grow in woodlands dominated by ramsons or dog's mercury but thrives amongst bluebells or ivy. Its reluctance to grow among ramsons or dog's mercury is strange – in my garden it grows happily amongst vigorous ground cover plants and is slowly spreading, though it will be some time before I have enough for a decent meal.

The leaves appear very early in the year, often in January, and form robust clumps by the early spring. The flower spikes don't appear until the leaves have died back. In some places, the displays consist of many thousands of plants. Yet, even despite their tall stems bearing flowers over the last third, the display is not a conspicuous one. The flowers are white and green, and seem to disappear in the dappled sunlight of high summer woodlands. But close up, caught in a sun spot against a dark forest background, individual flowers are most impressive.

Several other species of *Ornithogalum*, *O. angustifolium*, *O. nutans* and *O. umbellatum* are found in the wild in Britain, but since they are popular garden plants, most of these populations have escaped from cultivation. However, it is possible that *O. angustifolium* is a native in the Breckland, an area of dry open heaths on sandy soil covering parts of Norfolk and Suffolk and famous for its unusual flora. It's easy to confuse the species in this collection of stars of Bethlehem, particularly *O. umbellatum* and *O. angustifolium*, so it's difficult to be certain of the true distribution of each of these plants or their status as natives.

Spiked star of Bethlehem or Bath asparagus. They were so abundant around Bath in the southwest of England that, until recently, the flower buds were eaten as a vegetable.

GRAPE HYACINTHS AND SQUILLS

Another group of popular garden plants that frequently escape to the wild are the grape hyacinths, *Muscari*. These bulbs, bearing spikes of deep-blue globular flowers resembling miniature bunches of grapes, are sold in almost every garden centre and recommended for naturalizing in the garden, so it's not surprising they also do so well in the wild. However, one species, *M. neglectum*, is sometimes regarded as a native in parts of eastern England. But, as with the stars of Bethlehem, there are several very similar species. *M. armeniacum* is more common as a garden plant and is often confused with *M. neglectum*, so again the true distribution of our possible native grape hyacinth is not accurately known.[43]

Muscari species are common around the Mediterranean, where they flower very early in the year, before the land is baked by the summer sun that attracts millions of sun-worshippers from northern Europe. Most people who visit Mediterranean countries, therefore, do not see the local flora at its best. That needs an early spring visit or alternatively one in autumn, since late flowering is another adaptation to the Mediterranean climate, when autumn rains once again green the hillsides and vineyards.

Our two species of squill illustrate both of these patterns, spring squill, *Scilla verna*, flowering in early spring and autumn squill, *S. autumnalis*, flowering at the end of summer. Spring squill is found widely around the western coasts of Britain and along Scotland's wild north coast, where it grows in short turf on clifftops, often close enough to the sea to be doused by salt spray. In these exposed places, the plants are often tiny, hugging the ground, keeping their heads out of the wind, yet they can be very abundant and in the early spring sunshine their blue flowers mirror the sea below them.

Photographing spring squill sometimes calls for a good head for heights, since some of the best displays are on narrow ledges or on steep

Below and right: Spring squill.

grassy slopes that end in a precipitous drop. But whether growing on the magnificent Pembrokeshire coast or above isolated Cornish coves, it's always worth clambering around the clifftops in early spring to admire this plant.

Autumn squill is a much scarcer plant, restricted to the south-west of England, where it usually grows in open coastal grasslands. The Lizard Peninsula in the far south-west of Cornwall is a good place to search for autumn squill when it opens its flowers, usually between July and September. Away from the coast, it also grows in a few dry grasslands along the Thames. There's even a colony in Hampton Court, growing precariously close to the area that is trampled flat by plant enthusiasts each year during the Hampton Court Flower Show. Closer to my home in Bristol, there are scattered colonies in the Avon Gorge, where it joins an impressive list of rare plants. The population in the Avon Gorge was badly affected by the building of Isambard Kingdom Brunel's iconic suspension bridge, which was completed in 1864. Brunel's wife pointed out the threat posed to the autumn squill by her husband's ambitious construction plans, and the engineer had those plants that lay in the way of the building work dug up, to be replanted after the bridge was complete. Even so, autumn squill seems to have been eradicated from the Somerset side of the gorge.[44] It is also threatened by invasive species of wild garlics (see pages 410–11).

Squill species, like the *Gagea* species explored earlier, are numerous and complicated. They too are evolving rapidly and their taxonomy is as tangled as a Gordian knot. Spring squill is part of a particularly complex group of species, most of which are so similar they can only be told apart by genetic analysis.[45] This complex of cryptic species is found mostly around the western Mediterranean, where some members of the *S. verna* complex have tiny ranges. For example, *S. pavi* grows only in the Sierra de Cazorla of south-east Spain, while *S. merinoi* is restricted to coastal dunes in north-west Spain.[46] Only one species, *S. verna* itself, reaches far

enough north to have colonized the British Isles, which makes life a lot less confusing for British botanists.

The western Mediterranean and the Iberian Peninsula are home to several such species complexes. Some are more adapted to the drier climate of the Mediterranean and include the spectacularly large *S. peruviana*, not, as its name might suggest, a denizen of South America but a Portuguese species and a familiar garden plant. Other complexes are adapted to the wetter Atlantic climate of the western edge of Europe. Overall there are perhaps 125 species of *Scilla*[47] and 70 per cent of them occur in western Europe, 6 per cent of them on the Iberian Peninsula,[48] which gives some indication of the complexity of this group of plants. Some botanists have suggested that climate change will favour the Mediterranean species complexes at the expense of the Atlantic ones, so eventually we might find new species heading towards the British Isles.

Autumn squill is also a confusing plant. Across its wide range in Europe there are many different varieties. These differ in ploidy levels but also in the fact that some have extra segments added to their chromosomes[49] or different chromosome arrangements. Ten different 'chromosome races' have been described, and though the plants look identical to the field naturalist, some have 68 per cent more DNA than others.[50] Even so, they are all still classified as a single species, though in reality there may be lots of cryptic species, just as in spring squill. But the distribution of these races can help us deduce the history of autumn squill since the last Ice Age.

Most races occur on Crete, which, along with Greece and the Balkans was part of a refuge for those plants fleeing south before the glaciers. The number of races found here suggests that this was where autumn squill survived the Ice Age and from where it spread to colonize most of Europe again when the ice retreated. But our plants may not have come from this area. Distinct types of autumn squill occur in the Iberian Peninsula, the southern extremities of which were another glacial refugium. This was a more likely source of the plants that eventually colonized the south-west of Britain. But even in Britain we have two types of autumn squill. Most of our plants are tetraploid (with four copies of each chromosome), but the plants from Guernsey and the south of Cornwall belong to a hexaploid (six copies) race.[51] So perhaps there were several colonizations, or perhaps the hexaploid variety arose more recently in Britain – another twist in the tangled knot of evolution in the squills.

The two broad types of Mediterranean plants, spring- and autumn-

Autumn squill.

flowering species, often have other differences. The spring type, called the 'crocus type' by botanists, have their ovaries underground, which protects the seeds as they lie dormant through the summer and winter, to germinate in the following spring. The autumn type has been called the 'urginea type' after *Urginea maritima*, a Mediterranean plant related to the squills and often called the sea squill, which puts up a spectacular flower spike late in the year. In this case, the ovaries are above ground and release their seeds as soon as they are mature, to germinate immediately. Many of these autumn 'urginea' plants produce leaves in the spring, which die back in summer followed by the appearance of a leafless flower in the autumn.[52]

Autumn squill falls into this category, though in Britain the flowers and leaves appear at the same time. Nevertheless, its seeds germinate quickly, adapted for late-autumn germination.[53] In Israel autumn squill flowering is triggered by the falling temperatures of autumn which means that those growing on north-facing slopes are the first to flower[54] – the opposite of the more usual experience in Britain of searching for the first flowers on warm south-facing slopes.

The squills are closely related to two other early spring plants that will be familiar to gardeners, *Pushkinia* and *Chionodoxa*. The latter is the evocatively named Glory of the Snow, which flowers in alpine areas just as the snow is melting. Some botanists even include these species within *Scilla*. Glory of the Snow can be naturalized in lawns to form spectacular displays. There is a fine example in Kew Gardens but occasionally it also manages to naturalize itself in the wild.

WILD TULIPS

Despite appearances, the last plant I'm going to consider in this chapter is closely related to the first species we discussed, those in the genus *Gagea*. Tulips are familiar to everyone, usually as the bloated and blousy cultivars which seem to exist in endless gross variety. But they can't compare to the delicate beauty of the wild species. Some of these, like *Tulipa bakeri*, are also readily available in garden centres, so there's no excuse for not growing the more elegant wild forms. There are 70–100 species of wild tulips ranging from North Africa to Central Asia. But only one species has become naturalized in Britain, where it is known simply as the wild tulip, *T. sylvestris*.

Left: Naturalized glory of the snow form impressive carpets.

Overleaf: Wild tulips.

Because they have been admired for so long, many tulips have been carried beyond their native ranges for centuries. Less than half the tulips growing wild in Turkey are natives; many of the others were brought by the Seljuk tribes as they occupied Turkey in the eleventh century. By the twelfth century Persian poets like Omar Khayyam were celebrating the beauty of tulips, [55] though almost certainly the spectacular displays on the steppes would have been known long before that.

Some authors think that there are no native tulips west of the Balkans, which means that the wild tulip is naturalized across its entire European range. Others think that *T. sylvestris* subsp. *australis* is native in the mountains of Portugal, Spain and North Africa. But certainly throughout much of western Europe, the wild tulip is naturalized. In Britain it is scattered across many areas, in chalk pits, grassy roadsides and waste ground. It doesn't set much seed, but local populations seem to be quite long-lived. It always reminds me of a peeled banana, as its outer tepals peel back from the flower, but it's an attractive plant – and adds a touch of the exotic in the odd spots where it occurs.

Wild tulips were cultivated in Britain by the end of the sixteenth

century and were found growing wild by the end of the eighteenth. During that period tulips grew to be such a craze that many people invested a lot of money in them. An export trade for many species and hybrids grew up, first in France and then in the Netherlands, reaching a peak in 1636. Then, just three years later, over-supply caused the market to crash. Fortunes were lost, many people went bankrupt and governments introduced trading restrictions on tulips. It wasn't the last of the plant crazes. As we saw earlier, the Victorians were particularly prone to such manias for all kinds of plant from snowdrops to orchids and ferns (see pages 167 and 317).

The 'lilies' of open ground is the last of the main groups of plants that I set out to photograph back in 2012 when I conceived this project. Tracking down all these plants in the field right across the British Isles has been an enormously rewarding experience, in the course of which I not only learned a lot about their natural history but also how best to capture their beauty in photographs. In the following appendix, I'll explore a little of the history of plant photography, which dates back to the very dawn of photography, and share some of the techniques I used to obtain the photographs for this book.

Appendix
Photographing Wildflowers

Wildflowers might seem like the easy option for a wildlife photographer, since they are rooted to the spot. And as a wildlife film-maker for this past thirty years, I can see some merit in that suggestion. There's none of the time-consuming hassle of moving a hide into position, only to find the animal in question has decided to move to the other side of the valley. And there's no risk of one's stealthy approach being thwarted by some inadvertent noise, as happened to me in Tasmania when a particularly loud stomach rumble frightened off a quoll (a small predatory nocturnal marsupial) who we'd been sneaking up on for the past hour. But wildflowers do present their own challenges.

With wildflowers, there's time to plan your shot to make the best of the situation, so there's no excuse for shots grabbed on the spur of the moment. The flower can be lit in whatever elaborate or artistic manner you wish or you can wait until the natural light is perfect. You can even check where sunrise or sunset will be and pick a plant that makes a dramatic silhouette in these extreme conditions. You can scope out a site and mark specimens that are close to opening, so you can return when the flower has just opened and is pristine (unless it has been eaten in the meantime). And, armed with a large umbrella, you can create some very effective images in the rain, so there is never any excuse for the keen wildflower photographer to stay tucked up warm and dry at home. In short, there is no end of creative or artistic ways of approaching wildflower photography.

In this chapter I'll explore the various techniques I've used to create the photographs in this book. This is by no means an exhaustive or definitive guide to shooting wildflowers; it's intended simply to give the reader inspiration to try their own ideas. Every situation is different, so there's no magic formula. Yet each different situation offers its own possibilities for satisfying end results. But first I'm going to look at the work of some other plant photographers who have provided me with inspiration.

PLANTS: A KEY ROLE IN THE HISTORY OF PHOTOGRAPHY

Perhaps not surprisingly, plants were the subject of some of the very first photographs of all, for the simple reason that they don't move and early photography demanded very long exposures – sometimes hours! One of the pioneers of photography was Henry Fox Talbot (1800–77), who lived at Lacock Abbey in Wiltshire. The village of Lacock is so beautifully preserved that it now earns a good living as a set for period dramas and films. But as the very latest digital movie cameras capture scenes of the village, just down the road in the museum at Lacock Abbey (now run by the National Trust) are some of the first-ever photographs to be produced. Strictly speaking, they aren't photographs but photograms.* But either way, they are very beautiful.

Fox Talbot had discovered that if paper was impregnated with salt, then brushed with a solution of silver nitrate it turned black in sunlight. He began to experiment by placing the foliage of plants, like ferns or asparagus which had intricate leaves, on to his treated paper. He pressed them flat with a sheet of glass and then exposed them to sunlight. The sheet remained white where light was blocked by the leaf, but turned black elsewhere, producing a negative outline of the leaf that captured the very finest of details. But once the leaf was removed, the image soon faded as light hit the undarkened areas. Fox Talbot found that further treatment with salt could halt the darkening and fix the image, giving him a perfect record of his botanical specimens. He called these 'photogenic drawings' and he made his first as early as 1834.

---

* A picture produced with photographic materials, such as light-sensitive paper, but without a camera.

With modern cameras, a similar effect can be achieved, though by an entirely different process. Simply flatten a leaf under glass on a light box and photograph it. The image can then easily be turned into a negative using image manipulation software such as Photoshop. It's a lot simpler and less messy than Fox Talbot's technique, but it is a good way of producing very graphic images of certain kinds of plants.

Fox Talbot went on to develop true photography, using a camera and lens to capture negative images of three-dimensional objects. The end result of the process he invented is called a calotype. At about the same time, in France, Louis Daguerre (1787–1851) invented an entirely different system for capturing images in a camera. The end product of his process is called a daguerreotype. Whether France or England could claim the glory of inventing photography was hotly contested at the time, a rivalry given added spice by the fact that the Battle of Waterloo, fought just twenty years earlier, was still a recent memory. In any case, both of these inventions spurred others to perfect photographic processes and to apply their ingenuity in creating beautiful and artistic images of the natural world.

In 1928 a remarkable photographic book appeared in Germany. It showcased the work of Karl Blossfeldt, who at the time was sixty-three. Over the preceding three decades he had been photographing images of flowers, leaves, buds, twigs, tendrils and seed capsules to highlight their extraordinary architecture. During this time, he taught sculpture at a Berlin art school and used his photographs to instruct students about design elements in nature. Towards the end of his career his works were compiled into a book, originally called *Urformen Der Kunst: Photographische Pflanzenbilder*, literally 'Fundamental Forms of Art – Photographic Plant Pictures', but which appeared in English as *Art Forms in Nature*. It contained only 120 photographs from around 6,000 that he had taken over the years. But it became an instant bestseller and made Blossfeldt famous. It's still seen as one of the seminal photographic books. In 1932, the year of his death, a second book appeared under the title *Wundergarten der Natur* ('Wonders of the Garden of Nature'). Blossfeldt is less well known today, but his work still stands up to modern techniques and should be far more widely known.

His books, along with later compilations of his work, are still in print,[1, 2] and his photographs are still exhibited. I would urge any would-be plant photographer to buy one of these books or, better still, visit an exhibition. I went to see such an exhibition recently at Nature in Art, a museum of natural history artwork at Wallsworth Hall, Twigworth, in the Gloucestershire countryside. Reproduced at larger sizes than would be possible in a book, the photographs are stunning, both technically and artistically. Blossfeldt chose his specimens carefully to show off the varied forms of plants and arranged multiple specimens in imaginative ways. But the images he produced are both pin-sharp and have an extraordinary depth of field. That is, all parts of his subject are in focus, giving his images an almost computer-generated feel. As a photographer he was self-taught and produced his striking photographs on home-made cameras with lenses that could magnify his subjects up to thirty times. But I have no idea how he achieved the results he did – still remarkable for today, let alone for a century ago.

Blossfeldt's work remains an inspiration, but all the more so when set in the context of its time. Around the time that Blossfeldt was photographing his plants there was an art movement in Germany known as *Neue Sachlichkeit* ('New Objectivity'). In essence, this saw the camera's only role as that of capturing objective reality. The camera could record objects with scientific realism, but art should be left to the artists. Of course, Blossfeldt's work encapsulates both art and science in equal and copious measure. As Blossfeldt himself once remarked:

> *The plant never lapses into mere arid functionalism; it fashions and shapes according to logic and suitability, and with its primeval force compels everything to attain the highest artistic form.*

Again, it's possible to produce images that technically resemble those of Karl Blossfeldt using the modern process of image stacking. Whether you can match Blossfeldt's artistry is down to the ingenuity of each photographer! I'll cover the technical aspects of image stacking later in this chapter.

Since Blossfeldt's time, plant photography has, to use the obvious expression, blossomed and many modern photographers are producing imaginative images of plants the world over. The International Garden Photographer of the Year competition showcases many of these, from amateur to professional, while the prestigious Wildlife Photographer of the Year competition has a category for plant photography, which is of the very highest standard. I'll pick just one modern photographer whose work I greatly admire – Sandra Bartocha. She is based in Potsdam, not far from Berlin, where Karl Blossfeldt produced his work. Bartocha's work is regularly exhibited in 'Wildlife Photographer of the Year' and she has contributed to the international photographic project 'Wild Wonders of Europe'. She uses all the possibilities offered by modern digital cameras to great effect, in particular double exposures. It's easy to make a very messy image with this technique (I know, I've produced plenty!), but Bartocha seems to have an eye for compositions that work extremely well. It is well worth looking at the works of photographers like Bartocha and others to get a sense of the endless possibilities of plant photography.

While there's a special joy in tracking down and photographing rare species, it's also well worth looking at common plants or even weeds with an eye to their artistic worth. In my experience all plants have something to offer a creative photographer and some of the most familiar offer some of the most exciting photographic possibilities. There's also no problem with picking or dissecting such common plants to photograph them in unusual and revealing ways. The common ragwort, *Jacobaea vulgaris*, a plant also unkindly called 'stinking willie', is more often reviled as a noxious weed, but its yellow flowers are beautiful in extreme close-up. In such detail, the 'flower' is revealed to be a head of multiple flowers or florets, those around the outside bearing a petal (the 'ray florets') to draw the attention of pollinators to the flowers in the centre ('disc florets'), which are reduced to just their basic reproductive organs.

Lesser celandines, *Ficaria verna*, are among the first flowers to open in the spring, a yellow that shines as bright as their near relatives, the buttercups. They are predominantly woodland plants but sometimes invade roadside verges, even urban ones, in such numbers that they form a bright carpet and create yet more opportunities for creative photography. In wet grasslands, ragged robin, *Lychnis flos-cuculi*, often grows in spectacular abundance too, but each flower on its own is a work of art. The thin, branching and twisting petals that are responsible for the description 'ragged' also make an elegant portrait.

To create images that satisfy, both technically and artistically, means understanding how your camera works and what it can do. There are many excellent books that cover this for all the different kinds of cameras available, and it would be impossible to do this justice here. Nor will I delve into the technical aspects of the various bits of software that can be used to enhance images. Again, these are dealt with in other books and, in many cases, online as well. My intention in this short chapter is simply to give suggestions for different ways to approach plant photography along with some of the tips and tricks I've discovered along the way. First, I'll deal with 'in camera' techniques, then with other techniques that require some post-shooting processing with various kinds of software.

IN-CAMERA TECHNIQUES I:
PERSPECTIVE AND FOCUS

The first choice you face when picking up your camera is which lens to use. Many books will tell you that a macro lens is invaluable and certainly you'll need such a lens if you want to photograph details of plants. I frequently use a macro lens, particularly in my studio, but the two lenses I use the most in the field are a telephoto lens and a fisheye lens.

I use a 300mm telephoto, with a close focus of under 2 metres (6.5 ft). For most plants this allows me to fill the frame with either the whole plant or the flower spike of larger plants. I use a long lens like this to throw the background far out of focus. Some manufacturers, like Tamron and Sigma, make telephoto zoom lenses that reach 300mm at the long end of the zoom and which are also macro lenses, though not, strictly speaking, true macro lenses. True macro lenses should be able to render the subject life size on the camera sensor, described as 1:1. These telephoto macro lenses only achieve 1:2. However, they do combine the close-up effects of a macro lens with the soft focus background of a long lens. Personally, I don't use such lenses as the image quality is better on a prime (fixed focal length) lens, though as lens design continues to improve, those differences are becoming less and less obvious. And if publication or exhibition quality is not your goal, then these lenses give a greater degree of flexibility.

Although not absolute, one golden rule of all wildlife photography is to shoot the subject from its level, not yours. For most plants, this means sprawling along the ground. Using a long lens in this position will create a background of abstract shades of green and brown with no details, against which all the subtleties of the subject stand out. But it also opens up even more artistic possibilities. When many people begin plant photography, they try to capture as much as possible in focus, just as Blossfeldt achieved. This can be done by stopping the lens down to small apertures (F16 or 22), though using very small apertures will lower the quality of the image as light is diffracted around the tiny opening. But often what's *not* in focus is what makes the picture. Shooting on a long lens which is wide open or almost so (for example F5.6, 4 or 2.8 depending on the lens) will give you only a very narrow plane of focus and it's what you choose to have in focus that makes or breaks the picture.

It is possible to get into a deep discussion with a serious photographer, not only about how sharp a lens is, but also how it renders out-of-focus areas. This even has a name – *bokeh* –which comes from a Japanese word meaning 'haze' or 'blur'. The out-of-focus areas of some lenses have a more satisfying appearance than others. So from an artistic point of view, when choosing a lens, it's worth considering both how sharp it is and the quality of its bokeh. In general, the more blades a lens has in the aperture diaphragm, the rounder the hole will be when the lens is partially stopped down. This results in better transitions between blurred areas in the background, or better bokeh.

It might seem obvious to choose a clear path to your subject to give an unobstructed view, but it's often more effective to shoot through vegetation. All this vegetation will be out of focus but can produce wonderful abstract patterns in the foreground and create a frame around the subject. But it can also be a real mess! To create something artistic means spending time trying many different positions and angles, then making small adjustments to the camera position, so that the part of the subject you are interested in is both visible and in the part of the frame where you want it. Since the camera is often right at ground level, you need to accept a stiff neck or invest in a right-angle viewfinder that attaches to the camera's viewfinder.

A similar effect can sometimes be achieved with multiple exposures. Depending on your camera, you can set it to take two or more exposures which will be superimposed on each other. This was always a tricky technique with film cameras, requiring careful calculations to make sure the final exposure on the film was correct. But digital cameras make it easy. They do all the calculations, leaving you to work on the artistry. One effective technique is to hold the camera in a fixed position then adjust the focus of the lens between each exposure, in each one focusing on a different subject. This works well in dense stands of plants such as bluebells, wild daffodils or ramsons. Just as with shooting through vegetation, there's a lot of trial and error with this technique. You can control the end result to some extent, by choosing where you place focus for each exposure, but with digital cameras you can view the end result immediately and make further adjustments to your technique. You can also shoot and superimpose entirely different scenes, to give very different effects. The permutations are endless, limited only by your imagination.

Digital SLRs and increasingly the newer compact cameras have a variety of choices for the file format of the image produced. One very useful tip if experimenting with large areas of soft focus is to shoot uncompressed RAW files rather than JPEGs. JPEGs are compressed files, meaning that to make the file size smaller, some information from the camera's sensor is thrown away. On an image with lots of very subtle gradations of colour and no sharp details, this lack of information can result in an ugly banding pattern. RAW files keep all the information. Your camera may have a setting for 'lossless compressed RAW', which is also fine. This format uses a very clever way of packaging the data in such a way that it's a smaller file than uncompressed RAW, but all the information can be retrieved again when needed.

IN-CAMERA TECHNIQUES II
DELIBERATE CAMERA MOVEMENT

Another in-camera technique that can produce beautiful abstract images, which sometimes even look like paintings, involves deliberate camera movement while taking the shot. Most photographers strive to reduce any camera movement that might cause image blur and lens manufacturers have gone to a great deal of trouble to produce lenses with image stabilization that compensates for any accidental camera shake. But in photography, rules were made to be broken.

Before playing with this technique, turn off any image stabilization on the lens. Deliberate camera movement involves even more trial and error than the other techniques I've mentioned so far. The idea is to create a blurred image that nevertheless retains enough context to be recognisable. The exact effect depends on how long the shutter is open and how fast you move the camera. And you'll need to pick the right kind of subject, one which has a basic simplicity or is already slightly abstract. Bluebells growing under beech trees is a good example – a simple image, with a wash of blue across the forest floor, little or no messy understory and light-grey straight trunks. Though not British, another good example is the longleaf pine forest of Florida and Georgia. Here the understory is often a uniform spread of bright-green palmettos, with the long, dark trunks of the pines rising in regimented stands. The final effect also depends on which way you move the camera. In this last example, a vertical camera movement keeps the regimented structure of the trees and a sense of the green carpet of palmettos.

The camera can also be rotated; for example, when looking into the canopy of a forest. This technique can be combined with flash to freeze some portion of the image. In the case of rotating the camera while looking along a tree into the canopy, a flash fired at some time during the movement will produce a sharper image of the trunk. Meanwhile, the canopy will be rendered as an abstract swirl. You might need to experiment with the power output of the flash to achieve a good balance of exposure between the canopy and those parts of the trunk lit by the flash.

Finally, if using a zoom lens, the lens can be zoomed while the shutter is open. This creates a tunnelling effect something like a starship jumping to light speed. Again, certain subjects work better than others. My best advice for working with any form of deliberate camera movement is to experiment widely with different subjects and with different combinations of shutter speeds and speeds of movement – and have fun.

IN-CAMERA TECHNIQUES III:
FISHEYES AND TILT-SHIFT LENSES

The second lens I find myself turning to frequently is a fisheye. These lenses are ultra-wide with close on a 180-degree field of view, so wide that often the biggest problem is keeping parts of yourself or your shadow out of the picture. At the opposite extreme from isolating a subject against an abstract background, these lenses are great for placing a plant in a landscape. Generally, these lenses also focus very close, and combined with a small aperture can create pictures where subject and background are all in focus. Fisheye lenses distort the final image, curving vertical and horizontal lines, sometimes to dramatic effect, but often creating an unnatural look. This can be removed or greatly improved by using some form of fisheye correction software. Photoshop has a built-in version, but there are a number of third-party programs that either work as plug-ins for Photoshop or as stand-alones. I've found 'Fish-eye Hemi', from Image Trends, to be the most effective. It removes most of the artefacts without cropping too much of the picture.

A much more specialist kind of lens, but one very useful for plant photographers is a tilt-shift lens, sometimes called a perspective control lens. This lens can be tilted with respect to the camera body as a way of maximizing depth of field for certain subjects. For example, when looking obliquely across a display of flowers like snake's head fritillaries in a meadow or bluebells in a woodland, this lens allows sharp focus from front to back. These lenses are not cheap and only useful in certain circumstances, but are very effective in these cases. Recently a Chinese company, Venus Optics, has begun producing a series of low cost but unique lenses that look like they are becoming an indispensable part of my kit. The Laowa 15 mm. macro has no real counterpart elsewhere. It is a true macro, giving a 1:1 magnification, but is nearly as wide as my fisheye lens, without the distortion. However, it's a lens you'll need to get used to. At full magnification, the subject is only 4 mm from the front element, so it's hard to avoid the camera casting a shadow. Also, these lenses are completely manual (hence the reasonable price bracket) so you'll need to turn off all that sophisticated programming in your DSLR and do it the old way. There is also a Laowa 25 mm. zoom macro lens, which is actually a lot more than 'macro'. It goes from a 2.5:1 magnification all the way to 5:1, which you would normally have to achieve with a cumbersome bellows system.

Whatever lens you use, a polarizing filter is very useful. Many photographers use one to enhance the depth of colour in the sky, but it's also very effective in bringing out the greens of plants. A polarizer is less effective on really wide shots since you will see a change in darkness across the sky as the angle of polarization of the light from the sky changes.

IN-CAMERA TECHNIQUES IV:
LIGHTING

Lighting is a key ingredient for a successful image. Usually, bright overcast conditions work better than direct sunlight, especially with more abstract images shot on a long lens. That's because these generally look best with low contrast with no heavy shadows. Even though you can't control the weather, you aren't stuck with what nature offers. In sunlight, a fold-out diffuser can be used to shadow the plant and soften the contrast. The background might still be lit by the sun, but if this is very abstract (as described above), this sometimes creates a very effective image. Contrast can also be softened by using a reflector or by fill lighting. Carrying a fold-out reflector along with your diffuser is always a good idea. Many come with two different reflective sides, but often even a piece of white card positioned at just the right angle will reflect enough light back into the image to create a softer contrast. In other cases, it might be more effective to use a light source to fill in shadows. Flashes have been around for a long time and have grown ever more sophisticated. Modern flashes have a variety of automatic settings which when combined with the camera's settings take all the trial and error out of fill lighting.

Today there are alternatives in the form of low-cost LED panels that come in a range of sizes. If you are prepared to spend a little more, there are even LED sheets that can be rolled up. The panels come in a range of sizes and outputs, but for close-up work, even the smallest ones work well. They are perfect for providing a gentle fill light, or if positioned behind the subject, create subtle back-lighting to make petals and leaves glow or pick out hairy stems. And the advantage over flash is that you can see exactly what effect they are having and make adjustments as needed. Larger panels can light quite large areas and although they can't turn a dull scene into a sunlit one, they can lift light levels over a big enough area to make a difference. I often use large LED panels when shooting for documentaries, for example in rainforests or in dense woodland. This style of lighting blends well with natural light and the scene never looks artificially lit.

Full sun creates a harsher, high-contrast image with distracting heavy shadows or bright highlights. However, fisheye images often work well when shot into bright sun, with the starburst around the sun as a key feature in the image. But shooting into the sun can cause exposure problems. If the sky and sun are exposed well, the subject may be heavily under-exposed or vice versa. There is a way round this and that brings us to a whole suite of techniques that require some work after you've returned from your photographic trip.

POST-SHOOTING TECHNIQUES I: HIGH DYNAMIC RANGE

The first is HDR – or high dynamic range. It's a way of creating an image that captures more levels of light and dark than a single camera exposure can. Our eyes have a much higher dynamic range than most cameras. In other words, we can see more detail in shadows and highlights in a high-contrast situation than a camera could capture. So, although some more purist photographers regard HDR techniques as cheating, in fact they help create scenes that more resemble those we see with our eyes, at least if used subtly. If over applied, this technique can result in garish and unreal images. A kinder description of over-applied HDR is 'painterly' and if you search for HDR images online, you'll find plenty like this. In most cases I aim for a level of subtlety such that the viewer isn't aware that they are looking at an HDR image. So how does it work?

Some compact and smartphone cameras (and a few digital SLRs) offer an 'in camera' HDR feature, but you don't have much control over the end product. To achieve the best results means shooting a series of images of different exposure that are later combined under your control. The number of images needed depends on the degree of contrast in the scene. Usually five to seven is enough in most circumstances. Digital SLRs generally have a bracket feature, in which you select the number of shots and also the exposure difference between shots. I normally leave this set to 1 F-stop difference between each image, which is the maximum on my camera, and then shoot the set number of shots. You should use a tripod, if possible, to prevent movement between shots, though most HDR programs can align shots that have moved slightly, which means you can shoot with the camera hand-held on a wider image if you have a reasonably steady hand.

You'll end up with a series of differently exposed shots that between them should contain all the information from the very darkest areas to the very lightest, though if you are shooting into the sun, the sun's disc itself may still be overexposed, which is not usually a problem in final compositions featuring the sun. Now all you have to do is combine all the correctly exposed areas in each shot into a single final image that contains details in all areas of light and dark. Luckily there are several programs that do this for you.

Photoshop has a built-in HDR feature, but I use a stand-alone program called Photomatix, which has a large number of presets, from realistic to surreal, so if one of these preset looks appeals, it's just a simple press of a button to create and save the HDR image. But it also has controls that allow the user a lot of flexibility over the final look and it's usually worth the extra effort to get a bespoke finish. The bank of controls in this and other similar programs looks daunting, but it's easy enough to play around with each slider to see what effect it has, then home in on the look you want. Nothing is fixed until you save the image. As with all these techniques there are also many excellent video tutorials online, from beginner level to advanced.

One of the biggest problems with this technique is movement between the different shots. The software works by first superimposing all the different exposures on top of each other. So if a plant is blowing in the wind, it will be in different positions in each image. If not corrected, this will result in 'ghosts' in the final image. The software offers a way of reducing this by manually painting over or outlining any ghosts, which forces the software to use just one image in that area. But, the more the plants are moving during shooting, the worse this problem will be, so it's best to pick calm conditions to experiment with HDR photography.

I won't go into detail about what each control in the software does, since they are arranged differently in different programs and it's best just to play around with each one to see how it affects the look. It's not a precise science! But one word of warning; as you work, check the image at high magnification. A common artefact in HDR processing is halos around areas of high contrast, such as leaves against the sky, though these aren't always visible when the whole picture is displayed on the screen. Leaves on distant trees against a bright sky blowing in the wind are a particular problem. It's impossible to paint over them all, to choose the information from just one image, and in any case this is likely to be a high-contrast area where you need information from several different exposures to contribute to the final image. If you look at the leaves at high magnification, you'll often find a mess of superimposed images. I've not found a sure-fire way around this, other than shooting in very calm conditions and hoping. Sometimes it works, sometimes it doesn't.

A less technical version of this involves blending just two exposures together. This is most useful on wide shots where you have a frame including land and sky, and the exposure between the two is very different. Take two shots, one exposed for the sky and one for the land. These can be put together in HDR software (Photomatix for example has an 'exposure fusion' setting). Or you can blend the two together manually in Photoshop, using the gradient tool to mix between the two images. This is the equivalent of using a graduated filter on the lens (the only solution in the days of film), but mixing two exposures allows a lot more flexibility over where the join between the two exposures lies, and it doesn't have to be a straight line. Photoshop's brush tool allows you to make fine adjustments over the shape of the join between the two layers.

I've already mentioned the tip of shooting RAW files. Because of the way the information is stored, a single RAW file actually contains quite a bit of extra information in the highlights and the shadows. Sometimes this is enough to capture all the tonal gradations in a high-contrast scene without resorting to HDR. The way to check that it does is to look at the histogram of the image on the camera. This is a representation of how the pixels are distributed across all the tonal levels in your image, from black at the left to white at the right. A hump in the left side of the histogram means most pixels are representing darker tones, so the image will appear dark or underexposed. If some of the histogram appears piled up against either end, you'll have lost information from either the blacks or the highlights. But if all the histogram is contained between the left and right side, it will be possible to process the image to regain all the tonal information.

A RAW file will need processing in any case in order to save it as one of the universal picture formats, usually a JPEG or a TIFF. That means going through a RAW converter. Some camera manufacturers ship a basic converter with their cameras, but perhaps the most commonly used is Adobe Camera Raw, which is part of Adobe's Photoshop, Lightroom or Elements packages. This allows a lot of flexibility over enhancing the basic image. Shadows can be lifted to reveal hidden detail and likewise highlights brought down. Colour can be enhanced, along with many other subtle (and some not so subtle) tweaks. You can also apply a digital version of a graduated filter to better balance exposure between land and sky. Even a sophisticated package like Adobe Camera Raw is not as daunting as it first appears and there are several excellent workbooks to take you through the basic operations, as well as online video tutorials.

POST-SHOOTING TECHNIQUES II:
FOCUS STACKING

There are also various kinds of software available for image stacking, a technique that gets around some of the basic compromises and limitations in photography. Two of the most widely used are Helicon Focus and Zerene Stacker. Often plant pictures look good when the subject stands out against a soft background as described above. This can be achieved by working with a wide aperture and consequent shallow-depth field. But this means there is

only a narrow plane of focus, so only part of the subject will be sharp. You might, quite reasonably, decide that you want all of the plant to be in focus. Normally, you achieve this by stopping the lens down to a small aperture. This increases the depth of field, which means a greater depth of the image comes into focus. But this affects the whole image, which means the arty abstract background is brought nearer focus and instead becomes messy and distracting. On top of that, stopping a lens down to a small aperture also increases the effects of diffraction, which ultimately softens the image. Lenses are at their sharpest somewhere in the middle of their exposure range, not stopped all the way down or wide open.

The way round this compromise is to shoot with a wide aperture, but take multiple images, moving the focus between each shot, starting with the farthest point you want to be in focus and finishing with the nearest or vice versa. The camera's autofocus system will need to be turned off, as will any vibration reduction on the lens. In fact, vibration reduction should be turned off any time the camera is on a tripod. The change in focus can be effected by moving the manual focus on the lens a fraction between each picture, but it's hard to be precise with this technique. It's far better to invest in a focus slide, which allows the camera to be physically racked forwards or backwards by small increments. Some of the latest high-end digital SLRs, for example the Nikon D850, have a focus-stacking setting which will automatically change the focus over a series of shots, so making focus-stacking a lot easier. The focus adjustments need to be small enough so that there is some overlap in the areas in focus between each shot. This might need a large number of shots, much larger than the exposure stacks used for HDR processing. Often I end up with sixty or seventy shots on really big close-ups where depth of field is most limiting. Again, there are various software tools to do the processing. The company that developed Helicon Focus have also developed various software and hardware tools that automate the process of shifting the focus. So if you plan to do a lot of image stacking, it's worth checking out their website. In most software packages, there are various settings to choose from, though less than with HDR processing and, as with HDR techniques, it's a case of trial and error to find the best setting.

Depending on the image, there might be quite a bit of manual tidying up to do, usually in two stages. Areas further back in the image will, when in focus, be masked by closer areas, which are soft. This often results in blurred outlines around overlapping edges. In the first stage of tidying, the stacking software allows you to paint into the final image from the image of your choice in the stack. Some of the blurring can be reduced by finding the image that is sharp at that point and painting it into the final. But inevitably some blurred edges are left. The only way round this is to open the image in Photoshop or other editing software and copy from a similar sharp area into the blurred area using the clone tool. In a complex image, this can be quite time-consuming, but hopefully the end result is worth it.

Shots for image stacking can be done in the field, but wind movement often creates problems for the software. It's often better to shoot in a studio where the plant can be firmly clamped. And this is essential for really big close-up work, where image stacking really comes into its own. A studio can be anything from a purpose-built space to a kitchen work surface. But bringing plants indoors opens up a lot more possibilities, particularly for abstract work. Backgrounds can be simplified to either pure white or pure black which can be very effective with some specimens. White is best achieved by shooting against a lightbox. Many lightboxes are battery-powered, so can even be used in the field for specimens that can't be picked and taken home. In both cases, you usually need to over-expose by a stop or more to get the background to appear true white. It's the 'snow problem' familiar to many outdoor photographers. The camera's metering system tries to expose the dominant area of the image as a neutral grey and therefore underexposes the white background. For black backgrounds, good quality black velvet is by far the best. Other cloths or black card reflect some light and it's very difficult to get a pure black.

You'll soon accumulate all kinds of other useful bits and pieces that help with studio shooting, but two essentials to start with are a laboratory stand and clamp and a flexible clamp. There is a low-cost, custom-built version of the latter, the Wimberley 'Plamp', which is also very handy in the field for stabilizing stems waving in the breeze. Laboratory stands are readily available from many suppliers online.

Then, armed with an ample supply of Blu-Tac and ingenuity, you can create some stylish images. You can arrange plants so the image looks like an old herbarium pressed specimen, you can partially dissect flowers to reveal the hidden beauty of stamens and styles or you can indulge in some artistic flower arranging. As with many of the techniques I've mentioned, once you start experimenting, the possibilities are endless.

SMARTPHONES AND GOPROS

So far I've assumed you're using a digital SLR, but today there are other kinds of cameras that produce high-quality images and can be used in different ways from DSLRs. Most smartphones have excellent cameras and produce large images. Their tiny lenses also create images with a large depth of field. But they really come into their own when producing panoramas. Panoramas can, of course, be created with a DSLR, by carefully shooting a sequence of images, overlapping by about a third or so, then stitching the separate images in Photoshop or with specialized stitching software, of which there are several choices available. But smartphones assemble panoramas directly as the phone is panned. For big landscape shots this can even be done hand-held, using an on-screen guide to keep the camera level.

Smartphones are excellent for taking close-up, wide-angle panoramas. They can focus on foreground subjects, but their large depth of field means much of the background will also be in focus. The only problem is that, with a lot of foreground close to the camera, the stitching program struggles to build the panorama if the panning movement is at all erratic. You can end up with something that looks more like a Cubist painting than a photograph. The solution is to buy a smartphone holder that has a tripod attachment and set the phone on a video tripod head that has a smooth fluid motion. It's much easier to pan the phone smoothly on a video head, especially if you need the camera to be close to the ground, to get close to the foreground plants. In this position, it would be all but impossible to hand-hold the phone anyway, unless you are a contortionist.

A smartphone can also be placed in positions where a DSLR would be too bulky, for example flat on the ground looking up through a display of flowers to the sky or trees beyond. This is where 'selfie' mode is useful. This flips the camera to the same side of the phone as the controls, so you can position the phone exactly where you want it. Then all you have to do is press the 'shutter', whilst trying to avoid appearing in the picture yourself – the opposite of what the phone manufacturers intended with selfie mode! There are also a variety of apps which can control your smartphone remotely from a second phone or tablet, which means you don't have to be quite such a contortionist.

Another approach for these kinds of images is to use a GoPro or similar miniature camera. These are mainly intended as video cameras, usually attached to helmets of climbers or skydivers, or mounted on drones or surfboards, for high-action, adrenaline-fuelled footage. But the latest incarnations of these cameras can produce pretty good quality stills. A 4k GoPro, for example, can shoot 12 megapixel (3000 x 4000 pixels) publication-quality images. And again there are apps available that allow the camera to talk via WiFi to a smartphone or tablet. This allows you to see what the camera sees, with a range of tens of metres and to control the camera settings remotely. So you can position the camera accurately, then retreat to a safe distance to trigger it.

INFRARED PHOTOGRAPHY

DSLRs are constantly changing and with each new model come yet more 'must-have' features: bigger images, faster chips, quicker autofocus. Hopefully I have made it clear in this chapter that technology is merely the servant of creativity. Even so, as you get more serious about stills photography, it's always a help to use the latest technology. So what do you do with your old DSLR? Rather than letting it gather dust on a shelf, consider converting it for infrared photography. On normal cameras, there is a filter in front of the image sensor which serves to block infrared from reaching the sensor. This long wavelength of light, invisible to our eyes, would otherwise degrade the image. Specialist companies can replace this filter with one which blocks all visible light and only lets through infrared. This filter appears black to our eyes, but the sensor is sensitive to infrared wavelengths.

Now, objects that reflect infrared will appear white in the image; those that absorb it appear black. Green foliage reflects infrared, so leaves appear white. This can produce beautiful, ethereal images. But it can also tell you something more about the plants. When photographing a field of dandelions in infrared, I noticed something peculiar. Most had finished flowering and the heads had closed up as the seeds matured, before opening again to reveal the fluffy seed head – the dandelion clock familiar from childhood. Most of the image was, as expected, in shades of white as grass and dandelion leaves reflected infrared light. But the closed flower heads were all black. Perhaps, in absorbing infrared, the closed flowers were warming themselves, to speed up the maturation of their seeds.

MONOCHROME PHOTOGRAPHY

Because the camera is only sensing one wavelength of light, infrared images are monochrome. But sometimes it's worth exploring monochrome images shot with a normal camera. Colour images can be converted to black-and-white (one kind of monochrome) either in the RAW converter, in Photoshop or in dedicated conversion software. All of these techniques give much more control over the final image than was possible in the past by shooting on black and white film. To achieve the best results on film means using various colour filters to enhance local contrast. There are also many techniques and tricks for getting the best out of prints made from black-and-white negatives. Printing your own black-and-white photographs is addictive and I've lost whole days in the darkroom in the past. Black-and-white photography is a real art form in every sense, and it is worth looking at the work of black-and-white photographers past and present for inspiration. Digital black-and-white photography might be less organic, but with a bit of creative thought you can still produce some striking images.

Converting from a colour digital still on a computer allows the photographer to experiment widely with many different settings to achieve the most dramatic result. Often monochrome images look good in high contrast (which can also be adjusted during conversion) as this brings out the architecture or texture of the subject. Indeed, without distracting colours, monochrome photography is much the best way of highlighting plant form, as dramatically illustrated by the work of Karl Blossfeldt.

Monochrome doesn't have to mean black-and-white. Subtle colour washes can also be added and some software allows you to create antique-looking sepia images. The conversion software usually also allows the creation of duotones – sometimes called split toning. This means adding a faint colour wash to the shadows and a second, complementary one, to the highlights. The conversion controls allow for any two colours to be added, for example making the shadows blue and the highlights yellow, and for adjusting the transition point between the two colours. At first glance, these images might look like black-and-white, but they are often more subtle and can enhance textural or architectural details. The creative possibilities are endless. Randomly converting stills from your collection can produce some surprising results, but in general, if you want to work with monochrome, I would recommend that you shoot new images, and that you have some idea of what you want to achieve before you do so. In a single and relatively short chapter such as this, I cannot offer a comprehensive guide to plant photography, but I hope I have managed to suggest a few potential avenues of approach. For a more comprehensive overview of all these topics, along with background details on basic camera functions and some inspiring images, I recommend *Digital Plant Photography* by Adrian Davies, published by Bloomsbury. However, a brief search on the internet will throw up a large range of books on all aspects of nature photography, along with books that look at image-processing techniques, from basic adjustments to advanced manipulation. And there are an ever-growing number of video tutorials that cover all these techniques.

The works of pioneers like Karl Blossfeldt are truly inspirational, but modern digital photography has opened up new vistas of creativity undreamed of even a few decades ago. More importantly, a camera is the perfect excuse for spending long hours in the field and is a great way of opening your eyes to the beauty in every wildflower.

References

PART I: WOODLANDS

INTRODUCTION

1. Augustin, L., et al., 'Eight glacial cycles from an Antarctic ice core' *Nature*, 2004. 429: pp. 623–628.
2. Berger, A. and M.-F. Loutre, 'An exceptionally long interglacial ahead?' *Science*, 2002. 297(5585): pp. 1287–1288.
3. 'Next Ice Age Delayed by Rising Carbon Dioxide Levels', 2007 [12 August 2018]. Available from: www.sciencedaily.com/releases/2007/08/070829193436.htm.
4. Rackham, O., *The History of the Countryside: the Classic History of Britain's Landscape, Flora and Fauna*, 1986: Phoenix Press, London.
5. Smout, C., 'The History and the Myth of Scots Pine' RSFS *Scottish Forestry*, 2014: p. 68.
6. Lake, S., et al., *Britain's Habitats: A Guide to the Wildlife Habitats of Britain and Ireland*, 2015: Princeton University Press.
7. Peterken, G.F., *Natural Woodland: Ecology and Conservation in Northern Temperate Regions*, 1996: Cambridge University Press.
8. Lake, S, et al., 2015.
9. Baarda, P., 'Atlantic oakwoods in Great Britain: Factors influencing their definition, distribution and occurrence' *Botanical Journal of Scotland*, 2005. 57(1): pp. 1–19.
10. Rackham, O., *Woodlands*, 2009: HarperCollins, UK.
11. Mitchell, F.J.G., 'How open were European primeval forests? Hypothesis testing using palaeoecological data' *Journal of Ecology*, 2005. 93(1): pp. 168–177.
12. Mitchell, F.J.G., 2005.
13. Batchelor, C.R., et al., 'The timing and causes of the Neolithic elm decline: New evidence from the Lower Thames Valley (London, UK)' *Environmental Archaeology*, 2014. 19(3): pp. 263–290.
14. Lake, S, et al., 2015.
15. Hopkins, J.J. and K.J. Kirby, 'Ecological change in British broadleaved woodland since 1947' *Ibis*, 2007. 149: pp. 29–40.

16. Keith, S.A., et al., 'Taxonomic homogenization of woodland plant communities over 70 years' *Proceedings of the Royal Society of London B: Biological Sciences*, 2009. 276(1672): pp. 3539–3544.
17. Rackham, O., *Hayley Wood*, 1975: Cambridgeshire and Isle of Ely Naturalists' Trust.
18. Rackham, O., 2009.
19. Verheyen, K. and M. Hermy, 'The relative importance of dispersal limitation of vascular plants in secondary forest succession in Muizen Forest, Belgium' *Journal of Ecology*, 2001. 89(5): pp. 829–840.
20. Bossuyt, B., M. Hermy and J. Deckers, 'Migration of herbaceous plant species across ancient–recent forest ecozones in central Belgium' *Journal of Ecology*, 1999. 87(4): pp. 629–638.
21. Rackham, O., 2009.

I   WOODLAND LILIES

1. Cullen, K.E., 'Carl Linnaeus (1707–1778): binomial nomenclature system', in *Biology: The People Behind the Science*, 2006: Infobase Publishing, pp. 28–43.
2. Jardine, N., J.A. Secord, and E.C. Sparey, eds. *Cultures of Natural History*, 1996: Cambridge University Press.
3. de Jussieu, A.L., *Antonii Laurentii de Jussieu Genera plantarum: secundum ordines naturales disposita, juxta methodum in Horto regio parisiensi exaratam, anno M.DCC. LXXIV.* 1789 [cited 5th March 2017]. Available from: http://www. biodiversitylibrary.org/item/7125#page/1/mode/1up.
4. Lindley, J., *An introduction to the natural system of botany: or, A systematic view of the organisation, natural affinities, and geographical distribution, of the whole vegetable kingdom: together with the uses of the most important species in medicine, the arts, and rural or domestic economy.* 1830: Longman, London.
5. Bjerketvedt, D.K., et al., 'The growth and

phenology patterns of herb paris (*Paris quadrifolia* L., Trilliaceae): relation to soil and air temperatures' *Ekologija*, 2003. 1: pp. 75–80.
6. Jacquemyn, H. and R. Brys, 'Density-dependent mating and reproductive assurance in the temperate forest herb *Paris quadrifolia* (Trilliaceae)' *American Journal of Botany*, 2008. 95(3): pp. 294–298.
7. Jacquemyn, H., et al., 'Sexual reproduction, clonal diversity and genetic differentiation in patchily distributed populations of the temperate forest herb *Paris quadrifolia* (Trilliaceae)' *Oecologia*, 2006. 147(3): pp. 434–444.
8. Kranczoch, J., 'Struktur und Dynamik in dichten Beständen von *Paris quadrifolia* (Trilliaceae)' 1997.
9. Wright, J., 'An ecological basis for the conservation management of *Polygonatum verticillatum* (L.) All. (Convallariaceae)' *Botanical Journal of Scotland*, 1997. 49(2): pp. 489–500.
10. Tybjerg, H. and P. Vestergaard, 'Growth Dynamics in the Rhizomatous Herb *Polygonatum verticillatum*' *Oikos*, 1992. 65(3): pp. 395–408.
11. Kosiński, I., 'Generative reproduction dynamics in populations of the perennial herb *Polygonatum multiflorum* (Asparagaceae)' *Annales Botanici Fennici*, 2012. BioOne.
12. Perttula, U., 'Untersuchungen über die generative und vegetative Vermehrung der Blütenpflanzen in der Wald-, Hain-, Wiesen- und Hainfelsenvegetation' *Suomalainen Tiedeakatemia*, 1941.
13. Arens, P., et al., 'Clonal diversity and genetic differentiation of *Maianthemum bifolium* among forest fragments of different age' *Plant Ecology*, 2005. 179(2): pp. 169–180.
14. Czarnecka, B., 'Clonal organization of populations of *Asarum europaeum* and *Maianthemum bifolium* in contrasting woodland habitats' *Vegetatio*, 1996. 125(1): pp. 51–62.
15. Honnay, O., et al., 'Consequences of

prolonged clonal growth on local and regional genetic structure and fruiting success of the forest perennial *Maianthemum bifolium*' *Oikos*, 2006. 112(1): pp. 21–30.

16. Ietswaart, J.H. and J.W. Schoorl, 'Fructification in Dutch *Maianthemum bifolium* populations' *Acta Botanica Neerlandica*, 1985. 34(4): pp. 381–391.

17. Tumidajowicz, D., 'Effectiveness of generative reproduction of some forest plants from chosen communities of Southern Poland' *Bulletin. Serie des sciences biologiques*, 1977.

18. Kosiński, I., 'Long-term variability in seed size and seedling establishment of *Maianthemum bifolium*' *Plant Ecology*, 2008. 194(2): pp. 149–156.

19. Oinonen, E., 'The time table of vegetative spreading in oak fern (Carpogymnia dryopteris (L.) LÖVE & LÖVE) and may-lily (Maianthemum bifolium (L.) F. W. SCHMIDT) in Southern Finland' *Acta Forestalia Fennica*, 1971. 118: pp. 1–37.

20. *The Natural History of the Scarborough District*, 1953: Scarborough Naturalists.

21. Chwedorzewska, K.J., H. Galera, and I. Kosiński, 'Plantations of *Convallaria majalis* L. as a threat to the natural stands of the species: genetic variability of the cultivated plants and natural populations' *Biological Conservation*, 2008. 141(10): pp. 2619–2624.

22. Nelson, E.C. and R.A. Stalley, 'Medieval naturalism and the botanical carvings at Corcomroe Abbey (County Clare)' *Gesta*, 1989: pp. 165–174.

23. Oinonen, E., 'The time table of vegetative spreading of the lily-of-the-valley (*Convallaria majalis* L.) and the wood small-reed (*Calamagrostis epigeios* (L.) Roth) in southern Finland' *Acta Forestalia Fennica*, 1969. 97: pp. 1–35.

24. Araki, K., K. Shimatani, and M. Ohara, 'Floral distribution, clonal structure, and their effects on pollination success in a self-incompatible *Convallaria keiskei* population in northern Japan' *Plant Ecology*, 2007. 189(2): pp. 175–186.

25. Ponert, J., ed. Convallaria. *Flora Europaea*, ed. V.H. Haywood. Vol. 5. 1980.

26. Vandepitte, K., et al., 'Extremely low genotypic diversity and sexual reproduction in isolated populations of the self-incompatible lily-of-the-valley (*Convallaria majalis*) and the role of the local forest environment' *Annals of Botany*, 2010. 105(5): pp. 769–776.

27. Oinonen, E., 1969.

28. Vandepitte, K., et al., 2010.

29. Ehrlen, J. and O. Eriksson, 'Toxicity in fleshy fruits: a non-adaptive trait?' *Oikos*, 1993: pp. 107–113.

30. Ehrlen, J. and O. Eriksson, 1993.

31. Alcock, J., *An Enthusiasm for Orchids. Sex

and Deception in the Plant World, 2006: Oxford University Press.

32. Williams, G.C. and R. Dawkins, *Adaptation and Natural Selection: A Critique of Some Current Evolutionary Thought*, 2019: Princeton University Press.

33. Dennett, D.C., *Darwin's Dangerous Idea: Evolution and the Meanings of Life*, 1995: Simon and Schuster.

34. Franková, L., et al., 'Biochemical and physiological aspects of developmental cycle of *Colchicum autumnale* L.' *Biologia plantarum*, 2003. 47(4): pp. 509–516.

35. Sundov, Z., et al., 'Fatal colchicine poisoning by accidental ingestion of meadow saffron-case report' *Forensic Science International*, 2005. 149(2–3): pp. 253–256.

36. Klintschar, M., et al., 'Colchicine poisoning by accidental ingestion of meadow saffron (*Colchicum autumnale*): pathological and medicolegal aspects' *Forensic Science International*, 1999. 106(3): pp. 191–200.

37. Peters, F.T., et al., 'Colchicine poisoning after mix-up of Ramsons (*Allium ursinum* L.) and meadow saffron (*Colchicum autumnale* L.)' *Toxichem Krimtech*, 2004. 71: pp. 156–160.

38. Grigson, G., *The Englishman's Flora*, 1955: Phoenix House, London.

39. Butcher, R., '*Colchicum Autumnale* L.' *The Journal of Ecology*, 1954: pp. 249–257.

40. Jung, L.S., et al., '*Colchicum autumnale* L.' *Perspectives in Plant Ecology, Evolution and Systematics*, 2011. 13(3): pp. 227–244.

41. Butcher, R., 1954.

42. Jung, L.S., et al., 2011.

43. Adriaens, D., et al., 'Conservation of remnant populations of *Colchicum autumnale* – The relative importance of local habitat quality and habitat fragmentation' *Acta Oecologica*, 2009. 35(1): pp. 69–82.

44. Jung, L.S., et al., 2011.

45. Butcher, R., 1954.

46. Poutaraud, A. and P. Girardin, 'Alkaloids in meadow saffron, *Colchicum autumnale* L.' *Journal of Herbs, Spices & Medicinal Plants*, 2002. 9(1): pp. 63–79.

47. Poutaraud, A. and P. Girardin, 'Seed yield and components of alkaloid of meadow saffron (*Colchicum autumnale*) in natural grassland and under cultivation' *Canadian Journal of Plant Science*, 2003. 83(1): pp. 23–29.

48. Poutaraud, A. and P. Girardin, 'Influence of chemical characteristics of soil on mineral and alkaloid seed contents of *Colchicum autumnale*' *Environmental and Experimental Botany*, 2005. 54(2): pp. 101–108.

2 RAMSONS

1. Mabey, R., *Flora Britannica*, 1996: Reed International Books.

2. Griffiths, D., *Vikings of the Irish Sea*, 2010: The History Press.

3. Mabey, R., 1996.

4. Oborny, B., et al., 'Population ecology of *Allium ursinum*, a space-monopolizing clonal plant' *Acta Botanica Hungarica*, 2011. 53(3): pp. 371–388.

5. Kovács, J.A., 'Data to the Vegetation Biology and Coenological Relations of *Allium ursinum* L. Stands in Eastern Transylvania' *Kanitzia*, 2007. 15: pp. 63–76.

6. Morschhauser, T., et al., 'Density-dependence in the establishment of juvenile *Allium ursinum* individuals in a monodominant stand of conspecific adults' *Acta Oecologica*, 2009. 35(5): pp. 621–629.

7. Kricsfalusy, V. and G. Budnikov, 'Threatened vascular plants in the Ukrainian Carpathians: current status, distribution and conservation' *Thaiszia – Journal of Botany*, 2007. 17: pp. 11–32.

8. Oborny, B., et al., 2011.

9. Ernst, W.H.O., 'Population Biology of *Allium ursinum* in Northern Germany' *Journal of Ecology*, 1979. 67(1): pp. 347–362.

10. Trémolières, M., V. Noël, and B. Hérault, 'Phosphorus and nitrogen allocation in *Allium ursinum* on an alluvial floodplain (Eastern France). Is there an effect of flooding history?' *Plant and Soil*, 2009. 324(1–2): pp. 279–289.

11. Rychnovská, M. and V. Bednár, 'Floodplain forest: herb layer as indicator of its ecological status' *Acta Universitatis Palackianae Olomucensis: Facultas Rerum Naturalium: Biologica*, 1998. 36: pp. 7–15.

12. Ernst, W.H.O., 1979.

13. Eggert, A., 'Dry matter economy and reproduction of a temperate forest spring geophyte, *Allium ursinum*' *Ecography*, 1992. 15(1): pp. 45–55.

14. Grime, J.P., Hodgson, J.G. Hodgson and Hunt, R., *Comparative Plant Ecology: A Functional Approach to Common British Species*. 1988: London, Allen and Unwin, p. 742.

15. Morschhauser, T., et al., 2009.

16. Oborny, B., et al., 2011.

17. Djurdjevic, L., 'Allelopathic potential of *Allium ursinum* L.' *Biochemical Systematic and Ecology*, 2004. 32: pp. 533–544.

18. Ernst, W.H.O., 1979.

19. Puxbaum, H. and G. König, 'Observation of dipropenyldisulfide and other organic sulfur compounds in the atmosphere of a beech forest with *Allium ursinum* ground cover' *Atmospheric Environment*, 1997. 31(2): pp. 291–294.

20. Preuss, H.G., et al., 'Wild garlic has a greater effect than regular garlic on blood pressure and blood chemistries of rats' *International Urology and Nephrology*, 2001. 32(4): pp. 525–530.

21. Błażewicz-Woźniak, M. and A. Michowska,

'The growth, flowering and chemical composition of leaves of three ecotypes of *Allium ursinum* L.' *Acta Agrobotanica*, 2011. 64(4): pp. 171–180.

22. Schmitt, B., et al., 'Chemical Characterization of *Allium ursinum* L. Depending on Harvesting Time' *Journal of Agricultural and Food Chemistry*, 2005. 53(18): pp. 7288–7294.

23. Mabey, R., 1996.

24. Salisbury, A., 'Impact, host range and chemical ecology of the lily beetle, *Lilioceris lilii*', 2008: Imperial College, London.

25. Sapáková, E., et al., 'The intensity of infestation of garlic by *Lilioceris merdigera* and *Oprohinus suturalis*' *Acta Universitatis Agriculturae et Silviculturae Mendelianae Brunensis*, 2014, p. 62.

26. Hövemeyer, K., 'Trophic links, nutrient fluxes, and natural history in the *Allium ursinum* food web, with particular reference to life history traits of two hoverfly herbivores (Diptera: Syrphidae)' *Oecologia*, 1995. 102(1): pp. 86–94.

27. Speight, M.C.D., '*Portevinia maculata* (Fal.): last instar larva and puparium, with notes on the relationship between this hoverfly and its larval host plant, *Allium ursinum* (Diptera, Syrphidae)' *Nouvelle Revue d'Entomologie*, 1986. 3: pp. 37–43.

28. Rotheray, G.E. and F. Gilbert, *The Natural History of Hoverflies* 2011: Forrest Text, Cardigan. p. 334.

29. Jandl, R., H. Kopeszki, and G. Glatzel, 'Effect of a dense *Allium ursinum* (L.) ground cover on nutrient dynamics and mesofauna of a *Fagus sylvatica* (L.) woodland' *Plant and Soil*, 1997. 189(2): pp. 245–255.

30. Jandl, R., et al., 1997.

31. Andersson, M.E., 'Aluminium Toxicity as a Factor Limiting the Distribution of *Allium ursinum* (L.)' *Annals of Botany*, 1993. 72(6): pp. 607–611.

32. Trémolières, M., et al., 2009.

33. Oborny, B., et al., 2011.

---

3 **BLUEBELLS**

1. House, H. (ed.), *The Journals and Papers of Gerard Manley Hopkins*, 1959: Oxford University Press.

2. Ingrouille, M.J., *Historical Ecology of the British Flora*, 1995: Chapman and Hall.

3. Thompson, P.A. and S.A. Cox, 'Germination of the Bluebell (*Hyacinthoides non-scripta* (L.) Chouard) in Relation to its Distribution and Habitat' *Annals of Botany*, 1978. 42(1): pp. 51–62.

4. Grundmann, M., et al., 'Phylogeny and taxonomy of the bluebell genus, *Hyacinthoides*, Asparagaceae [Hyacinthaceae].' *Taxon*, 2010. 59(1): pp. 68–82.

5. Thompson, P.A. and S.A. Cox, 1978.

6. Wilson, J.Y., 'Verification of the Breeding System in the Bluebell *Endymion nonscriptus* (L.) Garcke' *Annals of Botany*, 1959. 23(1): pp. 201–203.

7. Corbet, S.A., 'Fruit and seed production in relation to pollination and resources in bluebell, *Hyacinthoides non-scripta*' *Oecologia*, 1998. 114(3): pp. 349–360.

8. Thompson, P.A. and S.A. Cox, 1978.

9. Knight, G.H., 'Some Factors Affecting the Distribution of *Endymion nonscriptus* (L.) Garcke in Warwickshire Woods' *Journal of Ecology*, 1964. 52: pp. 405–421.

10. Vickers, A.D. and I.D. Rotherham, 'The response of bluebell (*Hyacinthoides non-scripta*) to seasonal differences between years and woodland management' *Aspects of Applied Ecology*, 2000. 58: pp. 351–356.

11. Blackman, G.E. and A.J. Rutter, '*Endymnion non-scriptus*' *Journal of Ecology*, 1954. 42: pp. 629–638.

12. Roisin, P., *Le Domaine Phytogéographique Atlantique d'Europe* 1969: Editions J. Duculot.

13. Pigott, C.D., 'The experimental study of vegetation' *New Phytologist*, 1982. 90(3): pp. 389–404.

14. Newsham, K.K., A.H. Fitter, and A.R. Watkinson, 'Multi-functionality and biodiversity in arbuscular mycorrhizas' *Trends in Ecology & Evolution*, 1995. 10(10): pp. 407–411.

15. Sebastiaan Van Der, V., et al., 'Over the (range) edge: A 45-year transplant experiment with the perennial forest herb *Hyacinthoides non-scripta*' *J Ecol*, 2007. 95(2): pp. 343–351.

16. Belitt, B., *The Forgèd Feature: Toward a Poetics of Uncertainty: New and Selected Essays*, 1994: Fordham University Press.

17. Hopkins, G.M. and W. Gardner, *Poems and Prose*. 2008: Penguin.

18. Harris, S. and D.W. Yalden, eds., *Mammals of the British Isles: Handbook*. 4th Edition, 2008: The Mammals Society.

19. Kohn, D.D., et al., 'Are native bluebells (*Hyacinthoides non-scripta*) at risk from alien congenerics? Evidence from distributions and co-occurrence in Scotland' *Biological Conservation*, 2009. 142(1): pp. 61–74.

20. Cooke, A.S., 'Effects of grazing by muntjac (*Muntiucus reevesi*) on bluebells (*Hyacinthoides non-scripta*) and a field technique for assessing feeding activity' *Journal of Zoology*, 1997. 242(2): pp. 365–369.

21. Tubbs, C.R., *The New Forest*. New Naturalist Series. 1986, London: Collins.

22. Kirby, K.J., 'The impact of deer on the ground flora of British broadleaved woodland' *Forestry*, 2001. 74(3): pp. 219–229.

23. Watson, A.A., et al., '*Glycosidase-inhibiting pyrrolidine alkaloids* from *Hyacinthoides non-scripta*' *Phytochemistry*, 1997. 46(2): pp. 255–259.

24. Littlemore, J. and S. Barker, 'The ecological response of forest ground flora and soils to experimental trampling in British urban woodlands' *Urban Ecosystems*, 2001. 5(4): pp. 257–276.

25. Surprisingly few detailed studies on this topic have been carried out, though one in 2011 by the Department for Environment, Food and Rural Affairs) and the Forestry Commission suggested that currently wild boar were having little effect on bluebell displays.

---

4 **WILD DAFFODILS**

1. Willis, D., *Yellow Fever: A Prospect of the History and Culture of Daffodils*. 2012: David Willis.

2. Dalton, J. *The English Lent Lily* [18/10/2014]. Available from: http://thedaffodilsociety.com/wordpress/wp-content/uploads/2013/03/Jan-Dalton-The-English-Lent-Lily.pdf.

3. Dweck, A., 'The Folklore of Narcissus', in *Narcissus and Daffodil: The Genus Narcissus* (Medicinal and Aromatic Plants – Industrial Profiles), G.R. Hanks, Editor. 2002: CRC Press, p. 452.

4. Mabey, R., *The Cabaret of Plants: Botany and the Imagination*, 2015: Profile Books.

5. Pliny, *Naturalis Historia*: Book XXI, Chapter 75.

6. Willis, D., 2012.

7. Dalton, J., 2014.

8. Rivera, D., et al., 'The biogeographical patterns of floral form in wild daffodils and their contribution to the cultivar groups of *Narcissus* L. subgenus *Ajax* Spach (Amaryllidaceae)', in *Floriculture, Ornamental and Plant Biotechnology*, J.A. Teixeira da Silva, Editor. 2006.

9. Willis, D., 2012.

10. Preston, C.D., D.A. Pearman, and T.D. Dines, *New Atlas of the British and Irish Flora: An Atlas of the Vascular Plants of Britain, Ireland, The Isle of Man and the Channel Islands*. 2002: Oxford University Press.

11. Preston, C.D., et al., 2002.

12. Curtis, W., *The Botanical Magazine*. Vol. IV. 1795, London: William Curtis.

13. Vickery, R., *The Dictionary of Plant Lore*. 1995: Oxford University Press.

14. Kingsbury, N. and J. Whitworth, *Daffodils*. 2013, London, Portland: Timber Press, p. 220.

15. Willis, D., 2012.

16. Willis, D., 2012.

17. Wordsworth, D., *The Grasmere and Alfoxden Journals*, 2002: Oxford University Press.

18. Preston, C.D., et al., 2002.

19. Bastida, J., R. Lavilla, and F. Viladomat, 'Chemical and Biological Aspects of

Narcissus Alkaloids', in *The Alkaloids: Chemistry and Biology*, A.C. Geoffrey, Editor. 2006: Academic Press, pp. 87–179.

20. Willis, D., 2012.

21. Gerard, J., *The Herball or Generall Historie of Plantes*, 1597: John Norton, London.

22. Mabey, R., *Flora Britannica*. 1996: Reed International Books.

23. Barkham, J.P., 'Population Dynamics of the Wild Daffodil (*Narcissus pseudonarcissus*): I. Clonal Growth, Seed Reproduction, Mortality and the Effects of Density' *Journal of Ecology*, 1980. 68(2): pp. 607–633.

24. Barkham, J.P., 'Population Dynamics of the Wild Daffodil (*Narcissus pseudonarcissus*): II. Changes in Number of Shoots and Flowers, and the Effect of Bulb Depth on Growth and Reproduction' *Journal of Ecology*, 1980. 68(2): pp. 635–664.

25. Barkham, J.P., 1980 (I).

26. Barkham, J.P., 1980 (I).

27. Barkham, J.P., 'Population Dynamics of the Wild Daffodil (*Narcissus pseudonarcissus*). IV. Clumps and Gaps' *Journal of Ecology*, 1992. 80(4): pp. 797–808.

28. Barkham, J.P. and C.E. Hance, 'Population Dynamics of the Wild Daffodil (*Narcissus pseudonarcissus*): III. Implications of a Computer Model of 1000 Years of Population Change' *Journal of Ecology*, 1982. 70(1): pp. 323–344.

29. Fuller, R.J. and M.S. Warren, *Coppiced Woodlands: Their Management for Wildlife*. 1993: Joint Nature Conservation Committee, London.

30. Colling, G., et al., 'Population genetic structure of wild daffodils (*Narcissus pseudonarcissus* L.) at different spatial scales' *Plant Systematics and Evolution*, 2010. 287(3–4): pp. 99–111.

31. Barkham, J.P., 1992.

32. Jones, D., *The Tenby Daffodil; The Remarkable Story of the True Welsh Daffodil* 1992: Tenby Museum, p. 28.

33. Jones, D., 1992.

34. Jones, D., 1992.

35. Pugsley, H.W., '*Narcissus obvallaris* at Tenby' *Journal of Botany*, 1942, p. 79.

36. Etnier, S.A. and S. Vogel, 'Reorientation of daffodil (*Narcissus*: Amaryllidaceae) flowers in wind: Drag reduction and torsional flexibility' *American Journal of Botany*, 2000. 87(1): pp. 29–32.

---

5 SNOWDROPS & SNOWFLAKES

1. Lledó, M.D., et al., 'Phylogenetic analysis of *Leucojum* and *Galanthus* (Amaryllidaceae) based on plastid matK and nuclear ribosomal spacer (ITS) DNA sequences and morphology' *Plant Systematics and Evolution*, 2004. 246(3–4): pp. 223–243.

2. Meerow, A.W., et al., 'Phylogenetic Relationships and Biogeography within the Eurasian Clade of Amaryllidaceae Based on Plastid ndhF and nrDNA ITS Sequences: Lineage Sorting in a Reticulate Area?' *Systematic Botany*, 2006. 31: pp. 42–60.

3. Preston, C.D., D.A. Pearman, and T.D. Dines, *New Atlas of the British and Irish Flora; An Atlas of the Vascular Plants of Britain, Ireland, The Isle of Man and the Channel Islands*. 2002: Oxford University Press.

4. Preston, C.D., et al., 2002.

5. 'Panjutin's snowdrop' [29 December 2015]. Available from: http://www.kew.org/science-conservation/plants-fungi/galanthus-panjutinii-panjutin%E2%80%99s-snowdrop.

6. Aschan, G. and H. Pfanz, 'Why Snowdrop (*Galanthus nivalis* L.) tepals have green marks?' *Flora – Morphology, Distribution, Functional Ecology of Plants*, 2006. 201(8): pp. 623–632.

7. Aschan, G. and H. Pfanz, 2006.

8. Rønsted, N., et al., 'Snowdrops falling slowly into place: An improved phylogeny for *Galanthus* (Amaryllidaceae)' *Molecular Phylogenetics and Evolution*, 2013. 69(1): pp. 205–217.

9. Bishop, M., J. Grimshaw, and A.P. Davis, *Snowdrops: A Monograph of Cultivated Galanthus*. 2001: Griffin Press.

10. Gerard, J., *The Herball or Generall Historie of Plantes*. 1597: London, John Norton.

11. Cox, F., *A Gardener's Guide to Snowdrops*. 2013: Crowood.

12. Smith, J.E. and J.J. Römer, *Flora Britannica*. Vol. I 1804: typis Henrici Gessneri.

13. Crellin, J.R. 'Species account: *Leucojum aestivum*. Botanical Society of the British Isles' www.bsbi.org.uk. [2 Jan 2016]. Available from: http://sppaccounts.bsbi.org.uk/content/leucojum-aestivum-0.

14. Parolo, G., et al., 'Biological flora of Central Europe: *Leucojum aestivum* L.' *Perspectives in Plant Ecology, Evolution and Systematics*, 2011. 13(4): pp. 319–330.

15. Preston, C.D., et al., 2002.

16. Mabey, R., *Flora Britannica*. 1996: Reed International Books.

17. Farrell, L., 'The Distribution of *Leucojum aestivum* L. in Ireland' *The Irish Naturalists' Journal*, 1982. 20(11): pp. 483–489.

18. Farrell, L., 1982.

19. Crellin, J.R., 2016.

20. Servigne, P., 'Étude expérimentale et comparative de la myrmécochorie: le cas des fourmis dispersatrices *Lasius niger* et *Myrmica rubra*', 2008, Université libre de Bruxelles.

21. Newton, R.J., F.R. Hay, and R.H. Ellis, 'Ecophysiology of seed dormancy and the control of germination in early spring-flowering *Galanthus nivalis* and *Narcissus pseudonarcissus* (Amaryllidaceae)' *Botanical Journal of the Linnean Society*, 2015. 177(2): pp. 246–262.

22. Rejšková, A., et al., 'Temperature distribution in light-coloured flowers and inflorescences of early spring temperate species measured by infrared camera' *Flora-Morphology, Distribution, Functional Ecology of Plants*, 2010. 205(4): pp. 282–289.

23. Büdel, A., 'The microclimate of flowers blooming near the ground' *Zeitschrift für Bienenforschung*, 1959. 4: pp. 131–140.

24. Kevan, P. 'Thermoregulation in Arctic insects and flowers: adaptation and co-adaptation in behaviour, anatomy, and physiology' in *Proc Int Symp Thermal Physiol*. Elsevier, Amsterdam. 1989.

25. Ščepánková, I. and J. Hudák, 'Leaf and tepal anatomy, plastid ultrastructure and chlorophyll content in *Galanthus nivalis* L. and *Leucojum aestivum* L' *Plant Systematics and Evolution*, 2004. 243(3–4): pp. 211–219.

26. Rejšková, A., et al., 2010.

27. Farrer, R., *In a Yorkshire Garden* 1909: Edward Arnold.

28. Cox, F., 2013.

29. Maak, K. and H. von Storch, 'Statistical downscaling of monthly mean air temperature to the beginning of flowering of *Galanthus nivalis* L. in Northern Germany' *International Journal of Biometeorology*, 1997. 41(1): pp. 5–12.

30. Roetzer, T., et al., 'Phenology in central Europe – differences and trends of spring phenophases in urban and rural areas' *International Journal of Biometeorology*, 2000. 44(2): pp. 60–66.

31. Roetzer, T., et al., 2000.

32. Gerard, J., 1597.

33. Plaitakis, A. and R.C. Duvoisin, 'Homer's moly identified as *Galanthus nivalis* L.: physiologic antidote to stramonium poisoning' *Clinical neuropharmacology*, 1983. 6(1): pp. 1–5.

34. Heinrich, M. and H. Lee Teoh, 'Galanthamine from snowdrop—the development of a modern drug against Alzheimer's disease from local Caucasian knowledge' *Journal of Ethnopharmacology*, 2004. 92(2–3): pp. 147–162.

35. Shellard, E.J., 'Alkaloids from snowdrops' *The Pharmaceutical Journal*, 2000. 264: p. 883.

36. Heinrich, M., 'Snowdrops: The heralds of spring and a modern drug for Alzheimer's disease' *The Pharmaceutical Journal*, 2004.

37. Özhatay, N., 'Diversity of bulbous monocots in Turkey with special reference to chromosome numbers' *Pure and Applied Chemistry*, 2002, p. 547.

38. Demir, A., 'Medical Resource Value Appraisal for *Leucojum aestivum* in Turkey' *American Journal of Alzheimer's Disease and Other Dementias*, 2014.

39. Gussev, C., et al., 'Conservation of *Leucojum aestivum* (Amaryllidaceae) in

Bulgaria' *Bocconea*, 2003. 16(2): pp. 815–821.

40. Gussev, C., et al., 'Resource assessment of *Leucojum aestivum* L.(Amaryllidaceae) populations in Bulgaria' *Bocconea*, 2007. 21: pp. 405–411.

41. Stevanov, Z., 'Eco-biological and phytochemical investigations of natural populations and introduced origins of summer snowflake (*Leucojum aestivum* L.) in Bulgaria' 1990, NIHFI: Sofia.

42. Berkov, S., et al., 'The geographic isolation of *Leucojum aestivum* populations leads to divergation of alkaloid biosynthesis' *Biochemical Systematics and Ecology*, 2013. 46(0): pp. 152–161.

43. Abeli, T., et al., 'Restoring population structure and dynamics in translocated species: Learning from wild populations' *Plant Ecology*, 2015. pp. 1–10.

44. Jovanović, F., D. Obratov-Petković, and M. Mačukanović-Jocić, 'Nectar production in species of the Genus *galanthus* L. (Amaryllidaceae) from Serbia' *Glasnik Šumarskog fakulteta*, 2014. 109: pp. 85–96.

45. Newton, R.J., et al., 2015.

46. Newton, R.J., et al., 2015.

PART II: GRASSLANDS

INTRODUCTION

1. Pilkington, M., *Wildflower Meadows*. 2012, Winterbourne: Papadakis.

2. Peterken, G., *Meadows*. 2017: Bloomsbury Publishing.

3. King, M., 'The Kepp Vera Conference; the case for creating new wood pastures' *British Wildlife*, 2017. 29(1): pp. 27–33.

4. Vera, F.W., E.S. Bakker, and H. Olff, *Large herbivores: Missing partners of western European light-demanding tree and shrub species?* Conservation Biology Series, Cambridge, 2006. 11: p. 203.

5. Hodder, K.H., et al., 'Naturalistic Grazing and Re-Wilding in Britain – Perspectives from the Past and Future Directions' *British Wildlife*, 2009. 20(5, Special Supplement).

6. Marshall, A., 'A Legacy of the Crusaders' *BSBI News*, 1991. 58: pp. 33–34.

7. Majeský, Ľ., et al., 'The pattern of genetic variability in apomictic clones of *Taraxacum officinale* indicates the alternation of asexual and sexual histories of apomicts' *PLoS ONE*, 2012. 7(8): p. e41868.

6 BUTTERCUPS

1. Benn, M. and L.J. Yelland, 'Ranunculin' *Canadian Journal of Chemistry*, 1968. 46(5): pp. 729–732.

2. Blackmore, S., *Buttercups*. Shire Natural History. 1985: Aylesbury, Shire Publications Ltd.

3. He, J., et al., 'Survival tactics of Ranunculus

species in river floodplains' *Oecologia*, 1999. 118(1): pp. 1–8.

4. Wells, T. and D. Barling, '*Pulsatilla vulgaris* Mill. (*Anemone pulsatilla* L.). *Journal of Ecology*' 1971. 59(1): pp. 275–292.

5. Jones, E., 'The decrease of *Pulsatilla vulgaris* in England' *Biological Conservation*, 1969. 1(4): pp. 327–328.

6. Hensen, I., C. Oberprieler, and K. Wesche, 'Genetic structure, population size, and seed production of *Pulsatilla vulgaris* Mill. (Ranunculaceae) in Central Germany' *Flora-Morphology, Distribution, Functional Ecology of Plants*, 2005. 200(1): pp. 3–14.

7 FRITILLARIES

1. Mabey, R., *Flora Britannica*. 1996: Reed International Books.

2. Zhang, L., 'Vegetation ecology and population biology of *Fritillaria meleagris* L. at the Kungsängen nature reserve, eastern Sweden' *Acta phytogeographica Suecica*, 1983.

3. Oswald, P., 'The fritillary in Britain; a historical perspective' *British Wildlife*, 1992. 3(4): pp. 200–210.

4. Mabey, R., 1996.

5. Zhang, L., 1983.

6. Pratt, K. and M. Jefferson-Brown, *The Gardener's Guide to Growing Fritillaries*. 1997: David and Charles.

7. Zhang, L., 1983.

8. Zych, M., et al., 'The most effective pollinator revisited: Pollen dynamics in a spring-flowering herb' *Arthropod-plant Interactions*, 2013. 7(3): pp. 315–322.

9. Zych, M. and M. Stpiczyńska, 'Neither protogynous nor obligatory out-crossed: Pollination biology and breeding system of the European Red List *Fritillaria meleagris* L. (Liliaceae)' *Plant Biol* (Stuttg), 2012. 14(2): pp. 285–294.

10. Stpiczyńska, M., M. Nepi, and M. Zych, 'Secretion and composition of nectar and the structure of perigonal nectaries in *Fritillaria meleagris* L. (Liliaceae)' *Plant Systematics and Evolution*, 2012. 298(5): pp. 997–1013.

11. Zych, M., et al., 2013.

8 GENTIANS

1. Winfield, M., et al., 'A brief evolutionary excursion comes to an end: The genetic relationship of British species of *Gentianella* sect. *Gentianella* (Gentianaceae)' *Plant Systematics and Evolution*, 2003. 237(3–4): pp. 137–151.

2. Lennartsson, T. 'Demography, reproductive biology and adaptive traits in *Gentianella campestris* and *G. amarella*: Evaluating grassland management for conservation by using indicator plant species' 1997. Available from: http://agris.fao.org/agris-search/

search.do?recordID=SE9711699.

3. Milberg, P., 'Germination ecology of the endangered grassland biennial *Gentianella campestris*' Biological Conservation, 1994. 70(3): pp. 287–290.

4. Lennartsson, T. and J.G.B. Oostermeijer, 'Demographic variation and population viability in *Gentianella campestris*: Effects of grassland management and environmental stochasticity' *Journal of Ecology*, 2001. 89(3): pp. 451–463.

5. Juenger, T., T. Lennartsson, and J. Tuomi, 'The evolution of tolerance to damage in *Gentianella campestris*: Natural selection and the quantitative genetics of tolerance' *Evolutionary Ecology*, 2000. 14(4): pp. 393–419.

6. Lennartsson, T., P. Nilsson, and J. Tuomi, 'Induction of overcompensation in the field gentian, *Gentianella campestris*' *Ecology*, 1998. 79(3): pp. 1061–1072.

7. Huhta, A.-P., et al., 'Grazing tolerance of *Gentianella amarella* and other monocarpic herbs: Why is tolerance highest at low damage levels?' *Plant Ecology*, 2003. 166(1): pp. 49–61.

8. Marren, P., *Britain's Rare Flowers*. 1999, London: T. & A. D. Poyser Natural History, p. 337.

9. Marren, P., 1999.

10. Winfield, M., et al., 2003.

11. Rich, T., et al., 'Hybridisation between *Gentianella amarella* (L.) Boerner and *G. anglica* (Pugsley) EF Warb. (Gentianaceae)' *Watsonia*, 1997. 21(4): pp. 313–326.

12. Fischer, M. and D. Matthies, 'Mating structure and inbreeding and outbreeding depression in the rare plant *Gentianella germanica* (Gentianaceae)' *American Journal of Botany*, 1997. 84(12): pp. 1685–1685.

13. Elkington, T., '*Gentiana Verna* L.' *Journal of Ecology*, 1963. 51(3): pp. 755–767.

14. Marren, P., 1999.

15. Miller, G., C. Geddes, and D. Mardon, 'Response of the alpine gentian *Gentiana nivalis* L. to protection from grazing by sheep' *Biological Conservation*, 1999. 87(3): pp. 311–318.

16. Geddes, C. and C. Miller, 'Long-term changes in the size of an Alpine Gentian, *Gentiana nivalis* L., population in Scotland' *Watsonia*, 2010. 28(1): p. 65.

9 PRIMULAS

1. Horn, P., 'Old names for British Primulas' *BSBI News*, 1992. 62: pp. 37–38.

2. *The Phytologist: A Popular Miscellany of Botany*, 1842. 1(11): p. 191.

3. Doubleday, H., 'Letter from Henry Doubleday to Charles Darwin' May 3 1860.

4. Darwin, C.R., 'On the specific differences between *Primula veris*, Brit. Fl. (var. officinalis, of Linn), *P vulgaris*, Brit. Fl. (var

acaulis, Linn) and *P. elatior,* Jacq.; and on the hybrid nature of the common oxlip' *Journal of the Linnean Society of London, Botany,* 1868. 10: pp. 437–454.

5. Dijk, v.W., 'La decouverte de l'heterostylie chez Primula par Ch. de l'Ecluse dt P. Reneaulme' *Nederlandsch Kruidhundig Archief,* 1943. 53: pp. 81–85.

6. Barrett, S.C.H. and J.S. Shore, 'New Insights on Heterostyly: Comparative Biology, Ecology and Genetics' in *Self-Incompatibility in Flowering Plants* 2008, Springer Berlin Heidelberg. pp. 3–32.

7. Darwin, C.R., *The Different Forms of Flowers on Plants of the Same Species.* 1877: London, John Murray.

8. Wallace, A.R., 'The Debt of Science to Darwin' *The Century,* 1883. XXV: pp. 420–432.

9. Richards, A.J., *Primulas of the British Isles.* Shire Natural History, 1989: Shire Publications Ltd.

10. Shivanna, K.R., J. Heslop-Harrison, and Y. Heslop-Harrison, 'Heterostyly in *Primula.* 3. Pollen water economy: A factor in the intramorph-incompatibility response' *Protoplasma,* 1983. 117(3): pp. 175–184.

11. Shivanna, K.R., J. Heslop-Harrison, and Y. Heslop-Harrison, 'Heterostyly in *Primula.* 2. Sites of pollen inhibition, and effects of pistil constituents on compatible and incompatible pollen-tube growth' *Protoplasma,* 1981. 107(3–4): pp. 319–337.

12. Piper, J. and B. Charlesworth, 'The evolution of distyly in *Primula vulgaris' Biological Journal of the Linnean Society,* 1986. 29(2): pp. 123–137.

13. Schou, O.L.E., 'The distyly in *Primula elatior* (L.) Hill (Primulaceae), with a study of flowering phenology and pollen flow' *Botanical Journal of the Linnean Society,* 1983. 86(3): pp. 261–274.

14. Barrett, S.C.H., 'Sexual interference of the floral kind' *Heredity,* 2002. 88(2): pp. 154–159.

15. Barrett, S.C.H. and J.S. Shore, 2008.

16. de Vos, J.M., et al., 'Heterostyly accelerates diversification via reduced extinction in primroses' *Proceedings of the Royal Society of London. B: Biological Sciences,* 2014. 281(1784).

17. Brys, R., et al., 'Reduced reproductive success in small populations of the self-incompatible *Primula vulgaris' Journal of Ecology,* 2004. 92(1): pp. 5–14.

18. Crosby, J.L., 'High proportions of homostyle plants in populations of *Primula vulgaris' Nature,* 1940. 145: pp. 672–673.

19. Boyd, M., J. Silvertown, and C. Tucker, 'Population ecology of heterostyle and homostyle *Primula vulgaris*: Growth, survival and reproduction in field populations' *Journal of Ecology,* 1990. 78: pp. 799–813.

20. Jacquemyn, H., et al., 'Biological Flora of the British Isles: *Primula vulgaris* Huds. (P. acaulis (L.) Hill)'. *Journal of Ecology,* 2009. 97(4): pp. 812–833.

21. Boyd, M., et al., 1990.

22. Richards, A.J., 1989.

23. Boyd, M., et al., 1990.

24. Boyd, M., et al., 1990.

25. Piper, J.G., B. Charlesworth, and D. Charlesworth, 'Breeding system evolution in *Primula vulgaris* and the role of reproductive assurance' *Heredity,* 1986. 56(2): pp. 207–217.

26. Arnold, E.S. and A.J. Richards, 'On the occurrence of unilateral incompatibility in *Primula section Aleuritia Duby* and the origin of *Primula scotica Hook' Botanical Journal of the Linnean Society,* 1998. 128(4): pp. 359–368.

27. Melderis, A., 'Some parallels between the British and Scandinavian mountain floras', *The Changing Flora of Britain,* J.E. Lousley, Editor. 1953: T. Bunde & Co. Ltd: Arbroath. pp. 89–104.

28. Guggisberg, A., et al., 'Evolution of biogeographic patterns, ploidy levels, and breeding systems in a diploid–polyploid species complex of *Primula.' New Phytologist,* 2006. 171(3): pp. 617–632.

29. Boonkerd, T., 'Eco-physiology of *Primula farinosa* Linn: and some allied species.' 1987: Durham University.

30. Dovaston, H.F., '*Primula scotica* Hook., A relict species in Scotland', Royal Botanic Gardens, Edinburgh, 1955. 21: pp. 289–291.

31. Bullard, E.R., '*Primula scotica' BSBI Scottish Newsletter,* 1995. 17: p. 25.

32. Bullard, E.R., '*Primula scotica*: A Conservation Problem' *BSBI News,* 1993. 63: p. 15.

33. Ritchie, J., '*Primula scotica* Hook' *The Journal of Ecology,* 1954. 42: pp. 623–628.

34. Bullard, E.R., et al., 'Survival and flowering of *Primula scotica* Hook' *Journal of Ecology,* 1987.

35. Bullard, E.R., et al., 1987.

36. Bullard, E.R., et al., 1987.

37. Glover, B.J. and R.J. Abbott, 'Low genetic diversity in the Scottish endemic *Primula scotica* Hook' *New Phytologist,* 1995. 129(1): pp. 147–153.

38. Hambler, D. and J. Dixon, '*Primula farinosa* L.' *Journal of Ecology,* 2003. 91(4): pp. 694–705.

39. Boonkerd, T., 1987.

40. Manley, G., 'Meteorological observations on Dun Fell, a mountain station in north England' *Quarterly Journal of the Royal Meteorological Society,* 1942. 68: pp. 151–162.

41. Toräng, P., J. Ehrlén, and J. Ågren, 'Habitat quality and among-population differentiation in reproductive effort and flowering phenology in the perennial herb *Primula farinosa' Evolutionary Ecology,* 2010. 24(4): pp. 715–729.

42. Reisch, C., A. Anke, and M. Röhl, 'Molecular variation within and between ten populations of *Primula farinosa* (Primulaceae) along an altitudinal gradient in the northern Alps' *Basic and Applied Ecology,* 2005. 6(1): pp. 35–45.

43. Ehrlén, J., S. Käck, and J. Ågren, 'Pollen limitation, seed predation and scape length in *Primula farinosa' Oikos,* 2002. 97(1): pp. 45–51.

44. Vanhoenacker, D., J. Ågren, and J. Ehrlén, 'Spatio-temporal variation in pollen limitation and reproductive success of two scape morphs in *Primula farinosa' New Phytologist,* 2006. 169(3): pp. 615–621.

45. Vanhoenacker, D., J. Ågren, and J. Ehrlén, 'Spatial variability in seed predation in *Primula farinosa*: Local population legacy versus patch selection' *Oecologia,* 2009. 160(1): pp. 77–86.

46. Madec, C., 'Genetic Variation and Evolution of Floral Display in *Primula farinosa'*, Faculty of Science and Technology, 2014, University of Uppsala: Uppsala. p. 40.

47. Valentine, D., 'Studies in British *Primulas* II. Ecology and Taxonomy of Primrose and Oxlip (*Primula vulgaris* Huds. and *P. Elatior* Schreb.)' *New Phytologist,* 1948. 47(1): pp. 111–130.

48. Taylor, K. and S.R.J. Woodell, 'Biological Flora of the British Isles: *Primula elatior* (L.) Hill' *Journal of Ecology,* 2008. 96(5): pp. 1098–1116.

49. Whale, D.M., 'Habitat Requirements in *Primula* Species' *New Phytologist,* 1984. 97(4): pp. 665–679.

50. Christy, M., '*Primula elatior* in Britain: Its Distribution, Peculiarities, Hybrids, and Allies' *Journal of the Linnean Society of London, Botany,* 1897. 33(229): pp. 172–201.

51. Meyer, H. and D. Meyer, 'The distribution of *Primula elatior* (L.) Hill.', *The Study of the Distribution of British Plants,* J.E. Lousley, Editor. 1951: Botanical Society of the British Isles: Oxford, pp. 80–81.

52. Rackham, O., 'The woods 30 years on: Where have all the Primroses gone?' *Nature in Cambridgeshire,* 1999. 41: pp. 73–87.

53. Rackham, O., 1999.

54. Gurney, M., et al., 'Hybridisation between Oxlip *Primula elatior* (L.) Hill and Primrose *P. vulgaris* Hudson, and the identification of their variable hybrid *P. xdigenea* A. Kerner' *Watsonia,* 2007. 26: pp. 239–251.

55. Keller, B., J.M. de Vos, and E. Conti, 'Decrease of sexual organ reciprocity between heterostylous primrose species, with possible functional and evolutionary implications' *Annals of Botany,* 2012. 110(6): pp. 1233–1244.

56. Jacquemyn, H., et al., 2009.

57. Jacquemyn, H., et al., 2009.

58. Valdés, A. and D. García, 'Recruitment limitations in *Primula vulgaris* in a

fragmented landscape' *Basic and Applied Ecology*, 2013. 14(7): pp. 565–573.

59. Valverde, T. and J. Silvertown, 'A Metapopulation Model for *Primula Vulgaris*, A Temperate Forest Understorey Herb' *Journal of Ecology*, 1997. 85(2): pp. 193–210.

60. Taylor, K. and S.R.J. Woodell, 2008.

61. Valdés, A. and D. García, 2013.

62. Valverde, T. and J. Silvertown, 'An Integrated Model of Demography, Patch Dynamics and Seed Dispersal in a Woodland Herb, *Primula vulgaris*' *Oikos*, 1997. 80(1): pp. 67–77.

63. Jacquemyn, H., et al., 2009.

64. Taylor, K. and S.R.J. Woodell, 2008.

10 ORCHIDS

1. Bateman, R.M., 'Burnt tips and bumbling bees: how many orchid species currently occur in the British Isles?' *Journal of the Hardy Orchid Society*, 2004. 31: pp. 10–18.

2. Bateman, R.M. 'How many orchid species are currently native to the British Isles?' *Current Taxonomic Research on the British & European Flora*, ed. J. Bailey and R.G. Ellis. 2006.

3. Darwin, C.R., *On the Various Contrivances by which British and Foreign Orchids are Fertilised by Insects*. 1862: London, John Murray.

4. Tabb, K., 'Darwin at Orchis Bank: Selection after the *Origin*' *Studies in History and Philosophy of Science Part C: Studies in History and Philosophy of Biological and Biomedical Sciences*, 2016. 55: pp. 11–20.

5. Mondragón-Palomino, M. and G. Theißen, 'MADS about the evolution of orchid flowers' *Trends in Plant Science*, 2008. 13(2): pp. 51–59.

6. Foley, M. and S. Clarke, *Orchids of the British Isles*. 2005: Griffin Press in association with the Royal Botanic Garden, Edinburgh.

7. Darwin, C.R., 1862.

8. Bateman, R.M. and R. Sexton, 'Is spur length of *Platanthera* species in the British Isles adaptively optimized or an evolutionary red herring?' *Watsonia*, 2008. 27: pp. 1–21.

9. Bateman, R.M. and P.J. Rudall, 'Evolutionary and morphometric implications of morphological variation among flowers within an inflorescence: a case-study using European orchids' *Annals of Botany*, 2006. 98(5): pp. 975–93.

10. Bateman, R., K. James, and P. Rudall, 'Contrast in levels of morphological versus molecular divergence between closely related Eurasian species of *Platanthera* (Orchidaceae) suggests recent evolution with a strong allometric component' *New Journal of Botany*, 2012. 2(2): pp. 110–148.

11. Bateman, R., et al., 2012.

12. Darwin, C.R., 1862.

13. Jersáková, J., S. Johnson, and P. Kindlmann, 'Mechanisms and evolution of deceptive pollination in orchids' *Biological Reviews*, 2006. 81(2): pp. 219–235.

14. Dafni, A., Y. Ivri, and N.J.M. Brantjes, 'Pollination of *Serapias vomeracea* Briq. (Orchidaceae) by imitation of holes for sleeping solitary male bees (Hymenoptera)' *Acta Botanica Neerlandica*, 1981. 30: pp. 69–73.

15. Dafni, A. and Y. Ivri, 'The flower biology of *Cephalanthera longifolia* (Orchidaceae)—pollen imitation and facultative floral mimicry' *Plant Systematics and Evolution*, 1981. 137(4): pp. 229–240.

16. Roubik, D.W., 'Deceptive orchids with *Meliponini* as pollinators' *Plant Systematics and Evolution*, 2000. 222(1): pp. 271–279.

17. Nilsson, L.A., 'Mimesis of bellflower (*Campanula*) by the red helleborine orchid *Cephalanthera rubra*', *Nature*, 1983.

18. Newman, R.D., et al., 'Hand pollination to increase seed-set of red helleborine *Cephalanthera rubra* in the Chiltern Hills, Buckinghamshire, England' *Conservation Evidence*, 2007. 4: pp. 88–93.

19. Mant, J.G., et al., 'A Phylogenetic Study of Pollinator Conservatism among Sexually Deceptive Orchids' *Evolution*, 2002. 56(5): pp. 888–898.

20. Breitkopf, H., et al., 'Pollinator shifts between Ophrys sphegodes populations: Might adaptation to different pollinators drive population divergence?' *Journal of Evolutionary Biology*, 2013. 26(10): pp. 2197–2208.

21. Ayasse, M., et al., 'Evolution of Reproductive Strategies in the Sexually Deceptive Orchid *Ophrys spegodes*: How Does Flower Specific Variation of Odor Signals Influence Reproductive Success?' *Evolution*, 2000. 54(6): pp. 1995–2006.

22. Sonkoly, J., et al., 'Higher seed number compensates for lower fruit set in deceptive orchids' *Journal of Ecology*, 2016. 104(2): pp. 343–351.

23. Jersáková, J., et al., 2006.

24. Johnson, S.D. and L.A. Nilsson, 'Pollen carryover, geitonogamy, and the evolution of deceptive pollination systems in orchids' *Ecology*, 1999. 80(8): pp. 2607–2619.

25. Johnson, S.D., C.I. Peter, and J. Agren, 'The effects of nectar addition on pollen removal and geitonogamy in the non-rewarding orchid *Anacamptis morio*' *Proceedings of the Royal Society of London. Series B: Biological Sciences*, 2004. 271: pp. 803–809.

26. Wallace, L.E., 'The Cost of Inbreeding in *Platanthera leucophaea* (Orchidaceae)' *American Journal of Botany*, 2003. 90(2): pp. 235–242.

27. Gigord, L.D.B., et al., 'The potential for floral mimicry in rewardless orchids: an experimental study' *Proceedings of the Royal Society of London. Series B: Biological Sciences*, 2002. 269(1498): pp. 1389–1395.

28. Scopece, G., et al., 'Pollination Efficiency and the Evolution of Specialized Deceptive Pollination Systems' *The American Naturalist*, 2010. 175(1): pp. 98–105.

29. Scopece, G., et al., 2010.

30. Scopece, G., F. Schiestl, and S. Cozzolino, 'Pollen transfer efficiency and its effect on inflorescence size in deceptive pollination strategies' *Plant Biology*, 2014. 17(2): pp. 545–550.

31. Sonkoly, J., et al., 2016.

32. Schiestl, F.P. and M. Ayasse, 'Post-mating odor in females of the solitary bee, *Andrena nigroaenea* (Apoidea, Andrenidae), inhibits male mating behavior' *Behavioral Ecology and Sociobiology*, 2000. 48(4): pp. 303–307.

33. Schiestl, F.P. and M. Ayasse, 'Post-pollination emission of a repellent compound in a sexually deceptive orchid: A new mechanism for maximising reproductive success?' *Oecologia*, 2001. 126(4): pp. 531–534.

34. Ayasse, M., et al., 2000.

35. Stejskal, K., et al., 'Functional significance of labellum pattern variation in a sexually deceptive orchid (*ophrys heldreichii*): Evidence of individual signature learning effects' *PLoS ONE*, 2015. 10(11): p. e0142971.

36. Scopece, G., et al., 2014.

37. Sletvold, N., et al., 'Strong pollinator – mediated selection for increased flower brightness and contrast in a deceptive orchid' *Evolution*, 2016.

38. Darwin, C.R., 1862.

39. Sumpter, J., et al., 'The current status of military (*Orchis militaris*) and monkey (*Orchis simia*) orchids in the Chilterns' *Watsonia*, 2004. 25(2): p. 175–184.

40. Qamaruz-Zaman, F., et al., 'Genetic fingerprinting studies of *Orchis simia* and *O. militaris*.' Unpublished report from Royal Botanic Gardens Kew to English Nature, 2002.

41. Fay, M.F., et al., 'Genetic diversity in *Cypripedium calceolus* (Orchidaceae) with a focus on north-western Europe, as revealed by plastid DNA length polymorphisms' *Annals of Botany*, 2009. 104(3): pp. 517–25.

42. Harrap, S., '*Spiranthes romazoffiana* (Irish lady's tresses): A Wild Goose Chase' *BSBI News*, 2017. 135: pp. 49–50.

43. Jacquemyn, H., et al., 'A spatially explicit analysis of seedling recruitment in the terrestrial orchid *Orchis purpurea*' *New Phytologist*, 2007. 176(2): pp. 448–459.

44. Machon, N., et al., 'Relationship between genetic structure and seed and pollen dispersal in the endangered orchid *Spiranthes spiralis*' *New Phytologist*, 2003. 157(3): pp. 677–687.

45. Lang, D. and L. Spalton, '*Serapias lingua* in south Devon (vc 3)' *BSBI News*, 1998(79):

pp. 20–21.

46. Lang, D., *Britain's Orchids*. 2004, Old Basing, Hampshire: Wildguides Ltd.

47. Chalk, M., 'The sawfly orchid (*Ophrys tenthredinifera*) on the Dorset coast: A first for the British Isles' *BSBI News*, 2014. 127: p. 32.

48. Wohlleben, P., *The Hidden Life of Trees: What They Feel, How They Communicate–Discoveries from a Secret World*. 2016: Greystone Books.

49. Ramsay, M.M. and J. Stewart, 'Re-establishment of the lady's slipper orchid (*Cypripedium calceolus* L.) in Britain' *Botanical Journal of the Linnean Society*, 1998. 126(1–2): pp. 173–181.

50. Stewart, J., 'The Sainsbury orchid conservation project: The first ten years' *Curtis's Botanical Magazine*, 1993. 10(1): pp. 38–43.

51. Dearnaley, J.D.W., 'Further advances in orchid mycorrhizal research' *Mycorrhiza*, 2007. 17: pp. 475–486.

52. Cameron, D.D., et al., 'Mycorrhizal Acquisition of Inorganic Phosphorus by the Green-leaved Terrestrial Orchid *Goodyera repens*.' *Annals of Botany*, 2007. 99(5): pp. 831–834.

53. Wohlleben, P., 2016.

54. McKendrick, S.L., J.R. Leake, and D.J. Read, 'Symbiotic germination and development of myco-heterotrophic plants in nature: Transfer of carbon from ectomycorrhizal *Salix repens* and *Betula pendula* to the orchid *Corallorhiza trifida* Châtel through shared hyphal connections' *New Phytologist*, 2000. 145: pp.: 539–548.

55. McKendrick, S.L., et al., 'Symbiotic germination and development of the myco-heterotrophic orchid *Neottia nidus-avis* in nature and its requirement for locally distributed *Sebacina* spp.' *New Phytologist*, 2002. 154: pp. 233–247.

56. Waud, M., et al., 'Specificity and localised distribution of mycorrhizal fungi in the soil may contribute to co-existence of orchid species' *Fungal Ecology*, 2016. 20: pp. 155–165.

57. Webster, A.D., *British Orchids*. 1898: J S Virtue & Co.

58. Sumpter, J., et al., 2004.

59. Sumpter, J., et al., 2004.

60. Willems, J. and L. Bik, 'Long-term dynamics in a population of *Orchis simia* in the Netherlands', *Population Ecology of Terrestrial Orchids*. SPB Academic Publishing, The Hague, 1991: pp. 33–45.

61. Bateman, R.M., R.J. Smith, and M.F. Fay, 'Morphometric and population genetic analyses elucidate the origin, evolutionary significance and conservation implications of *Orchis× angusticruris* (*O. purpurea× O. simia*), a hybrid orchid new to Britain' *Botanical Journal of the Linnean Society*, 2008. 157(4): pp. 687–711.

62. Bateman, R., 'Where Does Orchid Conservation End and Gardening Begin?' *Journal of the Hardy Orchid Society*, 2010. 7: pp. 119–133.

63. Carey, P.D., 'Changes in the distribution and abundance of *Himantoglossum hircinum* (L.) Sprengel (Orchidaceae) over the last 100 years' *Watsonia*, 1999. 22: pp. 353–364.

64. Kull, T. and M.J. Hutchings, 'A comparative analysis of decline in the distribution ranges of orchid species in Estonia and the United Kingdom' *Biological Conservation*, 2006. 129(1): pp. 31–39.

65. Darwin, C.R., 1862.

66. Jacquemyn, H., et al., 'Does nectar reward affect rarity and extinction probabilities of orchid species? An assessment using historical records from Belgium and the Netherlands' *Biological Conservation*, 2005. 121(2): pp. 257–263.

67. Dressler, R.L., *Phylogeny and Classification of the Orchid Family*. 1993: Cambridge University Press.

68. Ramirez, S.R., et al., 'Dating the origin of the Orchidaceae from a fossil orchid with its pollinator' *Nature*, 2007. 448(7157): pp. 1042–5.

69. Poinar, G., J.R. Finn, and N. Rasmussen, 'Orchids from the past, with a new species in Baltic amber' *Botanical Journals of the Linnaean Society*, 2017. 183: pp. 327–333.

70. Ramirez, S.R., et al., 2007.

71. Foley, M., 'The current distribution and abundance of *Orchis ustulata* L. in southern England' *Watsonia*, 1990. 18(1): pp. 37–48.

72. Pillon, Y., et al., 'Genetic diversity and ecological differentiation in the endangered fen orchid (*Liparis loeselii*)' *Conservation Genetics*, 2006. 8(1): pp. 177–184.

73. Campbell, V.V., et al., 'Genetic differentiation amongst fragrant orchids (*Gymnadenia conopsea* s.l.) in the British Isles' *Botanical Journal of the Linnean Society*, 2007. 155(3): pp. 349–360.

74. Foley, M. and S. Clarke, 2005.

75. Campbell, V.V., et al., 2007.

76. Mant, J.G., et al., 2002.

77. Breitkopf, H., et al., 'Multiple shifts to different pollinators fuelled rapid diversification in sexually deceptive *Ophrys* orchids' *New Phytologist*, 2015. 207(2): p. 377–389.

78. Borg-Karlson, A.-K., et al., 'Form-specific fragrances from *Ophrys insectifera* L. (Orchidaceae) attract species of different pollinator genera: Evidence of sympatric speciation?' *Chemoecology*, 1993. 4(1): pp. 39–45.

79. Vereecken, N., S. Cozzolino, and F. Schiestl, 'Hybrid floral scent novelty drives pollinator shift in sexually deceptive orchids' *BMC Evolutionary Biology*, 2010. 10(1): p. 103.

80. Bateman, R., 'Systematics research into hardy orchids: Recent successes and future prospects' *Journal of the Hardy Orchid Society*, 2018. 15: pp. 114–132.

81. Pillon, Y., et al., 'Evolution and temporal diversification of western European polyploid species complexes in *Dactylorhiza* (Orchidaceae)' *Taxon*, 2007. 56(4): pp. 1185–1208.

82. Bateman, R. and I. Denholm, 'Taxonomic reassessment of the British and Irish tetraploid marsh-orchids' *New Journal of Botany*, 2013.

83. Hedren, M. and S. Nordstrom, 'Polymorphic populations of *Dactylorhiza incarnata* s.l. (Orchidaceae) on the Baltic island of Gotland: Morphology, habitat preference and genetic differentiation' *Annals of Botany*, 2009. 104(3): pp. 527–542.

84. Bateman, R., 'When orchids challenge an island race... Part 2: The British Isles' *Orchid Review*, 2006. 114(1267): pp. 36–41.

85. Paun, O., et al., 'Stable epigenetic effects impact adaptation in allopolyploid orchids (Dactylorhiza: Orchidaceae)' *Molecular Biology and Evolution*, 2010. 27(11): pp. 2465–2473.

PART III: OPEN GROUND

INTRODUCTION

1. Gagné, J.-M. and G. Houle, 'Facilitation of *Leymus mollis* by *Honckenya peploides* on coastal dunes in subarctic Quebec, Canada' *Canadian Journal of Botany*, 2001. 79(11): pp. 1327–1331.

2. Sánchez Vilas, J., 'Sexual dimorphism in ecological and physiological traits in the subdioecious dune plant *Honckenya peploides* (L.) Ehrh'.2007: University of Santiago de Compostela.

3. Hatch, P.J., *'A Rich Spot of Earth': Thomas Jefferson's Revolutionary Garden at Monticello*. 2012: Yale University Press.

4. Bridges, R., 'When first we met we did not guess / That Love would prove so hard a master', *Shorter Poems*. 2016: Portable Poetry p. 82.

5. Stewart, N. and R. Randall, 'The past and present distribution of *Mertensia maritima* (L.) SF Gray in the British Isles (Exhibition Meeting Report)' *BS BJ. News*, 1988. 49: p. 51.

6. Gardiner, T., 'Response of shrubby sea-blite *Suaeda vera* to cutting on a sea wall flood defence at Goldhanger, Essex, England' *Conservation Evidence*, 2011. 8: pp. 1–5.

7. Marchant, C., 'Evolution in *Spartina* (Gramineae): I. The history and morphology of the genus in Britain' *Botanical Journal of the Linnean Society*, 1967. 60(381): pp. 1–24.

8. Gray, A.J., D. Marshall, and A. Raybould, 'A century of evolution in *Spartina anglica*'

in *Advances in Ecological Research*. 1991, Elsevier. pp. 1–62.
9. Lake, S., et al., *Britain's Habitats: A Guide to the Wildlife Habitats of Britain and Ireland*. 2015: Princeton University Press.

11 BUTTERWORTS, BLADDERWORTS & SUNDEWS

1. Brewer, J.S., et al., 'Carnivory in plants as a beneficial trait in wetlands' *Aquatic Botany*, 2011. 94(2): pp. 62–70.
2. Bailey, T. and S. McPherson, *Carnivorous Plants of Britain and Ireland*. 2016, Poole: Redfern Natural History Productions.
3. ' "Killer Petunias" Should Join the Ranks of Carnivorous Plants, Scientists Propose' *Science Daily* [2009 24/10/11]. Available from: http://www.sciencedaily.com/releases/2009/12/091204103747.htm.
4. Darwin, C. and F. Darwin, *Insectivorous Plants*, 1888: J. Murray.
5. Chapman, T., 'Observations on the life history of *Trichoptilus paludum* Zell' *London Transactions of the Entomological Society*, 1906: pp. 133–154.
6. Matthews, D., 'The sundew plume moth, *Buckleria parvulus* (Barnes & Lindsey) (Lepidoptera: Pterophoridae)' *Southern Lepidopterists' News*, 2009. 31: pp. 74–77.
7. Jennings, D.E., et al., 'Evidence for competition between carnivorous plants and spiders' *Proceedings of the Royal Society of London. Series B: Biological Sciences*, 2010. 277(1696): pp. 3001–8.
8. Anderson, B. and J.J. Midgley, 'Food or sex: Pollinator–prey conflict in carnivorous plants' *Ecology Letters*, 2001. 4(6): pp. 511–513.
9. Anderson, B., 'Did *Drosera* evolve long scapes to stop their pollinators from being eaten?' *Annals of Botany*, 2010. 106(4): pp. 653–657.
10. Vincent, O., et al., 'Ultra-fast underwater suction traps' *Proceedings of the Royal Society of London. Series B: Biological Sciences*, 2011. 278(1720): pp. 2909–2914.
11. Heard, S.B., 'Pitcher-Plant Midges and Mosquitoes: A Processing Chain Commensalism' *Ecology*, 1994. 75(6): pp. 1647–1660.
12. Król, E., et al., 'Quite a few reasons for calling carnivores "the most wonderful plants in the world"' *Annals of Botany*, 2012. 109(1): pp. 47–64.
13. Chase, M.W., et al., 'Murderous plants: Victorian Gothic, Darwin and modern insights into vegetable carnivory' *Botanical Journal of the Linnean Society*, 2009. 161(4): pp. 329–356.

12 SAXIFRAGES

1. Chase, M.W., et al., 'Murderous plants: Victorian Gothic, Darwin and modern insights into vegetable carnivory' *Botanical Journal of the Linnean Society*, 2009. 161(4): pp. 329–356.
2. Nicholls, K.W., B.A. Bohm, and R. Ornduff, 'Flavonoids and affinities of the cephalotaceae' *Biochemical Systematics and Ecology*, 1985. 13(3): pp. 261–263.
3. Welch, D., 'The establishment of recovery sites for *Saxifraga hirculus* L. in NE Scotland' *Botanical Journal of Scotland*, 2002. 54(1): pp. 75–88.
4. Wiggington, M.J., *British Red Data Books, – Vascular Plants*. British Red Data Books. Vol. 1. 1999, Peterborough: Joint Nature Conservation Committee.
5. Preston, C.D., D.A. Pearman, and T.D. Dines, *New Atlas of the British and Irish Flora; An Atlas of the Vascular Plants of Britain, Ireland, The Isle of Man and the Channel Islands*. 2002: Oxford University Press.
6. Scott, M., *Mountain Flowers*. British Wildlife Collection, Vol. 4, 2016, London, New York: Bloomsbury.
7. Wiggington, M.J., 1999.
8. Rhind, P. and B. Jones, 'The vegetation history of Snowdonia since the late glacial period' *Field Studies*, 2003. 10: pp. 539–552.
9. Barnard, K., 'Monitoring Populations of *Saxifraga cespitosa* in Scotland' *Sibbaldia: The Journal of Botanic Garden Horticulture*, 2014(12): pp. 99–110.
10. Kay, P. and T. Deacon. 'UK: Is it getting too warm for the Tufted Saxifrage?' 2010 [04/04/2018]. Available from: http://www.plant-talk.org/uk-tufted-saxifrage-snowdonia-wales.htm.
11. Walker, K., 'The last thirty-five years: recent changes in the flora of the British Isles' *Watsonia*, 2007. 26(3): pp. 291–302.
12. Preston, C.D., et al., 2002.
13. Reisch, C., 'Genetic structure of *Saxifraga tridactylites* (Saxifragaceae) from natural and man-made habitats' *Conservation Genetics*, 2007. 8(4): pp. 893–902.

13 ALLIUMS

1. Stearn, W.T., 'How many species of *Allium* are known?' *Curtis's Botanical Magazine*, 1992. 9(4): pp. 180–182.
2. Li, Q.-Q., et al., 'Phylogeny and biogeography of *Allium* (Amaryllidaceae: Allieae) based on nuclear ribosomal internal transcribed spacer and chloroplast rps16 sequences, focusing on the inclusion of species endemic to China' *Annals of Botany*, 2010. 106(5): pp. 709–733.
3. Stace, C., *New Flora of the British Isles*. 4th Edition 2019: C&M Floristics.
4. Stearn, W.T., 'European species of *Allium*

and allied genera of Alliaceae: A synonymic enumeration' Ann. Mus. Goulandris, 1978. 4: pp. 83–198.
5. Treu, R., et al., '*Allium ampeloprasum* var. *babingtonii* (Alliaceae): an isoclonal plant found across a range of habitats in S.W. England' *Plant Ecology*, 2001. 155(2): pp. 229–235.
6. Harding, S., 'Inflorescence Development in *Allium ampeloprasum* var. *babingtonii* (Babington's Leek). 2004, University of Worcester/Cardiff University.
7. Treu, R., et al., 2001.
8. Ellstrand, N.C. and M.L. Roose, 'Patterns of Genotypic Diversity in Clonal Plant Species' *American Journal of Botany*, 1987. 74(1): pp. 123–131.
9. Stearn, W.T., 1978.
10. Block, E., *Garlic and Other Alliums: the Lore and the Science*. 2010: Royal Society of Chemistry. p.480.
11. Hirschegger, P., et al., 'Origins of *Allium ampeloprasum* horticultural groups and a molecular phylogeny of the section *Allium* (Allium: Alliaceae)' *Molecular Phylogenetics and Evolution*, 2010. 54(2): pp. 488–497.
12. Hirschegger, P., et al., 2010.
13. Hirschegger, P., et al., 2010.
14. Lovatt, C., 'The history, ecology and status of the rare plants and the vegetation of the Avon Gorge, Bristol'. 1982, PhD. Thesis. University of Bristol: Bristol, UK.
15. Bailey, E., et al., 'A botanical survey of the distribution and state of the rare plants in the Avon Gorge, Bristol. Part I. Clifton side' , Unpublished report, Department of Botany, University of Bristol: Bristol, 1972.
16. Frost, L., et al., '*Allium sphaerocephalon* L. and introduced *A. carinatum* L., *A. roseum* L. and *Nectaroscordum siculum* (Ucria) Lindley on St Vincent's Rocks, Avon Gorge, Bristol. *Watsonia*, 1991. 18: pp. 381–384.
17. Frost, L., et al., 1991.
18. White, J.W., *The Bristol Flora*. 1912, Bristol: John Wright & Sons.
19. Lovatt, C., 1982.
20. Bennett, D. and K. House, 'A Botanical Survey of the Rare Plants of the Avon Gorge, Bristol with Particular Reference to the Drought of 1976, Unpublished Report, Department of Botany, University of Bristol: Bristol, 1977.
21. Houston, L., 'Population count in 1987, 1988 and 1989 of rare and uncommon plants in the Avon Gorge, Bristol, with analysis and comments' in *Avon Gorge Project Report*, 1991, University of Bristol: Bristol.
22. Beckett, A., L. Houston, and L.C. Frost, 'New host records for *Puccinia allii* Rud' *Plant Pathology*, 1992. 41(1): pp. 83–85.
23. White, J.W., 1912.
24. Marren, P., *Britain's Rare Flowers*, 1999: London, T. & A. D. Poyser Natural History. p.337.

25. Micklewright, S.D. and L.C. Frost, 'Historical land use of the Bristol Downs as common of pasture' in *The Avon Gorge*, A.E. Frey, Editor. 1989: Bristol. pp. 21–26.

26. Najjaa, H., et al., 'Essential oil composition and antibacterial activity of different extracts of *Allium roseum* L., a North African endemic species' *Comptes Rendus Chimie*, 2007. 10(9): pp. 820–826.

27. Štajner, D., et al., 'Exploring *Allium* species as a source of potential medicinal agents' *Phytotherapy Research*, 2006. 20(7): pp. 581–584.

28. Lazarević, J.S., et al., 'Chemical composition and antioxidant and antimicrobial activities of essential oil of *Allium sphaerocephalon* L. subsp. *sphaerocephalon* (Liliaceae) inflorescences' *Journal of the Science of Food and Agriculture*, 2011. 91(2): pp. 322–329.

29. Guetat, A., et al., 'Genetic diversity in Tunisian rosy garlic populations (*Allium roseum* L.) as evidenced by chloroplastic DNA analysis: Sequence variation of non-coding region and intergenic spacers' *Biochemical Systematics and Ecology*, 2010. 38(4): pp. 502–509.

30. Najjaa, H., et al., 2007.

31. Otto, S.P., 'The evolutionary consequences of polyploidy' *Cell*, 2007. 131(3): pp. 452–462.

32. Marcucci, R. and N. Tornadore, 'Intraspecific variation of *Allium roseum* L. (Alliaceae)' *Webbia*, 1997. 52(1): pp. 137–154.

33. Fialová, M. and M. Duchoslav, 'Response to competition of bulbous geophyte *Allium oleraceum* differing in ploidy level' *Plant Biology*, 2014. 16(1): pp. 186–196.

34. Åström, H. and C.-A. Hæggström. 'Chromosome numbers of *Allium scorodoprasum* and *A. vineale* from SW Finland and W Ukraine' in *Annales Botanici Fennici*. 2003. 40(1): pp. 1–3.

35. Åström, H. and C.-A. Hæggström. 'Generative reproduction in *Allium oleraceum* (Alliaceae)', *Annales Botanici Fennici*. 2004. 41(1): pp. 1–14.

36. Duchoslav, M. and H. Staňková, 'Population genetic structure and clonal diversity of *Allium oleraceum* (Amaryllidaceae), a polyploid geophyte with common asexual but variable sexual reproduction' *Folia Geobotanica*, 2015. 50(2): pp. 123–136.

37. Duchoslav, M., L. Šafářová, and M. Jandová, 'Role of adaptive and non-adaptive mechanisms forming complex patterns of genome size variation in six cytotypes of polyploid *Allium oleraceum* (Amaryllidaceae) on a continental scale' *Annals of Botany*, 2013. 111(3): pp. 419–431.

38. Duchoslav, M., L. Šafářová, and F. Krahulec, 'Complex distribution patterns, ecology and coexistence of ploidy levels of *Allium oleraceum* (Alliaceae) in the Czech Republic' *Annals of Botany*, 2010.

39. Ježilová, E., V. Nožková-Hlaváčková, and M. Duchoslav, 'Photosynthetic characteristics of three ploidy levels of *Allium oleraceum* L. (Amaryllidaceae) differing in ecological amplitude' *Plant Species Biology*, 2015. 30(3): pp. 212–224.

40. Duchoslav, M., et al., 2013.

41. Marcucci, R. and N. Tornadore, 1997.

42. Håkansson, S., '*Allium vineale* L. as a weed: With special reference to the conditions in south-eastern Sweden.' 1963, Department of Plant Husbandry, Agricultural College of Sweden: Uppsala.

43. Duchoslav, M., 'Effects of contrasting habitats on the phenology, seasonal growth, and dry-mass allocation pattern of two bulbous geophytes (Alliaceae) with partly different geographic ranges' *Polish Journal of Ecology*, 2009. 57(1): pp. 15–32.

44. Richens, R., 'Biological flora of the British Isles. *Allium vineale* L.' *Journal of Ecology*, 1947. 34: pp. 209–26.

45. Ceplitis, A., 'Genetic and environmental factors affecting reproductive variation in *Allium vineale*' *Journal of Evolutionary Biology*, 2001. 14(5): pp. 721–730.

46. Fialová, M. and M. Duchoslav, 2014.

47. Fialová, M., et al., 'Biology of the polyploid geophyte *Allium oleraceum* (Amaryllidaceae): Variation in size, sexual and asexual reproduction and germination within and between tetra-, penta- and hexaploid cytotypes' *Flora – Morphology, Distribution, Functional Ecology of Plants*, 2014. 209(7): pp. 312–324.

48. Ronsheim, M.L., 'Dispersal distances and predation rates of sexual and asexual propagules of *Allium vineale* L.' *American Midland Naturalist*, 1994: pp. 55–64.

49. Duchoslav, M., 'Small-scale spatial pattern of two common European geophytes *Allium oleraceum* and *A. vineale* in contrasting habitats' *Biologia*, Bratislava, 2001. 56(1): pp. 57–62.

50. Ceplitis, A., 'The Importance of Sexual and Asexual Reproduction in the Recent Evolution of *Allium vineale*' *Evolution*, 2001. 55(8): pp. 1581–1591

51. Ceplitis, A. and B.O. Bengtsson, 'Genetic variation, disequilibrium and natural selection on reproductive traits in *Allium vineale*' *Journal of Evolutionary Biology*, 2004. 17(2): pp. 302–311.

52. Ronsheim, M., 'Distance-dependent performance of asexual progeny in *Allium vineale* (Liliaceae)' *American Journal of Botany*, 1997. 84(9): pp. 1279–1284.

53. Maynard Smith, J., *The Evolution of Sex*. 1978: Cambridge University Press.

54. Åström, H. and C.-A. Hæggström, 2004.

55. Richens, R., 1947.

56. Defelice, M.S., 'Wild Garlic, *Allium vineale* L. – Little to Crow About' *Weed Technology*, 2003. 17(4): pp. 890–895.

57. Ceplitis, A., 2001.

58. Duchoslav, M., '*Allium oleraceum* and *A. vineale* in the Czech Republic: Distribution and habitat differentiation' *Preslia*, 2001. 73(2): pp. 173–184.

59. Fenwick, G.R. and A.B. Hanley, 'The genus *Allium* – part 3' *CRC Critical Reviews in Food Science and Nutrition*, 1985. 23: pp. 1–73.

60. Defelice, M.S., 2003.

61. Lazenby, A., 'Studies on *Allium Vineale* L.: I. The Effects of Soils, Fertilizers and Competition on Establishment and Growth of Plants from Aerial Bulbils' *Journal of Ecology*, 1961. 49(3): pp. 519–541.

62. Richens, R., 1947.

63. Defelice, M.S., 2003.

64. Lazenby, A., 'Studies on *Allium Vineale* L.: II. Establishment and Growth in Different Intensities of Competition' *Journal of Ecology*, 1961. 49(3): pp. 543–558.

65. Lazenby, A., 'Studies on *Allium Vineale* L. III. Effect of Depth of Planting' *Journal of Ecology*, 1962. 50(1): pp. 97–109.

66. Richens, R., 1947.

67. Guetat, A., et al., 2010.

14 LILIES OF OPEN GROUND

1. Streeter, D., et al., *Collins Flower Guide* 2009, London: HarperCollins.

2. Woodhead, N., '*Lloydia serotina*' *Journal of Ecology*, 1951. 39(1): pp. 198–203.

3. Marren, P., *Britain's Rare Flowers*, 1999: London, T. & A.D. Poyser Natural History. p. 337.

4. Peterson, A., I.G. Levichev, and J. Peterson, 'Systematics of *Gagea* and *Lloydia* (Liliaceae) and infrageneric classification of *Gagea* based on molecular and morphological data' *Molecular Phylogenetics and Evolution*, 2008. 46(2): pp. 446–465.

5. Jones, B. and C. Gliddon, 'Reproductive biology and genetic structure in *Lloydia serotina*' *Plant Ecology*, 1999. 141(1–2): pp. 151–161.

6. Peterson, A., et al., 2008.

7. Rix, E. and R. Woods, 'Gagea bohemica (Zauschner) J.A. & J.H. Schultes in the British Isles, and a general review of the *G. bohemica* species complex' *Watsonia*, 1981. 13(4): pp. 265–270.

8. Peterson, A., et al., '*Gagea bohemica* (Liliaceae), a highly variable monotypic species within *Gagea* sect. *Didymobulbos*' *Plant Biosystems*, 2010. 144(2): pp. 308–322.

9. Slater, F., '*Gagea bohemica*; Biological Flora of the British Isles' *Journal of Ecology*, 1990. 78(2): pp. 535–546.

10. Černý, T., et al., 'Vegetation with *Gagea bohemica* in the landscape context' *Plant Biosystems – An International Journal Dealing*

with *All Aspects of Plant Biology*, 2011. 145(3): pp. 570–583.

11. Černý, T., et al., 2011.

12. Peterson, A., et al., 2010.

13. Ray, J., *Historia Plantarum (History of Plants)*. Vol. 1. 1686, London: Clark.

14. Slater, F., 1990.

15. Pfeiffer, T., et al., 'Reproductive isolation vs. interbreeding between *Gagea lutea* (L.) Ker Gawl. and *G. pratensis* (Pers.) Dumort. (Liliaceae) and their putative hybrids in Mecklenburg-Western Pomerania (Germany)' *Plant Species Biology*, 2013. 28(3): pp. 193–203.

16. Peruzzi, L., et al., 'On the Phylogenetic Position and Taxonomic Value of *Gagea trinervia* (Viv.) Greuter *and Gagea* sect. *Anthericoides* A. Terracc. (Liliaceae). *Taxon*, 2008. 57(4): pp. 1201–1214.

17. Botschantzeva, Z.P., *Tulips: Taxonomy, Morphology, Cytology, Phytogeography and Physiology*, 1982: CRC Press.

18. Peruzzi, L., 'Chromosome diversity and evolution in the genus *Gagea* (Liliaceae)' *Bocconea*, 2012. 24: pp. 147–158.

19. Pfeiffer, T., et al., 2013.

20. Pfeiffer, T., et al., 'Does sex make a difference? Genetic diversity and spatial genetic structure in two co-occurring species of *Gagea* (Liliaceae) with contrasting reproductive strategies' *Plant Systematics and Evolution*, 2011. 292(3–4): pp. 189–201.

21. Pfeiffer, T., et al., 'No sex at all? Extremely low genetic diversity in *Gagea spathacea* (Liliaceae) across Europe' *Flora – Morphology, Distribution, Functional Ecology of Plants*, 2012. 207(5): pp. 372–378.

22. Peterson, A., et al., 2010.

23. Gargano, D., et al., 'Preliminary observations on the reproductive strategies in five early-flowering species of *Gagea* Salisb. (Liliaceae)' *Bocconea*, 2007. 21: pp. 349–358.

24. Manicacci, D. and L. Despres, 'Male and hermaphrodite flowers in the alpine lily *Lloydia serotina*' *Canadian Journal of Botany*, 2001. 79(9): pp. 1107–1114.

25. Eckstein, R.L. and P.S. Karlsson, 'Variation in nitrogen – use efficiency among and within subarctic graminoids and herbs' *New Phytologist*, 2001. 150(3): p. 641–651.

26. Kudo, G., et al., 'Does seed production of spring ephemerals decrease when spring comes early?' *Ecological Research*, 2004. 19(2): pp. 255–259.

27. Nishikawa, Y., 'The function of multiple flowers of a spring ephemeral, *Gagea lutea* (Liliaceae), with reference to blooming order' *Canadian Journal of Botany*, 1998. 76(8): pp. 1404–1411.

28. Nishikawa, Y., 'Significance of intra-inflorescence variation on flowering time of a spring ephemeral, *Gagea lutea* (Liliaceae), under seasonal fluctuations of pollinator

and light availabilities' *Plant Ecology*, 2009. 202(2): pp. 337–347.

29. Sunmonu, N., T.Y. Ida, and G. Kudo, 'Photosynthetic compensation by the reproductive structures in the spring ephemeral *Gagea lutea*' *Plant Ecology*, 2013. 214(2): pp. 175–188.

30. Hagerup, O., '"Rain Pollination" Det Kgl. Danske Videnskabernes Selskab' *Biologiske MeddeleLser*, 1950. 18(5).

31. Malone, F., et al., 'Bog asphodel (*Narthecium ossifragum*) poisoning in cattle' *Veterinary Record*, 1992. 131(5): pp. 100–103.

32. Angell, J. and T. Ross, 'Suspected bog asphodel (*Narthecium ossifragum*) toxicity in cattle in North Wales' *Veterinary Record*, 2011. 169(4): pp. 102.

33. Summerfield, R.J., 'The growth and productivity of *Narthecium ossifragum* on British mires' *Journal of Ecology*, 1973. 61(3): pp. 717–727.

34. Malmer, N., *Studies on Mire Vegetation in the Archaean Area of Southwestern Götaland (South Sweden)*, 1962: Almqvist and Wiksell.

35. Spink, A.J. and A.N. Parsons, 'An experimental investigation of the effects of nitrogen deposition to *Narthecium ossifragum*' *Environmental Pollution*, 1995. 90(2): pp. 191–198.

36. Kay, Q., E. Davies, and T. Rich, 'Taxonomy of the western European endemic *Asparagus prostratus* (A. officinalis subsp. prostratus) (Asparagaceae)' *Botanical Journal of the Linnean Society*, 2001. 137(2): pp. 127–137.

37. King, H. and B. Edwards, 'Hand pollination of a single female wild asparagus *Asparagus prostratus* plant near Ferrybridge in Dorset, using pollen taken from plants in Cornwall, southwest England' *Conservation Evidence*, 2007. 4: pp. 73–76.

38. Anido, F.L. and E. Cointry, '*Asparagus*', in *Vegetables II*, 2008, Springer, pp. 87–119.

39. Castro, P., et al., 'Assessment of genetic diversity and phylogenetic relationships in *Asparagus* species related to *Asparagus officinalis*' *Genetic Resources and Crop Evolution*, 2013. 60(4): pp. 1275–1288.

40. Hill, D. and B. Price, '*Ornithogalum pyrenaicum* L.' *Journal of Ecology*, 2000. 88(2): pp. 354–365.

41. Hill, D. and B. Price, 2000.

42. Martínez-Azorín, M., M.B. Crespo, and A. Juan, 'Taxonomic revision of *Ornithogalum* subg. *Beryllis* (Hyacinthaceae) in the Iberian Peninsula and the Balearic Islands' *Belgian Journal of Botany*, 2009: pp. 140–162.

43. Preston, C.D., D.A. Pearman, and T.D. Dines, *New Atlas of the British and Irish Flora: An Atlas of the Vascular Plants of Britain, Ireland, The Isle of Man and the Channel Islands*, 2002: Oxford University Press.

44. Crouch, H. 'Somerset Rare Plant Register Account: *Scilla autumnalis*'. Available from:

www.somersetrareplantsgroup.org.uk.

45. Da Silva, R.M.A. and Rosselló, J.A., 'Anatomical studies on the *Scilla verna* (Hyacinthaceae) complex' *Israel Journal of Plant Sciences*, 1999. 47(2): pp. 103–110.

46. Da Silva, R.M.A., et al., 'The Iberian Species of *Scilla* (Subfamily Scilloideae, Family Asparagaceae) under Climatic Change Scenarios in Southwestern Europe' *Systematic Botany*, 2014. 39(4): pp. 1083–1098.

47. Banciu, C., et al., 'In Vitro Propagation of Critically Endangered Species *Scilla autumnalis* L. – Biochemical Analyses of the Regenerants' *Analele Universitatii din Oradea – Fascicula Biologie*, 2010. 17(2).

48. Da Silva, R.A.M., et al., 2010.

49. Jamilena, M., et al., 'Inheritance and fitness effects analysis for a euchromatic supernumerary chromosome segment in *Scilla autumnalis* (Liliaceae)' *Botanical Journal of the Linnean Society*, 1995. 118(3): pp. 249–259.

50. Vaughan, H., S. Taylor, and J. Parker, 'The ten cytological races of the *Scilla autumnalis* species complex' *Heredity*, 1997. 79(4): pp. 371–379.

51. Preston, C.D., et al., 2002.

52. Dafni, A., A. Shmida, and M. Avishai, 'Leafless autumnal-flowering geophytes in the Mediterranean region— phytogeographical, ecological and evolutionary aspects' *Plant Systematics and Evolution*, 1981. 137(3): pp. 181–193.

53. Marques, I. and D. Draper, 'Seed germination and longevity of autumn-flowering and autumn-seed producing Mediterranean geophytes' *Seed Science Research*, 2012. 22(04): pp. 299–309.

54. Dafni, A., et al., 1981.

55. Christenhusz, M.J.M., et al., 'Tiptoe through the tulips – cultural history, molecular phylogenetics and classification of *Tulipa* (Liliaceae)' *Botanical Journal of the Linnean Society*, 2013. 172(3): pp. 280–328.

APPENDIX

1. Blossfeldt, K., *Art Forms in the Plant World* (Dover Pictorial Archive) 1986: Dover Publications Inc.

2. Blossfeldt, K. and H.C. Adam, *Blossfeldt: The Complete Published Work* (Bibliotheca Universalis), 2014: Taschen GmbH.

Bibliography

GUIDES

Bailey, T. and McPherson, S., *Carnivorous Plants of Britain and Ireland* (Redfern Natural History Productions Ltd, 2016)

Blamey, M., Fitter, R. and Fitter, A., *Wild Flowers of Britain and Ireland*, Second edition (Bloomsbury Natural History , 2013)

Foley, M.J.Y. and Clarke, S.J., *Orchids of the British Isles* (Griffin Press, 2005)

Harrap, S., *Harrap's Wild Flowers* (Bloomsbury Natural History , 2018)

Harrap, A. and Harrap, S., *Orchids of Britain and Ireland: A Field and Site Guide, Field & Site Guides* (Bloomsbury Natural History, 2018)

Johnson, O., *Collins Tree Guide* (William Collins, 2016)

Kuhn, R., Pedersen, H. and Cribb, P., *Field Guide to the Orchids of Europe and the Mediterranean* (Kew Publishing, 2019)

Lang, D., *Britain's Orchids*, Wild Guides (Princeton University Press, 2004)

Stace, C., *New Flora of the British Isles*, Fourth edition (C&M Floristics, 2019)

Poland, J. and Clement, E.J., *The Vegetative Key to the British Flora* (John Poland, 2009)

Price, D., *A Field Guide to Grasses, Sedges and Rushes* (The Species Recovery Trust, 2017)

Raven, S. and Buckley, J., *Sarah Raven's Wild Flowers* (Bloomsbury Publishing, 2011)

Rose, F., *Colour Identification Guide to the Grasses, Sedges, Rushes and Ferns of the British Isles and North Western Europe* (Viking, 1989)

Rose, F. and O'Reilly, C., *The Wild Flower Key – How to identify wild plants, trees and shrubs in Britain and Ireland*, revised edition (Warne, 2006)

Streeter, D., *Collins Wild Flower Guide*, Second edition (William Collins , 2016)

GENERAL READING

Averis, B., *Plants and Habitats: An Introduction to Common Plants and Their Habitats in Britain and Ireland* (Ben Averis, 2013)

Cox, F., *A Gardener's Guide to Snowdrops* (The Crowood Press Ltd, 2018)

Dunn, J., *Orchid Summer: In Search of the Wildest Flowers of the British Isles* (Bloomsbury Publishing, 2018)

Jones, D., *Tenby Daffodil* (Tenby Museum, 1992)

Kilpatrick, J. and Harmer, J., *The Galanthophiles: 160 Years of Snowdrop Devotees* (Orphans Publishing, 2018)

Kingsbury, N. *Daffodil: the Remarkable Story of the World's Most Popular Spring Flower* (Timber Press, 2013)

Lake, S., Liley, D., Still, R. and Swash, A., *Britain's Habitats: A Guide to the Wildlife Habitats of Britain and Ireland*, Wild Guides (Princeton University Press, 2014)

Lloyd, C., *Meadows* (Timber Press, 2004)

Mabey, R., *Flora Britannica* (Chatto & Windus / Sinclair Stevenson, 1996)

Marren, P., *Britain's Rare Flowers* (Poyser Natural History) (A & C Black Publishers Ltd, 2005)

Marren, P., *Chasing the Ghost: My Search for all the Wild Flowers of Britain* (Square Peg, 2018)

Peterken, G., Meadows, *British Wildlife Collection* (Bloomsbury Natural History, 2018)

Preston, C.D., Pearman, D. A. and Dines, T. D., *New Atlas of the British and Irish Flora: An Atlas of the Vascular Plants of Britain, Ireland, The Isle of Man and the Channel Island* (Oxford University Press, 2002)

Proctor, M., *Vegetation of Britain and Ireland, Collins New Naturalist Library*, Book 122 (William Collins, 2013)

Rackham, O., *Woodlands*, Collins New Naturalist Library, Book 100 (William Collins, 2006)

Rackham, O., *Trees and Woodland in the British Landscape* (Weidenfeld & Nicolson, 2001)

Rackham, O., *The History of the Countryside* (Weidenfeld & Nicolson, 2001)

Scott, M., *Mountain Flowers*, British Wildlife Collection (Bloomsbury Natural History, 2016)

Slade, N., *Plant Lovers Guide to Snowdrops*, Plant Lover's Guides (Timber Press, 2014)

Stace, A. and Crawley, M.J., *Alien Plants*, Collins New Naturalist Library, Book 129 (William Collins, 2015)

Thompson, K., *Darwin's Most Wonderful Plants: Darwin's Botany Today* (Profile Books, 2018)

Acknowledgements

My sincere thanks to David Parker for his comments on saxifrages and for providing details of his work with this group of plants. Thanks also to Clive Lovatt for reading and commenting on the alliums chapter and for graciously sharing his unrivalled knowledge of the intriguing history of plants and botany in the Avon Gorge in Bristol. I am also extremely grateful to Richard Bateman who read and commented on the orchids chapter. His knowledge of this confusing and complex family of plants is encyclopaedic and I thank him for keeping me on the straight and narrow as I wound a path through the orchid story.

In taking the photographs for this book I am indebted to the many reserve wardens and local naturalists who helped me track down the best locations for many species. In particular, I'd like to thank Tony Hughes of the Hardy Orchid Society, who sadly died in 2015. He was no slouch himself when it came to photographing orchids and he kindly showed me some of his favourite spots for a wide variety of species. Many thanks to Nick Wray, curator of the University of Bristol Botanic Gardens for allowing me to photograph some of the south-west's rarest plants which are held in their collection and where it is far easier (or at least less nerve-wracking than being perched half way up a cliff) to compose artistic shots.

I also owe thanks to Keith Turner for reading each chapter as I completed the first drafts and for his comments both as a knowledgeable ecologist and an avid reader of popular natural history books. And thanks to my wife, Vicky Coules, whose self-professed botanical knowledge runs to daffodils and 'not-daffodils', at least until she ploughed through the whole manuscript. I'm very grateful for her comments and guidance in helping me keep the book accessible for non-specialists and for her continued support during what turned out to be a far longer and more complex project than originally envisioned. I'm also grateful for her company on some of our photographic expeditions, from Devon and Kent in the south of England to the Outer Hebrides and the far north of Sutherland in Scotland.

Finally, thanks to Kate Hordern, my literary agent, without whom this book would never have come to fruition. Her deep understanding of the book world proved invaluable in shaping the final structure of the book, as well as in finding the perfect publisher in Head of Zeus. I thank Isambard Thomas who designed the book and who created a visual impact far beyond my expectations. At Head of Zeus, my thanks also to Clémence Jacquinet, who was responsible for the book's production, and Florence Hare. And my heartfelt thanks to Richard Milbank, Publishing Director at Head of Zeus, for his meticulous work in editing the text. His empathy with my vision for the project not only vastly improved on my original work but made the whole editing process a real pleasure and a fitting culmination to many years research and travelling.

Index of Plant Names

General Index

This is an Apollo book,
first published in the UK in 2019
by Head of Zeus Ltd

Copyright © 2019 Steve Nicholls
for text and photography

The moral right of Steve Nicholls to be identified as the author
of this work has been asserted in accordance with the Copyright,
Designs and Patents Act of 1988.

3 5 7 9 10 8 6 4 2

A CIP catalogue record for this book is available from
the British Library.

Extract from *When We Were Very Young* by A.A. Milne.
Text copyright © The Trustees of the Pooh Properties 1924.
Published by Egmont UK Ltd and used with permission.

Extract from *Inside the Brightness of Red* by Mary McCrae.
Published by Second Light Publications, 2010
and used with permission.

Extract from 'The Road Not Taken' published in
Mountain Interval by Robert Frost.
Published by Henry Holt & Co, 1916.

Every effort has been made to trace copyright holders
to obtain their permission for the use of copyright material.
The publishers shall, if notified, rectify any omissions
in a future reprint of this book.

ISBN [HB] 9781789540543
ISBN [E] 9781789540680

Designed by Isambard Thomas / Corvo
Printed in Slovenia

Head of Zeus Ltd
5–8 Hardwick Street
London ECIR 4RG
www.headofzeus.com

An Apollo Book